Carolina's Historical Landscapes

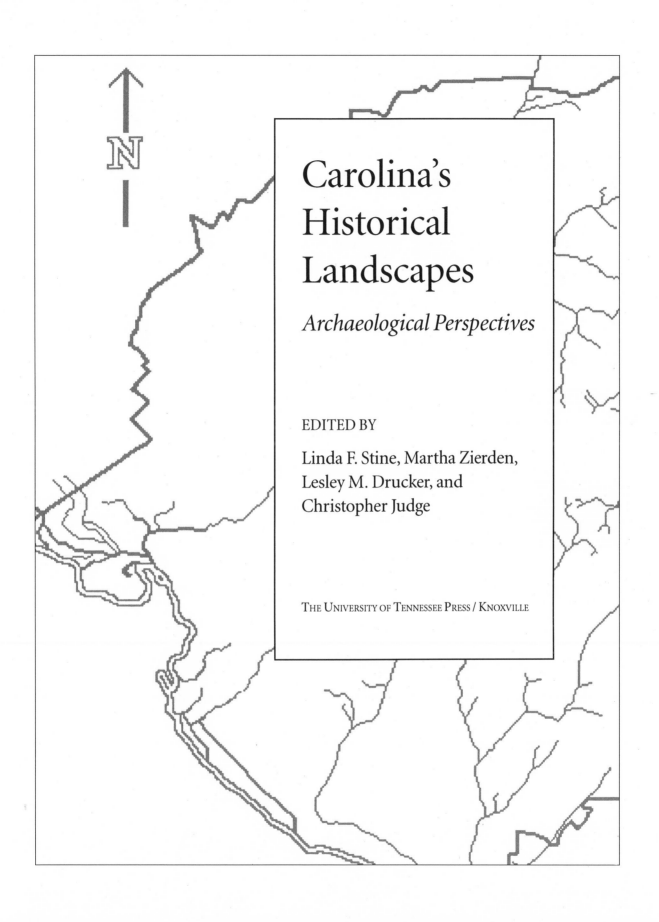

Carolina's Historical Landscapes

Archaeological Perspectives

EDITED BY

Linda F. Stine, Martha Zierden,
Lesley M. Drucker, and
Christopher Judge

THE UNIVERSITY OF TENNESSEE PRESS / KNOXVILLE

Library of Congress Cataloging-in-Publication Data

Carolina's historical landscapes : archaeological perspectives /
      edited by Linda F. Stine ... [et al.]. — 1st ed.
            p. cm.
      Includes bibliographical references and index.
      ISBN 0-87049-976-9 (cloth: alk. paper)
      1. Landscape archaeology—South Carolina. 2. South Carolina—
      Antiquities. I. Stine, Linda F. (Linda France), 1956– .
      F271.C37 1997
      911'.757—dc20   96-35709
                                         CIP

CONTENTS

ILLUSTRATIONS

PREFACE

Carolina historical archaeologists at universities, research institutes, government management agencies, and private companies have worked hard to communicate the results of their projects to the public and to one another. As members of the Council of South Carolina Professional Archaeologists (COSCAPA), they have shared ideas, results, and hopes for a synthesis of South Carolina historical archaeology.

A preliminary workshop was held at The Charleston Museum on September 10, 1988, to develop strategies and research topics for this synthesis. The South Carolina Department of Archives and History recommended funding the "South Carolina Archaeological Synthesis Project" through a National Park Service survey and planning grant (1991–1992 cycle). These chapters have their genesis in papers given at the COSCAPA symposium on South Carolina's historical landscapes on September 13, 1991, and Society for Historical Archaeology meetings (SHA) in Kingston, Jamaica, in January 1992. The volume has been revised in light of new research spurred by spirited panel and audience discussions and subsequent debates. Its primary focus is on *landscape*—as a unifying theoretical perspective, a tool for cultural resource managers, and as an interpretive device.

The volume has been strengthened by exposure to the perspectives of several people, among them Lee Tippett, Steve Skelton, Nancy Meriwether, and Mary Parramore of the South Carolina Department of Archives and History, Ken Driggers of Palmetto Conservation Foundation, and Julie Flowers of the South Carolina Department of Parks, Recreation, and Tourism. Many thanks to Ruth Ann Mitchell of the National Parks Service for pointing out the need for a preservation plan for South Carolina historical archaeology. She, Steve Smith, and Linda Stine have enjoyed discussing the potential of using a landscape approach to develop preservation contexts. Additional insights have been offered by Kenneth Robinson of the North Carolina Department of Transportation, Charles D. Hocksmith of the Kentucky Heritage Office, Keith Derting and Stanley South of the South Carolina Institute of Archaeology and Anthropology, Chris Espenshade and Paul Brockington Jr. of Brockington and Associates, and Ismael Williams, formerly of New South Associates. Francis Marion National Forest Service archaeologist Robert Morgan and forest archaeologist Robert Wise provided needed data and information. The authors would like to also thank the staff of the South Carolina Historical Society in Charleston and Caroliniana librarians at the University of South Carolina, Columbia.

The editors would like to thank our anthropologist, historian, and geographer colleagues for their participation. The contributors have synthesized, summarized, and selected avenues for future research. The Council of South Carolina Professional Archaeologists (COSCAPA) has shown continued interest and support for this project. University of Tennessee Press reviewers offered important suggestions toward improving this book. In particular, editor Meredith Morris-Babb guided our efforts to transform symposia presentations into a unified volume of written work. The patience and support of our families and friends is deeply appreciated. Special thanks are due to Roy S. Stine for his insightful suggestions and continuing forbearance.

Introduction: Historical Landscapes through the Prism of Archaeology

MARTHA ZIERDEN AND LINDA F. STINE

The word *landscape* evokes images of the natural world, but a world altered by human beings. In this volume, scholars from diverse disciplines explore the way South Carolinians changed and were changed by their interaction with the land. The focus is on historical landscapes, seen through the prism of South Carolina's historical archaeology. Historical archaeologists are synthesizing years of regional research, guided by a landscape perspective.

Landscape studies are the exploration of how people shaped and were shaped by the land within a dynamic cultural and natural context. The evolving paradigm of landscape archaeology is a response to critiques that archaeologists have been neglecting symbolic and ideological factors in their interpretations.[1] A landscape perspective attempts to form linkages among material, social, behavioral, ideological, and natural elements in a region of study. Crumley defines regions as "an arbitrary areal classification whose limits are defined by the researchers, for the purpose of studying phenomena within its boundaries."[2] She notes that regions (such as the Carolinas) can be viewed as homogeneous, heterogeneous, or both, depending upon the goals of the archaeologist and the chosen scale of analysis.

The landscape archaeologist also adds the dimension of perception to the classic archaeological dimensions of space, time, and form to regional studies.[3] This topic is relatively new in historical archaeology, but published landscape studies have already produced promising results. A variety of definitions for the term landscape are implicit in previous studies and in those presented here.

A simple definition from geography is "that portion of the earth that the eye can comprehend in a single view."[4] Stilgoe elaborates that it is not natural land but shaped land, land modified for permanent human occupation, for dwelling, agriculture, manufacturing, government, worship, and for pleasure—not by chance, but by contrivance, premeditation, or design. Landscape is above all a shared space, evolving to serve a community. J. B. Jackson suggests that the collective character of the landscape is agreed upon by all generations and all points of view.[5]

A simple definition of archaeology is that it is the study of past peoples and cultures through their material remains. This broad definition implies a holistic study of past groups, from the functional to the ideological. The material remains are generally called artifacts and traditionally are the fragmentary materials (e.g., "artifacts," "ecofacts") and soil changes (e.g., "features," "strata") removed through excavation.

But neither concept—landscape or artifact—is so simple. James Deetz was the first to broaden our definition of artifact to include documents, and even the "spoken word" and body movements.[6] Likewise, Dell Upton has challenged Stilgoe's definition of landscape, suggesting that the colonial gentry's landscape in particular was meant to be experienced dynamically; the visitor passed from one contrived setting to another; its meaning could *not* be comprehended in a single view.[7] The viewer was meant to piece together information from myriad, multiplex symbols.

Thus archaeologists now include the landscape itself in the category of artifact. Paul Shackel and Barbara Little suggest that as an artifact, landscapes are more than ornament; they are expressions of ideals, of emulation, and assertions of power. They were vehicles used to display control and reinforce hierarchy. Elizabeth Kryder–Reid notes that landscapes are particularly powerful symbolic artifacts because they are three–dimensional spaces, volumes literally entered into and experienced.[8]

The landscape as artifact consists of an overlapping and interrelated series of elements, subject to study in a variety of ways. The same landscape was viewed and used in different ways by the various groups who inhabited it. The archaeology of landscape, then, is a study of linkages, of articulation.[9] First, as Henry Miller notes, there are a variety of elements in even the vernacular landscape. Each requires different techniques of study, from intensive excavation to "minimalist archaeology" to critical use of other sources—documents, art, oral history.[10] Second, the physical features are articulated with their encoded messages; they might reveal a display of financial resources, a display of knowledge, or a display of power.[11] Landscape archaeology is thus an avenue to the elucidation of the dominant ideology. Third, it includes the process of linking the dominant ideology of the landscape to the subordinate ones.

In its simplest form, for instance, the colonial landscape consisted of a work environment shaped by the needs of a functioning household, but also deeply influenced by tradition, the social setting, and the cultural perspectives of the residents.[12] Prominent elements included:

1. Houses and other structures, the center of most human activity.
2. Fences and other barriers that physically structured open spaces.
3. Specialized activity areas.
4. Doors, gateways, paths, and roads, the access routes that linked each element.

These elements leave varying archaeological signatures. The gentry landscape, with its formal gardens and contrived vistas, centers of commerce, worship, and government, was even more complex, and its message of power was more pervasive.[13] Dell Upton has engaged in a concurrent analysis of the gentry world and the overlapping lower-class sphere of colonial Virginia.[14] He notes that these various groups shared the same physical structures but constructed very different mental landscapes from them. To the gentry, the landscape was a complete, articulated network. To their bonded laborers, the same landscape was a "ragged patchwork of free and controlled spaces," a series of spots where social relations were in effect. Thus the landscape is, as Bernard Herman has noted, "a vast text subject to the contributions of many authors, the interpretations of many readers, and the discourses of many critics."[15]

Landscape creation and use, then, held multiple purposes simultaneously, from food production through formal design to explicit statements of social position. James Deetz has warned against trying to separate these levels, for the technomic farm fields of English settlers in South Africa became, for example, powerful statements of cultural identity, to be seen and understood by others as such.[16]

Landscape archaeology in the United States has its roots in the study of gardens, such as those examined by William Kelso at Monticello.[17] In keeping with the definitions provided, this certainly involved excavating areas with minimal archaeological signatures. Landscape archaeology is no longer simply the archaeology of landscaping and gardening practices. The field has quickly expanded to embrace broader topics. Urban archaeology often encompasses a landscape approach; fill is accepted as an artifact in its own right, and the massive filling operations that characterize urban development result in a highly manipulated landscape. Just as current landscape studies are broad in scale, so too do they often involve a large number of scholars working on an interdisciplinary project. Published landscape studies incorporate the research efforts of palynologists, ethnobotanists, zooarchaeologists, historians, architects, and geographers.

Historical archaeology in South Carolina is the study of complex society, of the "modern world system."[18] The archaeology of the historic period encompasses many different types of sites, in various sections of the state, occupied for varying lengths of time. A temporal approach, dividing the state into centuries, or even eras, is inappropriate. Too many of the state's sites span more than one division, making a temporal approach at once arbitrary and repetitive. Similar problems plague a topical or geographical approach. A new thematic perspective is needed in South Carolina historical archaeology.

The present volume had its genesis in a series of symposia that explored the landscape approach as a unifying theme to help synthesize historical archaeological studies of South Carolina. Scholars from the fields of anthropology, history, and geography came together to discuss the concept of landscape and the notion of interdisciplinary research in landscape archaeology. The chapters in Part I of this volume arose out of that debate. These essays provide a theoretical framework and interdisciplinary overview of landscape studies. Geographer John Winberry, in the first chapter, sets the stage by reviewing the conceptual history of "landscape" in geography. He notes that archaeologists have yet to find similar agreement on the definition of land-scape in archaeological research. Winberry demonstrates that archaeologists in this volume use a landscape perspective in three distinct ways. The first is to provide a contextual basis to tie regional studies to larger cultural patterns, the second as an ecological approach to understand combined natural and cultural effects on the land, and third, as a way to preserve those modern physical landscapes that retain material remnants of the past.

In the next two chapters, anthropologists specializing in archaeology offer their own definitions of landscape and discuss methodological and theoretical implications of archaeological landscape research. Stan Green emphasizes the important interdisciplinary nature of landscape archaeology. He discusses the potential of using the landscape as a unit of analysis. Green argues that archaeologists must reconsider their use of fundamental concepts, such as site and feature, and basic tools, such as sampling designs. He believes that archaeologists should also use the landscape approach to consider areas that did not serve as the primary locus of human activities, opening archaeology to broader spatial and ultimately cultural studies. In her essay, Carole Crumley explains how the dialectical method can enhance landscape archaeology. She also sees landscape research as a means to bridge the natural and cultural sciences through the common use of five concepts: landscape, region, scale, complexity, and diversity. The next essay is by historian Peter Wood. He has worked with a number of archaeologists in the region and discusses the problems and promises of interdisciplinary research. Wood finds that historians and archaeologists have to learn how to appreciate the unique skills that members of each discipline practice. A shared interest in interpreting the past, and especially a shared focus on understanding historical landscape formation and change, necessitates improved communication between historians and archaeologists.

In the last chapter in Part I, anthropologist Ken Lewis views landscape investigation as an approach that broadens archaeological definitions and interpretations of settlement pattern studies. Lewis compares and contrasts results of his research on frontier landscapes in South Carolina and Michigan to illustrate his points. He recognizes four important common factors in frontier landscape studies: environmental conditions, land acquisition, production and marketing systems, and motivations for colonization.

In the case studies in Part II archaeologists have limited their region of landscape study based on each author's research focus. Two chapters, detailing the development of landscapes related to iron making (Ferguson and Cowan) and tar and pitch production (Harmon and Snedeker), take the broadest regional perspective. Their respective studies combine the results of archaeological investigations in both North and South Carolina. In contradistinction, Wayne's archaeological and historical research on brick making focuses on production in a smaller physiographic region, the lowcountry of South Carolina. Each author seeks to describe the broad patterns of human activity that occurred during production and the resulting impact on the physical landscape.

Chapters by Joseph, Beard, Crass and Brooks, and Joseph and Reed are about developing rural landscapes in South Carolina. In his essay on plantation landscapes, Joseph compares and contrasts land use patterns through space and time. Joseph examines the economic, ideological, and environmental factors that led to the development of distinctive backcountry and lowcountry plantation systems. He discusses how these systems changed over time as a response to dynamic environmental and social factors. Beard's essay details the related development of causeways and landings in the lowcountry landscape during the plantation period. He also offers a developmental typology of these features to enable better communication between terrestrial and underwater archaeologists and preservation planners. The essay by Crass and Brooks on changing historical settlement patterns in the sandhills provides data from a different physiographic area. Their chapter illus-

trates how a landscape perspective helps to broaden interpretation of settlement data, even if these data are preliminary, collected at a survey level. This contrasts to Reed and Joseph's site-specific chapter detailing results from an intensive data-recovery project in the backcountry of South Carolina. In their essay on the Finch Farm in Spartanburg County, Joseph and Reed use a landscape perspective to tie the archaeological signature of the turn-of-the-century farmstead to transforming social mores. Changes in the orientation and presentation of the farmstead buildings and associated features such as roads, activity areas, and landscaping are viewed as symbols of burgeoning, national ideological debates.

The effectiveness of landscape archaeology in an urban setting is discussed in the last two case studies by Zierden and Joyce. Zierden discusses the growth of urban archaeological studies in South Carolina and explains why most recorded urban studies have focused on Charleston. Landscape archaeology offers a broader, interdisciplinary perspective for urban archaeologists, and Zierden demonstrates this by summarizing many seasons of archaeological investigations in Charleston, detailing and explaining changes in the built environment, land use, and ideology over time and space. Joyce, in her restricted study of land use in one ward in antebellum Charleston, seeks a correspondence between dynamic social hierarchies and changes in land patterns and the built environment.

The last essays in Part III of this volume discuss how a landscape perspective can improve archaeological interpretation and management for cultural resource managers and the public. Stine and Stine briefly summarize the history of archaeological landscape studies in South Carolina and discuss the impetus of landscape archaeology for new interpretive and management techniques. They describe how technological innovations from geography, such as global positioning satellites, remote sensing, and geographic information systems should be integrated into landscape studies. The ramifications of landscape archaeology for integrating the goals of conservationists and preservationists, for preservation planning, and for National Register of Historic Places review is explored. In his essay, Errante explains how any study of lowcountry landscapes must include riverine and coastal environments and subsequent human modifications. He has coined the term "waterscape" to highlight the importance of ports, landings, harbors, and haul-overs for fully understanding social, economic, and transportation systems of plantations. He believes that Carolina preservationists should increase their interactions with both terrestrial and underwater archaeologists and treat both the plantation "landscape" and "waterscape" as a single cultural system. Drucker writes that preservationists should also think more holistically and seek to preserve South Carolina's historical landscape remnants. She argues that a landscape approach to preservation will better integrate the different needs of planners, archaeologists, tourists, and the general public.

In the last chapter in the volume, Stine undertakes a comparative case study of archaeological sites recorded for Charleston and York counties in South Carolina. Differences in the types of sites recorded and judged worthy of preservation are discussed in light of differential biases about the importance of particular types of sites to the history of the backcountry and lowcountry. The next section of the essay is formulated around a series of formal (and informal) discussions between 1991 and 1996 among Carolina university anthropologists, geographers, and historians, research institute archaeologists, cultural resource managers and archaeologists, and government preservationists about the value of using a landscape perspective in historical preservation. She ends her chapter with a discussion of the techniques and perspectives of landscape archaeology—as a tool for improving our understanding of the state's past and as a tool for better managing the state's archaeological resources.

NOTES

1. Hodder 1986.
2. Crumley 1979.
3. Crumley 1979:143–44; Spaulding 1960.
4. Stilgoe 1982:3.
5. Jackson 1984:7–8.
6. Deetz 1977.
7. Upton 1990.
8. Shackel and Little 1994; Kryder–Reid 1994.
9. Upton 1990.
10. Deetz 1977; Deetz 1990; Kelso and Most 1990; Miller 1994.
11. Upton 1990; Kryder–Reid 1994.
12. Miller 1994.
13. Deetz 1990; Kryder–Reid 1994.
14. Upton 1990.
15. Herman 1989; Zierden and Herman 1996.
16. Deetz 1990:2.
17. Kelso and Most 1990.
18. Wallerstein 1980.

WORKS CITED

Crumley, Carole L.
1979   Three Locational Models: An Epistemological Assessment for Anthropology and Archaeology. In *Advances in Archaeological Method and Theory,* vol. 2, edited by Michael B. Schiffer, pp. 141–73. Academic Press, New York.

Deetz, James
1977   Material Culture and Archaeology—What's the Difference? In *Historical Archaeology and the Importance of Material Things,* edited by Leland Ferguson. Special Publications Series No. 2, Society for Historical Archaeology, Tucson.
1990   Prologue: Landscapes as Cultural Statements. In *Earth Patterns,* edited by William Kelso and Rachel Most, pp. 1–4. Univ. Press of Virginia, Charlottesville.

Hodder, Ian
1986   *Reading the Past: Current Approaches to Interpretation in Archaeology.* Cambridge Univ. Press, Cambridge.

Jackson, James Brinckerhof
1984   *Discovering the Vernacular Landscape.* Yale Univ. Press, New Haven.

Kelso, William, and Rachel Most (editors)
1990   *Earth Patterns: Essays in Landscape Archaeology.* Univ. Press of Virginia, Charlottesville.

Kryder-Reid, Elizabeth
1994   As Is the Gardener, So Is the Garden: The Archaeology of Landscape as Myth. In *Historical Archaeology of the Chesapeake,* edited by Paul Shackel and Barbara Little, pp. 131–48. Smithsonian Institution Press, Washington, D.C.

Miller, Henry
1994   The Country's House Site: An Archaeological Study of a Seventeenth-Century Domestic Landscape. In *Historical Archaeology of the Chesapeake,* edited by Paul Shackel and Barbara Little, pp. 65–84. Smithsonian Institution Press, Washington, D.C.

Shackel, Paul, and Barbara Little
1994   Introduction: Plantation and Landscape Studies. In *Historical Archaeology of the Chesapeake,* edited by Paul Shackel and Barbara Little, pp. 97–100. Smithsonian Institution Press, Washington, D.C.

Spaulding, Albert
1960   The Dimensions of Archaeology. In *Essays on the Science of Culture in Honor of Leslie A. White,* edited by Gertrude Dole and Robert Carneiro, pp. 437–56. Thomas Y. Crowell, New York.

Stilgoe, John R.
1982   *Common Landscape of America, 1580–1845.* Yale Univ. Press, New Haven.

Upton, Dell
1990   Imagining the Early Virginia Landscape. In Earth Patterns, edited by William Kelso and Rachel Most, pp. 71–88. Univ. Press of Virginia, Charlottesville.

Wallerstein, Immanuel
1980   *The Modern World System II: Mercantilism and the Consolidation of the European World Economy, 1600–1750.* Academic Press, New York.

Zierden, Martha, and Bernard L. Herman
1996   Charleston Townhouses: Archaeology, Architecture, and the Urban Landscape, 1750–1850. In *Landscape Archaeology: Reading and Interpreting the American Historical Landscape,* edited by Rebecca Yamin and Karen Bescherer Metheny. Univ. of Tennessee Press, Knoxville.

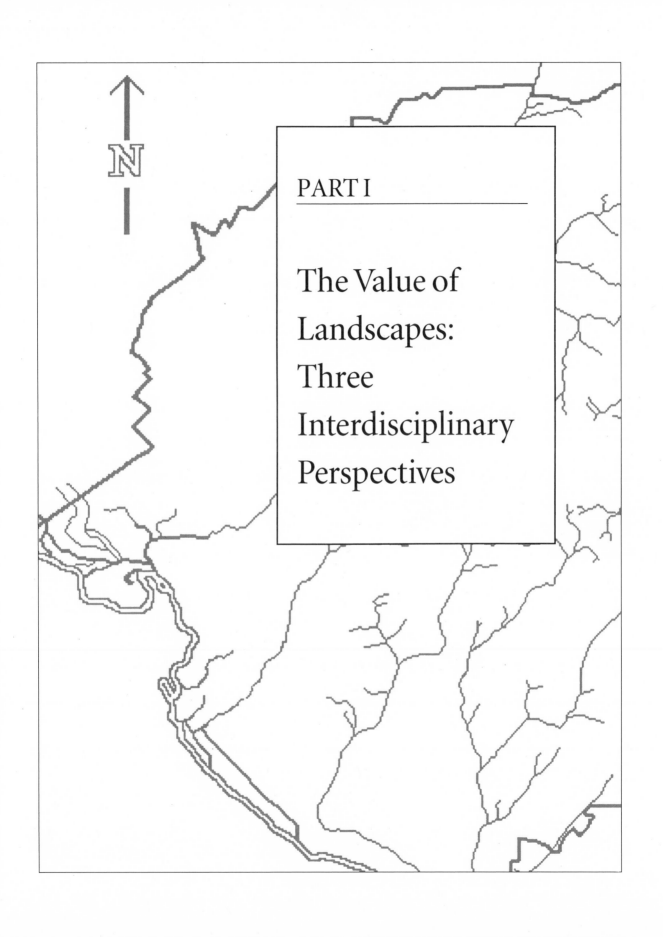

PART I

The Value of
Landscapes:
Three
Interdisciplinary
Perspectives

1. The Geographic Concept of Landscape: The History of a Paradigm

John J. Winberry

The concept of landscape has received a great deal of attention lately from archaeologists, as evidenced by the many chapters in this volume that incorporate the word into their titles.[1] It is a term that has been and is used by a number of different disciplines, including art and architecture. It was introduced into American geography about seventy years ago in Carl Sauer's seminal paper, "The Morphology of Landscape," and has been the subject of debate among geographers regarding its nature and approach. Despite the apparent simplicity of the concept, questions early were raised about its exact definition, and recently the term has faced the challenge of the "new" cultural geography and its rejection of the traditional approaches to the study of landscape. Despite these differences, geographers agree on what essentially is meant by landscape but continue to argue over how it is to be studied. Archaeology, on the other hand, adopted the idea of landscape recently, but the field seems to be at an early stage in clarifying the concept and uncertain about its meaning and application.

This chapter therefore has a twofold purpose. First, it will review the concept of landscape as it developed in geography, citing the early debates regarding its precise definition and later criticisms of how it was to be studied. This latter theme will address especially the position put forward by the "new" cultural geography. I will argue that the criticisms that it presents actually fail to acknowledge the changes that have taken place in the approach of traditional cultural geographers to landscape study, especially over the last few decades. Instead of the intellectual discontinuity that the "new" cultural geography claims, these changes create a continuous and unbroken evolution in the concept of landscape. While its foundation rests in Sauer's original ideas, this changing approach has gone beyond his early position and actually preempts, I argue, the essential criticisms offered by the "new" cultural geography. Second, this chapter will consider the use of landscape in the chapters that make up the bulk of this volume in an attempt to identify the archaeological definition of the term. The basic point is that archaeology has not yet reached a generally accepted definition of landscape, whereas geography, despite earlier debates and the many changes in how landscape is viewed, has established a clear meaning for the concept.

Carl Sauer and the Beginnings of Landscape Study

When geography began reentering the universities of the United States with the formation of geography departments at a number of major institutions at the turn of the twentieth century, it was strongly influenced by the Darwinian Revolution and the thesis of environmental determinism.[2] Though having its roots set deeply in the writings of Hippocrates and maintaining a strong explanatory power through the nineteenth century, expressed especially in the work of the German geographer Karl Ritter and his students, environmental determinism had an impact on American geography primarily through William Morris Davis. Trained as a geologist and physical geographer, Davis was a leading figure in the early development of geography in the United States. His presidential address to the Association of American Geographers in 1906 defined geography as the study of the responses of organisms, including humans, to the natural environment. Davis stated, "I am disposed to say that any statement is of geographical quality if it contains a reasonable relation between some inorganic element of the earth on which we live, acting as a control, and some fact concerning the existence or growth of behavior or distribution of the earth's organic inhabitants, serving as a response."[3] Later presidential addresses to the Association of American Geographers by Albert Perry Brigham, Harlan Barrows, and Charles Dryer, while cautious in the face of Davis's dominant influence, began to move away from a purely deterministic role for the natural environment and set the stage for Carl Sauer's contribution.[4]

Sauer received his Ph.D. from the University of Chicago almost a decade after Davis's address and joined the Department of Geography at the University of Michigan, where he remained for seven years. In 1923, he accepted the professorship of geography at the University of California—Berkeley and shortly thereafter published "The Morphology of Landscape." In it, he sought to bring the ideas of European geographers to the attention of American geography, introduced the concept of landscape, and rejected finally the rubric of environmental determinism, which, by the mid-1920s, was being questioned especially by younger geographers. As James and Martin point out, this younger generation was "ready to accept a change of paradigm, [and w]ith enthusiasm they turned to the study of landscapes."[5] Sauer's "Morphology" included some important points. First, he argued that geography, like any discipline, had to base itself on "a naively given section of reality," and to Sauer that was the study of area or chorology, a distinctly geographic theme. Chorology in turn was to focus on the theme of landscape, which Sauer identified as "the unit concept of geography" and defined "as an area made up of a distinct association of forms, both physical and cultural." Second, he divided landscape into the natural and cultural and stated that "[t]he cultural landscape is the geographic area in the final meaning," a collection of features that is the product of human activity. He believed that "[c]ulture is the agent, the natural area is the medium, and the cultural landscape the result. Under the influence of a given culture, itself changing through time, the landscape undergoes development, passing through phases, and probably reaching ultimately the end of its cycle of development."[6] One should note especially Sauer's emphasis on the role of culture and the relegation of the environment to being little more than a medium for its operation.

His definition of geography, with its focus on landscape, was actually a variation of regional geography that sought to identify culture areas across the world on the basis of "generic" landscapes. He argued that "landscape is not simply an actual scene viewed by an observer [but] a generalization derived from the observation of individual scenes." Sauer emphasized that the landscape and not the process behind its formation was the focus of research for the geographer: "we are not concerned in geography with the energy, customs, or beliefs of man but with man's record upon the landscape."[7]

Sauer continued developing the theme of landscape in 1931 with an encyclopedia entry that gave a clearer definition of the concept, a definition that has changed little since. He wrote, "Cultural geography is therefore concerned with those works of man that are inscribed into the earth's surface and give to it characteristic expression." It clearly emphasized that the focus of geography would be the material components of place analyzed from a historical perspective, but that the overall goal of the discipline still remained an areal understanding of the earth's surface. Sauer explained, "Cultural geography then implies a program which is unified with the general objective of geography; that is, an understanding of the areal differentiation of the earth. It rests largely on direct field observations. . . . Its method is developmental, specifically historical in so far as the material permits, and it therefore seeks to determine the successions of cultures that have taken place in an area."[8]

The writings of his students also reflected the developing intellectual parameters of Sauer's geographical philosophy regarding landscape. Fred Kniffen's 1936 paper on Louisiana house types employed a "quantitative and qualitative consideration of the cultural forms of the landscape," in this case rural house types, to define culturogeographic regions. These regions, he argued, were based on the spatial distribution of landscape traits and differed from geographic regions "in that only cultural forms are considered." Kniffen noted the influence of the Swedish ethnologist Erland Nordenskiold and his use of cultural traits "in arriving at culture regions."[9] House forms were readily visible in the landscape and could be associated with different cultural groups occupying one or another part of Louisiana. Kniffen saw this approach as not just description and mapping of distributions but "also an attempt to get at an areal expression of *ideas* regarding houses—a groping toward a tangible hold on the geographic expression of culture." The focus, however, remained on the forms in the landscape rather than their functions.

John Leighly's 1937 article contributed to the continued development of the landscape concept by presenting a clear statement regarding its contents and defining how geographers should study it. In contrast to earlier emphases on whole landscapes as the basis of analysis, Leighly identified individual landscape features, as had Kniffen, as the appropriate subjects of study. He wrote, "[The geographer] will be concerned with dwellings and other structures intended to shelter human beings and their possessions; with roads, bridges, and lines of division of the land; with features molded of the stuff of the earth itself—ditches, walls, furrows; in general with the *immobilia* among the products of culture and with the patterns in which they are arranged on the ground."[10]

Leighly criticized specifically the regional perspective, arguing that good regional description, even synthesis, was the work of the artist rather than the scientist. To describe a region, "[t]here must be a selection of items, and selection presupposes guiding principles," but "the criterion of selection lies outside any discipline that concerns itself, by definition, with regions as such."[11] Leighly reiterated Sauer's point as to the importance of a historical perspective: "we can work toward a historical understanding of anything [that culture] has contributed to the landscape." In other words, the scientific approach that was being advocated focused on the elements of the landscape, their ultimate origin, and how they came to be a part of the present-day landscape, whether by diffusion, migration, or even persistence as palimpsests from previous landscapes. This approach to geography, with its emphasis on cultural landscape and the historical perspective, typified the work of Sauer and his students and came to be referred to as the Berkeley School.

What Is Landscape?

After the demise of environmental determinism as a paradigm for geography, the field sought to establish a new identity and carve out its distinctive focus of study. One of the most influential statements in this debate was a monograph entitled *The Nature of Geography,* in which Richard Hartshorne combined a historical and wide-ranging analysis of the literature of geography, primarily from Europe, and argued that the discipline should be defined as "the study of areal differentiation." He devoted one chapter of the book to a critique of Sauer's focus on landscape and the question of its actual meaning.[12] Hartshorne's argument began with the definition of the word *landschaft,* the German root of "landscape," and he criticized those who had introduced the term into American geography without clearly defining it. The word, he pointed out, carried a plethora of meanings in its original German and could be defined, for example, as "the appearance of a piece of land as we perceive it, or simply a restricted piece of land."

Hartshorne targeted Sauer's "Morphology" and noted, "The more often this essay is studied . . . the more difficult it is to perceive just what the difference is between 'landscape' and 'area.'"[13] Later in the same chapter, Hartshorne wrote, "[I]t seems desirable for American geographers, at least, to attempt to come to some agreement of what the word 'landscape,' as a technical term in our field, shall denote."[14] There had been some confusion in the "Morphology" itself regarding the interpretation of the word, but Sauer had clearly defined landscape in his 1931 paper. Leighly had limited the term to the cultural immobilia on the surface of the earth in his article, and both had been published before Hartshorne came out with his study. In addition, Hartshorne criticized Sauer's concept of landscape because it excluded what was not visible on the surface of the earth, arguing that these non-material variables constituted equally significant geographic facts.

Sauer addressed some of Hartshorne's comments in his presidential address to the Association of American Geographers in 1941. For instance, he clearly defined landscape, although admitting its limitations:

> We have available . . . an immediately useful restriction to the material culture complex that is expressed in the 'cultural landscape.' This is the geographic version of the economy of the group, as providing itself with food, shelter, furnishings, tools, and transport. The specific geographic expressions are the fields, pastures, woods, and mines, the productive land on the one hand, and the roads and structures on the other. . . . Though I should not argue that these terms include all of human geography, they are the core of the things that we know how to approach systematically.[15]

He also re-emphasized the diachronic as the proper approach to landscape study, arguing that "The geographer cannot study houses and towns, fields and factories, as to their where and why without asking himself about their origins."[16]

Sauer therefore defined the landscape as the material artifacts of place, the visible human imprint on the surface of the earth, and argued that geographers should use a historical perspective in its analysis. This included, first, the determination of origins and explanations of how features had become a part of the assemblage of material traits that gave character to a particular area and, second, the reconstruction of past landscapes through field and archival research. The ultimate purpose of the study of landscape therefore was the understanding of places, and the emphasis seemed increasingly to be on an idiographic orientation, notwithstanding the use of general principles such as culture, diffusion, and historical change.

By this time, the concept of landscape as the works of man inscribed into the surface of the earth was well established in the geographical literature. Philip Wagner and Marvin Mikesell in their edited collection of readings in cultural geography clearly separated cultural landscape from culture area (or region), the confusion which Hartshorne had noted much earlier. They defined the latter as a "unit in space, characterized by relative internal homogeneity in regard to certain criteria," while landscape was described as "the typical association of concrete geographic features within a region, or in any other spatial subdivision of the earth."[17] They reiterated the importance of the diachronic approach in the studying the landscape and stated: "The evolution of a landscape is a gradual and cumulative process—it has a history."[18] Wagner and Mikesell also accepted Hartshorne's recommendation that the term "landscape" be derived from the German *landschaftsbild,* a word that "refer[s] to the appearance of an area, not to the area itself as a delimited entity," instead of from *landschaft,* which had areal connotations.

Throughout the introduction to their book, the two editors frequently mentioned the concept of culture. In one oft-cited statement, however, they limited the extent of the geographer's interest in it: "The cultural geographer is not concerned with explaining the inner workings of culture or with describing fully patterns of human behavior, even when they affect the land, but . . . studies the distribution in time and space of cultures and elements of culture."[19] This really was a repetition of Sauer's earlier-expressed position in the "Morphology" that "we are not concerned in geography with the energy, customs, or beliefs of man but with man's record upon the landscape."

The concept of landscape therefore had undergone many interpretations during the first decade or so after Sauer had introduced it into American geography. But with time it had come to have a distinctive definition and one that is generally accepted by geographers today. While agreement had been reached on the definition of landscape, the approach to its study would soon become the subject of considerable debate. This was foreshadowed by two papers, one calling for a more theoretical orientation to the study of geography and the other criticizing the imposed intellectual limits of human geography. Around them would coalesce the challenges to the traditional study of landscape by the "new" cultural geography, which began in the 1980s.

Theory, the New Cultural Geography, and the Landscape

The debate over the focus of geography in the United States had involved many scholars, but, as noted above, one of the most influential was Hartshorne. He defined geography as "the study of areal differentiation," emphasizing the regional approach, the uniqueness of individual places, and

the discipline's essentially idiographic character. In 1953, Fred Schaefer questioned this position, arguing that geography instead "had to be conceived as the science concerned with the formulation of the laws governing the spatial distribution of certain features on the surface of the earth."[20] This presaged a major intellectual change as geography was challenged to join the social sciences and become a theory-based discipline with an emphasis on quantitative analysis. For the most part, the work of traditional cultural geographers did not fit this model, and they continued to study landscape as they had, finding themselves increasingly excluded from this developing nomothetic paradigm. In David Harvey's words, "[The cultural geographer] can either bury his head, ostrich-like, in the sand grains of an idiographic human history, conducted over unique geographic space, scowl upon broad generalization. . . . Or he can become a scientist and attempt, by the normal procedures of scientific investigation, to verify, or modify, the stimulating and exciting ideas which his predecessors presented him with."[21]

A second major criticism concerned cultural geography's reliance on description and lack of interest in understanding the inner workings of culture to explain the how and why of the formation of landscapes. Harold Brookfield especially cited the Berkeley School and stated that American geographers tended to limit their inquiry into the understanding of culture and "scarcely ever seek explanations in matters such as human behavior, attitudes and beliefs, social organization, and the characteristics and interrelationships of human groups."[22] He added that they instead accepted culture as a force of its own with little or no further analysis, but "I have so far found little reason for restricting the search for explanation . . . so as to exclude the varieties of human behavior and social organization."[23] He concluded that geographers had to adopt a perspective that involved "the diligent and unfettered search for satisfying answers to meaningful and rigorously formulated questions" and take a more critical approach to the delineation of culture and human behavior in the creation of the cultural landscape.

These two articles foreshadowed the rise of the "new" cultural geography in the 1980s, which began criticizing the traditional approach to studying landscape, calling on one hand for a more theoretical orientation and on the other for the rejection of the superorganic concept of culture and its replacement with an awareness of the social and political underpinnings of human behavior. To the "new" cultural geography, the traditional approach "was limited to the interpretation of historical, rural, and relict landscapes and to a static mapping of the distribution of cultural traits, from barns and cabins to field systems and graveyards."[24] "Their concerns were dominantly rural and antiquarian, narrowly focused on *physical artifacts*,"[25] while the "new" cultural geography saw the landscape as a complex expression, formed in different media and allowing for a broader interpretation of the content and its symbolism: "Landscape is a cultural image, a pictorial way of representing, structuring or symbolizing surroundings. This is not to say that landscapes are immaterial. They may be represented in a variety of materials and on many surfaces—in paint on canvas, in writing on paper, in earth, stone, water and vegetation on the ground."[26] The specific definition of landscape, "those works of man that are inscribed into the earth's surface," remained unchanged, however, but the manner of approaching it was seen as more interactive with its human occupants and more theoretical in its orientation. The landscape was not merely a collection of material artifacts, each with a particular history; it actually comprised a set of symbols that reinforced the political, economic, and social structure within the society. Denis Cosgrove criticized the morphological approach, associated with the Berkeley School, when he said, "Morphological analysis, with its concentration on empirically defined forms and their integration, can operate only at a surface level of meaning.... Below this lie deeper meanings which are culturally and historically specific.... Formal morphology remains unconvincing as an account of *landscape* to the extent that it ignores such symbolic dimensions."[27]

One theme growing out of this new analytic approach was to view landscapes as text, defining them as to "how they are constructed on the basis of a set of texts, how they are read, and how they act as a mediating influence, shaping behavior in the image of this text."[28] Seeking a more nomothetic orientation beyond mere description, the "new" cultural geography argued, "Virtually any landscape can be analyzed as a text in which social relations are inscribed."[29] The nomothetic dimension of landscape was not to be expressed in the generic delineation of landscape, as Sauer had spelled out in the "Morphology"; instead, the nomothetic generalizations would grow out of the relationship between the forms of landscape and the principles of social theory. "Cosgrove offers a critical alternative to the extreme subjectivity of much landscape research, reinserting the landscape into contemporary political and ideological debates."[30] Despite the common agreement among geographers on the contents of landscape, the "new" cultural geography saw itself as a totally different intellectual construct. It rejected the former "tradition of cultural landscape geography for its untheoretical adherence to a superorganic view of culture" and argued that it offered a wholly new approach.[31]

Another criticism by the "new" cultural geography, which had been addressed by Brookfield two decades earlier, involved the reliance of the Berkeley School on the superorganic concept of culture. Sauer's use of the superorganic and the apparent rejection of the workings of culture as a concern of landscape study was unacceptable to the "new" cultural geographers who studied the social and political substructure of landscape formation. Usually associated with his colleague in anthropology at Berkeley, Alfred Kroeber, the superorganic was adopted by Sauer and his students and used as the mechanism to explain how landscapes were formed. Its historical approach emphasized diffusion as a mode of cultural change, providing the means by which cultural traits became a part of the landscape. To the "new" cultural geographers, this mystical nature attributed to the superorganic without any attempt to understand its workings agreed with a perspective that considered only the morphology of landscape. The "new" cultural geography, however, identified the superorganic as a bankrupt concept, noting that it even had been abandoned by cultural anthropologists. To the "new" cultural geographers, "Culture [i.e., the superorganic] was viewed as an entity above man, not reducible to actions by individuals who are associated with it, mysteriously responding to laws of its own."[32] "To the extent that cultural geographers take culture to be a determining force, other types of explanation do not appear to be necessary.... We find little or no attempt to find empirical evidence of the processes by which cultural patterns are generated."[33] The emphasis on the homogeneity of human behavior, the lack of attention given to individual decision making, and the limited number of questions that could be applied to understanding human behavior constituted an issue of considerable import to the "new" cultural geographers. They argued that "[t]he superorganic implies a view of man as relatively passive and impotent. If the individual is considered atomistic and isolated then the binding forces between men must be external to them. Individuals making choices, interacting, negotiating, imposing constraints on one another are, then, largely ignored."[34]

In a recent article refuting the criticisms by the "new" cultural geography, Marie Price and Martin Lewis identify the Berkeley School as a department and graduate program rather than an intellectual heritage and really do not consider its philosophical identity with traditional landscape study as outlined above. As a result, their argument is that the Berkeley program has changed, citing the new faculty in the Berkeley department, their different research interests, and the development of such new approaches as cultural ecology.[35] The authors do not mention, however, the changes that also have occurred in the study of landscape by traditional cultural geographers. Many of these cultural geographers, however, were not products of the Berkeley department but, I feel, did share its traditional approach.[36] They have given landscape study a very different nature from what had been long associated with the Berkeley School and

identified by Mikesell in his presidential address of 1978.[37] These developments ironically could be seen as moving landscape study into a position actually to become a base for the "new" cultural geography rather than leaving a chasm separating the two approaches. The approach to studying landscape had not been static since 1962, when Wagner and Mikesell published their collection of readings, but it has matured to incorporate new ideas and interpretations—but still with its base in Sauer's early definition. The approach to landscape today, therefore, has been the product of an evolutionary process rather than the sudden adoption of a new paradigm as argued by the "new" cultural geography.

Changes in the Traditional View of Landscape

Cultural geography remains a viable intellectual endeavor, rooted in the model developed by the traditional Berkeley School approach to the study of landscape. Many criticisms of that approach, however, have focused on its rural, antiquarian, and atheoretical character and tendency to accept the superorganic concept of culture. While these criticisms have a certain validity with regard to the early history of landscape analysis, as noted above, they fail to consider the changes and developments that have characterized landscape study especially since the 1960s. A number of cultural geographers began to adopt new approaches to the cultural landscape, in many instances anticipating some of the criticisms that would come later. While not necessarily students of Sauer, many saw themselves as part of that tradition. Among the themes introduced was a new epistemological approach to landscape, a focus on contemporary and urban landscapes and their interpretation, a call to read the landscape with a sensitivity for its symbolic content rather than just describe it morphologically, and an attempt to derive a new definition of the workings of culture and the role of the individual in the formation of landscape.

David Lowenthal's seminal work on geography

and epistemology did not focus on landscape per se, but it introduced an important concept to that study that had a major impact on geographical thinking. Lowenthal argued that the landscape that we see is the product of a complex mental filtering of information that we receive through our senses: "Every image and idea about the world is compounded, then, of personal experience, learning, imagination, and memory.... The surface of the earth is shaped for each person by refraction through cultural and personal lenses of custom and fancy."[38] Landscapes therefore were not monolithic but were perceived uniquely by different individuals and groups, based on their precepts, percepts, and experiences. One could no longer talk of a landscape that was simply a collection of objects, but one had to consider how different groups perceived and used that landscape and how their perception of it affected their behavior. Sauer had presaged this theme in his 1941 article on historical geography, noting that a geographer "needs the ability to see the land with the eyes of its former occupants, from the standpoint of their needs and capacities."[39]

Just as landscapes had a certain relativity with regard to the process of perception, they also conveyed different types of information. Landscapes, in fact, were repositories of information about the people who created them, and they could and should be read like a book. Peirce Lewis wrote, "Our human landscape is our unwitting autobiography, reflecting our tastes, our values, our aspirations, and even our fears, in tangible, visible form."[40] The landscape, therefore, was not just the complex of material traits that gave character to an area but a collection of objects rich in meaning and ready for interpretation by the careful reader/observer.

Lewis had no hesitancy about studying modern as well as past landscapes and urban as well as rural landscapes, broadening the approach to landscape study that long had been tied more intimately to the past and to rural settings. The work of J. B. Jackson in landscape study developed this direction even further; as Donald Meinig wrote in a review of his work, "Jackson points the way in his insistence on looking the modern scene squarely in the face; and

his admonition is not simply for us to be comprehensive and tolerant, but to see the ordinary landscape of the automobile, mobile home, supermarket, and shopping center as legitimately 'vernacular' ... [u]nderlying that, of course, is his basic principle of evaluating landscapes in terms of *life*."[41]

In a more recent work, Lowenthal emphasized that even relict features from past landscapes could not be understood at only one level. Such features represented the past, but their preservation and recognition reflected the values and expectations of the present: "Every trace of the past is a testament not only to its initiators but to its inheritors, not only to the spirit of the past, but to the perspectives of the present."[42] Landscapes therefore were being seen and described by traditional cultural geographers as complex entities with specific histories, layered symbolization, deeper meanings, and iconographic images that communicated a great deal to the reader/observer. This developing idea of landscape, however, did not necessitate a structuralist interpretation of social, economic, and political theory, but such an approach could not be excluded from the analysis.

Just as students of landscape began approaching it with a perspective that broadened its meaning, geographers were taking a new look at the concept of culture itself. Both Wagner and Mikesell moderated their previous indifference to the issue, with Wagner noting, "I am sure that the idea of culture needs rethinking, in order that it may become a tool for larger tasks."[43] Milton Newton and Linda Pulliam-di Napoli sought to give a more creative interpretation to culture, defining it not as a superorganic determinant of values, as had been the case in the past, but tying it more to the interaction of individuals, each carrying his or her experiences and models into a dialogue. They wrote, "Where in a public occasion, each individual of the party holds his own practical syllogisms, and in which the largely conventional relations among men are factors as much as the environmental situation, the resolution of the potentialities of the occasion takes the form of rhetoric."[44] Marwyn Samuels furthermore questioned the biography of landscape and considered more carefully the role of the individual in its formation.[45]

Based on the works of these and many other geographers contributing to this evolutionary development, the broader concept of landscape and how it was to be studied were going through change even before the "new" cultural geography had begun its critical attacks on the Berkeley School. Not only was the landscape being analyzed for its meaning, but attempts were being made to provide a new interpretation of the workings of culture, anticipating the criticisms that would be voiced in the 1980s. Landscape study had not moved toward social geography and a structuralist underpinning, however, and it was this approach that would become central to the "new" cultural geography, but I would argue that traditional cultural geographers had laid the foundation for adopting such a critique.

Since its introduction into the geographic literature some seventy years ago, the concept of the cultural landscape has been the subject of debate, from early disagreements on its definition to later criticisms of the approaches to its study. Despite all this, the content of landscape was clearly defined and early accepted by the geography community as "those works of man that are inscribed into the earth's surface and give to it characteristic expression." Whether that imprint was to be seen as a collection of cultural artifacts for historic analysis or symbols for iconographic interpretation, the product of a faceless superorganic or of individual decisions, landscape became a paradigm, a major organizing principle in geographic study, and has remained a central concept of modern cultural geography.

Landscape and Archaeology

While geographers appear to have agreed on a clear definition of landscape, the chapters presented in this volume suggest that archaeologists have not reached such a consensus, even though many incorporate landscape into the titles of their essays. In a recent article, B. K. Roberts defined landscapes "as the assemblages of real-world features—natural,

semi-natural and wholly artificial—[that] give character and diversity to the earth's surface and *form the physical framework within which human societies exist* (emphasis added)."[46] In the same article, the author notes the difficulty of defining landscape, and his discussion presents a number of different ideas of what landscape includes. This gives the impression that the term is not clearly and specifically defined in archaeology nor that it agrees with the definition used by geographers. The contributions in this book also give landscape a number of different meanings, and some even ascribe more than one definition or approach to the concept. There seem to be three dominant themes that are presented by the authors in the following chapters that vary from what could be considered the geographic concept of landscape presented above:

1) Perhaps the most important concept for archaeologists is the "site," which traditionally has been the focus of their study and analysis. Such a narrow orientation has been found inadequate, however, because sites do not exist in a vacuum but have links with larger areas of human activity and resource exploitation. Archaeologists, therefore, have begun to think at a different scale, and, as Stine and Stine note, "a landscape perspective leads to a holistic investigation." Furthermore, "Landscape theory seeks to make connections between material remains, social institutions, natural resources, and human perceptions." This latter perspective is echoed by Joyce, who views "landscape and the production of space as a rudimentary element of social relations. Social relations are not only reflected in the landscape, the expressed landscape actively shapes those relations. It is the *process* by which a landscape is produced and encoded that is of critical importance for understanding past social relations." Errante states that landscape is associated with a more holistic approach and emphasizes the need to study it at a scale that allows the delineation of patterns.

Joseph and Reed allude to this issue of scale, arguing that the analysis of a larger area is necessary to understand a number of themes related to landscapes, including "the division of labor, social and socioeconomic relationships, the control of nature, and changing attitudes and responses toward refuse disposal and sanitation." Joseph points out that the landscape perspective focuses on the changes in social structure that modify and shape settlement patterns and the insights provided by settlement patterns into the social relationships and ideology of the groups that fashioned them. In other words, landscape is seen by archaeologists to consider the larger picture, what goes beyond the specifics of a single site; it is a liberating concept that gives archaeology a more emic nature as it links its analysis of the material trait or artifact with broader social and economic patterns.

This definition, however, raises two issues, both of which relate to methodology. First, there is no clear idea of what scale Errante or Joseph and Reed are referring to in their search for patterns; is it a regional scale? If so, what is the role of the site and archaeological procedure within this context? Second, none of the authors offers a methodology that allows one to move from observation of material traits to interpretation of the landscape to insights into the socioeconomic and ideological variables that created them. In fact, there seems to be almost an a priori assumption regarding these traits and their socioeconomic meanings rather than a logical and empirically based explanation of meaning and relationship.

2) Another definition of landscape suggested by Roberts in the quotation above and presented in the following chapters is related more to cultural ecology as it incorporates the interaction between humans and the natural environment. As Stine and Stine argue, "By focusing on the relations between the natural and cultural worlds, landscape alters our perspective to reach beyond description." Harmon and Snedeker, Crass and Brooks, and Wayne incorporate this ecological perspective into their analyses respectively of tar kilns, settlement patterns on the Savannah River Site, and brick making in the South Carolina lowcountry. Errante coined the term "waterscape" to show "the interaction of humans and the presence of any bodies of water." Again,

such a definition gives archaeologists a more emic base to their analysis by bringing in other variables, this time the natural environment. But this approach seems to involve more of a study of ecological relationships than an analysis of the features of human occupation.

3) A last theme involves the concept of the "historical landscape" and its intellectual reconstruction and actual preservation. Drucker posits that the preservation not just of individual sites but of communities is critical to creating a sense of place and that planners can incorporate cultural geographic features to create a community portrait that represents "one or more historical landscapes."

While important to planners, this seems to be a limited approach to the analysis of past landscapes and involves a desire not for interpretation but for the preservation of the past in its own right, but at a scale that gives it meaning. Geographers study the present-day landscape with a realization that it is a composite of past landscapes and current patterns. The palimpsests therefore allow us to understand the present-day landscape and its dynamic change and do not just constitute the basis for recreating what went before. But a further problem is what to preserve and how. Are we creating a true landscape of the past, or are we creating our particular and perhaps irrelevant version of it? Are we fooling ourselves with an image of the past that is false? And even the question of what time period should be the theme of preservation could become a sensitive issue. In fact, "the landscape may tell us more about the past [that] people wanted to preserve than about the past as it was experienced."[47]

What comes across in reading the following essays therefore is a great many meanings that are being applied to landscape in the archaeological literature. A couple of chapters see it as more "context" for understanding individual sites and for interpreting broader social and institutional patterns of behavior; others see it as an ecological perspective, bringing together culture and natural environment and considering also the perceptions carried by different groups; some use it to focus on slices of time as expressed in the structures and historic context from one or more periods as a means of creating a sense of place. It seems, therefore, that these authors actually have identified three separate theoretical approaches that really are not landscape, at least as defined by geographers. They could more accurately be identified respectively as "site context," "cultural ecology," and "historic preservation/ reconstruction." Each includes some aspects of the geographic theme of landscape, but none can be equated to it.

Where, then, does this leave the concept of landscape? Geographers have grappled for some seventy years with its meaning and the approaches to its study. It has been a complex odyssey, but through much of that time they seem to have shared a clear idea of what is meant by the term. Historical archaeologists, however, need to define more precisely what is meant by landscape for their own purposes and for interacting with the practitioners of other disciplines. I strongly support interdisciplinary work and believe that geography and historical archaeology do share considerable common ground, most importantly the central importance of material culture, and have a lot to say to and learn from each other, as indicated by the rich collection of essays that follow. But effective communication requires that the two disciplines share not only words but also the meanings of those words. In this case, a common understanding "will provide an important bridge between the varied traditions of scholarship which find a shared interest, if not always shared objectives, in the study of the landscapes wrought by human societies."[48]

NOTES

1. See also Wagstaff 1987.
2. Herbst 1961; Trindell 1969.
3. Davis 1906.
4. Brigham 1915; Dryer 1920; Barrows 1923.
5. James and Martin 1981:332.
6. Sauer 1963b:343.
7. Sauer 1963b:342n. 6.
8. Sauer 1931:624.
9. Kniffen 1962.
10. Leighly 1937:134.
11. Leighly 1937:129n. 10.
12. Hartshorne 1939.
13. Hartshorne 1939:155n. 12.
14. Hartshorne 1939:158n. 12.
15. Sauer 1963a:358.
16. Sauer 1963a:360n. 15.
17. Wagner and Mikesell 1961:9–10.
18. Wagner and Mikesell 1961:13n. 17.
19. Wagner and Mikesell 1961: 5n. 17.
20. Schaefer 1953:227.
21. David Harvey quoted in Johnston 1991:88.
22. Brookfield 1964:283.
23. Brookfield 1964: 287n. 22.
24. Jackson 1989:1.
25. Cosgrove and Jackson 1987:96.
26. Daniels and Cosgrove 1988:1.
27. Denis Cosgrove 1985:17–18.
28. Duncan and Duncan 1988:120.
29. Duncan and Duncan 1988:123n. 28.
30. Jackson 1989:43n. 24.
31. Cosgrove 1990:562.
32. Duncan 1980:182.
33. Duncan 1980:191n.32.
34. Duncan 1980:190–191n. 32.
35. Price and Lewis 1993.
36. Rowntree 1996:131.
37. Mikesell 1978:4.
38. Lowenthal 1961:260. See also Tuan 1974.
39. Sauer 1963a:362n. 15.
40. Lewis 1979:12.
41. Meinig 1979b:235.
42. Lowenthal 1985:412.
43. Wagner 1975:8. See also Mikesell 1978:10–12n. 36.
44. Newton and Pulliam-di Napoli 1977:365.
45. Samuels 1979:51–88.
46. Roberts 1987:79.
47. Johnston 1991:182n. 21.
48. Roberts 1987:77–95n. 44.

Works Cited

Barrows, Harlan
1923   Geography as Human Ecology. *Annals of the Association of American Geographers* 13:1–14.

Brigham, Albert Perry
1915   Problems of Geographic Influence. *Annals of the Association of American Geographers* 5:3–25.

Brookfield, H. C.
1964   Questions on the Human Frontiers of Geography. *Economic Geography* 40:283–303.

Cosgrove, Denis E.
1985   *Social Formation and Symbolic Landscape.* Barnes and Noble, Totowa, New Jersey.

Cosgrove, Denis E., and Peter Jackson
1987   New Directions in Cultural Geography. *Area* 19:95–101.

1990   "...Then We Take Berlin": Cultural Geography 1989–90. *Progress in Human Geography* 14:560–68.

Daniels, Stephen, and Denis Cosgrove
1988   Introduction: Iconography and Landscape. In *The Iconography of Landscape,* edited by Denis Cosgrove and Stephen Daniels, pp. 1–10. Cambridge Univ. Press, New York.

Davis, William Morris
1906   An Inductive Study of the Content of Geography. *Bulletin of the American Geographical Society* 38:67–84.

Dryer, Charles
1920   Genetic Geography. *Annals of the Association of American Geographers* 10:3–16.

Duncan, James S.
1980   The Superorganic in American Cultural Geography. *Annals of the Association of American Geographers* 70:181–98.

Duncan, James, and Nancy Duncan
1988   (Re)Reading the Landscape. *Environment and Planning D: Society and Space* 6. pp. 117–26.

Hartshorne, Richard
1939   *The Nature of Geography.* Association of American Geographers, Lancaster.

Herbst, Jergen
1961   Social Darwinism and the History of American Geography, *Proceedings of the American Philosophical Society* 105:538–44.

Jackson, Peter H.
1989   *Maps of Meaning.* Unwin Hyman, London.

James, Preston, and Geoffrey Martin
1981   *All Possible Worlds: A History of Geographical Ideas.* Second Edition. Wiley and Sons, New York.

Johnston, R. J.
1991   *Geography and Geographers: Anglo-American Geography Since 1945.* 4th ed., Edward Arnold, London.

Kniffen, Fred
1962   Louisiana House Types. In *Readings in Cultural Geography,* edited by Philip Wagner and Marvin Mikesell, pp. 157–69. Univ. of Chicago Press, Chicago. Originally published in 1936 in *Annals of the Association of American Geographers.*

Leighly, John
1937   Some Comments on Contemporary Geographic Method. *Annals of the Association of American Geographers* 27:125–41.

Lewis, Peirce F.
1979   Axioms for Reading the Landscape: Some Guides to the American Scene. In *The Interpretation of Ordinary Landscapes,* edited by Donald W. Meinig, pp. 11–32. Oxford Univ. Press, New York.

Lowenthal, David
1961   Geography, Experience, and Imagination: Towards A Geographical Epistemology. *Annals of the Association of American Geographers* 51:241–60.

1985   *The Past Is a Foreign Country.* Cambridge Univ. Press, New York.

Meinig, Donald W.
1979b   Reading the Landscape: An Appreciation of W. G. Hoskins and J. B. Jackson. In *The Interpretation of Ordinary Landscapes,* edited by D. W. Meinig, pp. 195–244. Oxford Univ. Press, New York.

Mikesell, Marvin W.
1978   Tradition and Innovation in Cultural Geography. *Annals of the Association of American Geographers* 68:1–16.

1979b   Reading the Landscape: An Appreciation of W. G. Hoskins and J. B. Jackson. In *The Interpretation of Ordinary Landscapes,* edited by D. W. Meinig, pp. 195–244. Oxford Univ. Press, New York.

Newton, Milton B., and Linda Pulliam-di Napoli
1977   Log Houses as Public Occasions: A Historical Theory. *Annals of the Association of American Geographers* 67:360–83.

Price, Marie, and Martin Lewis
1993   The Reinvention of Cultural Geography. *Annals of the Association of American Geographers* 83:1–17.

Roberts, B. K.
1987   Landscape Archaeology. In *Landscape and Culture: Geographical and Archaeological Perspectives,* edited by J. M. Wagstaff, pp. 77–95. Basil Blackwell, New York, and T. J. Press Ltd., Padstow, Cornwall, Great Britain.

Rowntree, Lester
1996   The Cultural Landscape Concept in American Geography. In *Concepts in Human Geography,* edited by Carville Earle, Kent Mathewson, and Martin Kenzer. Rowman and Littlefield, Lanham, Maryland.

Samuels, Marwyn S.
1979   The Biography of Landscape: Cause and Culpability. In *The Interpretation of Ordinary Landscapes: Geographical Essays,* edited by D. W. Meinig, pp. 51–88. Oxford Univ. Press, New York.

Sauer, Carl Ortwin
1931   Cultural Geography. *Encyclopedia of the Social Sciences* 6:621–24.
1963a   Foreword to Historical Geography. In *Land and Life: A Selection from the Writings of Carl Ortwin Sauer,* edited by John Leighly, pp. 351–79. Univ. of California Press, Berkeley. Originally published in 1941.
1963b   The Morphology of Landscape. In *Land and Life: A Selection from the Writings of Carl Ortwin Sauer,* edited by John Leighly, pp. 315–50. Univ. of California Press, Berkeley. Originally published in 1925 in Univ. of California Publications in Geography (vol. 2, no. 2):19–53.

Schaefer, Fred K.
1953   Exceptionalism in Geography: A Methodological Examination. *Annals of the Association of American Geographers* 43:226–49.

Trindell, Roger T.
1969   Franz Boas and American Geography. *Professional Geographer* 21:328–32.

Tuan, Yi-Fu
1974   *Topophilia.* Prentice-Hall, Englewood Cliffs.

Wagner, Philip L.
1975   The Themes of Cultural Geography Rethought. *Yearbook of Pacific Coast Geographers* 37:7–14.

Wagner, Philip, and Marvin Mikesell (editors)
1961   *Readings in Cultural Geography.* Univ. of Chicago Press, Chicago.

Wagstaff, J. M.
1987   *Landscape and Culture: Geographical and Archaeological Perspectives.* Basil Blackwell, Oxford.

2. Reuniting the Truth: Integrating Anthropology, Geography, and History through Landscape Archaeology

STANTON W. GREEN

Geography, History and Anthropology are a
trilogy to be broken with a severe loss of truth.
—H. J. FLEURE AND H. J. PEAKE

By bringing together geographers, historians, and anthropologists, this volume moves us several steps in the direction of Fleure and Peake's "truth." In this essay, I would like to explore landscape archaeology as an approach capable of integrating these fields—these artificially divided areas of inquiry—with the objective of providing a unifying framework for archaeological method and theory.

To illustrate my points, I will use both prehistoric and contemporary examples. I will also use examples from Europe. This is not totally without design, for, indeed, landscape approaches in archaeology have a longer history in Europe. The implications of landscape archaeology, however, must be understood as general and applicable to all areas of anthropological study. This book illustrates how such an approach can be particularly powerful within the realm of historical archaeology in the Carolinas.

How do we approach landscapes archaeologically? As Deetz suggests, we can start methodologically. He argues, "It is most likely that the cultural landscape is the largest and most pervasive artifact with which we as archaeologists must deal, yet much remains to be done and much thinking about the ways to do it must be indulged. . . . [T]his is a very positive thing because it forces us out of the traditional five foot square mentality by raising new questions that must be answered through new and different field techniques and analytical methods."[1]

This effort to define landscape as artifact and feature has important methodological implications, as it quite literally broadens the scope of archaeological inquiry. We can begin to conceptualize archaeological methods in terms of sampling, collecting, analyzing, and interpreting landscapes, as we traditionally do with artifacts and features. It also opens up management and conservation issues as we talk of preserving landscapes and perhaps even defining National Historic Landscapes as the British do—for example, in Julian Richards's work on the Stonehenge environs.[2] However, a focus on landscape has much broader implications with regard to archaeological theory and practice.

If we begin with the example of landscape taphonomy, we see the integration of geomorphological and archaeological studies—in a sense behavioral archaeology writ large.[3] Rather than solely concentrating on the formation of discrete sites, landscape taphonomy focuses on the geo-morphogical and archaeological processes that form over large continuous areas of the landscape. This focus includes those areas that had limited or no human use. A shift in the unit of inquiry from "site" to "landscape" requires conceptual as well as methodological and technical changes. It opens up both theoretical and methodological discussions on the basics of archaeological inquiry: the relationship between space, time, and form.[4] The landscape, although an arbitrary region of space, is more than simply a larger version of a traditional archaeologi-cal site. The use of landscape as a unit of analysis allows archaeologists to deal with the general problem of understanding space as a continuous dimension.[5]

Although this shift in emphasis from site to landscape may appear simplest at the methodologi-cal level, even here we see the potential revolution-ary effects of how landscape can change the way we think about and do archaeology. This is because landscape methods challenge the fundamental assumptions of the site concept.[6] The site concept has been challenged by those advocating a nonsite or anti-site approach to archaeology. Practitioners explicate the difficulties of following traditional site by site or distributional perspectives in both management and research.[7] As Dunnell and Dancey explain, focusing a survey only on sites is limiting, leaving large areas of people and environmental interaction unexplored, unrecorded, and thus unexplained.[8]

The problem for archaeologists is discovering how to move beyond the methodological to the interpretive level. It is fine to develop sampling methodologies to sample large areas such as prescribed by so-called "Total regional analysis," but sound inquiry and interpretation requires a theo-retical frame of reference.[9] Site models rely on theories that relate the locus of archaeological evidence (i.e., the site) to a place where people were engaged in activities such as cooking, sleeping, or manufacturing material goods. Sites are inferred to represent archaeological settlements, which in turn are interpreted as cultural communities. But the discreteness required by these site models is often (if not usually) unsatisfactory because human activities do not typically occur within such well-defined spaces. Moving, however, methodologically to the regional distribution of artifacts, landscape, as the spatial unit of analysis, does not solve the inferential problem of changing from emphasis on "locus" to refocusing on "behavior." If archaeolo-gists continue to turn to the landscape as a unit of analysis, where should scholars seek conceptual models and theories? The beauty of the landscape approach lies in the available broad, deep, and interdisciplinary theoretical literature in landscape studies.

The Theoretical Tenets of Landscape Archaeology

The conceptual power of landscape results from its incorporation of three elements basic to the study of the spatial dimension of human social organization and ecology—integration, continuity, and view of the lands. First, it takes into account the *integration* of natural and cultural factors. Second, it takes into account *continuity* in the human use of space. These first two characteristics of the landscape derive from general geographic theory. An agricultural geogra-pher, for example, does not examine fields as independent sites, but views fields as parcels of space within a continuous land use system. More-over, the relationship between natural factors (e.g., soils, slope, drainage) are understood to interact with cultural factors (e.g., crop demand, transpor-tation costs) that affect the need for and use of the land.[10] Finally, the third and most thought-provok-ing conceptual element of the landscape approach derives from the literal meaning of landscape—the *view of the land*. This element brings in humanity as a determining factor in the dialectic between culture and nature, by including both the *perception* of the land and its *use*.

This final aspect is illustrated through the following narrative description of the prehistoric Avebury landscape of southern England and its environs. This is, of course, a region of many monuments and archaeological sites. However, the quote reorients the reader from the sites themselves and moves her or him toward an understanding of the landscape: how people were viewing and using it, capturing what it might have been like to be in Avebury in 2600 B.C.

> In 2600 B.C. the stone temples of Avebury were the wonder of the British Isles. One day's journey to the south, skirting the marshes and then up the slopes of Salisbury Plain, and a traveler would come to Stonehenge, its low irregular bank enclosing a ring of freshly cut pits. . . . North-westward, fourteen days along the trackways overlooking rivers and forests, then a crossing of the sea, and he would have arrived at the Irish valley of the river Boyne where a multitude of circular tombs, one of them walled white with quartz, clustered together, some of them on hillocks higher than trees. Many had carved kerbstones around their bases, decorated in patterns that few people understood. Inside each tomb a passage led to a dark chamber, its roof rising high above the head, and in the gloomy side-cells the dead that had been laid, burned, their bones placed on stone basins in the blackness. It was said that at midwinter dawn, the sun penetrated the sepulchre, bringing life to the bones. A further two weeks more, this time northwards past the islands green in the Atlantic waters, and the voyager would have come to the Orkneys and to another tomb, Maes Howe, aligned on the midwinter sunset, and close to a pair of rings of standing stones put up in the narrow land between two lochs.[11]

Two important insights can be derived from this description. One is the continuity of this landscape even as it crosses bodies of water. A second is the author's attempt to regain the point of view within its historical context by describing the journey in historically relevant space/time units. This includes, in this case, days and the natural and cultural landmarks of the time. What emerges is a landscape that is greater than the sum of its megaliths. The significance of the Avebury landscape lies in its connectivity, and not in its particular, if awe-inspiring, sites. Within this type of interpretive framework, archaeologists would never consider a henge monument, a barrow, a dolmen, or a megalith in the British Isles or Ireland as redundant because another one exists around the bend or upriver. Indeed, the meaning of a particular monument is to a great extent defined through its spatial, temporal, and formal relationships in regards to other monuments. Quite literally, the view of the land is greater than the sum of its spatial parts. This brings us into the realm of the landscape as a visual concept.

Landscape as Differing Views of the Land

The geographer Tuan has heuristically divided the landscape into vertical views and horizontal views.[12] The vertical view represents the vantage point of the observer, in our case the archaeologist. The archaeological interpretation of the landscape requires an explication of where we are "standing." Our descriptive and analytical view must be explicit. To begin, we have to take into account where we are physically standing. An urban area, for example, will look different from the center of the main city than it does from the periphery in an agricultural field. In order to analyze and interpret a landscape we have to decide what or what kind of a map or Geographic Information System (GIS) overlay we are examining and how we are viewing and orienting this spatial representation. We also must be clear about which aspects of the environs we are "viewing." Are we trying to interpret the political landscape, the economic landscape, the natural landscape, the agrarian landscape, and/or the urban landscape? This is the analytical view. The vertical view sets the archaeologist's position as a context for investigation and interpretation. This calls for a critical or reflexive perspective as the archaeologist judges the way he or she observes, analyzes, and ultimately interprets past landscapes.

The horizontal view, in Tuan's terms, is the view

of the people inhabiting the landscape—that is, the view of those people we are observing either through their behavior or the residues of their behavior. The term horizontal captures the notion that the participant in the landscape is seeing things from the inside. With a little modification, the description of the Neolithic British Isles as viewed from Avebury could be written as a horizontal view. Ultimately, the horizontal view places the landscape within its social and historical contexts. Recognizing the importance of explicitly seeking and combining vertical and horizontal views moves us toward the interpretive potential of landscape archaeology.

The geographer Patrick McGreevy offers an example of the power of this approach.[13] In his study, McGreevy "imagines" Niagara Falls in terms of its geographic remoteness, its association with death (and death-defying deeds), its place in nature, and finally in the way it affected people's view of the future. He found this perspective especially useful in light of people's fears and hopes related to economic and technological development. By studying "how people have imagined Niagara Falls (and determining) the meanings they have attributed to the place," McGreevy applies Tuan's concepts as a basis for understanding the place of Niagara within its culture historical context. His use of the word "imagine" is powerful because it implies both cause and effect. It captures the notion that landscape is both a motivator of human behavior as well as a consequence of it.

Over the past decade, archaeologists have indeed been broadening their imaginations. We can see this when comparing the types of studies in Bender's (1994) recent landscape volume, *Landscape: Politics and Perspectives,* to those included in Wagstaff's (1987) *Landscape and Culture.* Wagstaff's integration of geographical and archaeological approaches began with studies of ecology and economy and moved on to symbolic and political interpretations of landscape. Bender's volume would seem to begin where Wagstaff leaves off. Her book includes studies ranging from the political through cosmological interpretations of

historic and prehistoric landscapes.[14] The combined sequence of studies in these volumes moves us through the three levels of landscape theory: culture-ecological integration, spatial continuity, and visual relativity.

Let me conclude with a brief foray into broader-ranging theory in order to summarize the potential theoretical power of the landscape approach. I will do this through a brief and hopefully provocative recasting of the classic problem of agricultural origins.

We have come a long way in our understanding of the development of farming, viewing it much more than as the result of isolated technical or even economic change. Archaeologists are beginning to investigate this development as a social process.[15] The landscape approach, I believe, can take us yet further. When people adopt farming in their cultural systems, they are not just adopting an economic system; they are, in fact, choosing a new landscape. I do not mean this in the simplistic sense of choice (i.e., choosing from a set of possibilities with knowledge of short- and long-term consequences and perfect information). Rather, I am proposing that a community's use and view of the land is in large part the actual medium for occurring social and ecological changes. It is to a great degree the medium through which the choice is made and the consequences felt. As in McGreevy's sense, the landscape is both a cause and an effect.

This theoretically engages the spatial dimension into the process of agricultural development. People live, in many ways, through their view of their environment. Moreover, their view of change is often understood in terms of change of their visual surroundings. The visual structure of the landscape is not just a passive consequence of culture change; it is acted upon and reacted to by communities as they promote and cope with change. There is a visual aesthetic component to culture change. We see this repeatedly with regard to economic development. Economic development may do lots of things to people and to the environment, but one thing that people react to, perhaps more than anything else, is how changing economies affect the visual structure of the land—how it changes their visual surroundings. One thing we cannot overlook is how the adoption of agriculture physically, aesthetically, and symbolically changed the landscape.[16] Agriculture changed the way people "imagined" their world. By moving us beyond the site concept, landscape archaeology can contribute to the way archaeologists imagine culture change.

NOTES

1. Deetz 1990:1.
2. Richards 1990.
3. Schiffer 1976. Taphonomy is the delineation of natural and/or cultural processes that effect organic remains, such as bone, after death.
4. Spaulding 1960.
5. Green and Perlman 1980.
6. Green 1976.
7. Dunnell 1992; Ebert 1986; Thomas 1975.
8. Dunnell and Dancey 1983.
9. Fish and Kowalewski 1990; Green 1992.
10. Chisholm 1970.
11. Burl 1979:1.
12. Tuan 1979.
13. McGreevy 1994.
14. Bender 1994; Wagstaff 1987.
15. Bender 1994.
16. Hodder 1990.

WORKS CITED

Bender, Barbara
1994   *Landscape and Politics.* Blackwell, Oxford.
Burl, Aubrey
1979   *Prehistoric Avebury.* Yale Univ. Press, New Haven.
Chisholm, Michael
1970   *Rural Settlement and Land Use.* 2d ed., Univ. Library of Geography. Aldine Publishing, Chicago. Originally published 1962, Hutchinson, London.
Deetz, James
1990   Prologue: Landscapes as Cultural Statements. In *Earth Patterns,* edited by William Kelso and Rachel Most, pp. 1–4. Univ. Press of Virginia, Charlottesville.
Dunnell, Robert
1992   The Notion Site. In *Space, Time and Archaeological Landscapes,* edited by J. Rossignol and L. Wandsnider pp. 21–42. Plenum Press, New York.
Dunnell, Robert C., and William S. Dancey
1983   The Siteless Survey: A Regional Scale Data Collection Strategy. In *Advances in Archaeological Method and Theory,* vol. 6, edited by Michael Schiffer, pp. 267–87. Academic Press, New York.
Ebert, James
1986   *Distributional Archaeology: Non-site Discovery Recording and Analytical Methods.* Ph.D diss., Dept. of Anthropology, Univ. of New Mexico.

Fish, Suzanne, Stephen Kowaleski (editors)
1990   *The Archaeology of Regions: A Case Study for Full-Coverage Survey.* Smithsonian Institution Press, Washington, D.C.
Green, Stanton W.
1976   What Is a Site? Paper presented at the Archaeological Colloquium Series, South Carolina Institute of Archaeology and Anthropology, Univ. of South Carolina, Columbia.
1992   Review of *The Archaeology of Regions,* edited by Suzanne K. Fish and Stephen A. Kowalewski *Winterthur Portfolio* 26(1):82–85.
Green, Stanton W., and Stephen M. Pearlman (editors)
1980   *The Archaeology of Frontiers and Boundaries.* Academic Press, Orlando.
Hodder, Ian
1990   *The Domestication of Europe.* Blackwell, London.
McGreevy, Patrick
1994   *Imagining Niagra: The Meaning and Making of Niagara Falls.* Univ. of Massachusetts Press, Amherst.
Richards, Julian
1990   *The Stonehenge Environs Project.* Historic Buildings and Monuments Commission for England, London.
Schiffer, Michael
1976   *Behavioral Archaeology.* Academic Press, New York.

Spaulding, Albert
1960   The Dimensions of Archaeology. In *Essays on the Science of Culture in Honor of Leslie A. White,* edited by Gertrude Dole and Robert Carneiro, pp. 437–56. Thomas Y. Crowell, New York.
Thomas, David H.
1976   Nonsite Sampling in Archaeology: Up the Creek without a Site? In *Sampling in Archaeology,* edited by James Mueller, pp. 61–81. Univ. of Arizona Press, Tucson.
Tuan, Yi-Fu
1979   Thought and Landscape: The Eye and the Mind's Eye. In *The Interpretation of Ordinary Landscapes,* edited by D. W. Menig, pp. 89–102. Oxford Univ. Press, Oxford.

3. A Dialectical Approach to Landscape

CAROLE L. CRUMLEY

In his exploration of particular attempts at synthesis in landscape studies, Green (this volume) mentions Bill Marquardt's and my dialectical approach; I wish to elaborate and briefly explain this approach.[1] Because of the divergence between the history of ideas in the United States and in Europe, the term dialectical is not very well understood in North America. Many people associate dialectical thinking with Marx and perhaps Hegel, and with complicated theories of oppositions and contradictions. Only infrequently is it seen as a method or tool of analysis. It is actually a very simple idea, not necessarily burdened with ideological baggage, and useful as a scheme to guide thinking.

The dialectical method can be of considerable utility in undertaking landscape archaeology and landscape studies in general. The dialectic has three forms, or "moments," which relate to and play off one another. The first two are epistemological and serve as a point of entry to the analysis. In defining something worthy of study, certain elements or criteria are chosen for inclusion and other elements are left out. For example, the vista of a managed forest may be defined as a rural landscape or it may not, depending on whether the definition of "rural" admits silviculture or is restricted to agricultural lands. In a definition, what an entity *is not* is as important as what it *is,* and constitutes a separate body of information to be analyzed; if human activity relative to the environment is to be understood, both the elements excluded from a definition and those included are important. Thus, the second moment constitutes the critical re-analysis of the elements initially chosen for inclusion in a definition. In the example, "rural" is re-defined to include managed forests, and the earlier, more restrictive definition rejected.

The third moment examines the assumptions in the organizational pattern employed in the first two, offering a critique and an alternative solution. Rather than continually redefining "rural" as additional evidence fails to fit the current definition, a scheme which rejects the rural/urban distinction but utilizes and reorganizes previously defined elements that make up the landscape (fields, managed forests) is formulated. In the new scheme, epistemological problems already encountered (what is "rural"?) could be abandoned, but not previously collected data (the characteristics of fields and forests) and landscapes could be characterized in categories other than rural and urban. This would, for example, be much more appropriate in parts of the world that are relatively densely populated but where a strong tradition of family garden plots beneath trees produces harvestable fruit, nuts, or wood (Amazonia, West Africa, Indonesia). This third transforming moment in the analysis is the most important; it is the synthesis of old data into a new formulation.

We need to move past the many oppositions we have constructed for ourselves, not only in our concepts but among colleagues who share a common research goal. Within archaeology, the division between historic and prehistoric archaeology is deserving of critical examination; even at the 1991 South Carolina Historical Landscape conference, where the landscape concept offered (as it were) common ground, few prehistorians attended the historic session and vice versa.

The human-environment relation is a subject many anthropologists, geographers, and environmental historians share, but interdisciplinary collaboration remains rare. Differences between and within these related fields of study can be traced to historic branching points: Boas's use of the concept of culture in the struggle against scientific racism; the post-World War II emphasis on statistical analysis; the realities of graduate training and extramural funding. Whatever the reason, all the aforementioned fields have tacitly or actively subscribed to a distinction between culture and nature. That definition of humans' place in the world has become increasingly untenable as, thanks to ozone holes, marine pollution, and the like, we come to realize that nowhere on earth is free of all signs of human activity. Scholars have begun to address this issue by re-analyzing the categories themselves.[2]

Despite a heightened awareness of the shortcomings of a scheme that posits a Nature unspoiled by humans, the environment continues to be placed at a distance and idealized. The Sierra Club still frames the pictures on Club calendars in such a way that a buyer does not see the interstate just out of the view. We still respond to a romanticized, "wild" landscape, even though it becomes more and more difficult to tease nature and culture apart. This problem has stopped otherwise very fruitful interaction with colleagues, especially those in the natural sciences.

Excepting the work of archaeologists, environmentally oriented anthropologists, and a few historians, collaboration between social scientists and natural scientists is all but nonexistent. Most natural and physical scientists consider human activities to be "noise" in their analyses of non-human biological and mechanical systems.[3] The behavior and habitat of the field mouse can still be studied apart from the farm field. Naturalists cling every bit as fiercely to the Nature/Culture distinction as do postmodernist ethnographers, albeit for entirely different reasons. Relatively little progress has been made toward rapprochement since C. P. Snow addressed the problem that he termed the two cultures in the 1950s.[4]

I wish to elaborate a set of concepts that could be understood across the humanities/social science–natural/physical science boundary. *Landscape* is one such term, offering a bridge to the natural and physical sciences and to others concerned about global scale issues; it is clear that solutions to enormous global problems that affect everyone will necessarily be interdisciplinary.

Until recently, geographers have been essentially alone in trying to ensure that a humanistic perspective is incorporated into physical and natural scientists' approaches to the national and international mitigation of global environmental change. Those of us interested in landscape analysis have a very important tool to aid the geographers' efforts. Chapters in this volume elaborate on this potential: Crass and Brook's contribution on microenvironment and climate and the role both play in settlement, Wayne's chapter on bricks, Harmon and Snedeker's chapter on pitch and tar, and Ferguson and Cowan's chapter on iron production. While natural, physical, and material sciences play an important explanatory role in these essays, the emphasis is on exploring human-environment relations through the dialectical analysis of changing landscapes.

I would like to add four other concepts that can bridge the natural–social science boundary. This volume treats the concept of *region,* which was developed by geographers and shared with archaeologists and anthropologists. A regional approach is implicit in much of this volume, inasmuch as it focuses on the Carolinas and the Southeast. The initial definition of "region" is not especially important if one employs a dialectical approach, as it simply begins the analysis. What is important is that the initial definition be contrasted with other possible definitions using different elements and different scales of time and space. Although the book is about South Carolina archaeology, some papers elaborate on connections to several other regions.

Besides landscape and region, *scale* is of critical analytic importance. Scale has long been an important tool in ecology.[5] As well as aiding us in the interpretation of archaeological stratigraphy, geologists work at scales both larger (soil chemistry) and smaller (landforms, lithic facies) than sites and necessitate archaeological interpretation beyond the traditional site-based analysis.

A fourth concept is *diversity;* an elegant argument can be made for the importance of both biological (species) and cultural diversity in the world today. The argument for cultural diversity is both ethical and practical, the latter being made primarily through anthropologists' and archaeologists' documentation of the outcomes (some happy, some not) of past human adaptive strategies.[6] Were such an argument to be made in collaboration with wildlife biologists who are (for the most part) working at shorter time intervals but who are also using historic and geographic data, its power would be matched only by its urgency.

Finally, it is important to look carefully at what we term the *structure,* or order, of society. The fluidity and variety of power relations are as important in understanding social organization and its spatial manifestation in the landscape as are the hierarchies elites seek to impose. A recent trend in social science research has focused analysis on individual competence, social transmission, and elaborately organized schemes of resistance— complex by any measure—in contrast to earlier

research that focused upon the idealized hierarchies of elites. It is time for archaeology to join this larger trend, to suspend uncritical acceptance of the assertions of unchallenged power that vanished elites have left in stone and on paper. Archaeologists must question the assumption (which has undergirded archaeology since its inception as a discipline) of the equivalence of spatial and social hierarchies and the unexamined value judgment of a steadily increasing "complexity." Heterarchical models (in which the elements are unranked or ranked in a variety of ways depending on the context) will be particularly important as a regional approach becomes more common, and the spatial identification of contiguous, interacting polities with very different systems of governance and power relations requires new methods.[7]

In archaeology's search for pattern in settlement and society, we have (like many of our sociocultural colleagues) become timid about arguing that a portion of the pattern (and, hence, a portion of its explanation) is a function of the environment. If we are going to understand settlement at a regional scale, we must develop different models of social organization and control over resources the landscape distribution of which is heterarchical. For example, some characteristics (location and quality of ore) of iron production are due to environmental factors, while others (who controls extraction sites, what is made) are cultural. But inasmuch as past human activity can also determine resource distributions (e.g., black earth sites in Amazonia), their relation is dialectical.

In the first half of the century researchers who introduced the concepts of landscape and region (e.g., Carl Sauer and others in the United States, the *Annales* historians in Europe) were equally capable in natural sciences, social sciences, and humanities scholarship. We now think of them as "renaissance" people, who mastered those fields when the knowledge base was still small enough to do so. But some of us, especially archaeologists, hold onto the idea that knowing something about a variety of fields is dangerous only if we presume to know everything. Although we have all been trained during a period of rigid disciplinization, more and more of us are asking Does it have to be this way? Do we really have to stay inside of these restrictive disciplinary boundaries? Must we learn only this? Most of us feel a growing, collective frustration that results from universities, publishers, and granting agencies forcing competition for fewer resources and more narrow venues.

I will end by suggesting the term "historical ecology" for a broad interdisciplinary activity employing the concepts discussed above. The noun *ecology* offers a means by which our natural science, materials, and physical science colleagues can be included from the start. The adjective *historical,* as Bruce Winterhalder points out, should not be necessary if the evolutionary potential of ecology were recognized; however, the practice of ecology in both the natural and social sciences is more functional (synchronic) than evolutionary (diachronic).[8] This is unfortunately true in archaeology as well. A part of every site report has a section on "the environment" but archaeologists have only recently begun to explore coeval environmental and cultural change and their implications.[9] *Historical* should not modify only Euro-American archaeology (as it does in the United States, privileging written accounts over oral or material witnesses to events); rather, events and conditions, recorded in a variety of ways, offer multiple lines of evidence to see how pasts were and are collectively shaped. Some figures in archaeology (W. W. Taylor for example) have attempted such a synthesis of diverse data. Maybe it's time to dust Taylor off and try again. If you do not like Taylor, read Marc Bloch or Carl Sauer. Perhaps we can retrieve something that, at the turn of the century and through the twenties and maybe even into the thirties, was still a part of the study of the past. If we can rework an approach that employs what geographers, anthropologists, archaeologists, and historians have been doing for a long time into a new synthesis, we will be prepared to address the global scale issues that loom before us.

NOTES

1. Crumley and Marquardt 1987.
2. Brown 1991; Ingerson 1994.
3. E.g., Naveh and Lieberman 1984.
4. Snow 1959.
5. Pielou 1984.
6. Denslow and Padoch 1988; Crumley 1994.
7. For example, Renfrew and Cherry 1986; Crumley 1987; Marquardt and Crumley 1987; Ehrenreich, Crumley, and Levy 1995.
8. Winterhalder 1994.
9. But see Gunn and Crumley 1991 and Gunn, Folan, and Robichaux 1995.

WORKS CITED

Brown, Donald E.
1991   *Human Universals.* McGraw-Hill, New York.

Crumley, Carole L.
1987   A Dialectical Critique of Hierarchy. In *Power Relations and State Formation,* edited by Thomas C. Patterson and Christine Ward Gailey, pp. 155–69. American Anthropological Association, Washington, D.C.

Crumley, Carole L. (editor)
1994   *Historical Ecology: Cultural Knowledge and Changing Landscapes.* School of American Research, Santa Fe.

Crumley, Carole, and William Marquardt (editors)
1987   *Regional Dynamics: Burgundian Landscapes in Historical Perspective.* Academic Press, New York and San Diego.

Denslow, Julie Sloan, and Christine Padoch (editors)
1988   *People of the Tropical Rainforest.* Univ. of California Press, Berkeley.

Ehrenreich, Robert M., Carole L. Crumley, and Janet Levy (editors)
1995   *Heterarchy and the Analysis of Complex Societies.* Archaeological Papers of the American Anthropological Association. No. 6. American Anthropological Association, Washington, D.C.

Gunn, Joel, and Carole L. Crumley
1991   Global Energy Balance and Regional Hydrology:
       A Burgundian Case Study. *Earth Surface Processes
       and Landforms* 16(7):579–92.
Gunn, Joel, William J. Folan, and Hubert R. Robichaux
1995   A Landscape Analysis of the Candelaria Watershed
       in Mexico: Insights into Paleoclimated affecting
       Upland Horticulture in the Southern Yucatan
       Peninsula Semi-Karst. *Geoarchaeology* 10:3–42.
Ingerson, Alice
1994   Tracking and Testing the Nature/Culture
       Dichotomy in Practice. In *Historical Ecology:
       Cultural Knowledge and Changing Landscapes,*
       edited by Carole L. Crumley, pp. 43–66. School of
       American Research Press, Santa Fe.
Marquardt, William H., and Carole L. Crumley
1987   Theoretical Issues in the Analysis of Spatial
       Patterning. In *Regional Dynamics, Burgundian
       Landscapes in Historical Perspective,* edited by
       Carole L. Crumley and William H. Marquardt,
       pp. 1–18. Academic Press, San Diego.

Naveh, Zev, and Arthur S. Lieberman
1984   *Landscape Ecology: Theory and Application.*
       Springer-Verlag, New York.
Pielou, Edith
1984   *The Interpretation of Ecological Data: A Primer on
       Classification and Ordination.* Wiley and Sons,
       New York.
Renfrew, Colin, and John F. Cherry (editors)
1986   *Peer Polity Interaction and Sociopolitical Change.*
       Cambridge Univ. Press, Cambridge.
Snow, C. P.
1959   *The Two Cultures and the Scientific Revolution.*
       Cambridge Univ. Press, New York.
Winterhalder, Bruce P.
1994   Concepts in Historical Ecology: The View from
       Evolutionary Theory. In *Historical Ecology:
       Cultural Knowledge and Changing Landscapes,*
       edited by Carole L. Crumley, pp. 17–42. School of
       American Research Press, Santa Fe.

4. Digging Down and Looking Backward: The Awkward Relation of History and Archaeology

Peter H. Wood

Repeated observation, limited personal experience, and simple common sense tell me, as a historian, that it is tough work to be an archaeologist. Digging in the ground is never easy, even under the best of conditions. Recently, when I visited with historical archaeologists excavating the site of a black Moravian church in Old Salem, North Carolina, their necks and arms had been bitten by mosquitoes. The following month, when I encountered a similar group in Kodiak, Alaska, exploring the site of the first Russian settlement in the Americas, their fingers and toes had been nipped by frost.

But it is also tough to be a historian. Archival dust clogs the lungs; grainy microfilm weakens the eyes; unending library work tires the butt. If archaeologists are somehow distantly related to ditch diggers and oilfield roughnecks, then historians are really glorified street sweepers and janitors, endlessly gathering and shuffling the discarded papers left behind by others. I sense that we historians dress and talk somewhat differently than archaeologists. We probably like different foods and order different drinks. We are turned on by rather different discoveries . . . and we certainly ache in different places.

But the fact is, we share a common fascination with the past, and it is encouraging to see that in recent years our two worlds have been coming closer together. Or, rather, we are waking up to the fact that historians and historical archaeologists have been inhabiting the same turf for some time. It is as though we rolled over in bed and suddenly discovered a familiar-looking stranger. We are each trying to hide our mixed feelings of surprise and concern, pleasure and embarrassment, while we try to figure out how we got here and how long we have been together. The past, like the present, can indeed create strange bedfellows.

Needless to say, this has not been a long and intimate relationship. Indeed, the traditional avoidance between historians and archaeologists, with all our common ancestry, has bordered upon an incest taboo. As someone particularly interested in the growth of the southern colonies, the evolution of Native American cultures, and the emergence of early African American society, I have had several experiences that have forced me to begin thinking about how to overcome this avoidance, so I hope you will indulge me if I address myself directly to archaeologists and would-be archaeologists.

In the early 1970s, while working as a foundation officer, I had the good fortune to be able to encourage interdisciplinary work on the seventeenth-century excavation site at St. Mary's City in

southern Maryland. I was impressed by the willing-
ness of archaeologists in the field to compare notes
with co-workers from the state archives in Annapolis,
and by the eagerness with which these same archival
historians connected their dusty documents to the
numbered fragments in the endless brown paper
lunch bags. Such cooperation seemed so logical and
simple. It must be this way everywhere, I thought.
Little did I know. . . .

A decade later, hoping to become more involved in such an interdisciplinary undertaking, I
signed on, in the summer of 1982, as the resident
historian for a project to excavate the slave dwellings
on Somerset Plantation in eastern North Carolina.
This extraordinary site had been carved from a
dense swamp by enslaved workers during the
generation after the American Revolution. The
persons forced to undertake this Herculean task—
cutting acres of virgin cypress trees and digging
miles of drainage canals—had been brought directly
from Africa. And the whites who exploited the labor
of these newcomers and of their descendants kept
copious records that have been preserved in the
Southern Historical Collection in Chapel Hill.

For all these reasons the site was ideal for
persons interested in early African American
culture. As with numerous southern plantations,
the Big House at Somerset was a state historical site
open to a daily flow of tourists. But the row of
vanished slave quarters was only a half-mown field,
totally ignored and thoroughly unexplored. Spurred
on by this obvious neglect and bias, we labored
willingly for months in the hot sun in order to
uncover traces of black life on this Carolina gulag.
By the end of the summer, I had learned a great deal
about Somerset's former residents, and about the
pros and cons of interdisciplinary research efforts.
The process was not as simple as I had hoped.

Moreover, my most startling discovery came
the following winter. Belatedly, I learned that three
weeks after we had cleaned our trowels and de-
parted, a black family reunion took place in the
adjoining campground. It brought together scores
of persons descended from a Somerset family that
had once inhabited the line of cabins we had just

located. No one told *us* that they were coming; no
one informed *them* that we had just been there—
and had unearthed the very hearth upon which
their great-great-grandparents prepared their
meals. We could have learned a great deal from each
other, but the opportunity was missed, as it has been
so often on the edge of an archaeological site.

Several years later, Dorothy Redford, another
descendent of Somerset slaves, would become
interested enough in that amazing plantation to
write a book about it *(Somerset Homecoming)*, and
she is now the director of the site, organizing
ongoing historical and archaeological research, as
well as biannual family reunions. Dot Redford is
neither an archaeologist nor historian by training.
Perhaps that is why she can see clearly the need that
these two disciplines have for each other. (With her
encouragement, and support from North Carolina
Historic Sites, a team led by Carl Steen and Trisha
Samford resumed excavations at Somerset in 1995.)

But it is no longer enough to rely on the
fortuitous intervention of outsiders. The time has
come for us to take it upon ourselves to examine our
complementary differences and explore what we
have to offer one another. We do not need to trip
ourselves so often on that little piece of ankle-high
string that separates history from archaeology. Let
me, as my modest contribution, mention several
broad aspects of archaeology that I admire, even
envy, and then describe a few attributes that
historical and archaeological research seem to have
in common.

What I envy the most in archaeology, I think, is
its enormous geographical scope. You have your
localisms, I know, and surely there are practitioners
who have put down their test probes in a single acre
and stayed there the rest of their lives. But your
training has taught you to think comparatively and
to visit, or at least talk about, every conceivable
terrain. You practice arid climate archaeology, high-
altitude archaeology, underwater archaeology. . . .
As a colonial American historian, my professional
inheritance is much more narrow. It stretches from
Plymouth Rock to Williamsburg—and back again!
If I want to consider French explorers in Louisiana,

Spanish missionaries in California, or Russian settlers in Alaska, I must rattle my cage somewhat. And if I wish to write about Africans in South Carolina and Jamaica or Native Americans in Florida and Hudson's Bay, I must saw through several bars.

Which brings me to the second point. For all their stratigraphic measurements and distribution coefficients, archaeologists are more humane than historians. "Humane" in the sense of being broadly interested in the human species, rather than remaining narrowly concerned, for the most part, with what is white and male, urban and literate. I exaggerate, of course, at the expense of some of my broadest and most creative historian colleagues. But if this generalization is not still depressingly relevant, then why is there such consternation abroad in the land—particularly among the powers that be—about the supposedly dangerous and disorienting practice of teaching about our North American past in all its ethnic, cultural, and gender diversity?

In 1992, Republican presidential hopeful Patrick Buchanan found this tendency so troubling that he referred to it disparagingly as "the landfill of multiculturalism." This anxiety about human diversity within our borders and beyond our customs barriers has become a hallmark of the 1990s. Historians, with our relatively new social interests and limited comparative skills, are not well equipped to fight the fight. We need considerable help and counsel from anthropologists and archaeologists—people who take diversity for granted.

I might go a step further and make an additional point: anthropologists are not only more accepting of human diversity; they are more conscious of mankind's actual position in the global environment. My open-air cousins with dirt under their nails come from a tradition that welcomed Charles Darwin and that revels in the intimate involvement of *Homo sapiens* in the natural world. My immediate academic family, the sons and daughters of Clio, has been far more careful about not spending too much time out of doors and about not welcoming Mr. Darwin into the parlor too quickly.

Let's face it, we historians are far from adventuresome when it comes to dealing with the world around us. We are taught to prefer the tick of a grandfather clock in the reading room to the ticks that infest southern fields in summertime. It is a function of my professional training at Harvard and Oxford that when I first visited Columbia, South Carolina, on a research trip in 1970, I spent most of my time in the beautiful confines of the South Caroliniana Library and in the cool chambers of the South Carolina State Archives on Senate Street, venturing out only to visit the driving range in late evening, after the temperature dropped below 80 degrees.

Still pursuing this line of thought, I want to express my esteem for the relatively collective nature of the archaeological enterprise. You rarely go into the field alone, and when you succeed it is invariably the result of a collaborative effort, even if one person claims credit for writing the essential grant proposal, uncovering the crucial pot fragment, or deciphering the inscrutable rune. You archaeologists, it seems to me, wear "Just Do It" T-shirts. We all know exceptions, but most of you find it necessary, natural, maybe downright enjoyable, to get along with people—colleagues and strangers, landowners and bartenders, lab assistants and backhoe operators.

In contrast, historians, I sometimes think, are enamored of the dead precisely because we have so much trouble confronting the living. Even our respect for the librarians and archivists who keep us supplied with books is too often the begrudging tolerance that addicts show toward their suppliers. We may co-author an article or share a reference now and then, but historical research (in contrast to the actual making of history) is not a team sport, and too few historians enjoy encountering new people and situations. Several years ago, when I drove across the United States in the dead of winter for a meeting of the American Historical Association in San Francisco, many of my disbelieving colleagues asked incredulously, "What on earth would you want to do that for?"

Finally, my list would be incomplete if I did not

also confess to a certain amount of envy toward the publicity many archaeologists seem able to generate for their work. This is not jealousy for the swash-buckling *Raiders of the Lost Ark* image. (I prefer as my Hollywood role models for truth-seekers the more cerebral images of John Houseman as a law professor in *The Paper Chase* or Peter Falk, as the detective in *Colombo*.) No, I refer to the startling degree of attention that a single artifact can gener-ate, in comparison to a single idea. Ever since Thomas Jefferson sliced through an Indian mound and Charles Willson Peale supervised the excavation of mastodon bones, the recovery of a material object has had a unique excitement for the American press and public. In recent times, how eagerly we awaited a second look at the *Titanic*, how avidly we peered into the waters of Pearl Harbor to glimpse the *Arizona*. I envy that direct connection between artifact and public.

Broad geographical horizons, an inclusive definition of humanity, an acceptance of our descent from apes, not angels, the inviting prospect of practical collaboration, the apparent ease of popular recognition.... Such are the differences that strike me, though you might dispute several of these and add a few distinctions of your own. But I am more struck by the similarities in our work, compatibilities that have too often been obscured by the separate professional dialects we still speak.

All of us, to begin with, are fascinated by, and wedded to, the basic idea of chronological change. Whether time is a circle or an arrow, a spiral or a pendulum, we might debate endlessly, but we each seek to find and elucidate the differences between "early" and "late," whether we are examining Catawba pottery, or Spanish fortifications, or the English slave trade, or FDR's foreign policy. Continuity—the relative lack of change—interests us too, but it only makes sense against this broader background, this unending kaleidoscope of sudden shifts and gradual modifications.

Our shared commitment to the study of chronological change is augmented by our common faith in interdisciplinary research. Individually, we each have our favorite tools and our preferred

questions. But all of us know that when we dig down into the past, whether literally or metaphorically, we ignore any aspect of human knowledge at our own risk. We have all had the experience (before, during, and sometimes after a research project) of telling ourselves, "If only I knew more about X," where X can be anything from A to Z, from aardvarks to zymurgy. (Zymurgy, the last word in my *Webster's Dictionary*, is "a branch of applied chemistry that deals with fermentation processes." Never having excavated a colonial brewery, I know nothing about it.)

Finally, we have at least one other thing in common that may not be entirely insignificant: our enormous fallibility as investigators and explicators. The broad scope of our studies, the thin and inconsistent nature of our evidence, and the cultural importance of our findings combine to make us all—both historians and archaeologists—repeat-edly susceptible to mistakes, deceptions, and fraud. This came home to me as I was reading the recent book by Stephen Williams, curator of North American Archaeology at Harvard's Peabody Museum. His volume, entitled *Fantastic Archaeology: The Wild Side of North American Prehistory*, re-counts a series of cautionary tales, ranging from the Cardiff Giant of 1869 to the Kensington Rune Stone of 1898.

A companion volume on "fantastic history" would not be difficult to construct. It would include such recent ruses as the "Hitler diaries," but it might also recount some of the places where historians and archaeologists have aided and abetted one another in their mistaken interpretations, as in the nine-teenth-century explorations of prehistoric mounds, described so effectively by Robert Silverberg in his book, *Mound Builders of Ancient America: The Archaeology of a Myth*.

For all our real and imagined differences, therefore, archaeologists and historians share a chronological mindset, an interdisciplinary pen-chant, and a recurrent gullibility. But this is only the beginning of a long list of common or complemen-tary traits. As our two disciplines become more familiar with each other, they will, I think, grow more accepting—less anxious to defend and criticize, more willing to listen and incorporate. The next step after panel discussions and co-edited volumes is certainly the extension of practical collaboration between our overlapping fields in the context of ongoing research projects.

Several years ago, in my hometown of Hillsborough, North Carolina, an archaeology team from nearby Chapel Hill excavated a contact-period site of the Occaneechi Indians in a bend of the Eno River, less than a mile from my house. I could not resist joining them. I was inspired by how different our approaches were to the same historical problem. The archaeology students could interpret evidence in the ground that I could hardly see; I could make use of John Lawson's eighteenth-century description of the village, which some of them had not even read. Together, as is often the case, the whole was better than the sum of the parts. I helped dig down in the earth; they helped look back through histori-cal records. My back got sore; their eyes got tired. It was an awkward, but respectful, relationship.

This renewed encounter with the sun-baked anthropologist "other" reminded me of an important lesson. We historians and historical archaeologists do not simply inhabit the same metaphorical terrain of the buried past. Instead, we literally share specific physical landscapes in our work, and we need to acknowledge that shared ground more readily and enthusiastically. The recent tendency of both historians and archaeologists to explore these common landscapes in new ways appears promising. Now if we can only begin to delve and examine *together* sometimes, we shall increasingly come to trust in, learn from, and even depend upon one another. I look forward, as I trust all persons interested in anthropology and public history do also, to broader and more frequent collaborations in the future.

NOTE

Previous versions of this chapter have been presented to the Society of Historical Archaeology and the National Council on Public History.

5. Historical Landscapes in Archaeology: The Development of the Frontier

KENNETH E. LEWIS

Archaeology and Landscapes

Archaeology involves the analysis of material evidence for the purpose of investigating behavior at various levels and scales. Accomplishing this task requires contexts within which to examine and compare data, as well as to recognize and interpret patterning. Two dimensions of archaeological research employed to define such contexts are space and time. These allow us to observe the distribution of phenomena, infer relationships among them, and postulate the nature of their evolution as reflected by temporal change. Crucial to this endeavor is the establishment of concepts and units, making it possible to measure changing spatial relationships and discover their meaning.

One such concept is that of landscape, a term that embodies several notions about the relationship between societies and the spaces they occupy. A landscape is the spatial manifestation of the adaptation of humans to their environments.[1] The nature of this adaptation varies with the organization of a society and the scale of its activities. Consequently, the definition of landscape is linked both to the nature of the social system under study as well as to those aspects of it around which the inquiry is focused. Landscape studies can involve larger or smaller regions and emphasize different cultural institutions depending on the questions asked.[2]

Cultural changes are a major factor in the evolution of landscapes over time. Each landscape, however, creates a physical component of which at least a portion usually survives. These remains form a sequence of archaeological landscapes that may be examined, at least in part, to reveal the chronological evolution of social, economic, and political systems.[3] The relationship between landscape change and cultural evolution is of great significance to the study of human adaptations in North America and of particular importance to the understanding of development during the historic period. The seventeenth, eighteenth, and nineteenth centuries were characterized by the expansion of European activities to gain possession of the continent and its resources. The progressive nature of this expansion created a series of landscapes in time as well as space, as regions were occupied, exploited, and reorganized, while new areas were continually being brought within the realm of this larger international economy. The importance of European colonization in the formation of North American landscapes has led to the adoption of frontier studies as a focus of historical research.

Because the components of these landscapes constitute the historical archaeological record, and an understanding of such landscapes is necessary to our comprehension of that record, the investigation of colonial landscapes and their formation has become, I believe, a central topic of historical archaeological research. My own work in South Carolina and Michigan, to which I will later briefly refer, resulted from an interest in understanding the landscapes that produced this material record.[4] Our ability to perceive historical landscapes is enhanced by the availability and extent of the documentary record, which provides a source of information entirely separate from material evidence in the ground. Employing an approach combining both types of data, we may more accurately model behavior and its spatial manifestations over time and, through the use of comparative data, postulate and seek to demonstrate the occurrence of processes accounting for the form, nature, and distribution of activities that produced the archaeological landscape.

The examination of processes dealing with landscape change immediately introduces the notion of scale. Just as the definition of a landscape is linked to the scale of activity under investigation, so should the nature of a process reflect the scope and extent of the behavior associated with a particular region. For example, if we were to study the colonization of North America as a whole, it is possible to generate models describing the development of landscapes on a scale that would emphasize the similarity of the individual regions within a larger area. If, on the other hand, we were interested in examining the occupation of a specific portion of North America, say Massachusetts Bay, the Ohio Western Reserve, Spanish East Florida, or the upper Pee Dee drainage, it becomes necessary to focus on a process that includes those factors relevant to the particular region under consideration. The scale employed in modeling change depends on the questions asked, but may also be affected by the evidence available.[5]

Archaeological data can reflect processes ranging in scope from intrasettlement to interconti-nental; however, to employ such material evidence effectively, it must be gathered in such a way as to obtain representative byproducts of the activities involved in a particular process. Because archaeology is site specific in nature, the acquisition of material evidence of regional processes becomes difficult unless the past function of the sites excavated can be reasonably well predicted. To be able to do this, it is necessary to understand beforehand the relationship between past processes and the settlement patterns they produce. By settlement pattern I refer to the distribution of, interrelations among, and function of settlement and activity components in a given region. Settlement patterning reflects the adaptation inherent in the creation of a landscape and identifies locations at which material evidence of this adaptation are likely to be situated. A knowledge of such patterning is crucial not only to investigating larger-scale processes archaeologically, but also to discovering the organization of historical landscapes.

Landscapes of Colonization

To illustrate the employment of these notions of landscape, pattern, and process, I would like to move to a discussion of colonization studies, a major topic in my research. My interest was focused initially on constructing a model of change that would account for the evolution of settlement patterning in frontier regions characterized by small farm or settlement plantation colonization. The resulting model, based on comparative cross-cultural evidence, defined a generalized landscape that contained an entrepôt linking the region to the outside world, together with a hierarchy, or "gradient," of settlements connected by a dendritic transportation and communications network. The size, form, content, distribution, and function of these settlements constitute adaptations to a low population density, attenuated social and political interaction, and nature and modes of production and transportation on the periphery of a world economy. The settlements evolve over time in response to population increase, intensification of production and land use, competition, and an alteration of marketing networks. Roles of individual settlements change, replacing the initial gradient with an integrated network of settlements supported by a more complex infrastructure typical of older, more stable regions. The former frontier region is consolidated as a portion of the parent state, or at least at a higher level in the larger world economy, as colonization proceeds to adjacent territories. The model describes a broad process characterized by settlement patterning that evolves through generalized phases as a region is colonized. The model explains the form and development of agricultural frontier landscapes as a consequence of economic processes associated with the region's initial isolation and identifies types of settlements whose sites might provide data for archaeological analyses relating to agricultural frontiers in general. Because of the model's scale, however, it is not capable of explaining why a particular region developed a specific pattern of settlement whose sites might provide material evidence relating to this landscape apart from others. The investigation of an individual frontier landscape requires the explanation of its settlement pattern, and this involves the modeling of agricultural colonization on a somewhat smaller scale.[6]

A frontier landscape is the result of the operation of general processes common to all such regions as well as factors distinctive of the time and place in which it develops. These factors include social and political as well as economic influences affecting frontier settlement. Briefly, these factors fall into four groups. The first involves *environmental conditions*, or rather their perception by the pioneer population. Images of the land and its characteristics vary not only with the technological capabilities of the intrusive society, but also with its philosophical view of nature and the role of humankind in it. Second, the manner of *land acquisition* and distribution considers not only the role of the colonizing state and its agents, official and unofficial, in making land available for settlement, but also the influence of the region's earlier residents, whose pacification and/or removal was necessary

before colonization could commence. Third, factors of *production and marketing* affect frontier settlement through the influences of market demand, strategies for production, commodity-processing needs, availability of labor, and the technologies of production and transportation. Indeed, the transformation of a frontier region into a component of the larger national or international economy has a dramatic impact on the nature of colonial production and the organization of settlement. Finally, there are the *strategies for colonization*, a factor sometimes difficult to define. Such strategies represent the manner in which immigrant populations adapt to the social as well as the economic environments of the frontier. They also link motivations that induced migration with the patterning and scheduling of settlement resulting from this process. These factors, while not changing the nature of agricultural colonization, are expected to alter its form, rate, and direction to create a distinctive landscape for a particular region.[7] The significance of these factors can be illustrated by reference to two regions with which I am familiar: South Carolina and the southern portion of Michigan's Lower Peninsula. Both were settled by agriculturalists of primarily British background and were, at the close of their colonization, characterized as commercial producers of staples. In each region a similar general pattern of settlement developed, characterized by a central entrepôt (Charleston and Detroit respectively), a series of inland centers, and smaller nucleated, semi-nucleated, and dispersed settlements connected by dendritic networks of transportation and communication. Clearly, both landscapes were formed by a similar large-scale process. In order to explain the settlement patterning that actually developed in each region, and thereby identify individual landscape components on which to conduct meaningful archaeological studies, it is necessary to go beyond merely recognizing this process and investigate how the factors mentioned earlier modified its footprint on the ground.[8]

I will not attempt to discuss in detail the influence of all of the factors affecting landscape formation; however, an example may be used to illustrate this point. The system of land distribution to individual colonists varied considerably between these two areas, although in both cases lands were ceded first by aboriginal peoples to colonial governments. In eighteenth-century South Carolina, as on much of the Eastern Seaboard south of New England, no general survey preceded the transfer of lands to colonists. Grants were made for a certain size tract usually situated within the bounds of a larger area, such as a township. Only after the individual inspected the land and had its boundaries surveyed was its location recorded, and then often impermanently because of the use of metes and bounds markers. While this system facilitated the dispersal of settlement typical of frontiers, it provided virtually no control over such spread and tended to bypass many areas, especially if they were perceived to be less desirable. Although South Carolina's occupation occurred in a generally northwestward direction spreading inland from the Atlantic coast, this movement was far from uniform. The availability and accessibility of land over a relatively wide region seems to have encouraged, or at least not prevented, expansion into any part of the interior, resulting in the early settlement of some distant inland areas and the delayed occupation of other regions nearer the entrepôt.[9]

By the third decade of the nineteenth century, when Michigan's settlement began in earnest, western frontier territories were under the nominal control of a central government in whose interest it was to promote settlement on available lands. In order to facilitate this process a system was established in the Northwest Ordinance of 1785 to survey accurately all new lands on a grid system prior to their sale. Not only were the lands precisely located, but the districts made available for settlement were opened at different times. This allowed a more

systematic transfer of lands as the sale of better and lesser quality lands together insured a more even dispersal of settlement over a given region. As a consequence, settlement patterning on the Michigan frontier, while characterized by the lower population density typical of such regions, tended to exhibit more compactness, possessing few large gaps in that portion of the Lower Peninsula opened to settlement. Particular characteristics of each region modified further the settlement patterning found in Michigan and South Carolina, creating additional distinctions in the frontier period landscapes of these two regions.[10]

The explanation of settlement patterning over time provides not only a key to the development of a landscape as a whole, but also establishes a necessary link between the components of that landscape and its entirety. This linkage has tremendous implications for interpreting the historical roles of individual settlements, activity sites, vacant spaces, and other landscape elements in the larger context of a region. The examination of landscapes on such a scale is also crucial to the investigation of historical archaeological sites. As the remains of settlement and activity components whose roles can only be understood in terms of the landscape of which they are a part, the sites also can be interpreted only in the context of the larger system. Indeed, the value of archaeological data with regard to providing evidence capable of answering specific questions about that system lies in our analyzing them in that context. Historical archaeology can no longer afford to approach questions dealing with the social, political, economic, and ideological aspects of past peoples on the basis of individual sites of uncertain context. To employ material data to address anthropological topics we must establish the context of our evidence in the past landscapes of which it was a part.

NOTES

1. The modern concept of landscape owes much to the work of geographers and particularly Carl O. Sauer, who emphasized the role played by humans in shaping the physical world. Rejecting earlier views of landscape that relied heavily on the importance of the natural environment, Sauer concluded that landscape was more than simply a region defined in physical terms. Rather, it is an area shaped in part by processes of which humans are an integral part. A landscape is a region "made up of a distinct association of forms, both physical and cultural" (Sauer 1963b: 25–26). See Sauer 1927:186–87. A discussion of Sauer's influence appears in James 1972:399–404; Winberry, this volume.

2. Marquardt and Crumley 1987:2–4.

3. Meinig 1979a:43–45 presents a useful discussion of the role of landscape in the investigation of historical processes, emphasizing the cumulative effect of past patterning on that of the present.

4. For summaries of the intellectual development of frontier studies, particularly in the United States, see Miller and Steffen 1977:3–10; and Savage and Thompson 1979:3–24. A discussion of comparative frontier studies from a world systems perspective and their relevance to archaeology is contained in Lewis 1984:Chap. 2. These studies have been concerned largely with investigating the nature of adaptive change undergone by expanding industrial societies. Others have also emphasized the value of using frontier studies as a context for examining social change among participating groups in situations of culture contact. See, e.g., Lightfoot and Martinez 1995:486–88.

5. The use of scale in historical regional studies is addressed by Oakes 1987:300–301 and Marquardt and Crumley 1987:2.

6. The terms "small farm" and "plantation" frontier were introduced by Leyburn 1935 and were recognized as functionally distinct from other forms of colonization by Thompson 1973:6–7. The distinction between agricultural settlement frontiers and other types of frontiers is treated at length in Steffen 1979:94–123 and Steffen 1980. The process of change in agricultural frontiers has been employed as a basis for modeling the historical development of colonial societies and discerning evidence of such change in the archaeological record, see Lewis 1984:19–27. The concept of "colonization gradient" was developed by Casagrande, Thompson, and Young 1964:312–14. Hudson 1969 modeled the patterning of settlements in agricultural frontiers, proposing successive stages characterized by random, clustered, and evenly spaced distributions. The occurrence of this sequential patterning in historical context has been demonstrated by Swedlund 1975 and Lewis 1985a:261–63.

7. These topics have been developed further in Lewis 1991a and Lewis 1991b.

8. For a discussion of settlement patterning and expansion in colonial South Carolina, see Petty 1975; Meriwether 1940; and Lewis 1984:Chap. 3. See also Kovacik and Winberry 1989:76–81. The most comprehensive treatment of the expansion of agricultural settlement in frontier Michigan is contained in Fuller 1916; see also Parkins 1918:Chap. 11. A more recent general account is contained in Dunbar 1980:Chaps. 8 and 9.

9. Colonial American systems of land division and their implications for settlements are examined in Hart 1975:54–55 and Bartlett 1974:68. The patterning of inland settlement in South Carolina before 1800 has been estimated on the basis of both documentary and archaeological evidence by Lewis 1984:66–69, 169–73.

10. The nature and implications of the rectangular land surveys for settlement in the West are discussed by Hibbard 1965:Chaps. 1 and 2; Bartlett 1974:69–75; Clawson 1970:46–56; and Rasmussen 1975:276–77. A spatial approximation of settlement spread in Michigan's Lower Peninsula during the first half of the nineteenth century appears in Hudgins 1961:n.p.

WORKS CITED

Bartlett, Richard A.
1974   *The New Country, a Social History of the American
         Frontier, 1776–1890.* Oxford Univ. Press, New
         York.

Casagrande, Joseph B., Stephen I. Thompson, and Philip
         D. Young
1964   Colonization as a Research Frontier. In *Process
         and Pattern in Culture, Essays in Honor of Julian
         H. Steward,* edited by Robert A. Manners, pp.
         281–315. Aldine, Chicago.

Clawson, Marion
1970   *Uncle Sam's Acres.* Greenwood Press, Westport.
         Originally published 1951, Dodd, Mead and Co.,
         New York.

Dunbar, Willis F.
1980   *Michigan, a History of the Wolverine State.* Revised
         edition by George S. May. William B. Eerdmans,
         Grand Rapids.

Fuller, George N.
1916   *Economic and Social Beginnings of Michigan, a
         Study of the Settlement of the Lower Peninsula
         during the Territorial Period, 1805–1837.*
         Wynkoop Hallenbeck Crawford Co.,
         Lansing.

Hart, James Frazer
1975   *The Look of the Land.* Prentice-Hall, Englewood
         Cliffs.

Hibbard, Benjamin Horace
1965   *A History of the Public Land Policies.* Univ. of
         Wisconsin Press, Madison.

Hudgins, Bert
1961   *Michigan, Geographic Backgrounds in the
         Development of the Commonwealth.* By the
         author, Detroit.

Hudson, John C.
1969   A Locational Model of Rural Settlement. *Annals
         of the Association of American Geographers*
         59:365–81.

James, Preston E.
1972   *All Possible Worlds: A History of Geographical
         Ideas.* Bobbs-Merrill, Indianapolis.

Kovacik, Charles F., and John J. Winberry
1989   *South Carolina: The Making of a Landscape.* Univ.
         of South Carolina Press, Columbia. Originally
         published in 1987 as *South Carolina: A Geogra-
         phy.* Westview Press, Boulder and London.

Lewis, Kenneth E.
1984   *The American Frontier: An Archaeological Study of
         Settlement Pattern and Process.* Academic Press,
         New York.
1985a   Functional Variation Among Settlements on the
         South Carolina Frontier: An Archaeological
         Perspective. In *The Archaeology of Frontiers and
         Boundaries,* edited by Stanton Green and Stephen
         Perlman, pp. 251–74. Academic Press, Orlando.
1991a   General Processes and Particular Variables in the
         Shaping of Frontier Settlement Patterns. In
         *Landscape, Architecture, and Artifacts: Historical
         Archaeology of Nineteenth Century Illinois,* edited
         by Erick K. Schroeder, pp. 1–13. Illinois Cultural
         Resources Study 15, Springfield.
1991b   Motivations for Colonization and their Effect on
         Settlement Patterning in Nineteenth Century
         Michigan. Paper presented at the 1991 Illinois
         Historical Archaeology Conference, Springfield.

Leyburn, James G.
1935   *Frontier Folkways.* Yale Univ. Press, New Haven.

Lightfoot, Kent G., and Antoinette Martinez
1995   Frontiers and Boundaries in Archaeological
         Perspective. In *Annual Review of Anthropology,*
         vol. 24, edited by William Durham, E. Valentine
         Daniel, and Bambi Schieffelin, pp. 471–92.
         Annual Reviews, Palo Alto, California.

Marquardt, William H., and Carole L. Crumley
1987   Theoretical Issues in the Analysis of Spatial
         Patterning. In *Regional Dynamics, Burgundian
         Landscapes in Historical Perspective,* edited by
         Carole L. Crumley and William H. Marquardt,
         pp. 1–18. Academic Press, San Diego.

Meinig, Donald W.
1979a   The Beholding Eye, Ten Versions of the Same
         Scene. In *The Interpretation of Ordinary Land-
         scapes,* edited by D. W. Meinig, pp. 33–48. Oxford
         Univ. Press, New York.

Meriwether, Robert L.
1940   *The Expansion of South Carolina, 1729–1765.*
         Southern Publishers, Kingsport, Tennessee.

Miller, David Harry, and Jerome O. Steffen
1977   Introduction. In *The Frontier, Comparative
         Studies,* edited by David Harry Miller and Jerome
         O. Steffen, pp. 3–10. Univ. of Oklahoma Press,
         Norman.

Parkins, Almon Ernest
1918 *The Historical Geography of Detroit.* Michigan Historical Commission, Lansing.

Petty, Julian J.
1975 *The Growth and Distribution of Population in South Carolina.* Originally published 1943, South Carolina State Planning Board, Columbia. Reprint, The Reprint Co., Spartanburg, South Carolina.

Rasmussen, Wayne D.
1975 Introduction, U.S. Land Policies, 1783–1840. In *Agriculture in the United States, a Documentary History,* vol. 1, edited by Wayne D. Rasmussen, pp. 273–80. Random House, New York.

Sauer, Carl Ortwin
1927 Recent Developments in Cultural Geography. In *Recent Developments in the Social Sciences,* edited by E. C. Hayes, pp. 186–87. J. P. Lippincott, Philadelphia.
1963b The Morphology of Landscape. In *Land and Life: A Selection from the Writings of Carl Ortwin Sauer,* edited by John Leighly, pp. 315–50. Univ. of California Press, Berkeley. Second printing 1965. Originally published in 1925 in Univ. of California Publications in Geography (vol. 2, no. 2):19–53.

Savage, William W., Jr., and Stephen I. Thompson
1979 The Comparative Study of the Frontier: An Introduction. In *The Frontier, Comparative Studies,* vol. 2, edited by W. W. Savage and S. I. Thompson, pp. 3–24. Univ. of Oklahoma Press, Norman.

Steffen, Jerome O.
1979 Insular Vs. Cosmopolitan Frontiers: A Proposal for Comparative Frontier Studies. In *The American West, New Perspectives, New Dimensions,* edited by Jerome O. Steffen, pp. 94–123. Univ. of Oklahoma Press, Norman.
1980 *Comparative Frontiers: A Proposal for Studying the American West.* Univ. of Oklahoma Press, Norman.

Swedlund, Alan C.
1975 Population Growth and Settlement Pattern in Franklin and Hampshire Counties, Massachusetts, 1650–1850. In *Population Studies in Archaeology and Biological Anthropology: A Symposium,* edited by Alan C. Swedlund, *American Antiquity,* Memoir 30:22–33.

Thompson, Stephen I.
1973 *Pioneer Colonization: A Cross-Cultural View.* Addison-Wesley Modules in Anthropology 33.

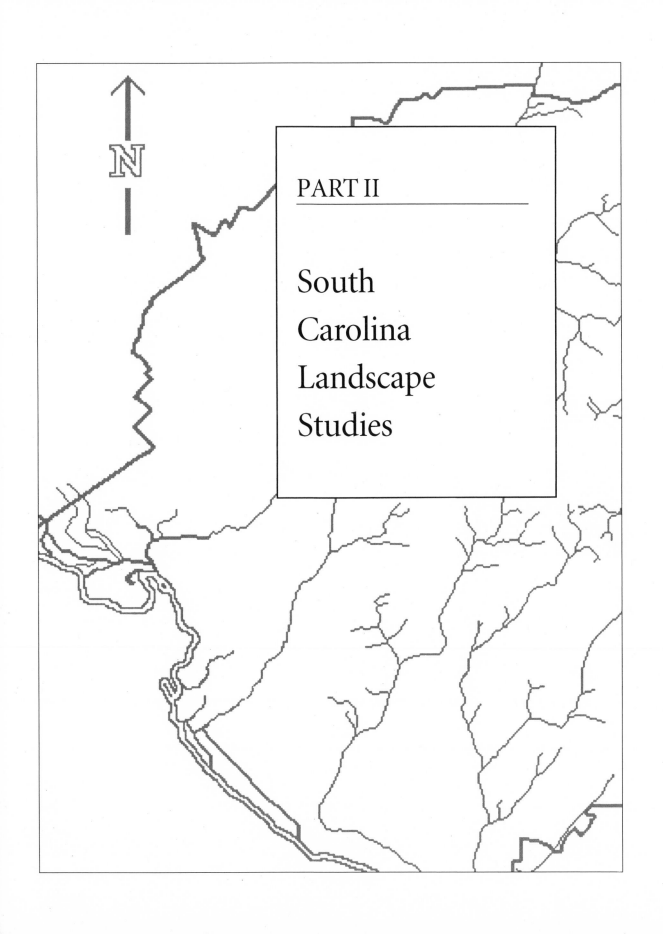

N

PART II

South
Carolina
Landscape
Studies

6. Building to Grow: Agrarian Adaptations to South Carolina's Historical Landscapes

J. W. Joseph

Southern history is agrarian history. Our knowledge of the South must thus be based in this agricultural heritage, since it is only through our understanding of how agriculture shaped and structured southern culture that we will be able to understand this culture as a whole. Agrarian history is landscape history. By its very nature, agrarian society was wed to the land, and changes within agrarian society can thus be read from the shifts in settlement patterning and in the changing relationship of humans to their environment.

This chapter seeks to examine historical agrarian adaptations to South Carolina within a landscape perspective, focusing upon those social transformations which in turn altered and shaped settlement trends and, more important, on the information which agricultural settlement provides concerning social structure and ideology.

In recognition of the scale and pervasiveness of the agrarian South, this essay has not confined itself to any specific manifestation or geographic location of South Carolina's agrarian past, but rather attempts to study agrarian culture as a whole. As one component of a larger synthetic effort aimed at illuminating the archaeological potential and direction of historical landscape analysis, this chapter also attempts to define gaps which exist in our current perception of South Carolina's agrarian past. The synthesis of previous archaeological research offered herein is directed most intently toward those studies which have also been landscape oriented, and it is hoped that more detailed synopses of the corpus of plantation and farmstead archaeology in South Carolina will be provided by papers which focus more directly on specific elements of those two cultural settlements. This essay begins at the beginning, with origins of plantation settlement along the South Carolina coastal plain, and winds its way through time and space to a small farm of the South Carolina piedmont at the dawn of the twentieth century.

Lowcountry Plantation Settlement

In referring to the cultural heritage and historical events which shaped the Deep South during the colonial era, folklorist Henry Glassie has noted that the South was more the northernmost point of the Caribbean than the southern extension of the Mid-Atlantic and New England. His analogy rests on both environmental and historical fact. South

Carolina's temperate climate was more comparable with that of the Caribbean than of New England, and the Lords Proprietors who oversaw the colonial settlement of South Carolina were themselves much a product of the English plantation enterprise in Barbados. Given these associations, plantation agriculture was introduced to South Carolina soon after the arrival of the Charleston settlers in 1670. As a defining characteristic of the plantation, slave labor was integral to its establishment, and both Native Americans and Africans were employed as the plantation's labor force. The importation of Africans by South Carolina planters was such that, by 1737, one visitor to the colony would remark that "Carolina looks more like a negro country than a country settled by white people."[1]

The emphasis of the colonial plantation economy shifted during the first half of the colonial era between rice and indigo, with cattle production serving as an important ancillary "crop" of the early years. Our image of colonial plantation settlement remains poorly defined, but the basic vision which emerges from archaeological and historical research is one of isolated plantations, disparate slave settlements, and a high degree of absentee management. This pattern may have first appeared within the formative period of plantation settlement, as Wood notes that the raising of cattle was frequently carried out by Africans living in the swampland wilderness on their own.[2] Indeed, open grazing was more familiar to South Carolina's African population than to the colony's European immigrants.

Excavations at Yaughan and Curriboo Plantations, Lesesne and Fairbank Plantations, Cotton Hope Plantation, Willtown Bluff, Charles Towne Landing, and ongoing research at Middleburg Plantation, Spring Island and Four Men's Ramble provide to date the best images of colonial eighteenth-century plantation settlement.[3] This research suggests that the English intention of establishing small, fortified communities from which the outlying plantations would be served quickly eroded as the colonists sought the independence and financial return which permanent plantation residence and/or management afforded

them.[4] The archaeological studies noted above also indicate that colonial plantations were relatively isolated, and situated on major rivers, which served as transportation arteries;[5] that settlements were dispersed across the plantation landscape to take advantage of topography and arable soils;[6] that slave settlements were in certain instances isolated from European American owner or overseer households; and that main house compounds were relatively rudimentary (at least when compared with later plantation settlements) and served to house either overseers or plantation owners who were frequently absent from residence.

The results of a recent survey within the Francis Marion National Forest of Charleston and Berkeley Counties supports the image of a colonial eighteenth-century rural settlement comprised of isolated and semi-independent African villages sites. Williams et al. document the presence of seven presumably eighteenth-century sites, whose assemblages are dominated by colonoware, to a single early eighteenth-century site possessing European ceramics. Assuming the colonoware sites reflect slave inhabitations and the European ceramic site a European American household, these results buttress the image of a disarticulated plantation settlement comprised largely of slave villages.[7] Such settlement would have been well suited to the production of rice and indigo, as well as to cattle rearing. Inland swamp rice agriculture, the dominant form of rice production in the colonial period, utilized seasonally drained inland swamp environments. Thus a settlement system in which worker's villages were established near these swamps would have presented the most economical means of displacing human resources across the coastal plain environment.

This pattern of plantation settlement is considered to reflect an adaptation to the South Carolina coastal plain influenced by African as well as European concepts of social space. This early settlement pattern does not appear to mirror the ancestral plantation settlement of the Caribbean. Tyson has presented a model for Caribbean plantation settlement composed of four parts: the Great

House Complex, the Factory Complex, the Worker's Village, and the Field System.[8] He notes that the first three of these were usually situated close together, on the sloping hillsides overlooking the coastal plain, and also observes that topography served to delineate social and economic status within such nucleated settlement. Slave villages were thus closely aligned with owner's housing and sugar plantation factories, and Tyson further records that most Caribbean plantations operated under the direct supervision of a resident owner or overseer.

In contrast, the social settlement model which emerges for colonial South Carolina plantation settlement features a European owner class largely settled in the urban environment of Charleston; rural plantations often operated on an absentee basis, with overseer's resident in supervisory command; and a further dispersal of worker's housing across the landscape of the plantation, situated to take advantage of environments conducive to inland swamp rice agriculture. While this settlement system is considered in many respects to be a product of environmental adaptation, the rural-urban dichotomy is one also reflected in African and European societies.[9] Further research should be directed to the broader patterns of society and settlement which were typical of Africa, England, and the Caribbean in the seventeenth and early eighteenth centuries, to determine the ways in which these settlement plans influenced the lowcountry's settlement structure.

The African aspects of such settlement have served as the focus of Wheaton and Garrow's analysis of acculturation at Yaughan and Curriboo Plantations.[10] They note that the earliest slave village at Yaughan revealed eight slave structures in association with an interpreted overseer's house. These slave structures were constructed of a post-in-wall trench architecture which Wheaton and Garrow interpreted as similar to West African "cobb-wall construction."[11] Wheaton and Garrow also observe that the structure of slave settlement at Yaughan and Curriboo shifted from a topographically derived model in which structures were located in relation to the existing slope contours to a more

rigidly imposed structure of parallel, aligned streets which appeared by the late eighteenth century.

The shift in slave settlement noted by Wheaton and Garrow represents but one aspect of broad-ranging change in plantation organization which has provoked an intense discussion regarding the mind of the plantation. This shift is characterized by a number of factors: 1) a change from impermanent and insubstantial architecture to more permanent and ornate structures; 2) a move away from an organic or loosely structured settlement plan to one which was highly structured; 3) a corresponding increase in the modification of the natural landscape to reflect this settlement structure; and 4) the nucleation of plantations and the formation of main house compounds.

While it is tempting to speak of these changes in terms of the transition from the colonial to federal world, they would appear to more properly reflect a transformation radiating outward from Charleston's urban hearth and bounded by the limits of the tidal surge within South Carolina's coastal waterways, whose effects were felt at varying times and distances. For example, the appearance of a landscaped settlement structure supporting substantial permanent architecture can be seen as early as the mid-eighteenth century at plantations such as Drayton Hall, Middleton Place, and others situated on the immediate periphery of Charleston,[12] while the effects of this settlement transformation appear to have reached the far corners of the lowcountry toward the latter end of the eighteenth century.[13]

In a series of reports and articles, Kenneth Lewis and others have focused on this shift in the organization and settlement of lowcountry plantations as an indicator of plantation ideology.[14] Lewis emphasizes the Georgian characteristics of the new plantation settlement, highlighting the importance of order, hierarchy, and symmetry as the organizational tenets of the new settlement system. Within this landscape ideology, the main house dominated the visual perception, both in size and appearance, and was flanked by its dependencies, both architectural and social. Slave dwellings were rarely immediately associated with the planter's home, and instead were placed in subservient positions, either behind the main house or along its flank. As presented by Lewis, such settlement dynamics served to illustrate the social dominance of planters.

Taking his perception from the opposite end of the social spectrum, Babson views this shift in settlement as evidence of heightened racism and social tension. He notes in particular the change in the location of slave villages from semi-isolated peripheral locations to nuclear mainhouse compounds and suggests that such resettlement indicates that planters were beginning to extend greater control over their dominion slaves, delimiting the boundaries of the plantation and in turn limiting the boundaries of negotiation. While thus also recognizing social power and control in this settlement reorganization, Babson suggests the object of this display was directed inward to the slave society, rather than outward to the society as a whole.

Echoing these views of change in settlement pattern as a product of ideological transformation, Joseph suggests that such transformations indicate the incorporation of management philosophies associated with the Industrial Revolution into the mind-set of the lowcountry's planters. Viewing ideology as a system of classification, Joseph presents the new plantation settlement as an expression of neo-agribusiness, arguing that labor specialization, social stratification within the slave community as permitted by the task labor economy,[15] and the reorganization of plantation settlement in concert with management concerns are all reflective of a shift in plantation ideology, away from a racially motivated settlement structure and toward a plan based on labor stratification and management.

All of the authors cited above recognize the influence of tidal-flow rice agriculture on this new settlement scheme, and Ferguson and Babson provide a persuasive analysis of tidal-flow's relationship to this new settlement plan.[16] Tidal-flow agriculture required enormous expenditures of labor and capital, creating a series of rice ponds and dikes which allowed rice production to reach exceptional levels of productivity. As rice ponds were self-fertilizing, this new system allowed labor to be concentrated in larger and more stable settlements placed at fewer locations. Finally, as an extremely productive economy, tidal-flow rice production also permitted the expansion and elaboration of mainhouse compounds and plantation support structures. While the ideological factors discussed above all may have been at play in this settlement transformation, it is doubtful that this settlement shift would have come about without the change to tidal-flow production.

This settlement shift in lowcountry plantation agriculture remains one of the most prominent targets for a landscape perspective in agrarian archaeology, and will doubtlessly garner further attention in the coming years. The transition from the late eighteenth to early nineteenth century has received much of the research devoted to plantation archaeology, and, given the social and economic transformations which this period brought on a global scale, it is certainly deserving of yet further thought and consideration.

This review of lowcountry plantation settlement archaeology suggests that other aspects of the plantation landscape require further study, however. Specifically, much greater effort should be applied to the issue of colonial settlement systems. We should recognize that since colonial plantations appear to have been characterized by a dispersed settlement plan featuring less substantial architecture than later plantations, and since the material culture of the colonial period may be overshadowed by the production which followed the Industrial Revolution, the archaeological evidences of these colonial plantations may not be as recognizable or impressive as their late-eighteenth- and nineteenth-century counterparts.[17] However, given the relative lack of cartographic images available for these plantations, archaeological documentation may offer the most powerful means of addressing colonial settlement.

Efforts to understand the plantation should

also be extended outside the limits of individual estates, and the broad environmental and social parameters which structured the locations of individual plantations should be given greater consideration. While South and Hartley's "deep water-high ground" association provides a reliable model of the colonial settlement system, Ferguson and Babson's cartographic research and Stine's archaeological landscape study provide the only attempts to date to address broad-scale settlement patterning in the nineteenth century.[18] Research needs to be extended to factor into our account the influence of roads, the development of interior towns, and the eventual introduction of the railroad. We are well aware that the structure of individual plantations changed over time; we know far less about the locations of these plantations within their region. Finally, the collapse of the plantation economy and the subsequent era of agriculture, the period of tenant agriculture in the piedmont, is poorly documented for the coastal plain.[19] While the forest industry and phosphates eventually consumed much of the former plantation lands, the shift and relation of the antebellum plantations to these industrial ventures has not received scrutiny. The lowcountry plantation landscape remains one of the best documented for agrarian South Carolina; yet, despite the considerable attention this settlement system has received, gaps still persist in our image and understanding of lowcountry plantation settlement.

Upcountry Plantation Settlement

The increasing worldwide demand for cotton spurred by the Industrial Revolution, the invention of the cotton gin and the hence greater utility and value of short-staple cotton, and the settlement of the South Carolina upcountry by colonists aware of the financial boom in process along the coast all combined to introduce plantation agriculture to the upcountry. Indeed, the plantation followed immediately on the heels, if not within the feet, of the

Indian traders who first settled the upcountry. Despite this early introduction, little is known of the colonial aspects of piedmont plantation settlement. The work of Scurry et al., Brooks, Lewis, and others suggests that these plantations featured nuclear settlements containing owner and slave dwellings, agricultural structures, and livestock pens. Indeed, until the era of Indian conflict had passed, such nuclear and even fortified settlements, such as those documented by Bastian, would have been a necessary condition of life on the piedmont frontier.[20]

The antebellum period of plantation agriculture, the era from the close of the Colonial period to the beginning of the Civil War, is also not well known archaeologically. This is in part because 1) antebellum plantations were frequently occupied into the postbellum era, and thus pre- and postwar components are difficult to segregate,[21] and because 2) the severe erosion which characterizes piedmont agriculture has been responsible for the loss of a number of piedmont plantation sites, and because 3) the settlement system of antebellum and postbellum piedmont plantations was dispersed and somewhat ephemeral.

In an effort to address both plantation and farmstead settlement systems within the piedmont, Gray proposed four settlement models, drawing from Prunty's seminal concepts regarding plantation settlement structure.[22] These include the nucleated, semi-nucleated, conglomerate, and dispersed forms. The nucleated form consisted of a single settlement site housing both main house and support facilities, while the semi-nucleated pattern featured an association, but not direct concentration, of these aspects, i.e., a plantation whose slave village was separated from the main house by a distance of no more than a few hundred yards. The conglomerate pattern featured several clusters of activity sites, while the dispersed model was characterized by almost randomly spaced sites which were largely independent. Gray noted that, based on her research in the Richard B. Russell Reservoir area, the conglomerate pattern appeared to represent the most accurate reflection of piedmont plantation settlement.

Expanding upon Gray's research, Joseph observed that the nature of piedmont soils and crop production was conducive to a shift from nucleated to conglomerate settlement.[23] Cotton was extremely exhaustive of soil nutrients, and cotton fields were thus rotated every three to five years. Over time the loci of slave villages on any piedmont plantation would thus be expected to shift from one settlement to another as new areas were cleared for crop production. Slave dwellings were thus usually of impermanent construction, with the log cabin appearing as the most common slave structure in the piedmont. Such repositioning of plantation activity sites over time would yield a conglomerate settlement form, with the main house compound continuing to exist, but the actual major activity centers being repositioned across the plantation to maximize soil production.

As both Gray and Joseph note, the archaeological record tends to incorrectly emphasize nuclear settlement, since main house compounds are most frequently identified and recorded, while outlying slave settlements are not. None of the slave settlements at either the Bannister Allen or McCalla plantations within the Russell Reservoir project were identified. Gray observes that such sites were dispersed across the plantation landscape, and Joseph notes that these slave sites were likely to leave only a sparse archaeological record, and hence may not be recognized at the survey level as potentially significant sites to be afforded further study. Indeed, Gray pinpointed the locations of a number of known historic archaeological sites within the McCalla Plantation's historic boundaries which represented potential slave settlements, but which did not receive further study because they were not accorded potentially significant status following their identification.

The scant research of antebellum piedmont plantations carried out to date suggests a dichotomy in the ways in which the landscape was viewed and treated by piedmont planters. For many, South Carolina was merely the current square in a game of transatlantic hopscotch. As historian James Oakes notes, "By the nineteenth century, westward

migration had become so much a part of upward mobility in the South that it took on a lure almost independent of the profitable potential of the actual move."[24] Seen from this perspective, there was little need to nurture or embellish the landscape; unfettered exploitation offered the promise of the greatest profit. Yet, for others, position in South Carolina society and their impress on the landscape were irrevocably linked. James Henry Hammond, South Carolina statesman and planter extraordinare, was torn by the attractions of land in the Southwest and the prospect that by moving he would "make double what I do"; yet Hammond ultimately refused to relinquish his plantation home at Redcliffe, instead pursuing the benefits of scientific agriculture, dredging marl clay from 12 miles downriver which could be applied to his plantation fields as fertilizer.[25] Trinkley et al.'s recent landscape study of Rosemont Plantation in Laurens County emphasizes the role which permanent and embellished piedmont plantations served in securing the social standing of their owners. As Trinkley et al. note, such substantial and elaborate piedmont plantations served as "seats" and centers of social and political discourse in their regions. The archaeological impress of those piedmont planters (and plantations) who ignored the pull of the West is deserving of further study, as is the split in southern ideology evidenced between those who went west and those who stayed behind.[26]

The conclusion of the Civil War and the end of legalized slavery is widely recognized by its impress on piedmont plantations. The introduction of tenancy led to a gradual shift from a conglomerate settlement system to one in which tenant dwellings were displaced across the landscape under the supervision and control of the plantation owner and main house compound. Prunty, Shlomowitz, Orser and Holland and Orser provide excellent discussions of the changing labor relations and corresponding agricultural settlement during the postbellum period, which should be referred to for more detailed analysis. Orser and Nekola's examination of Millwood Plantation's tenant settlement recorded that Millwood tenants were likely to live less than 0.3 miles from an intermittent stream, less than 0.5 miles from a stream confluence, and less than 0.3 miles from the nearest neighbor.[27] This last measure may mark one of the strongest correlations in tenant settlement, as tenants were likely to be established near other tenants and in particular near kin.[28] Thus, while seemingly dispersed and isolated when compared to the plantation settlement system, tenant settlement appears to have maintained a kin- or community-based social structure.

In summary, the transformations from slavery to tenancy addressed by the authors cited above are reflected by the gradual breakdown of the old plantation settlement system; tenant "squads" may have continued to function as labor units with an organization similar to antebellum slave villages at least for the years immediately following the war. Eventually, however, this labor structure broke down, so that individual tenant farm families became the common labor unit, and these families were scattered across the plantation landscape to take advantage of arable soils. The settlement shift from the antebellum to the postbellum era among piedmont plantations is eloquent for what it expresses regarding the desires of both planters and freedmen. Planters wanted and held power in the economic, social, and political world. Tenants sought and received independence in exchange for power, as reflected by their selections of house sites away from planter scrutiny and in their emphasis on kin and community. This shift in settlement can thus also be read as a factor of a changing ideology and of changing social relations.

Farmstead Agriculture

The discussion of farmstead settlement presented herein is not divided into lowcountry and upcountry sections, as was the review of the plantation landscape. Although representing the most common form of agriculture in the state, farmsteads have received little attention archaeologically. This is especially true of the lowcountry, where plantations have been the recipient of much of the archaeological research.

Brockington et al.'s Mark Clark study represents the only project of scale to focus on lowcountry farmstead sites, but, as the product of transportation corridor research, it unfortunately does not provide much discussion of settlement aspects. Farmsteads have received greater attention in the piedmont, as a result of compliance studies carried out for the Richard B. Russell Reservoir,[29] Clarks Hill Lake,[30] Lake Hartwell,[31] and the Savannah River Site;[32] highway transportation projects;[33] and graduate research.[34] Again, this research is limited in that it does not provide much information concerning antebellum farmsteads, and is focused most intently upon the postbellum era.

Drawing from Weaver and Doster, S. Smith et al., Newton, and J. Hart, Worthy provides a listing of attributes for piedmont farmstead settlements.[35] These include:

1. The random clustering of domestic and service operations, usually situated on hilltops or other prominent points. The relationships among structures are generally idiosyncratic and a factor of differing opinions regarding "convenience."
2. Buildings have individual functions, i.e., dwelling, storehouse, smokehouse, livestock pen: only rarely are functions combined.
3. Dwellings, wells, privies, storage sheds, and chicken houses are placed in close proximity as structures associated with household activities. The house yard is also frequently swept, further distinguishing this space.
4. Barns, animal pens, equipment buildings, forges, and other agricultural activity areas are situated at a slight distance from the domestic area. The approach to these structures is usually around, rather than through, the domestic yard.
5. The house faces the probable path of approach and is shaded by trees.
6. Fields are irregularly arranged and follow topography. Fields are sited to make best use of arable lands, while farms are placed to provide access to fields.

Stine, drawing from Trewartha, Glassie, Kniffen, and others, notes that southern farm settlement was less structured than farms of other regions and featured fewer and less substantial structures.[36] She characterizes the settlement form of these farms as "loosely dispersed," and further notes that open yard areas were used for a number of activities on upland South farms. Stine's ethnoarchaeological study of a North Carolinian piedmont farming community revealed that both interior and exterior spaces were multifunctional.

All of the authors cited above recognize that farmsteads featured segregated domestic and agricultural areas. In a study of folk housing in Middle Virginia, Glassie observes that "the old farm had two centers, the house and the barn, around which smaller dependencies were dropped. Beside the house are the outbuildings needed by the woman in order to get food on the table; beside the barn are the outbuildings needed by the man to keep the cattle fat."[37] This sexual dimorphism is also recognized by J. Adams, who places it in the context of farmstead production and the authority to dispose of such produce.[38] Adams notes that men controlled actions and products which contributed to farmstead capital, while women controlled household production. She thus suggests that the division between domestic and agricultural space, between female and male labor, reflects a division in the management and production of the farmstead.

Stine, however, argues that such division may be a reflection of Victorian ideology more than agricultural reality. She notes that this ideology served to separate and segregate the purity of the household and the sin and inequity of the working world, and thus gender separation represents the norm of such ideology. However, her research in North Carolina suggests a degree of crossover, such that women occasionally worked in agricultural fields; root cellars, which were used for the storage of food crops and would have been considered to be the domain of women were located in agricultural areas; smokehouses, which were operated by men, were placed in domestic settings. Her research is supported by studies in piedmont South Carolina,[39] indicating that caution should be exercised when considering such spatial segregation.

In their study of Finch Farm, a late-nineteenth- and twentieth-century farmstead in Spartanburg County, South Carolina, Joseph et al. suggest that the landscape may have been deliberately modified to express an ideology which emphasized the farmer's ability to control nature.[40] Finch Farm was landscaped and defined by an arc of large oaks situated in an area of open fields and was bordered by an orchard. Stone walls were built in the rear yard area to define yard edges. According to Joseph et al., the overall effect was to create a domestic oasis in the midst of agricultural fields, a landscape transformation which would demonstrate the farmer's ability to control nature. While the "landscape" aspect of agrarian settlement has received considerable attention in lowcountry plantation research, less effort has been exerted toward recognizing land modification and manipulation on historic farms; that is, toward distinguishing the fields from the trees.

In summary, the archaeology of farmstead settlement has demonstrated some degree of separation between domestic and agricultural space, the meaning of which, however, is debated. Too little work has been done to date to address the issues of adaptation and evolution in farmstead plan, differences between the coast and upcountry, status differences in farmstead settlement, or ethnic variation in farmstead settlement. Although a common feature of South Carolina's historic landscape, our archaeological vision of farmsteads is poorly defined.

Between 1670 and some point prior to World War II, the majority of South Carolina's citizenry was directly tied to the land and its agricultural production. The changes which have occurred in southern society in the past half-century are monumental in scope, yet they cannot obscure our common landscape history. It has been said, but bears re-emphasis, that southern history is agrarian history. It thus follows that southern historical archaeology should include agrarian historical archaeology.

Our research emphasis to date has focused on the lowcountry's tidal rice plantations of the late eighteenth and nineteenth century; on the fascinating dance which served to define the social relations between Africans and European Americans; and on the South's mad rush into the industrial era and the centuries of change that thus passed in a few decades. These plantation sites are marked by an intricate web laid out across the terrain, by the grid of rice ponds and dikes, the broad oak avenues, the classical symmetry of homes and grounds, and by the quiet and "orderly" presence of slave streets tucked slightly away from view. It is not surprising that these sites have been lavished with so much of our attention, for they are indeed noteworthy. They are not, however, truly agrarian.

For much of its history, for most of its people, South Carolina's agrarian past was best noted for its rather casual and exploitative relationship with the land. Settlements were dispersed to make best use of fertile ground and moved when the earth's productivity diminished: houses were built cheaply and impermanently; field clearing inspired rampant erosion;[41] settlers moved from one location to the next, often toward the west, in search of a better land. The ideology of this era, the ideology of South Carolina's agrarian settlements on the other side of that 15-mile-wide band which defined the limits of the tidal surge, is marked by its exploitation of the land and by the influence of the frontier on settlement and land use. By the late nineteenth century, as the lands to the west dwindled and the frontier ceased to exist, agrarian life took on a more permanent aspect, treated the land a little better in an effort to gain a greater yield, and eventually settled down. The contrast between the settlement and ideology of lowcountry rice plantations and this frontier philosophy presents one of the most promising research perspectives available to historical archaeology, yet it cannot be addressed because we simply know too little about too much of South Carolina's agrarian past.

As Hodder and Orton note, "Any map is, in a sense, an attempt at quantification. It provides empirical evidence on which some theory can be built. But such a map can be misleading due to the uneven way archaeological information survives and is collected."[42] Our archaeological map of South Carolina's agrarian past offers such a deception, because it emphasizes the structure, stability, and complexity of lowcountry rice plantations and disregards the shadowy nature of other agrarian sites. Pre tidal-flow rice plantations of the coast, cotton plantations of the piedmont, and small farmsteads would all appear to be characterized by a dispersed and opportunistic settlement scheme featuring relatively short-lived, impermanent, ephemeral occupations. All of these factors have served to diminish the archaeological recognition of such sites. It is suggested that greater attention should be given to historic artifact scatters at the survey level in an effort to define their function and meaning within the historic landscape. While these sites cannot perhaps be effectively identified by small-scale projects, more intensive surveys of larger tracts should make the effort to associate such sites with known historic occupations (plantations, communities, mills, and farms) and to explain the meaning of such sites within an overall agrarian landscape, before simply dismissing such occupations as "ineligible" to the National Register.

The ephemeral nature of certain agrarian sites, most notably tenant households, has already prompted a considerable debate in historical archaeology.[43] While such sites are now widely recognized as having the potential to yield important scientific data, the means of securing such data continue to be discussed. Agrarian archaeology has yet to develop, or even explore, the need for a common methodology, but this overview indicates that such need exists, particularly in the study of settlement. Joseph et al. have recently suggested that architecturally intact farmstead and tenant sites offer the best prospects for archaeological research, since such locations are less likely to have suffered conversion to agricultural fields and the corresponding loss of soil and archaeological remains. This recommendation is supported here, since those sites possessing standing architecture are obviously capable of landscape analysis, but this chapter also recognizes that pure archaeological sites can yield landscape data, if studied from a landscape perspective. The requirements of such study would appear to consist of at least shovel testing at a close-order interval to identify artifact concentrations, the recognition and notation of landscape modifications (such as terracing, etc.), the exposure of artifact concentrations through either block excavation or stripping to expose and examine feature patterning, and the collection and analysis of ethnobotanical and phytolith samples and close examination of the current vegetation to aid in the reconstruction of the historic landscape.

Beyond individual sites, little work has been done with agrarian settlement at the regional level. We thus do not have good models for predicting the locations of farmsteads and plantations, although fortunately we do have historic maps. However, these are only likely to indicate the locations of permanent structures, omitting the presence of slave cabins, nineteenth-century tenant house sites, and other less noteworthy features from the landscape. Again, large-scale surveys should seek not only to locate historic sites, but to identify them as well, through the combination of more detailed archival research at the survey level and through comparison of the historic sites and settlement recorded by such efforts. While such research will require the expenditure of a greater level of effort at the survey phase, it should yield more secure assessments of site significance and eventually produce data on settlement patterning, which in turn may yield more efficient and less costly survey requirements.

It is impossible to know our future, so we had best direct our attention to our past. Our efforts to reveal the past must recognize our own biases, both in terms of what is most represented archaeologically and with regards to what appear to us to be the most fascinating objects of study. Tenant sites, small farmsteads, and dispersed plantation settlements may seem mundane when cast in the glamour of the lowcountry's plantations, yet the information these sites possess—those scattered, eroded, non-diagnostic bits of information—provide a very real and very rare glimpse of the way it was for many of our ancestors. As we continue to study the past as a reality and not simply our perception of reality, we develop a better image of where we have been and, more important, of where we are going. For more than two centuries, most of South Carolina's agrarian settlers abused the landscape and gave little attention to its future health. It is interesting to speculate upon the linkage between their mind-set and the region's current inclination toward serving as the repository for much of this nation's nuclear and hazardous waste. We may not realize it, but the ideology of our forebears is still a part of our mental makeup, and we must consider this agrarian past if we are ever to understand the present and provide direction to the future.

NOTES

1. Wood 1974:132–33.
2. Wood 1974:30–31.
3. See Wheaton, Garrow, and Friedlander 1983; Zierden, Drucker, and Calhoun 1986; Trinkley 1990b; Herold 1980; South 1971; Babson 1987; Babson 1988; Affleck and Adams 1991; Trinkley 1990a; and Wayne and Dickinson 1990.
4. See also Stine 1992a and Smith 1988. For a Georgia perspective on a similar settlement shift among the Salzburgers at Ebenezer, see Smith 1986. for a discussion of South Carolina's and Georgia's vanishing colonial towns see Elliott 1990b and Elliott 1991.
5. South and Hartley 1980; Hartley 1984.
6. Joseph and Reed 1991.
7. Williams, Cable, and Reed 1992.
8. Joseph and Tyson 1989.
9. For discussions of the rural-urban dichotomy in African settlement, see Vlach 1975 and Vlach 1978.
10. Wheaton and Garrow 1985.
11. Wheaton and Garrow 1985:248.
12. See Lewis 1978 and Lewis 1985; Lewis and Hardesty 1979; Lewis and Haskell 1980.
13. See Lees 1980 and Wheaton, Garrow, and Freidlander 1983.
14. For the archaeology of plantation ideology, see

15. For discussions of task labor and its affect on the archaeological record, see Anthony 1989 and Joseph 1987.

16. Ferguson and Babson 1986.

17. See Drucker 1981; Joseph 1989; Zierden and Calhoun 1983.

18. See South and Hartley 1980; Ferguson and Babson 1986; Stine 1992a. For a valuable historic perspective on lowcountry plantation settlement, refer to Smith 1988.

19. See, however, Brockington et al. 1985; Trinkley and Caballero 1983a.

20. See Scurry, Joseph, and Hamer 1980; Scurry 1982; Brooks 1986; Brooks 1988a; Brooks 1988b; Lewis 1976; Bastian 1982.

21. For examples of the difficulty in separating antebellum and postbellum occupations, see Brooks 1986 and 1988a; Drucker, Meizner, and Legg 1982; Orser, Nekola, and Roark 1982; Orser 1988.

22. Gray 1983; Prunty 1955.

23. In Anderson and Joseph 1988.

24. Oakes 1982:76.

25. See Faust 1982:114–17.

26. Trinkley, Adams, and Hacker 1992.

27. See Shlomowitz 1979 and Shlomowitz 1982; Orser 1986; Orser and Holland 1984; Orser and Nekola 1985.

28. For an analysis of the influence of kinship on rural settlement, see Joyce 1981, and Crass and Brooks, this volume.

29. Farmstead archaeological projects undertaken for the Richard B. Russell compliance studies include Drucker, Meizner, and Legg's 1982 investigation of the Thomas Clinkscales Farm and Gray's 1983 Old Home Place study; see also Drucker and Anthony 1986; Anderson and Joseph's 1988 technical synthesis; Jackson and Drucker 1985.

30. Drucker et al. 1984.

31. Anthony and Drucker 1984.

32. See Brooks 1986, 1988a, and 1988b.

33. See Trinkley and Caballero 1983; Joseph, Reed, and Cantley 1991.

34. Resnick 1984.

35. Worthy 1983.

36. Stine 1989a.

37. Glassie 1975.

38. Adams 1987.

39. See Joseph and Reed, this volume.

40. Joseph, Reed, and Cantley 1991.

41. See Trimble 1974.

42. Hodder and Orton 1976.

43. Most notably, see the Anderson-Muse and Trinkley debate—Anderson and Muse 1982 and Anderson and Muse 1983; Trinkley 1983b.

Works Cited

Adams, Jane Helen
1987   *The Transformation of Rural Social Life in Union County, Illinois, in the Twentieth Century.* Ph.D. diss., Dept. of History, Univ. of Illinois, Urbana-Champaign.

Affleck, Richard, and Natalie Adams
1991   Plantation Settlement Pattern and Slave Architecture from the South Carolina and Georgia Lowcountry, 1670 to 1865. Paper presented at the symposium entitled Plantation Archeology of the Virginia and Maryland Tidewater Region and the Lowcountry of Georgia and South Carolina: A Synthesis and Comparison. 1991 Annual Meeting of the Society for Historical Archaeology Richmond, Virginia.

Anderson, David G., and J. W. Joseph
1988   *Prehistory and History Along the Upper Savannah River: Technical Synthesis of Cultural Resource Investigations, Richard B. Russell Multiple Resource Area.* Russell Papers 1988. Interagency Archeological Services, National Park Service, Atlanta.

Anderson, David G., and Jennalee Muse
1982   The Archaeology of Tenancy in the Southeast: A View from the South Carolina Lowcountry. *South Carolina Antiquities* 14:71–82.
1983   The Archaeology of Tenancy (2): A Reply to Trinkley. *Southeastern Archaeology* 2:65–68.

Anthony, Ronald W.
1989   *Cultural Diversity at Mid to Late 18th Century*

Lowcountry Plantation Slave Settlements. Master's thesis, Dept. of Anthropology, Univ. of South Carolina, Columbia.

Anthony, Ronald, and Lesley M. Drucker
1984   *Hartwell Destination Park: An Archaeological Study of a Piedmont Locality, Oconoee County, South Carolina.* Resource Studies Series 74. Carolina Archeological Services, Columbia.

Babson, David W.
1987   Plantation Ideology and the Archaeology of Racism: Evidence from the Tanner Road Site (38BK416), Berkeley County, South Carolina. *South Carolina Antiquities* 19(1, 2):35–47.

1988   *The Tanner Road Settlement: The Archaeology of Racism on Limerick Plantation.* Volumes in Historical Archaeology, Conference on Historic Sites Archaeology, vol. 4, edited by Stanley South. South Carolina Institute of Archaeology and Anthropology, Columbia. Reprint of 1987 Master's thesis, Dept. of Anthropology, Univ. of South Carolina, Columbia.

Bastian, Beverly
1982   *Fort Independence: An Eighteenth Century Homesite and Militia Post in South Carolina,* National Park Service, Atlanta.

Brockington, Paul, Jr., Michael Scardaville, Patrick H. Garrow, David Singer, Linda France, and Cheryl Holt
1985   *Rural Settlement in the Charleston Bay Area: Eighteenth and Nineteenth Century Sites in the Mark Clark Expressway Corridor.* Submitted to the South Carolina Dept. of Highways and Public Transportation. Garrow and Associates, Atlanta.

Brooks, Richard D.
1986   The Ashley Plantation (1876–1950): Research Domains and Results. *South Carolina Antiquities* 18 (1, 2):9–14.

1988a   *Synthesis of Historical Archaeological Sites on the Savannah River Plant, Aiken and Barnwell Counties, South Carolina.* South Carolina Institute of Archaeology and Anthropology, Columbia.

1988b   *250 Years of Historic Occupation on Steel Creek, Savannah River Plant, Barnwell County, South Carolina.* Submitted to the Savannah River Operations Office, U. S. Department of Energy. Savannah River Archaeological Research Program, South Carolina Institute of Archaeology and Anthropology, Columbia.

Drucker, Lesley M.
1981   Socio-economic Patterning at an Undocumented Late 18th Century Lowcountry Site: Spiers Landing, South Carolina. *Historical Archaeology* 15(2):58–68.

Drucker, Lesley M., and Ronald W. Anthony
1986   On the Trail: An Examination of Socioeconomic Status at Late Historic Piedmont Farmsteads. *South Carolina Antiquities* 18(1, 2):15–24.

Drucker, Lesley M., Ronald W. Anthony, Susan Jackson, S. Krantz, and Carl R. Steen
1984   *An Archaeological Study of the Little River-Buffalo Creek Special Land Disposal Tract, Clarks Hill Lake, McCormick County, South Carolina.* Submitted to the U.S. Army Corps of Engineers, Savannah District. Resource Studies Series 75. Carolina Archeological Services, Columbia.

Drucker, Lesley M., Woody C. Meizner, and James B. Legg
1982   *The Bannister Allen Plantation (38Ab102) and Thomas B. Clinkscales Farm (38Ab221): Data Recovery in the Richard B. Russell Multiple Resource Area, Abbeville County, South Carolina.* Russell Papers. Submitted to the National Park Service, Carolina Archaeological Services, Columbia.

Elliott, Daniel
1990b   *The Lost City Survey: Archaeological Reconnaissance of Nine Eighteenth Century Settlements in Chatham and Effingham Counties.* LAMAR Institute, Athens.

1991   Lost and Found: Eighteenth Century Towns in the Savannah River Region. *Early Georgia* 19(2):61–92.

Faust, Drew Gilpin
1982   *James Henry Hammond and the Old South: A Design for Mastery.* Louisiana State Univ. Press, Baton Rouge.

Ferguson, Leland G.
1992   *Uncommon Ground: Archaeology and Early African America, 1650–1800.* Smithsonian Institution Press, Washington, D.C.

Ferguson, Leland, and David Babson
1986   *Survey of Plantation Sites along the East Branch of Cooper River: A Model for Predicting Archaeological Site Location.* Ms. on file, Dept. of Anthropology, Univ. of South Carolina, Columbia.

Glassie, Henry
1975   *Folk Housing in Middle Virginia; Structural Analysis of Historic Artifacts.* Univ. of Tennessee Press, Knoxville.

Gray, Marlessa A.

1983   *"The Old Home Place," An Archaeological and Historical Investigation of Five Farm Sites Along the Savannah River, Georgia and South Carolina.* Russell Papers 1983. Submitted to the Interagency Archeological Services, National Park Service, Atlanta.

Hartley, Michael O.

1984   *The Ashley River: A Survey of Seventeenth Century Sites.* Research Manuscript Series 192. Institute of Archeology and Anthropology, Univ. of South Carolina, Columbia.

Herold, Elaine

1980   *Historical and Archeological Survey of Willtown Bluff Plantation, Charlestown County, South Carolina.* The Charleston Museum, Charleston.

Hodder, Ian, and Charles Orton

1976   *Spatial Analysis in Archaeology.* Cambridge Univ. Press, Cambridge.

Jackson, Susan H., and Lesley M. Drucker

1985   *An Archaeological Inventory Survey of Development Parcels in Four State Parks of the Richard B. Russell Multiple Resource Area, Abbeville and Anderson Counties, South Carolina.* Resource Studies Series 79. Carolina Archaeological Services, Columbia.

Joseph, J. W.

1987   Highway 17 Revisited: The Archaeology of Task Labor. *South Carolina Antiquities* 19(1–2):29–34.

1989   Pattern and Process in the Plantation Archaeology of the Lowcountry of Georgia and South Carolina. *Historical Archaeology* 23(1):55–68.

1991   White Columns and Black Hands: Class and Classification in the Plantation Ideology of the Georgia and South Carolina Lowcountry. Paper presented at the symposium entitled Plantation Archeology of the Virginia and Maryland Tidewater Region and the Lowcountry of Georgia and South Carolina: A Synthesis and Comparison. 1991 Annual Meeting of The Society for Historical Archeology, Richmond, Virginia.

Joseph, J. W., and George F. Tyson Jr.

1989   *A Phase I Cultural Resources Survey of the Virgin Islands Port Authority Property, Estate Negro Bay, St. Croix, U.S.V.I.* New South Associates Technical Report 5. Submitted to Bioimpact. New South Associates, Stone Mountain, Georgia.

Joseph, J. W., and Mary Beth Reed

1991   *An Inventory of Archeological Resources and Recommended Preservation and Research Plan, McLeod Plantation, James Island, South Carolina.* New South Associates Technical Report 59. Submitted to Jaeger/Pyburn. New South Associates, Stone Mountain, Georgia.

Joseph, J. W., Mary Beth Reed, and Charles E. Cantley

1991   *Agrarian Life, Romantic Death: Archeological and Historical Testing and Data Recovery for the I–85 Northern Alternative, Spartanburg County, South Carolina.* New South Associates Technical Report 39. Submitted to the South Carolina Dept. of Highways and Public Transportation. New South Associates, Stone Mountain, Georgia.

Joyce, Jane Sally

1981   *A Settlement Pattern Study of the War Eagle Creek Region, Madison County, Arkansas, During the Pioneer Period.* Master's thesis, Dept. of Anthropology, Univ. of Arkansas, Fayetteville.

Lees, William B.

1980   *Limerick, Old and in the Way: Archaeological Investigations at the Limerick Plantation, Berkeley County, South Carolina.* Anthropological Studies 5. South Carolina Institute of Archaeology and Anthropology, Columbia.

Lewis, Kenneth E.

1976   *Camden: A Frontier Town in 18th Century South Carolina.* Anthropological Studies 2, South Carolina Institute of Archaeology and Anthropology, Columbia.

1985b   Plantation Layout and Function in the South Carolina Lowcountry. In *The Archaeology of Slavery and Plantation Life,* edited by Theresa A. Singleton, pp. 35–65. Academic Press, Orlando.

Lewis, Kenneth E., and Donald L. Hardesty

1979   *Middleton Place: Initial Archaeological Investigations at an Ashley River Rice Plantation.* Research Manuscript Series 148. South Carolina Institute of Archeology and Anthropology, Columbia.

Lewis, Kenneth E., and Helen W. Haskell

1980   *Hampton II: Further Archeological Investigations at a Santee River Rice Plantation.* Research Manuscript Series 161. South Carolina Institute of Archeology and Anthropology, Columbia.

Lewis, Lynne

1978   *Drayton Hall: Preliminary Archaeological Investigation at a Lowcountry Plantation.* The Univ. Press of Virginia, Charlottesville.

1985   The Planter Class: The Archaeological Record at Drayton Hall. In *The Archaeology of Slavery and*

Plantation Life, edited by Theresa A. Singleton, pp. 121–40. Academic Press, Orlando.

Michie, James L.
1990   *Richmond Hill Plantation 1810–1868: The Discovery of Antebellum Life on a Waccamaw Rice Plantation.* The Reprint Company, South Carolina.

Oakes, James
1982   *The Ruling Race: A History of American Slaveholders.* Alfred A. Knopf, New York.

Orser, Charles E., Jr., Annette M. Nekola, and James L. Roark
1982   *Exploring the Rustic Life: Multidisciplinary Research at Millwood Plantation, a Large Piedmont Plantation in Abbeville County, South Carolina, and Elbert County, Georgia.* Russell Papers. Submitted to the National Park Service. Mid-American Research Center, Loyola Univ. of Chicago.

Orser, Charles E., Jr.
1986   The Archaeological Recognition of the Squad System in Postbellum Cotton Plantations. *Southeastern Archaeology* 5(1):11–20.
1988   *The Material Basis of the Postbellum Tenant Plantation, Historical Archaeology in the South Carolina Piedmont.* Univ. of Georgia Press, Athens.

Orser, Charles E., Jr., and Annette M. Nekola
1985   Plantation Settlement from Slavery to Tenancy: An Example from a Piedmont Plantation in South Carolina. In *The Archaeology of Slavery and Plantation Life,* edited by Theresa A. Singleton, pp. 67–94. Academic Press, Orlando.

Orser, Charles E., Jr., and Claudia C. Holland
1984   Let Us Praise Famous Men, Accurately: Toward a More Complete Understanding of Postbellum Southern Agricultural Practices. *Southeastern Archaeology* 3:111–20.

Prunty, Merle, Jr.
1955   The Renaissance of the Southern Plantation. *Geographical Review* 45:459–91.

Resnick, Benjamin
1984   *The Archaeology, Architecture, and History of the Williams Place: A Scotch Irish Farmstead in the South Carolina Piedmont.* Conference on Historic Sites Series, vol. 3, edited by Stanley South. South Carolina Institute of Archaeology and Anthropology, Columbia.

Scurry, James D.
1982   Archeological Investigations at Redcliffe Plantation, Aiken, South Carolina. *Notebook* 14(3–4):1–27.

Scurry, James D., J. Walter Joseph, and Fritz Hamer
1980   *Initial Archeological Investigation at Silver Bluff Plantation, Aiken County, South Carolina.* South Carolina Institute of Archeology and Anthropology Research Manuscript Series 168. Columbia.

Shlomowitz, Ralph
1979   The Origins of Southern Sharecropping. *Agricultural History* 53:557–75.
1982   The Squad System on Postbellum Cotton Plantations. In *Toward a New South? Studies in Post–Civil War Southern Communities,* edited by Orville Vernon Burton and Robert C. McMath Jr., pp. 265–80. Greenwood Press, Westport, Connecticut.

Smith, Henry A. M.
1988   *The Historical Writings of Henry A. M. Smith.* 3 Vols. The Reprint Company, Spartanburg, South Carolina.

Smith, Marvin T. (compiler)
1986   *Archaeological Testing of Sixteen Sites on the Fort Howard Tract, Effingham County, Georgia.* Garrow and Associates, Atlanta.

South, Stanley
1971   *Archeology at the Charles Towne Site (38CH1) on Albemarle Point in South Carolina.* 2 vols. Research Manuscript Series 10. South Carolina Institute of Archeology and Anthropology, Columbia.

South, Stanley, and Michael Hartley
1980   *Deep Water and High Ground: Seventeenth Century Low Country Settlement.* South Carolina Institute of Archaeology and Anthropology Research Manuscript Series 166, Columbia.

Stine, Linda France
1989a   *Raised Up in Hard Times: Factors Affecting Material Culture on Upland Piedmont Farmsteads Circa 1900–1940.* Ph.D. diss., Dept. of Anthropology, Univ. of North Carolina, Univ. Microfilms, Ann Arbor.
1992a   *Revealing Historic Landscapes in Charleston County: Archaeological Inventory, Contexts, and Management.* Submitted to the Charleston County Planning Dept. South Carolina Institute of Archaeology and Anthropology.

Trimble, Stanley W.

1974   *Man-Induced Soil Erosion of the Southern Piedmont, 1700–1970.* Soil Conservation Society of America, Ankeny, Iowa.

Trinkley, Michael

1983b   "Let Us Now Praise Famous Men"—If Only We Can Find Them. *Southeastern Archaeology* 2:30–36.

Trinkley, Michael (editor)

1990a   *The Second Phase of Archaeological Survey on Spring Island, Beaufort County, South Carolina: Investigations of Prehistoric and Historic Settlement Patterns on an Isolated Sea Island.* Chicora Foundation, Columbia.

1990b   *Archaeological Excavations at 38BU96, A Portion of Cotton Hope Plantation, Hilton Head Island, Beaufort County, South Carolina.* Chicora Foundation Research Series 21. Chicora Foundation, Columbia.

Trinkley, Michael, Natalie Adams, and Debi Hacker

1992   *Plantation Life in the Piedmont: A Preliminary Examination of Rosemont Plantation, Laurens County, South Carolina.* Chicora Foundation Research Series 29. Chicora Foundation, Columbia.

Trinkley, Michael, and Olga M. Caballero

1983a   *Additional Archaeological, Historical, and Architectural Historical Evaluation of 38Hr127 and 38Hr131, Horry County, South Carolina.* South Carolina Dept. of Highways and Public Transportation, Columbia.

Vlach, John M.

1975   Sources of the Shotgun House: African and Caribbean Antecedents to Afro-American Architecture. Ph.D. diss., Dept. of Folklore, Indiana Univ., Bloomington.

1978   *The Afro-American Tradition in the Decorative Arts.* Cleveland Art Museum, Cleveland, Ohio.

Wayne, Lucy B., and Martin F. Dickinson

1990   *Four Men's Ramble: Archaeology in the Wando Neck, Charleston County, South Carolina.* Submitted to Dunes West Development Corporation by SouthArc, Gainesville, Florida.

Wheaton, Thomas R., Jr.

1989   *Drayton Hall: Archeological Testing of the Orangerie.* Report submitted to the National Trust for Historic Preservation. New South Associates Technical Report 11. Stone Mountain, Georgia.

Wheaton, Thomas, R., Jr., Amy Friedlander, and Patrick H. Garrow

1983   *Yaughan and Curriboo Plantations: Studies in Afro-American Archaeology.* Soil Systems, Marietta, Georgia.

Wheaton, Thomas R., Jr., and Patrick H. Garrow

1985   Acculturation and the Archaeological Record in the Carolina Lowcountry. In *The Archaeology of Slavery and Plantation Life,* edited by Theresa A. Singleton, pp. 239–59. Academic Press, Orlando.

Williams, G. Ishmael, John S. Cable, and Mary Beth Reed.

1992   *An Archeological Survey of 2,195 Acres in the Cainhoy Area, Wambaw and Witherbee Districts, Francis Marion National Forest. Francis Marion National Forest Indefinite Services Survey Report 1.* New South Associates Technical Report 66. Submitted to the U.S. Dept. of Agriculture, Forest Service. New South Associates, Stone Mountain, Georgia.

Wood, Peter H.

1974   *Black Majority: Negroes in Colonial South Carolina from 1670 through the Stono Rebellion.* W. W. Norton and Company, New York.

Worthy, Linda (editor)

1983   *"All That Remains": Traditional Architecture and Historic Engineering Structures of the Richard B. Russell Multiple Resource Area, Georgia and South Carolina.* Russell Papers. Interagency Archeological Services Division, National Park Service, Atlanta.

Zierden, Martha A., and Jeanne A. Calhoun

1983   *An Archaeological Assessment of the Greenfield Borrow Pit, Georgetown County, South Carolina.* Charleston Museum Contributions 4. Charleston.

Zierden, Martha A., Lesley M. Drucker, and Jeanne Calhoun

1986   *Home Upriver: Rural Life on Daniel's Island, Berkeley County, South Carolina.* Submitted to the South Carolina Dept. of Highways and Public Transportation. A Joint Venture of Carolina Archaeological Services/The Charleston Museum, Columbia and Charleston.

7. "Good Wharves and Other Conveniences": An Archaeological Study of Riverine Adaptation in the South Carolina Lowcountry

David Beard

In this chapter I develop a typology for river landings and their associated structures, based on such variables as age, function, construction materials and techniques, artifact assemblages, and associated vessel remains. This synthesis, it is hoped, will augment the scope of research designs for investigating South Carolina's lowcountry plantations and other waterfront historical sites by adding a long overlooked, but significant, cultural resource to those studies.

Historical Overview

Since prehistoric times, the rivers, creeks, and embayments in South Carolina's lowcountry have served as major arteries for transporting people, supplies, and produce, as well as a means of defense. With the founding of Charles Towne in 1670, the English settlers were confronted with this special environment and began to adapt to it. The settlement was originally located on Albemarle Point, which was "defended by the main [Ashley] river with a brooke on the one side and inaccessible Marsh on the other [which] all at high tides is ever overflown: joyning to the mainland in a small neck not exceeding fiftie yards."[1]

By 1680 Charles Towne had relocated from Albemarle Point to Oyster Point (present-day Charleston). It was noted that the location was "so convenient for the public Commerce that it rather seems to be the design of some skillful artist than the accidental position of nature."[2] Small farmsteads had begun to spread out from the main settlement and a network of streams facilitated not only this expansion, but also trade with local Native American groups.[3] The Cooper River, for example, was navigable for 20 miles above Charleston by large ships and as much as 40 miles for smaller vessels.[4]

Indigo, naval stores, and deer skins procured from the Indians were the first export products exploited by English settlers.[5] Between the years of 1699 and 1715, over 53,000 deer skins a year were being traded and by 1750 accounted for 16 percent of the colony's exports.[6] These products had to be transported by water to Charleston where they could be loaded onto large ocean-going vessels for shipment to England and to English colonies in the Caribbean.

Rice and cotton were introduced to the lowcountry in the late seventeenth century and were to become the primary agricultural products of the region. Rice, however, was to become the crop of choice for most lowcountry planters. For example, between 1725 and 1731 exports tripled and continued to grow despite a slight decline during the 1740s caused by the effects of the War of Austrian Succession.[7] By the early nineteenth century, rice had superseded all other crops as the area's primary agricultural export.[8] Large-scale rice cultivation required a substantial maritime support network. More than ever, the lowcountry's rivers and creeks became the main avenues for transporting this crop to market.

Vessels of all descriptions, from dugout canoes to large sailing ships, plied this network of streams carrying goods. Every plantation bordering navigable water had one or more landings at which to load and unload cargoes. The few existing roads often had to cross numerous streams. Where bridges could not be built, or were not practical because of vessel traffic, ferries were used to transport people, livestock, and commercial goods.

This intensive maritime activity has left a substantial archaeological legacy. Shipwrecks, landing remains, and large concentrations of lost and discarded artifacts are scattered along the bottoms of South Carolina's rivers.

Landings Research

Recent work along South Carolina's rivers and creeks has focused on an important but neglected aspect of the state's maritime heritage: landing sites with their associated causeways and wharf/dock structures (e.g., fig. 7.1). For years these sites have been popular with sport divers searching for collectables under South Carolina's Sport Diver Archaeology Management Program. The artifacts collected at these sites have attracted much attention, but very little has been paid to the structures themselves or the archaeological potential of the surrounding waterways.

Between 1990 and 1992 the author, while employed by the Underwater Archaeology Division of the South Carolina Institute of Archaeology and Anthropology (SCIAA), undertook several research projects, seeking conclusions about the function of individual landing sites based on age, construction materials and techniques, artifact assemblages, and associated vessel remains.

One of the most frustrating problems with this research is the paucity of previous studies on this topic. It was not until 1994 that William Barr of

FIG. 7.1. 1840 Plat of the White House plantation, illustrating typical waterfront archaeological features.

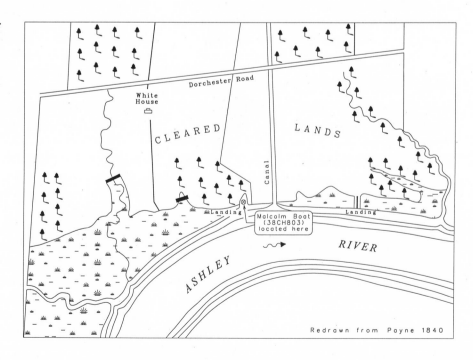

White House

Dorchester Road

CLEARED   LANDS

Canal

Landing   Landing

Malcolm Boat
(38CH803)
located here

ASHLEY   RIVER

Redrawn from Payne 1840

SCIAA investigated the northwest landing at Strawberry Ferry in any great detail.[9] While there are a number of other reports available about individual landing structures—mostly concerning large wharves in the northeastern and mid-Atlantic states—these are generally descriptive and make no effort toward any sort of synthesis.[10]

There has, however, been some good research concerning how landings and other waterfront constructs fit into the prevailing cultural scene.[11] James Errante, in particular, has made a significant contribution to these studies with the coining of the term "waterscapes" to describe 1) areas where human activities interface with riverine environments and 2) the physical alteration of that environment to meet certain needs.[12] These references and other general social histories provide information concerning detailed cultural contexts surrounding plantation waterscapes.

However, the landing sites themselves, i.e., the physical manifestations of these waterfront activities, have been virtually ignored. The present research is designed to address that problem. Initially it will be oriented toward description and development of a typology for these sites. By establishing a firm empirical foundation, archaeologists can pave the way for more diverse theoretical approaches which can be developed and tested.

Proposed Typology

To date, this author has conducted field investigations at several causeway and landing sites which represent different primary functions. Each of these exhibits distinct differences in associated structures. As yet, no systematic recovery of artifacts from these sites has been conducted, nor have the structures themselves been fully documented. Hundreds of other landing sites have been located through plat research and aerial photograph and terrain analysis, but have not been investigated in the field.

Based upon field observations, some general site characteristics have been formulated to develop a basic causeway and landing typology. These are general purpose plantation landings, special

purpose plantation landings, ferry landings, and shipyard landings. There are undoubtedly other classes of landings, but these have not been documented to date and will therefore not be discussed here. The archaeological features associated with these landings may include wharves, piers, filled cribbing, and causeways with fixed pierheads.

In order to subdivide these sites within the temporal ranges during which they may have been constructed and used, the author is currently using three very broad categories: colonial (ca. 1660–1780), antebellum (ca. 1780–1865), and postbellum (ca. 1865–1900). The physical characteristics of these sites may also fit into a number of broad categories. While incomplete, the following indicates the type of archaeological features which have been recorded so far, as well as certain variations within those types.

Under construction techniques I have divided the primary features into two groups: 1) wharves and piers and 2) causeways. Wharves and piers can consist of piling and cross-timber construction or log cribbing. These two construction methods can then be divided into categories of rough-hewn timbers or finished timbers. Causeways can consist of packed fill, packed fill around puncheons, or filled cribbing. The fill material may then consist of soil, brick, stone, shell, derelict vessels, and mixed fill.

Associated artifacts have been divided into function-specific and general categories. Function-specific artifacts are those items, such as shipwright tools, which are associated with the primary function of a particular landing site. Artifacts in the general category might consist of liquor bottles, smoking pipes, ceramics, and other domestic artifacts commonly found on most sites of the same period.

Construction Techniques and Site Function

As has been already mentioned, most previous studies have focused on wharves built in larger urban areas and intended for general commercial activities. While these studies can be useful for examining wharf remains located along Charleston's waterfront, for the most part they have very little in common with smaller riverine landings. There are, however, some similarities in construction tech-. niques used at large urban wharves and their smaller country cousins. In her studies on colonial wharf construction in New England, Andrea J. Heintzelman states that "[w]harf design and composition was related to the socio-economic conditions of the individual wharf owner and of the community; . . . availability of raw materials; and the environment at the time the wharf was built."[13] This view is supported by investigations of South Carolina landing structures.[14]

Probably the most common construction method for wharves and other landing structures was the filled log crib. These cribs can be of single or multipen construction, and may have been built in situ or at another location and sunk at the site. Both of these methods were used frequently in South Carolina, with variations dependent upon site function and environment.

Currently, there is some good functional evidence based upon certain physical characteristics which can be used to infer the function of particular causeways and landing structures. The Cedar Grove Plantation causeway/landing on the Ashley River (38DR155) appears to have been used for general plantation purposes. The causeway fill is packed and consists mostly of soil, but includes some shell, gravel, and a small amount of brick rubble. The pier/wharf structure at the causeway terminus seems to have been relatively lightly built, consisting of a series of small pilings and finished timbers, probably representing a fixed pierhead. A possible canal running along the upstream side of the causeway may have been used as a staging area for loaded or empty barges or other vessels.[15] In a contemporary account, the site was described as "a cause way, leading to a boat and wood landing in front of the house [which] connects the main-land" to the river.[16] This suggests that the plantation was also involved in timber production.

The Lexington Kiln Site causeways on Wagner Creek (38CH1086), a tributary of the Wando River,

had a specific purpose: a landing for loading bricks from nearby kilns.[17] The causeways' fill consists almost exclusively of brick rubble, possibly indicating that as brick production increased, the causeways were enlarged and strengthened by adding wasters from the kilns. Both causeways, as well as the surrounding area, are covered with brick rubble. The terminus of one causeway consists of rough log cribbing filled with brick rubble. Heavier finished timbers were apparently used as foundations for this cribbing. Between the two causeways is a canal which, like the one at Cedar Grove Plantation, may have been used to moor brick barges which were already filled or waiting to be filled.[18] It is also possible that within these canals exist undiscovered structures upon which barges could rest during low tides, making loading and unloading less dependent upon the tide. Similar structures have been documented in a tributary of the Delaware River near Philadelphia, Pennsylvania.[19]

At the Strawberry Ferry Southeast Landing site a very practical approach was taken to deal with fluctuating tides. A brick filled multipen cribbing structure was built on approximately a 20 degree slope, which allowed the ferry boats and other vessels to pull up and drop their ramps to unload passengers and cargo, no matter what the tide level. This structure extends into the river 20–30 feet below the low tide line. The northwest landing at Strawberry Ferry is slightly more substantial, incorporating a combination of log cribbing and puncheon and plank construction. This construct was filled with rubble and a patterned brick floor finished off its surface.[20]

The Lind's (Linn's, Lynn's) Shipyard Site causeway (38CH444) on Hobcaw Creek, another tributary of the Wando River, may have served a variety of purposes, but its method of construction reflects a considerable amount of ship-related activity . The causeway itself consists of very heavily built, finished timber cribbing filled almost entirely with ballast stone. This heavy construction may be the result of using available materials, such as heavy ship timbers and ballast stone from vessels under repair. It may have been a conscious effort to make a causeway strong enough to withstand the stress of supporting the mechanisms used to careen vessels and perform other heavy lifting operations.

The Paul Pritchard Shipyard Site (38CH1049), also on Hobcaw Creek, is somewhat different. A 1786 plat of the site drawn by Peter Boling indicates that it is located on a very well drained piece of high ground which comes right down to the water's edge. There is no marsh fronting the site, nor any indication that there ever was. In this case no causeway or filling of any kind was required. The remains of several wharf structures and a slipway for launching vessels are clearly visible abutting the shoreline at low tide.[21] These features are undoubtedly the remains of a substantial shipyard described as having "good Wharves and Other Conveniences Sufficient to Heave down Three Vessels at the same time."[22]

As has already been mentioned, some of the causeways and landings may have evolved as function and/or capacity needs changed. It may be possible, through archaeology, to trace the evolution of a causeway or landing from small-scale colonial plantation use, through massive antebellum rice or cotton agriculture, to postbellum phosphate mining. Research at Archdale Plantation (38DR153) may indicate a landing which went through such an evolution.[23]

Associated Artifacts as Indicators of Site Activities

Although construction techniques used on landing associated structures may offer some insight into the primary function of a particular landing site, it is the type and quantity of artifacts present on the site which will shed light on the types of other activities taking place.[24] For example, the main landing for a large plantation was the focal point of much socialization. Cargoes and passengers were loaded and unloaded, news from Charleston and surrounding plantations was exchanged, food and alcohol were consumed, and all manner of refuse was discarded. All of these things created an envi-

ronment conducive to the deposition of a wide variety of artifacts.

One of the problems inherent in assessing artifact assemblages from riverine sites is buoyancy. The artifact classes remaining on such sites tend to be heavy and are not susceptible to movement by the current. These prevailing natural forces therefore select the nature and location of artifact deposition.

Another problem is potential site contamination by materials washed in from other areas. Depending on the velocity of a particular stream, certain materials can be carried a considerable distance from their point of initial deposition. This situation has been reported by numerous divers, who have located large deposits of artifacts in natural catchment areas of certain rivers. These sites exhibit no physical evidence indicating that they were any sort of activity areas.

While it has been argued that the absence of artifacts in the water at certain landing sites is the result of prior collection by divers,[25] Lucy Wayne has suggested that the dearth of artifacts in Wagner Creek near the Lexington Kiln Site landing may be due to the fact that the major focus of social activities was located at the slave settlement south of the kilns. A multiroom habitation at the kiln site yielded very few artifacts, suggesting that slaves involved in the manufacture of bricks may have occasionally slept in these quarters, but socialized at the main slave complex.[26] Therefore, it is likely that at highly specialized sites, such as a brickyard landing, relatively few domestic artifacts were discarded.

At sites like the David Lind or Paul Pritchard shipyards, there is a high probability of encountering artifacts exclusively associated with the shipwright's trade. Artifacts that might be recovered from these sites are expected to include a variety of tools, metal fasteners, rigging elements, and other materials used in the building and repair of ships. Artifacts on such sites tend to be function specific, reflecting few general domestic categories.

A good example of artifacts located at a landing site attesting to the activities taking place at that location has come to light from research conducted along the Laurel Hill plantation waterfront on the Waccamaw River.[27] During underwater archaeological investigations of the site amid 1991 a number of iron rice hooks were recovered. It is interesting to speculate as to the reasons why these tools would be deposited in such profusion at this location. Were they lost as a result of accidents or possibly purposely discarded by the users as a means of getting out of an unpleasant task (rice harvesting) at a particular time?

The Ashley River at Archdale Plantation's landing holds an interesting clue to activities at this site. An underwater reconnaissance at the site located what appear to be the remains of a log raft. The presence of a wrought-iron "log dog" or "ring dog" amid this jumble of sawn hardwood logs adds some credibility to this assessment.[28] A 1791 plat of Archdale Plantation shows "Sawpit Creek," possibly indicating that log rafts may have been floated up the creek for processing into lumber at a plantation mill.

One important consideration when studying a collection of artifacts from a landing site, particularly a general purpose landing, is the potential for encountering items from cargoes lost during transfer to and from shore. A large collection of similar or identical ceramic vessels or other artifact types at a site is as likely to be the result of a mishap as of intentional disposal. Barring the presence of obvious packing containers or material, or finding nested or stacked artifacts, this will remain a problem in the analysis of artifact collections from landing sites.

Over the years, divers collecting artifacts from South Carolina rivers have reported such finds. In the Waccamaw River at Wachesaw Landing, for example, a diver recovered the remains of a straw-padded crate filled with a complete set of flow blue pearlware. More recently a diver reported recovering a collection of identical delftware bowls from the Ashepoo River, which included six bases, one nearly complete vessel, and one intact bowl, all from the same area. Some fairly bizarre items have been lost at these landings as well. A tombstone, complete with inscription, was found in the remains of its

wooden crate off the old wharf at Conway in the Waccamaw River.[29]

Landings and Derelict Vessel Abandonment

Since landings were high-traffic areas, it is reasonable to assume that at least a few old, worn-out vessels were abandoned in their vicinity. An interesting pattern has already emerged from research at ferry landings in other Atlantic Coast states.[30] Apparently, as ferry boats became worn out they were often scrapped very close to the landings. Two abandoned ferry boats were recorded in association with each of the above cited sites. In South Carolina this same pattern and quantity of abandoned ferry boats has been observed at the Browns Ferry Site (38GE57).

An even more dramatic example of this pattern is evident at the Laurel Hill Plantation landing (38GE251) on the Waccamaw River. At this site, no fewer than five wooden plantation barges, one possibly a large ferry boat, have been recorded in the river off the landing.[31] This particular method of vessel disposal is dependent upon deep water which takes the wrecks out of the way of other vessel traffic. While some of the vessels at Laurel Hill were probably abandoned during the heyday of the plantation period, others were likely abandoned during the Civil War with the collapse of the slave-based plantation economy.

The areas in the vicinity of plantation landings are proving to have a very high probability for derelict vessel abandonment. For example, just a few meters upstream from the landing at Boone Hall Plantation on Boone Hall Creek lie the remains of what appears to be a small keeled barge (38CH1209). Still in use today, this site was historically the principal landing for the plantation. The presence of the vessel remains in the vicinity of this landing gives rise to the likelihood that it was utilized by the plantation and then abandoned, for whatever reasons, close by.

More recently it has been discovered that the

site of the Malcolm Boat (38CH803) on the Ashley River was a landing associated with the White House Plantation (fig. 7.1). In this case the badly worm-eaten vessel had been abandoned in a small slough or creek located between the landing and the mouth of a canal running into the river.[32] There is, therefore, a high probability that these same patterns of derelict vessel abandonment may be repeated at other plantation landing sites.

Another, less well-defined pattern of vessel disposal may be coming to light in South Carolina. Farther up Hobcaw Creek from the Paul Pritchard and David Lind shipyard sites, the wreck of a sailing vessel approximately 12 meters long was discovered in 1991 by a crew building a private dock. Artifacts associated with this vessel, known as the Hobcaw Creek Plantation Vessel (38CH1289), date its use to the first quarter of the nineteenth century.[33] Interestingly enough, the Paul Pritchard shipyard ceased to operate in the early 1830s. Perhaps this vessel was at that yard for major repairs and was merely towed out of the way and abandoned when the shipyard shut down. This particular pattern of derelict vessel abandonment has been noted near small twentieth-century shipyards and waterman communities around Chesapeake Bay.[34] Further investigations of the Hobcaw Creek Plantation Vessel may shed light upon the reasons for its abandonment in the shallows of upper Hobcaw Creek.

Another pattern of derelict vessel deposition may also prove to be very common in South Carolina: shipwrecks as fill material. Large urban ports have yielded good evidence of the practice of filling in waterfront areas in order to expand usable land.[35] It is quite probable that this same method was used in waterfront development of peninsular Charleston. While current research focuses on landing sites in more rural agricultural areas, the development of port facilities in Charleston during the eighteenth and nineteenth centuries is inextricably tied to the plantation economy, and is therefore a corollary avenue of inquiry.[36]

In South Carolina's rural riverine systems, derelict vessels also appear to have been used as fill for land extensions. Along the South Carolina side of Back River near Savannah, Georgia, two interesting sites have recently been discovered. The first is a large rice barge which was filled with bricks and apparently used as a plantation landing. The second site, known as the Clydesdale Boat after the hunting club bordering the site, may be the wreck of a mid-eighteenth-century sailing vessel which was filled with soil and used to plug a hole in a rice levee.[37] As more research is done in South Carolina waterways, more examples of these types of vessel disposal will no doubt come to light.

The profusion of landing sites in South Carolina's rivers and creeks offers a rare opportunity to document variations of a site type in some detail with minimal expenditure of time, manpower, and site disturbance. Since many of the landing structures and shipwrecks are exposed at low tide, diving is not required for the majority of this work. The locations of many of these causeways and landings are well documented on archival maps. Some show up as distinct features on modern topographic maps and aerial photographs.

Future research plans include the continued survey of archival map collections to locate causeway and landing sites. These will be compared with modern topographic maps and aerial photographs. Any remaining structures at the sites will be physically inspected and documented. A pattern of easily identifiable attributes is expected from this research, so that when previously undocumented examples are encountered in the field a more accurate assessment of site age and function may be possible.

Hopefully, additional sites will be located to confirm the theorized pattern of derelict vessel abandonment. Archival research has pinpointed possible sites which have yet to be verified on the ground or beneath the waters.

It is also hoped that this research will encourage other related studies. It has been suggested that a study of Charleston's wharves, both physically and archivally, would be a good place to start. The two studies could then be tied together with a detailed examination of river traffic between the city and outlying plantations.[38]

Adaptation to South Carolina's riverine environment is once again on the rise. Residential development of tracts of land formerly occupied by plantations has spurred the construction of thousands of recreational piers and docks of all sizes, as well as the physical alteration of shorelines through filling and bulkheading. These modern developments pose a threat to the archaeological record left by the former inhabitants. While a great deal of attention has been given to the terrestrial components of these sites, most research has ended at the water's edge.[39] As pressure increases on these resources, archaeologists must consider all possible types of archaeological resources when they develop research designs for data recovery at planned developments.

NOTES

1. Cheeves 1897:196–97.
2. Mathews 1954:153.
3. Lewis 1984; Linda F. Stine 1992a.
4. Sellers 1970:5.
5. Orvin 1973:48–64.
6. Weir 1983:143.
7. Waterhouse 1973:123–25.
8. Orvin 1973:48–64.
9. Barr 1995:88–93.
10. Heintzelman 1986.
11. Ferguson and Babson 1986.
12. Errante, this volume. See also Errante 1989.
13. Heintzelman 1986.
14. Beard 1989; Beard 1990a; Beard 1990b; Beard 1991a; Beard 1991b.
15. Beard 1990b:7–9.
16. *Charleston Daily Courier*, Aug. 21, 1857.
17. Wayne and Dickinson 1989:Fig. 8–5.
18. Beard 1990a.
19. Cox 1985.
20. Barr 1995:90–91.
21. Beard 1989.
22. Salley 1912:177.
23. Zierden, Calhoun, and Hacker Norton 1985:42; Poplin and Beard 1991:28.
24. Beard 1991a:73.
25. Beard 1990a:8.
26. Wayne, personal communication 1991.
27. Harris 1992:47.
28. Poplin and Beard 1991:30.
29. Hampton Shuping, personal communication 1991.
30. Beard 1988; Watts and Hall 1989.
31. Harris 1992.
32. Amer et al. 1993:56–57.
33. Beard 1991b:1.
34. Donald Shomette, personal communication 1991.
35. Arnold 1990:108; Delgado 1986:106; Smith 1986:137.
36. Zierden 1986:33–40.
37. Watts 1995:119–27, 133–35; Leech and Wood 1994:188–96, 228.
38. Martha Zierden, personal communication 1992.
39. Errante, this volume.

WORKS CITED

Amer, Christopher, William Barr, David Beard, Elizabeth Collins, Lynn Harris, William Judd, Carl Naylor, and Mark Newell
1993   *The Malcolm Boat (38CH803): Discovery, Stabilization, Excavation, and Preservation of an Historic Sea Going Small Craft in the Ashley River, Charleston County, South Carolina.* Research Manuscript Series No. 217, South Carolina Institute of Archaeology and Anthropology.
Arnold, J. Barto, III
1990   The Survey for the *Zavala*, a Steam Warship of the Republic of Texas. In *Underwater Archaeology Proceedings from the Society for Historical Archaeology Conference,* edited by J. Broadwater, pp. 105–9. Tucson.
Barr, William B.
1995   Childsbury and Ashley Ferry Town: Elements of Control in the Economic Landscape of Colonial South Carolina. In *Underwater Archaeology Proceedings from the Society for Historical Archaeology Conference,* edited by Paul Forsythe Johnston, pp. 88–93. Tucson.

Beard, David V.

1988   *An Archaeological Survey of Selected Submerged Cultural Resources in Maryland.* Division of Archaeology, Maryland Geological Survey. Submitted to the Maryland Historical Trust, Baltimore.

1989   A Preliminary Reconnaissance of the Paul Pritchard Shipyard Site, Hobcaw Creek, Charleston County, S.C. Ms. on file, South Carolina Institute of Archaeology and Anthropology, Columbia.

1990a   Reconnaissance Survey Report: Underwater Archaeological Investigations of the Lexington Plantation Kiln Site Causeway in Wagner Creek, Charleston County, South Carolina. Ms. on file, South Carolina Coastal Council, Charleston.

1990b   *Underwater Archaeological Investigations of the Cedar Grove Plantation Causeway in the Ashley River, Dorchester County South Carolina.* Submitted to the South Carolina Coastal Council. South Carolina Institute of Archaeology and Anthropology, Columbia.

1991a   Causeways and Cribbing: Now You *Can* Get There from Here. In *Underwater Archaeology Proceedings from the Society for Historical Archaeology Conference,* edited by John Broadwater, pp. 73–77. Tucson.

1991b   *Preliminary Archaeological Investigations of the Hobcaw Creek Plantation Vessel Located in Hobcaw Creek, Charleston County South Carolina.* Submitted to the South Carolina Coastal Council. South Carolina Institute of Archaeology and Anthropology, Columbia.

Cheeves, Langdon, (editor)

1897   *Collections of the South Carolina Historical Society,* vol. 5. Jones, Book and Printer, Richmond.

Cox, Lee

1985   *Preliminary Survey to Analyze the Potential Presence of Submerged Cultural Resources in the Delaware and Susquehanna Rivers.* Master's thesis, Dept. of History, East Carolina Univ., Greenville, North Carolina.

Delgado, James P.

1986   Tasting Champagne. In *Archaeology in Solution, Proceedings of the Seventeenth Annual Conference on Underwater Archaeology,* edited by John W. Foster and Sheli O. Smith, pp. 104–7. Tucson.

Errante, James R.

1989   The Significance of Waterscapes in the Context of South Carolina's Tidal Rice Growing Plantations. In *Critical Approaches to Archaeology and Anthropology, Annual Papers of the University of South Carolina Anthropology Students Association,* vol. 4, edited by Kathleen Bolen, Kathy Forbes, and Ruth Trocolli, pp. 74–78. Univ. of South Carolina, Columbia.

Ferguson, Leland, and David Babson

1986   *Survey of Plantation Sites along the East Branch of Cooper River: A Model for Predicting Archaeological Site Location.* Ms. on file, Dept. of Anthropology, Univ. of South Carolina, Columbia.

Harris, Lynn

1992   *The Waccamaw–Richmond Hill Waterfront Project 1991.* South Carolina Institute of Archaeology and Anthropology, Univ. of South Carolina, Columbia.

Heintzelman, Andrea J.

1986   Colonial Wharf Construction: Uncovering the Untold Past. *The Log of Mystic Seaport.* Winter issue.

Leech, Richard W., Jr., and Judy L. Wood

1994   Archival Research, Archaeological Survey, and Site Monitoring Backriver Chatham County, Georgia, and Jasper County, South Carolina. U.S. Army Corps of Engineers, Savannah District.

Lewis, Kenneth

1984   *The American Frontier: An Archaeological Study of Settlement Pattern and Process.* Academic Press, New York.

Mathews, Maurice

1954   A Contemporary View of Carolina in 1680. *South Carolina Historical Magazine* 55:153–59.

Orvin, Maxwell Clayton

1973   *Historic Berkeley County, South Carolina, 1671–1900.* Comprint, Charleston.

Poplin, Eric, and David Beard

1991   *Archaeological Survey and Testing in a 23 Acre Tract in the Archdale Subdivision, Dorchester County, South Carolina.* Report on file, Brockington and Associates, Atlanta.

Salley, A. S., Jr.

1912   *Journal of the Commissioners of the Navy of South Carolina: October 9, 1776–March 1, 1779.* Historical Commission of South Carolina, Columbia.

Sellers, Leila

1970   *Charleston Business on the Eve of the American Revolution.* Arno Press, New York.

Smith, Sheli O.
1986   Excavation of the Ronson Ship. In *Archaeology in Solution, Proceedings of the Seventeenth Annual Conference on Underwater Archaeology,* edited by John W. Foster and Sheli O. Smith, pp. 137–38. Society for Underwater Archaeology, Tucson.

Stine, Linda France
1992a   *Revealing Historic Landscapes in Charleston County: Archaeological Inventory, Contexts, and Management.* Submitted to the Charleston County Planning Dept. South Carolina Institute of Archaeology and Anthropology.

Waterhouse, Richard
1973   *South Carolina's Elite: A Study of the Social Structure and Political Culture of a Southern Colony 1670–1760.* Univ. Microfilms, Ann Arbor.

Watts, Gordon P., Jr.
1992   *Remote Sensing and Low Water Survey: Back River and New Cut, Chatham County, Georgia, and Jasper Co., South Carolina.* Draft report submitted to the U.S. Army Corps of Engineers, Savannah District by Tidewater Atlantic Research, Little Washington, North Carolina.

Watts, Gordon P., Jr., and Wesley K. Hall
1989   *An Investigation of Blossums Ferry on the Northeast Cape Fear River.* Research Reports 1. East Carolina Univ., Greenville.

Wayne, Lucy B., and Martin F. Dickinson
1989   *Archaeological Survey, Dunes West Development, Charleston County South Carolina.* Submitted to Dunes West Development, Mount Pleasant, South Carolina by Environmental Services and Permitting, Jacksonville.

Weir, Robert M.
1983   *Colonial South Carolina: A History.* KTO Press, Millwood, New York.

Zierden, Martha
1986   The Rural-Urban Connection in the Lowcountry. *South Carolina Antiquities* 18(1–2):33–40.

Zierden, Martha, Jeanne Calhoun, and Debi Hacker Norton
1985   *Archdale Hall: Investigations of a Lowcountry Plantation.* Archaeological Contributions 10. The Charleston Museum, Charleston.

8. Settlement Patterning on an Agriculturally Marginal Landscape

DAVID COLIN CRASS AND RICHARD D. BROOKS

Settlement patterns are defined as the distribution of archaeological sites across a landscape. Settlement patterning is a response to widely held cultural needs; therefore, it offers a strategic starting point for the functional interpretation of archaeological cultures.[1] The analysis of settlement patterns is useful for several reasons. First, it is practical, since it is less labor-intensive than excavation. Second, it shows the spatial dimension of the human-environment interrelationship. Finally, it yields concrete clues regarding social organization, even if site-specific information pertaining to issues of class, race, gender, and ethnicity is scanty at a survey level of investigation.[2] This landscape study probes historical period settlement patterning on the Savannah River Site (SRS) through time within the framework of environmental history.

The Savannah River Site is situated 40 kilometers (25 miles) downstream of Augusta, Georgia, on the north side of the Savannah River (map 8.1). The study area is particularly well suited to settlement pattern studies because of its large size (approximately 780 square kilometers, or 300 square miles), its topography, which is dominated by the Savannah River proper and portions of five major stream drainages, and the nature of the available data,

which derive almost exclusively from survey-level field investigations. Over 470 square kilometers have been surveyed in the study area by Savannah River Archaeological Research Program (SRARP) personnel. As of 1989 these various surveys have resulted in the discovery of over 360 historic period archaeological sites representing 429 components, which date from the mid-eighteenth through the mid-twentieth centuries.[3] Testing at historic sites has ranged from controlled surface collection to limited shovel tests. In addition, 10 historic sites have received intensive subsurface testing or mitigation. The primary emphasis of the SRARP until 1989 was management of prehistoric archaeological sites; thus, the survey techniques used reflect a bias which may well have essentially dropped specific classes of historic sites out of the sample. Because of these factors, the interpretations contained herein are provisional.

Settlement pattern studies in South Carolina have approached spatial organization at several different scales. Site-specific and community-level settlement patterning have been examined by Trinkley and Lewis.[4] Large-scale or regional-level settlement studies have been relatively rare in South Carolina. The Richard B. Russell Reservoir Project in the upper piedmont of Georgia and South

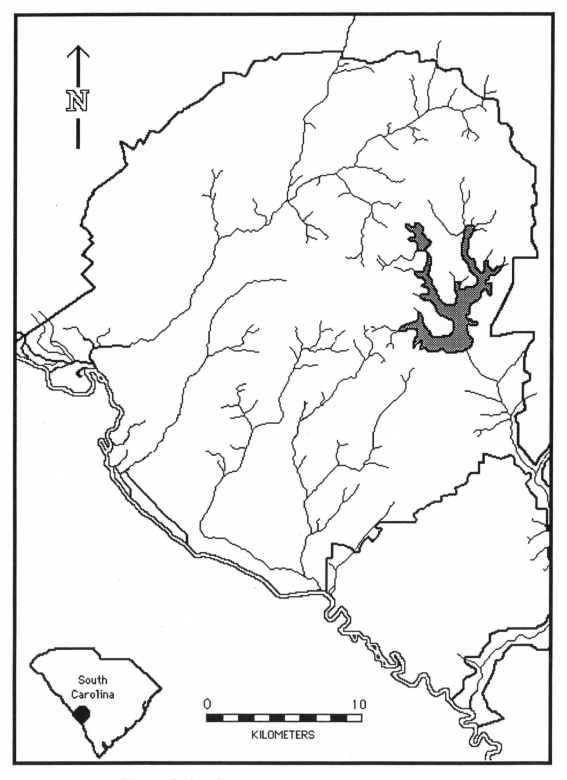

MAP 8.1. Location of Savannah River site.

Carolina yielded prehistoric and historic settlement data; unfortunately, the survey was restricted to pool level, and thus did not cover upland interfluves.[5] Lewis delineated the development of an insular frontier settlement pattern in his excellent *The American Frontier: An Archaeological Study of Settlement Pattern and Process*; however, much of the data were derived from archival sources, not from an archaeological survey.[6] Finally, South and Hartley investigated seventeenth-century settlement patterns on the Lower Coastal Plain.[7] This study represents the first large-scale historical period settlement pattern study based on archaeological data of the upper coastal plain.

Environmental Background

Rainfall in the study area is geographically spotty due to weather system interactions and the orographic effect.[8] Climatic records for the region from approximately 1869 to the present indicate an annual rainfall of about 45 inches, with an average growing season of 246 days. Between 1869 and 1903, yearly rainfall totals fell below 40 inches only once; totals for the other years ranged from 46 to 50 inches. However, the crucial growing-period precipitation is less consistent. For example, according to the Augusta figures, the relatively dry year 1904 had a wetter July and August—crucial for both cotton and corn—than did the relatively wet year 1888.[9] This is important because both cotton and corn require approximately 18 inches of rain during the prime growing season from early June to mid-September. In sum, rainfall is relatively spotty and unpredictable in the study area, both in terms of geographic distribution and amount.

The five drainages in the study area traverse the Aiken Plateau (the local aspect of the sandhills), then flow in a southwesterly direction to the river itself. The interfluves are composed of acidic, well to excessively drained soils. The topography of the study area can best be described as steep and dissected by numerous river, small stream channel, and terrace systems.[10]

The first recorded remarks concerning the soils of the SRS region were made in 1737 by an unnamed English surveyor, who reported that fertile and infertile lands lay next to each other, implying a patchy distribution of agriculturally productive land.[11] Robert Mills's statistical abstract of the state indicated that the soils in Barnwell District were mostly sand with a clay substrate.[12] In the nineteenth century members of the Beech Island Farmers Club lamented the poor quality of the soil, while twentieth-century assessments of the land include such remarks as more sand than loam.[13] A recent soil survey of the SRS has yielded data which support these earlier evaluations, particularly as regards soil fertility (map 8.2).[14]

Prime farmland is defined by the U.S. Department of Agriculture as land that is best suited to food, seed, forage, fiber, and oilseed crops. The soil qualities, growing-season length, and moisture supply are those needed for a well-managed soil to produce a sustained high crop yield using modern equipment on an economical basis.[15] Ten soil map units on the SRS meet these criteria; however, these soils make up just 15 percent (12,261 hectares or 30,275 acres) of the study area and, as noted above, are extremely patchy in distribution.[16] However, even those soils that are considered prime agricultural land today need intensive levels of management and fertilization. Without proper management, erosion control, and fertilization, modern crop yield figures would drop significantly, particularly on the acid, well-drained soils which are characteristic of the upland sandhills. Because of the historically documented lack of such management, as well as the patchy distribution of critical resources (in this case, fertile soil and rainfall), the study area is considered relatively marginal agricultural land.

Locational and Historical Data

A relatively narrow range of functional site types have been identified in the study area, consisting primarily of agricultural and mill sites. For the purposes of this study, archaeological components in the study area were classified by temporal

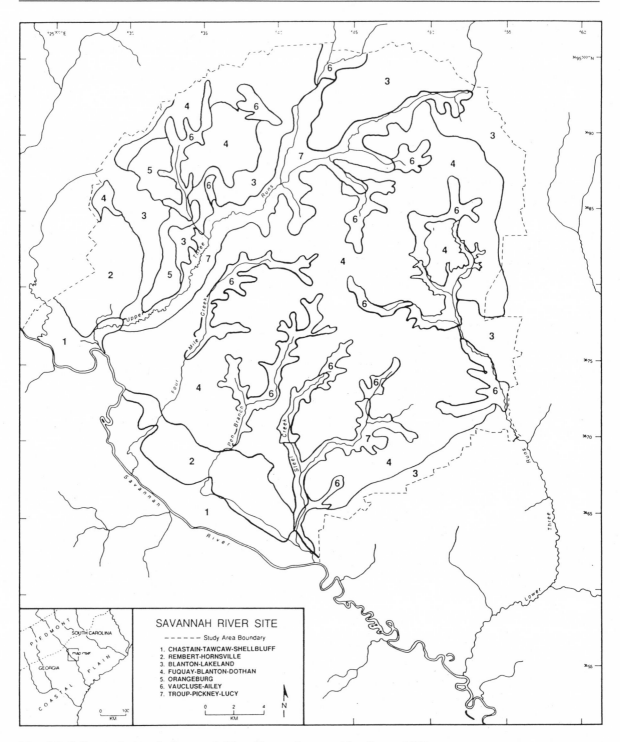

MAP 8.2. Soil associations in Savannah River Site study area. *After Rogers 1990.*

divisions based on diagnostic artifacts, including refined earthenwares, glass, and architectural hardware.[17] The archaeological components may be broken down into four broad temporal groups: those that date to the Colonial period (ca. 1730–1780), the Revolutionary War/Early National period (ca. 1780–1830), the Antebellum period (ca. 1830–1865), and the Postbellum/Modern period (ca. 1865–1952). The settlement pattern analysis results are summarized below.

The Colonial Period (ca. 1730–1780)

The earliest European settlement of the SRS appears to have taken place after initial settlement of Fort Moore in 1718. The major economic activities in the study area through the early decades of the eighteenth century were probably cattle ranching, lumbering, and mixed subsistence farming. Much of the early demand for cattle in the study area was driven by the Anglo-European taste for beef, while at least some of agricultural produce may have been sold to lowcountry planters for slave rations. Colonial period occupations, of which there are 64, represent approximately 15 percent of the identifiable historic components. Among the earliest known historic components on the SRS, 53 percent tend to be located close to the major tributaries (Rank 3 or greater) of the Savannah River, while 47 percent of the early components are located on the smaller Rank 1 and 2 streams (map 8.3). Maps of the period indicate that there was one road in the area which paralleled the river; most transport probably took place via boat.[18]

The Revolutionary War/Early National Period (ca. 1780–1830)

The subsistence agricultural nature of the area changed following the Revolutionary War because of the invention of the cotton gin. An influx of yeoman farmers into the region reduced the available open range for cattle, and a road net began to develop; however, pole boats and steam boats provided the bulk of transportation (map 8.4).[19] However, cotton cultivation may not have become

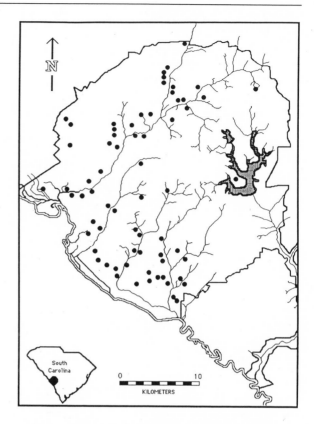

MAP 8.3. Colonial period component locations.

an important part of the study area's economy until the 1830s.[20] In fact, when Robert Mills traveled through Barnwell District in 1826 he mentioned that farmers in the area were rapidly destroying the fertility of the soil, and that foodstuffs were hard to obtain because they were raised not for market but for local consumption.[21]

In addition to cotton and subsistence farming, a small-scale, locally oriented milling industry serviced area farmers who harvested timber and ground their corn and other grain crops. This industry was characterized by a relative lack of technological innovation and low levels of capitalization, and it was probably operated part-time driven by local demand. These characteristics may in turn have been due to the agriculturally marginal nature of the soils in the study area, which made farming a risky enterprise. In the face of fluctuating demand, it would have made little sense for area

MAP 8.4. Barnwell
District roads.
From Mills 1825.

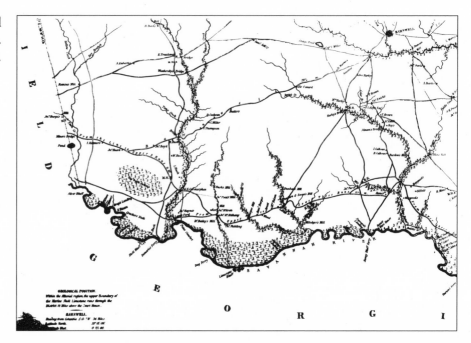

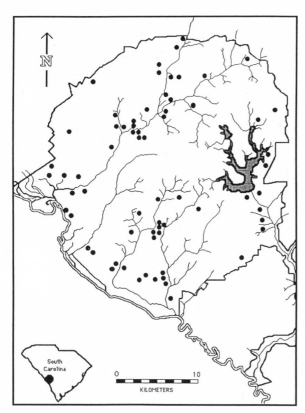

MAP 8.5. Revolutionary/Early National period
component locations.

millers to over-invest in state-of-the-art technology
when building their establishments. Revolutionary
War and Early National period components
represent approximately 22 percent of the identifiable historic occupations. A settlement trend away
from major streams began during this period, as 48
percent of the sites are located on Rank 3 and
smaller streams (map 8.5).

Antebellum Period (ca. 1830–1865)

During the Antebellum period the advance of
cotton plantations inland from the coast pushed the
ranching frontier west into Tennessee, although the
ranching nature of the study area probably lingered
until the 1840s.[22] Antebellum Period components are
not as numerous as are those of the Revolutionary
War/Early National period, but account for 20
percent of the identified historic occupations.

The settlement trend away from the major
tributaries continued during this period. Among
the components, 45 percent are located on Rank 3
or smaller streams (map 8.6). The majority of the
components away from water were located on or
close to roads constructed in the late 1780s by the
Winton County Government.[23]

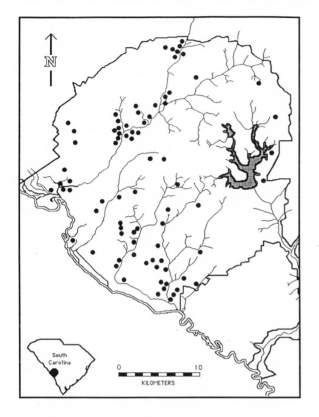

MAP 8.6. Antebellum period component locations.

Postbellum/Modern Period (ca. 1865–1952)

The Postbellum/Modern period in the study area was a time of radical change in some respects and continued stasis in others. The overall agricultural character of the economic landscape persisted.

However, patterns of land use changed. Perhaps the most significant change was a growing intensity in land use, as farmers plowed areas that had probably not been used in the Antebellum period for cotton (fig. 8.1). Thus, settlement patterns and locational data from this period reflect increasing use of the dry uplands and a progressive trend away from surface water. This took place simultaneously with changes in land ownership patterns, as tenancy became established and superseded previous freeholder/slave tenure systems.

In the 1930s these patterns began to shift again, as federal crop programs encouraged further diversification and crop yields increased due to the increased use of fertilizers, soil conservation measures, and mechanization. During the Postbellum/Modern period, some individual farmers were relatively successful.[24] However, fluctuating produce prices and, later, the Depression caused an outflow of population in the early twentieth century.[25] Timber became a more important industry, as marginal land finally became exhausted from 150 years of intensive agriculture and was planted in pine.[26] At the same time, increasing access to rail transport and improved road systems gave rise to small towns at important crossroads and railheads. This allowed cotton growers to move commodities to market centers like Atlanta, Georgia, and Charleston much more efficiently than had been the case using river transportation.

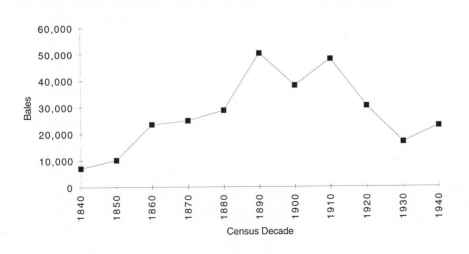

FIG. 8.1. Cotton production figures for Barnwell County in the Postbellum/Modern Period.

The trends of the late nineteenth and early twentieth centuries—growing agricultural intensification coupled with tenancy land tenure—are reflected in the archaeological record. Although areas along river and stream terrace systems continued to be occupied, archaeological sites in the sandhills are much more numerous than they were during earlier periods. This is particularly true for the northwest quarter of the study area, which is the southern edge of the Aiken Plateau (map 8.7). Postbellum/Modern components are the most numerous type of historical occupation in the study area, accounting for approximately 43 percent of total identifiable components.

Factors in Settlement Patterning

The historical cultures of the study area—indeed, culture in general—can be seen as adaptations shaped by specific environmental conditions and technologies.[27] Ecological studies of modern farmers have clearly demonstrated that control over resources can be the result of rational choices and not necessarily of built-in, culturally embedded patterns, as has been suggested by ethnographic studies of tribal societies.[28] This theoretical perspective, which emphasizes the role of decision making, is directly applicable to the historic period settlement of the SRS. Settlement patterns in the study area reflect conscious adjustments to both the distribution of resources and to associated social and cultural factors.[29] However, although spatial behavior is fundamentally rational in economic terms, it is never exclusively economic and only rarely optimal; thus, it seldom approaches minimax—that is, minimal effort for maximal return. Site location has to take into consideration a series of variables, including resource spaces and technology, scheduling, and demographic aggregation.[30] Maintenance of cooperative social ties is also critical.[31] In complex societies, social, political, and economic factors all condition the way in which human populations arrange themselves across the landscape.[32]

Because of the range of factors which enter into settlement patterning in a complex society, historical settlement studies may well be more complex than prehistoric models, particularly with regard to social constraints.[33] Within the study area, the overall settlement trend appears to be linked to a range of factors. Land availability appears to have been a particularly critical variable. The soils in the study area are generally marginal for agriculture using modern agricultural techniques; their viability under eighteenth- and nineteenth-century farming methods, which were labor-intensive and land-extensive, would have been even more precarious.

The data presented here indicate that component elevation is temporally sensitive (fig. 8.2). The preexisting trend toward use of upland areas appears to have accelerated during the transition to the Postbellum/Modern period, when intensive cotton farming and tenancy became an important part of the agricultural landscape. It seems likely

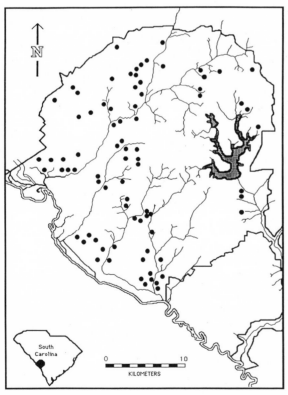

MAP 8.7. Postbellum/Modern component locations.

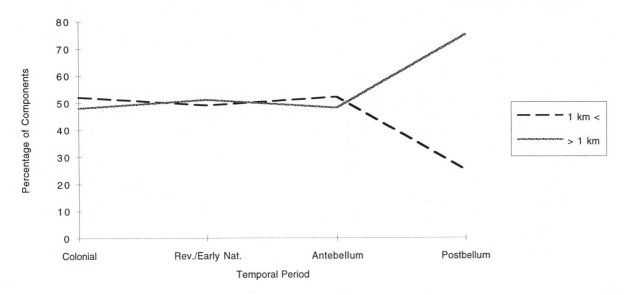

Fɪɢ. 8.2. Shifts in elevation of historic components through time.

that both of these factors—land tenure and intensive monocropping—contributed to the trend toward upland farming. Intensive cotton agriculture put substantial stress on the arable land, making marginal fields more economically viable. Further, tenancy, which was characterized by a shift from a nucleated or conglomerate pattern to a dispersed settlement pattern,[34] would have contributed substantially to this trend. Labor relations, which during the Revolutionary War/Early National and Antebellum periods were characterized by close control of slaves, shifted to a system in which tenants negotiated for greater autonomy and privacy during the Postbellum/Modern period. This meant that areas which were previously unoccupied, particularly on the Aiken Plateau, became more attractive. Add to these factors the patchy distribution of both good arable soil and rainfall and it seems clear that simple land availability was not the only factor determining settlement patterning and economic orientation. Prime farmland occurs either in thin ribbons along watercourses or in relatively spatially restricted loci in the study area (fig. 8.3). This distributional pattern may have militated against successful large-scale monocropping systems like those of the lowcountry.

Transportation system technology also played a strong role in determining settlement location. Early dependence on river transport for market goods in the eighteenth and early nineteenth centuries was superseded by rail and road systems. All of these left their mark on settlement patterns. Waterborne transport produced site clusters strung in a linear pattern along major streams. Roads appeared in conjunction with increasing settlement of the high interfluves. The appearance of rail systems gave rise to small-town development.

There is a clear relationship between settlement chronology and the location of major roads from the Colonial through Antebellum periods. The Postbellum/Modern period deviates radically from the previous three periods. This deviation may be the result of settlement decentralization associated with tenant land tenure. In addition, centers of exchange may have become more localized in the Postbellum/Modern period as larger landowners brought goods closer to the consumer. This economic diversification helped larger landowners during periods of economic stress by allowing them to acquire cheap land for future development through foreclosure. It also helped ensure control over the labor force.

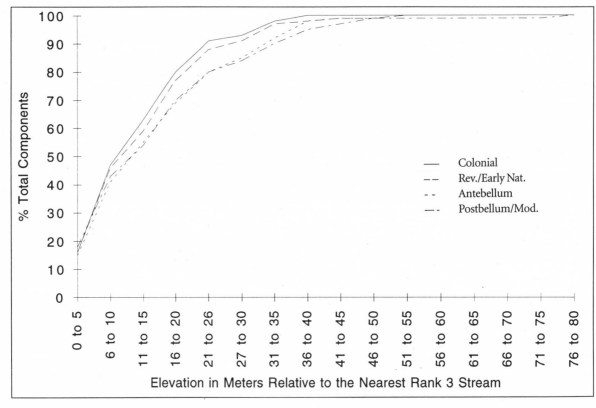

FIG. 8.3. Metric elevation relative to nearest rank 3 stream, Savannah River Site. *After Rogers 1990.*

In order to cope with these constraints, inhabitants of the study area may have hedged their economic bets by carefully maintaining social ties through kin-related land tenure. Preliminary research using land plats from the terminal period of occupation in the study area seems to point to the use of such a system, possibly as a risk-reduction behavior. Reciprocities and cooperation needed to accomplish such tasks as harvesting a crop, canning foods for the winter, or raising a barn are much more likely if one's neighbors are kin. Such techniques of social control are particularly prevalent in small, face-to-face societies, where the individual is on a first-name basis with many of his or her fellows.[35] The role of kinship in land-tenure systems during the nineteenth and early twentieth centuries has been documented elsewhere in the Southeast.[36] Data from the SRS support the notion that kinship was an important settlement factor, at least for landowners, in the study area as well.

In summary, the research carried out to date on historical period occupation of the SRS suggests that settlement patterns and economic trends were determined by a series of constraints, including 1) availability of arable land and the patchy distribution of what little arable land was available; 2) transportation technology; 3) exports from the area of animal products and agricultural commodities, especially beef and cotton; 4) land-tenure systems; and 5) kin relationships. As a result of these constraints, a diversified subsistence base and organizational flexibility appear to have constituted the major economic strategies for historical period occupants of the study area. This parallels the apparent strategy used during the prehistoric occupation of the area.[37] The cultural trajectory in the study area was in large part determined by the efforts of individual farmers to balance the goal of economic self-sufficiency with these constraints and conditioning factors.

NOTES

1. Willey 1953:1.
2. Chang 1967:95; Wilson 1988. In the present survey-level study, site-specific research on the history of each site, including the ethnicity and race of site inhabitants, has not been undertaken, due to factors of cost and the requirements of the project scope of work. However, some general comments on these social categories can be made from regional research, summarized in Crass and Brooks 1995:31–44. Historical accounts describe the Uchee Indians and the Creeks as early area inhabitants. The Chickasaws relocated in the vicinity in 1748. The relationships between these Native Americans and with other cultural groups remains unclear at the present time. The earliest European American settlers tended to be Protestants, especially Germans, Swiss, and some French Huguenots. Some people of English descent also moved into the area in the Colonial period. Although some of these settlers had African American slaves, their early numbers remain uncertain. The numbers of people of African descent reportedly grew over the National period. By 1809 the Barnwell District enumerator reported a total of 3,518 African Americans and 7,646 European Americans. By the Antebellum period, in 1860, African Americans out-numbered European Americans at 18,041 to 12,702. The majority of twentieth-century residents were farmers; in 1925 a total of 393 European Americans owned their farms as opposed to 138 African American farm owners and 1,395 black tenants.
3. Sassaman et al. 1989:67–91; Brooks et al. 1989.
4. Trinkley 1990a; Trinkley 1990b; Lewis 1982:1–12; Lewis 1989b:225–52.
5. Taylor and Smith 1978:210–27.
6. Lewis 1984.
7. South and Hartley 1980.
8. Plummer 1983:3.
9. Lovingood and Purvis n.d.
10. Sassaman et al. 1989:38.
11. Urlsperger 1972–81.
12. Robert Mills 1972.
13. Edgar 1981.
14. Rogers 1990.
15. Rogers 1990:43.
16. Rogers 1990:98.
17. South 1977; Fisher 1987:48–57; Jones and Sullivan 1985; Noël Hume 1980; Nelson 1968; Dreppard 1946; Blackall 1888:71–74; Price 1979; Jewitt 1970; Collard 1967; Williams 1978; Williams and Weber 1986.
18. Weaver 1972.
19. Brooks 1981; Brooks 1988b; Holcomb 1978.
20. Black 1864.
21. Mills 1972.
22. Lewis 1984:279–81; Brooks 1988b.
23. Holcomb 1978.
24. Edgar 1981:8–9.
25. Scott 1969.
26. Edgar 1981:11.
27. Moran 1979:52; Edgerton 1971.
28. Bennet 1969; Bennet 1976; Rappaport 1968; Nietschmann 1973:53.
29. Moran 1979:96.
30. Butzer 1982; Jochim 1983.
31. Wobst 1974.
32. Stine 1989a; Stine 1990; Zierden, Drucker, and Calhoun 1986.
33. Anderson and Joseph 1988.
34. Anderson and Joseph 1988:419–20.
35. Service 1975.
36. Joyce 1981; Stine 1989a:164–70.
37. Sassaman et al. 1989:36.

WORKS CITED

Anderson, David G., and J. W. Joseph
1988   *Prehistory and History Along the Upper Savannah River: Technical Synthesis of Cultural Resource Investigations, Richard B. Russell Multiple Resource Area.* Russell Papers 1988. Interagency Archeological Services, National Park Service, Atlanta.

Bennet, John
1969   *Northern Plainsmen.* Aldine, Chicago.
1976   *The Ecological Transition.* Pergamon Press, London.

Black, George R.
1864   "Black Family History, [ca. 1863–1864]." P MSS.
       Black Collection, South Caroliniana Library,
       Columbia.

Blackall, Henry
1888   Nails. *American Architect and Building News* 24
       (660):71–74.

Brooks, Richard D.
1981   *Initial Historic Overview of the Savannah River
       Plant, Aiken and Barnwell Counties, South
       Carolina.* Research Manuscript Series 170, South
       Carolina Institute of Archaeology and Anthro-
       pology, University of South Carolina, Columbia.

1988b *250 Years of Historic Occupation on Steel Creek,
       Savannah River Plant, Barnwell County, South
       Carolina.* Submitted to the Savannah River
       Operations Office, U. S. Department of Energy.
       Savannah River Archaeological Research
       Program, South Carolina Institute of Archaeol-
       ogy and Anthropology, Columbia.

Brooks, Mark, Richard D. Brooks, Kenneth Sassaman,
       George Lewis, and Glen Hanson
1989   *Archaeological Resource Management Plan of the
       Savannah River Archaeological Research Program.*
       Savannah River Archaeological Research
       Program, South Carolina Institute of Archaeol-
       ogy and Anthropology, Columbia.

Butzer, Karl
1982   *Archaeology as Human Ecology: Method and
       Theory for a Contextual Approach.* Cambridge
       Univ. Press, England.

Chang, K. C.
1967   *Rethinking Archaeology.* Random House, New
       York.

Collard, Elizabeth
1967   *Nineteenth Century Pottery and Porcelain in
       Canada.* McGill Univ. Press, Montreal.

Crass, David, and Mark Brooks (editors)
1995   *Cotton and Black Draught: Consumer Behavior on
       a Postbellum Farm.* Savannah River Archaeologi-
       cal Research Papers 5. Occasional Papers of the
       Savannah River Archaeological Research
       Program, South Carolina Institute of Archaeol-
       ogy and Anthropology, Univ. of South Carolina,
       Columbia.

Dreppard, Charles
1946   Spikes, Nails, Tacks, Brads, and Pins. *Early
       American Industries Association Chronicle* 3(8).

Edgar, Walter
1981   *Sleepy Hollow: The Study of a Rural Community.*
       Univ. of South Carolina, Columbia.

Edgerton, Robert
1971   *The Individual in Cultural Adaptation.* Univ. of
       California, Berkeley.

Fisher, Charles
1987   The Ceramic Collection from the Continental
       Army Cantonment at New Windsor, New York.
       Historical Archaeology 21:48–57.

Holcomb, Brian
1978   *Winton (Barnwell) County, South Carolina:
       Minutes of County Court and Will Book 1, 1785–
       1791.* Southern Historical Press, Easley, South
       Carolina.

Jewitt, Llewellyn
1970   *The Ceramic Art of Great Britain.* Ward Lock
       Repairs, London.

Jochim, Michael
1983   *Strategies for Survival: Cultural Behavior in
       Ecological Context.* Academic Press, New York.

Jones, Olive, and Catherine Sullivan
1985   *The Parks Canada Glass Glossary for the Descrip-
       tion of Containers, Tablewares, Flat Glass, and
       Closures.* Parks Canada, Ottawa.

Lewis, Kenneth E.
1982   Settlement and Activity Patterning on Two Rice
       Plantations in the South Carolina Low Country.
       *The Conference on Historic Site Archaeology Papers
       1979,* 14:1–12. South Carolina Institute of
       Archaeology and Anthropology, Univ. of South
       Carolina, Columbia.

1984   *The American Frontier: An Archaeological Study of
       Settlement Pattern and Process.* Academic Press,
       New York.

1989b Settlement Function and Archaeological Pattern-
       ing in a Historic Urban Context: the Woodrow
       Wilson House in Columbia, S.C. In *Studies in
       South Carolina Archaeology,* edited by Albert
       Goodyear and Glen Hanson, pp. 225–52. Anthro-
       pological Studies 9, South Carolina Institute of
       Archaeology and Anthropology, Columbia.

Lovingood, Paul E., Jr., and John C. Purvis
n.d.   The Nature of Precipitation: South Carolina,
       1941–1970. South Carolina Crop and Livestock
       Reporting Service, U.S. Dept. of Agriculture. Ms.
       on file, Dept. of Geography, Univ. of South
       Carolina, Columbia.

Mills, Robert
1972   *Statistics of South Carolina.* Originally published 1826. Reprint, Hurlbut and Lloyd, Charleston.

Moran, Emilio
1979   *Human Adaptability.* Duxbury Press, North Scituate.

Nelson, Lee
1968   Nail Chronology as an Aid to Dating Old Buildings. *History News* 23(11):495–6174.

Nietschmann, B.
1973   *Between Land and Water.* New York, Seminar Press.

Noël Hume, Ivor
1980   *A Guide to Artifacts of Colonial America.* Alfred A. Knopf, New York.

Plummer, G. L.
1983   *Georgia Rainfall: Precipitation Patterns at 23 places 1734–1982.* Georgia Academy of Science, Athens.

Price, Cynthia
1979   *19th Century Ceramics in the Eastern Ozark Border Region.* Center for Archaeological Research Monograph Series 1. Southwest Missouri State Univ., Springfield.

Rappaport, Roy
1968   *Pigs for the Ancestors.* Yale Univ. Press, New Haven.

Rogers, Virgil
1990   *Soil Survey of Savannah River Plant Area, Parts of Aiken, Barnwell, and Allendale Counties, South Carolina.* U.S. Dept. of Agriculture, Washington, D.C.

Sassaman, Ken, Mark Brooks, Glenn Hanson, and David Anderson
1989   *Technical Synthesis of Prehistoric Archaeological Investigations on the Savannah River Site, Aiken and Barnwell Counties, South Carolina.* Savannah River Archaeological Research Program, Aiken.

Scott, E.
1969   *Negro Migration During the War.* Arno Press/The New York Times, New York.

Service, Elman R.
1975   *Origins of the State and Civilization: The Process of Cultural Evolution.* W. W. Norton, New York.

South, Stanley
1977   *Method and Theory in Historical Archaeology.* Academic Press, New York.

South, Stanley, and Michael Hartley

1980   *Deep Water and High Ground: Seventeenth Century Low Country Settlement.* South Carolina Institute of Archaeology and Anthropology Research Manuscript Series 166, Columbia.

Stine, Linda France
1990   Social Inequality and Turn-of-the-Century Farmsteads: Issues of Class, Status, Ethnicity, and Race. In *Historical Archaeology of Plantations and Farms,* edited by Charles E. Orser Jr. *Historical Archaeology* 24(4):37–49.

1992a   *Revealing Historic Landscapes in Charleston County: Archaeological Inventory, Contexts, and Management.* Submitted to the Charleston County Planning Dept. South Carolina Institute of Archaeology and Anthropology.

Taylor, Richard, and Michael Smith
1978   *The Report of the Intensive Survey of the Richard B. Russell Dam and Lake, Savannah River, Georgia and South Carolina.* Research Manuscript Series 142. South Carolina Institute of Archaeology and Anthropology, Univ. of South Carolina, Columbia.

Trinkley, Michael (editor)
1990a   *The Second Phase of Archaeological Survey on Spring Island, Beaufort County, South Carolina: Investigations of Prehistoric and Historic Settlement Patterns on an Isolated Sea Island.* Chicora Foundation, Columbia.

1990b   *Archaeological Excavations at 38BU96, A Portion of Cotton Hope Plantation, Hilton Head Island, Beaufort County, South Carolina.* Chicora Foundation Research Series 21. Chicora Foundation, Columbia.

Urlsperger, Samuel (editor)
1972–   *Detailed Reports on the Salzburger Emigrants Who*
81   *Settled in America.* 8 vols. Univ. of Georgia Press, Athens.

Willey, Gordon
1953   *Prehistoric Settlement Patterns in the Viru Valley, Peru.* Bureau of American Ethnology Bulletin 155. Smithsonian Institution, Washington, D.C.

Williams, Petra
1978   *Staffordshire Romantic Transfer Patterns.* Fountain House East, Jeffersontown, Kentucky.

Williams, Petra, and Marguerite Weber
1986   *Staffordshire II Romantic Transfer Patterns.* Fountain House East, Jeffersontown, Kentucky.

Weaver, David
1972 *The Transport Expansion Sequence in Georgia and the Carolinas, 1670–1900: A Search for Spatial Regularities.* Ph.D. diss., Univ. of Florida, Gainesville.

Wilson, David
1988 *Prehispanic Settlement Patterns in the Lower Santa Valley, Peru.* Smithsonian Institution Press, Washington, D.C.

Wobst, Martin
1974 Boundary Conditions for Paleolithic Social Systems: A Simulation Approach. *American Antiquity* 39:147–78.

Zierden, Martha A., Lesley M. Drucker, and Jeanne Calhoun
1986 *Home Upriver: Rural Life on Daniel's Island, Berkeley County, South Carolina.* Submitted to the South Carolina Dept. of Highways and Public Transportation. A Joint Venture of Carolina Archaeological Services/The Charleston Museum, Columbia and Charleston.

9. "We Were Just Dirt Farmers": The Archaeology of Piedmont Farmstead Landscapes

J. W. JOSEPH AND MARY BETH REED

In 1856 . . . [David Golightly Harris] grew tired of trying to grow crops in the overly sandy soil of a particular field, so he dug through eighteen inches of sand to find good soil underneath. Despite the hard work required, he set his people to plowing with subsoil plows, and "In some places we go to the depth of three feet. . . . I am making a good piece of land out of poor but I am afraid it will not pay. The only way [to] find out is to try and experiment. . . ." Experience had not made him an optimist. Yet he persevered. He knew that he should return organic matter to the soil and made sure to plow under the crop stubble as deeply as possible. Also, he devised a system of horizontal ditches which crossed his fields to others that ran down the hills to carry off excess water. The upkeep of these ditches was time consuming but, unlike most of his neighbors, he believed that the time paid off in the long run.

—RACINE 1990:4

It was the nature of Piedmont soils that subsoil could be considered "good," and the nature of Piedmont farmers accustomed to a protracted battle with the earth that encouraged them to continue trying to make an agricultural existence on this barren land. Couple the Piedmont soil with the intransigent nature and innate stubbornness of a Scotch-Irish population, and place the whole on a heavily dissected topographic plane, and the severe erosion of the Piedmont is seen as the character, and not simply a characteristic, of Piedmont agriculture.

—JOSEPH, REED, AND CANTLEY 1991:256

The historical archaeology of South Carolina's piedmont farmsteads reflects in many respects the realizations of agrarian life. Historical archaeologists, too, have found South Carolina's piedmont clays unyielding and have bemoaned the loss of so much piedmont soil in an echo of the nineteenth-century farmer's lament. Despite the pervasiveness of piedmont farmsteads, despite the fact that farmsteads shaped the character of upcountry culture with as firm a hand as that exerted by plantations in the lowcountry, we know too little and expect much less of piedmont farmsteads. The archaeology of South Carolina's piedmont farmsteads is scant, and is represented by a few investigations undertaken as part of the compliance studies at the Russell Reservoir, Clarks Hill Lake, and Lake Hartwell; graduate research; and other isolated compliance investigations. Expanding the scope of farmstead archaeology into the neighboring states of Georgia and North Carolina, while adding some significant studies, does not appreciably change the magnitude of piedmont farmstead archaeology.[1]

Much of the futility of farmstead archaeology is a reflection of the degradation of the piedmont landscape, not merely in terms of the massive scale of soil erosion but also as reflected by the conversion of settlement loci to agricultural fields and by the expansive cycle of clear-cutting, agricultural use, and reforestation. Farmstead landscapes are difficult to reconstruct, and yet an understanding of these landscapes is elemental to the study of historic farmsteads. The piedmont's agrarian history is told within its relation with the land.

This chapter focuses on the internal and external dimensions of the piedmont farmstead landscape as developed through the study of one particular site, 38SP101, also known as the Finch Farm or Indian Ford Farm. The study reported herein was sponsored by the South Carolina Department of Transportation as part of the compliance archaeology undertaken for the I-85 Northern Alternative. This investigation was multidisciplinary in approach, providing for an ethnohistoric account of Finch Farm which interwove oral history, archaeology, architectural history, and the documentary base to provide a more comprehensive view of the social aspects of site settlement. The archaeological work made broad use of machine stripping in former occupation loci, which had been converted to use as agricultural fields following the collapse and abandonment of their historic structures. In the area of the surviving house and house yard, archaeological studies were conducted via traditional hand-excavated test units.

Perhaps the most salient aspect of this study, at least from a methodological perspective, should be emphasized at the outset. The machine-stripping excavations revealed that erosion in former activity areas had been so severe that only very large or very deep cultural features had survived. Based on the surviving remnants of these features, it is estimated that as much as two feet of subsoil had been washed away from the site. Within the intact house yard, however, feature preservation was far greater. For comparative purposes, the house yard produced one feature per 150 square feet, as opposed to one feature per 1,054 square feet in former activity areas which had reverted to use as agricultural fields. In compliance studies, there has been something of a divorce between architectural farmsteads and archaeological farmsteads, with archaeological work being advanced only toward those farm sites which no longer possess above-ground architecture. The findings from Finch Farm suggest that not only is such a divorce artificial, it is extremely prejudicial against farmstead archaeology. These findings indicate that the farmsteads best suited to receive archaeological study are those with standing structures, simply because the presence of such architecture eliminates field use and soil erosion. The presence of standing architecture also alleviates the need to expend time and money in an effort to archaeologically expose and interpret architectural remains, allowing farmstead archaeology to focus its attention on the landscape and material patterning.

The ethnohistorically reconstructed Finch Farm landscape lends itself to the consideration of several landscape topics: the division of labor, social and socioeconomic relationships, the control of nature, and changing attitudes and responses toward refuse disposal and sanitation. Each of these topics is discussed in greater detail below.

The Division of Labor

The Finch Farm complex is located just off South Carolina Highway 9 (Boiling Springs Road) and is confined largely to the ridgeline which divides the Shoally Creek and Lawson's Fork Creek drainages and which underlies the highway. Elevations within the farmstead range from a high of 830 feet AMSL to a low of 780 feet AMSL along the gully sides. The site is bordered to the north and west by a small intermittent drainage which is fed by at least two springs. The southwestern aspect of the site is gently sloping, leading to a small finger ridge knoll, and then more steeply sloping leading to a second unnamed intermittent drainage. Beyond this drainage the property crests to a small hillock which is bounded by Lawson's Fork Creek.

Historically, the site consisted of three separate activity areas: the main house complex, the agricultural complex, and the tenant farm (fig. 9.1). The main house was located on a slight rise adjacent to Highway 9 and is accessed by a single, unpaved road which divides as it reaches the house. The main house complex has the following features: a standing house; a historic yard area which once housed a smokehouse and garage, in addition to the surviving chicken coops and storage sheds; a reported fruit orchard located adjacent to the house yard; and the reported site of an African American farm employee, Will Lynch, whose house was said to be placed just beyond the rear of the yard. A second functional area was located southwest of the main house complex and housed the agricultural structures associated with the farmstead. Included in this complex were a frame barn, a log barn and cider mill, a log corn crib, a molasses mill, a blacksmith shop, a pig pen, and a spring. Only the log barn was standing at the time of the archaeological study. A final activity area comprised a small tenant farmstead which reportedly contained a house, barn, a spring and milk box, and a chicken coop. This tenant farm was visually separated from the main house and agricultural complexes by the finger ridge mentioned above. A hay barn was reportedly located on the north slope of this ridge, in a position intermediate to the tenant farm and the agricultural complex.

As outlined above, the farmstead expresses two settlement dichotomies, one which separated and opposed the agricultural and domestic activity areas, the other which emphasized the social distance and separate familial relationship of the Finches and their tenants, the Webbs. In neither case, however, are these separations absolute. The patterns of farm roads serve to delimit spatial boundaries and suggest the existence of intermediate spaces. The main house complex is surrounded by three ellipses, as formed by these roads. The first surrounds the main house proper, the second the house and farm yard, while the third adds Will Lynch's home, the molasses mill, and the frame barn. This third ellipse provides an intermediary connection between the domestic and agricultural spheres. Similarly, the hay barn and, to a lesser degree, the blacksmith's shop mediate the separation between the Webbs and the Finches and testify to their mutual co-dependence.

The separation between agricultural and domestic space has been characterized as a gender-based division. Commenting on the structure of middle Virginia farmsteads, folklorist Henry Glassie observed that "the old farm had two centers, the house and the barn, around which smaller dependencies were dropped. Beside the house are the outbuildings needed by the woman in order to get food on the table; beside the barn are the outbuildings needed by the man to keep the cattle fat."[2] This image of a gender-based settlement pattern has been challenged by Stine, who argues that it is partially a product of the Victorian "Cult of True Womanhood," which sought to separate the sin and inequity of the working world from the purity of the domestic household.[3] Stine contends that this ideal was promulgated through agricultural publications and land-grant college curricula, and that it thus partially explains the separation of domestic and agricultural space. However, she also notes a considerable degree of gender crossover in the use of domestic and agricultural space, citing the appearance of root cellars in agricultural areas which stored and supplied food for use in the household and the appearance of smokehouses—structures commonly associated with male activities—within house yards. Such overlap appears at Finch Farm, with the added twentieth-century male domain of the garage appearing in the domestic sphere.

An alternative view of the social behavior leading to this settlement structure is provided by Adams,[4] who emphasizes the means of production and the authority to dispose of produce as the

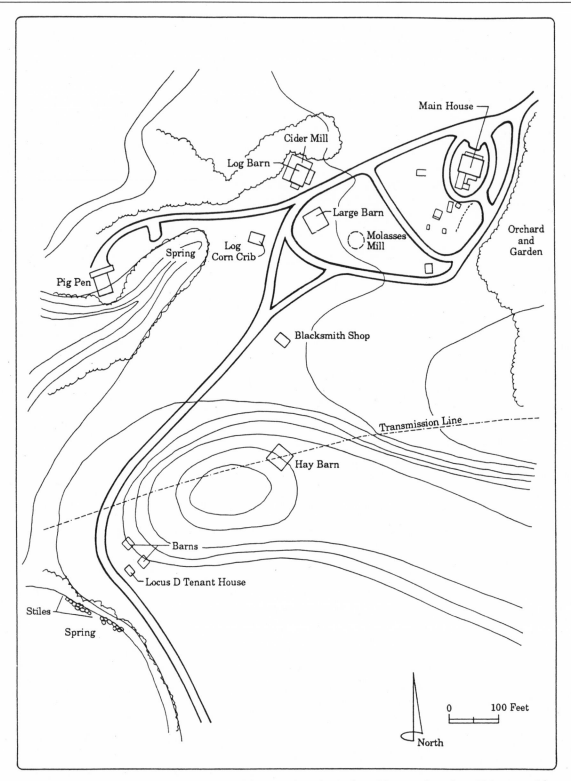

FIG. 9.1. Finch Farm site plan, as reconstructed from archaeological, architectural, and oral history evidence.

underlying basis for this settlement plan. Within Adams's model, structures and activities which contributed to farmstead capital were segregated from structures and activities which were geared toward domestic production. As men generally controlled products which contributed to farmstead capital and women controlled activities which contributed to the domestic production, this separation can assume the appearance of a gender relationship. Adams's model of settlement structure fits the pattern observed at Finch Farm and supports Stine's contention that the "rules" of gender separation were not strictly followed.

Social and Socioeconomic Relationships

The separation of the Finches from their tenants, the Webbs, would appear to be a factor of social and socioeconomic relationships as much as a division of labor. As noted above, the Webb tenant farm is sheltered from the view of Finch Farm by a small hillock. This visual isolation likely served both families; privacy appears to have been one of the most sought-after objectives of farm tenants and offers one explanation for the fragmentation of plantation settlements following the Civil War.

Interestingly, the socioeconomic index values calculated for the Finches and the Webbs do not indicate any great social distance,[5] as measured by the relative cost of ceramic vessels. Of the two families, the Webbs achieved the higher socioeconomic index ranking, at 1.32, while the Finches' ceramic assemblage was ranked at 1.24. Both of these index values are scaled toward the lower end of the socioeconomic index range. Assuming that the Webbs and Finches had equal access to goods, which both would have had from the shops in the nearby community of Boiling Springs, ceramics do not appear to have served as a measure of social status at Finch Farm. Rather, social rank appears to have been displayed by architecture and other outward possessions. This is interpreted to reflect the nature of social interaction within the farmstead. The

Finches would have dealt regularly with their tenants, the Webbs, but it is doubtful that the Webbs would have often been entertained within the Finch home. The Finches' social standing could thus best be displayed to the Webbs as well as other passersby in the scale and detail of their home, as well as by other outward material possessions, such as C. C. L. Finch's Model-T Ford. The absence of expensive ceramics within the Finch household suggests that the Finches rarely interacted socially with their peers. Rather, their relationships were with their tenants. This negated the necessity of demonstrating social standing through household objects and instead emphasized the importance of displaying status through outward symbols such as architecture and an automobile. This runs counter to Drucker et al.'s argument that wealth was not displayed through architecture on piedmont farmsteads. Drucker et al. suggest that the relative isolation of the piedmont leveled the architectural playing field; that all piedmont farmers were forced to rely upon a vernacular building tradition, which thus diminished the scale of variation among farmsteads.[6] While Drucker et al.'s contention that all (or certainly much) of piedmont architecture was vernacular in nature bears truth, their analysis fails to recognize the variation in form which vernacular architecture could achieve.

The study of piedmont farmsteads suggests that vernacular architecture could take on different appearances and particularly emphasizes the contrast between true vernacular structures, such as the log buildings at Finch Farm, and a more stylized architectural tradition which aspired toward formal design. While the 1896 Finch Farm house is a vernacular structure, designed and built by C. C. L. Finch himself, it aspires toward formal architecture in its plan and detailing. The "Folk Victorian" facade of this structure reflects a general architectural tradition touted in numerous agricultural journals of the era. Indeed, it closely resembles the facade of a stone structure published in Downing's *Architecture of Country Houses* in 1850. As the various agricultural periodicals published illustrations of ideal farmhouses in both plan and profile, it is difficult to say with certainty that the Finch Farm house was not adapted from such published plans. The January 4, 1870, issue of *Farmer and Artisan*, published in Athens and Atlanta, neatly summarizes the associations between architecture and status, as well as the transformation of the piedmont brought about by the closing of the western frontier:

> There is no feature of our civilization more closely allied with comfort, or more surely conducive to true refinement, than a neat and tasteful home. A person of culture may live in a very mean house, from necessity; but to so live from a lack of taste or energy to provide a good one, is a matter of reproach, as it also is a pretty sure evidence of a want of that higher civilizing influence which raises man above the nomadic habits of the Arab.... Our magnificent countryside wears an aspect of rudeness that is positively gloomy, simply from a neglect of taste in the erection of homes, and the arrangements of lawns, gardens, and orchards. In other days there were solid excuses, if not good reasons, for this neglect. Lands were cheap, and the great incentive was to exhaust a given area, and move bag and baggage to fresh fields and pastures new. This nomadic sort of existence discouraged a taste for the improvement of comfortable and substantial homes, and has left a large portion of our fairest domain a dull area of yawning gullies and rotting cabins. From the very poverty that has made us unable to buy fresh lands, is springing up a general purpose to improve our present possessions. As we bring our old fields back to their original productiveness, and abandon the idea of going West, there will grow up a love of home which will soon displace the old rotting cabin.

As the *Farmer and Artisan* essay makes clear, the linkage between architecture and social standing is not simply one of socioeconomic means, but

FIG. 9.2. Finch Farm house, 1989. *Courtesy of Richard T. Bryant.*

reflects the call of progressive farming, which developed as the frontier was filled and as piedmont farmers were forced to reconsider their farmsteads not simply as brief stopping points, but as homes. C. C. L. Finch—college-educated, a teacher, Sunday School superintendent, and progressive farmer—certainly would have been receptive to the *Farmer and Artisan*'s plea.

The design and ornamentation of the Finch Farm house reflect the tenets of progressive agriculture. The structure is a one-and-a-half-story, double-pile house built on brick piers, with an ell projecting from the rear of the house on its west side (fig. 9.2). The main part of the house is covered by a side-facing gable roof with a second gable clad with decorative fish-scale pattern shingles projecting over the doorway. The roof is covered with pressed-tin plates. A partial porch covered with a hipped roof lines the facade. This porch is supported by wood posts detailed by decorative brackets. Two interior brick chimneys, one stuccoed, pierce the main gable, while a third straddles the roof line of the rear ell. The placement of double-hung windows and the door is symmetrical. The appearance of the brackets, tin roof, and fish-scale shingles all post-date the original construction of the house, as indicated by a 1906 photograph (fig. 9.3). These ornamentations classify the house as Folk Victorian in style, a term coined by McAlester and McAlester to describe folk houses which incorporated Victorian detailing.[7]

The floor plan of the house reflects a basic central-hall configuration with rear additions (fig. 9.4). Room dimensions vary within this interior, however, in contrast to the Georgian ideal of this form. The presence of the hall, as well as the front porch, indicates the social dimensions of the house. As Glassie has noted, the introduction of the hallway to American homes provided a notable departure from the vernacular tradition brought over from England, establishing a barrier between the outside world and the house's inhabitants. Ames describes the hall as "a space which was neither wholly interior nor exterior but a sheltered testing zone which some passed through with ease and others never went beyond."[8] Thus, at Finch Farm, architecture reflects social position not only in its scale and appearance but also in its plan and design. Social position is also reflected in its landscaped environment.

The Control of Nature

The *Farmer and Artisan*'s plea that the piedmont be improved not only through the construction of substantial and tasteful homes, but also by "the arrangement of lawns, gardens, and orchards" was also heeded by C. C. L. Finch. Nature was employed to enhance the setting of the Finch Farm house and to distinguish it from the surrounding agricultural fields. When viewed from the major historic route through the area, the Boiling Springs Road (South Carolina Highway 9), the Finch Farm house would have been visually separated from its surrounding fields by its placement within a grove of large oaks. As the house was situated at the northern border of this oak grove and framed by an opening between the oaks, it would have maintained its prominence over the entire setting. The oak grove encircled the rear farm yard, forming a wooded enclave which was visually distinct from the surrounding open fields. Within this rear yard area, natural materials were further employed to create a civilized air by the construction of a stone retaining wall which formed the yard's eastern boundary. The presence of a fruit orchard to the east of the farm yard would have further lent to the cultured image of the farm.

That all of these "natural" elements of the farmstead's landscape in fact represent cultural creations is made clear by the 1906 photograph of the farmhouse. As is evident, the house was built on cleared land which itself had probably once been employed as agricultural fields. There are no trees visible beside or behind the farmhouse in this 1906 view. Thus, the oak grove, as well as the fruit orchard and other landscape elements, were clearly created by C. C. L. Finch as part of his overall scheme for the appearance of the farmstead. While at its most elemental level this landscaping simply serves to follow the admonitions of the *Farmer and Artisan* and improve the appearance of the countryside, such landscaping may also have been intended to enhance C. C. L. Finch's position within the community as a progressive farmer and to indicate his ability to control nature.

The economic existence of farmers in the piedmont was precarious, given the conditions of the piedmont's soils and the long-term effects of erosion. As all farmers succeeded or failed as a direct measure of their ability to control nature, as demonstrated by the production of their fields, it is argued that the visual demonstration of such control would have served to enhance social standing. Indeed, such landscaping, as witnessed not only within farm yards but also in the terracing of farm fields and the construction of drainage ditches and other devices to contain erosion, serves as one of the most visible characteristics of progressive farming. While such landscape efforts were intended to improve farm yields, when they were applied to agricultural fields, their application to farm yards seems to have been intended to demonstrate the power of progressive farming and to enhance the social standing of progressive farmers within their communities. In this respect, then, the farmstead landscape embodies a series of philosophical and intellectual concerns, and can be read as a measure of farmstead ideology.

Fig. 9.3. Finch Farm house and C. C. L. Finch family, ca. 1906. *Courtesy of Mary Collins Green.*

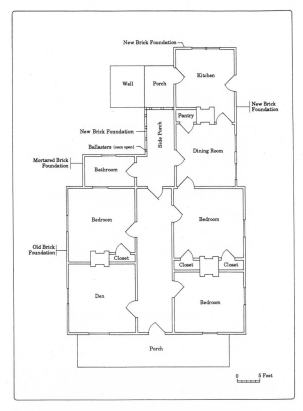

FIG. 9.4. Floor plan of the Finch Farm house.

Refuse Disposal Patterns

As a product of historical archaeology's concern with the recovery of material things, the analysis of refuse disposal patterns can be argued to represent historical archaeology's first, and still unique, contribution to landscape studies. Beginning with South's Brunswick Pattern of Refuse Disposal,[9] archaeologists have worked at defining and refining the ways in which trash was disposed of on piedmont farms. Lewis has provided farm and town residence models which reflect the distribution of peripheral refuse in terms of artifact pattern profiles.[10] Within Lewis's model, architectural debris is expected to cluster around structures and domestic debris between structures, while secondary refuse deposits are expected adjacent to kitchens and in isolated subterranean pit features. South suggests that the size and content of refuse will vary from location to location in farm yards.[11] He

proposes three refuse patterns: 1) "a Central Refuse Pattern composed of large and small refuse (cans, bottles, toy parts, junk) tossed beneath the house," 2) an "Adjacent Refuse Pattern composed of small fragments (such as ceramics and glass) in sometimes swept areas," and 3) a "Peripheral Refuse Pattern composed of large and small refuse (such as cans, bottles, toy parts, and junk) often along fence lines."

Evidence of four patterns of refuse disposal appear at Finch Farm: the Brunswick Pattern, wherein trash accumulated immediately surrounding structure openings; rear yard sheet midden accumulations, whereby trash was deposited on the ground surface along the rear margins of farm yards; Drucker et al.'s piedmont Refuse Disposal Pattern, in which trash was thrown downslope into the gullys surrounding piedmont farms; and trash burning, in which trash was burned as a means of disposal, as well as a source of soil nutrients. The appearance of these refuse patterns suggests an evolution in the relationship between sanitation and material culture.[12]

The appearance of the Brunswick Pattern at Finch Farm, a pattern defined by South as a measure of eighteenth-century British Colonial ideals regarding sanitation, is considered to be an anomaly and a factor in the transitional status of the farmstead. At the time of the archaeological study Finch Farm was still tenanted; however, the farmstead had been acquired by the Highway Department and its destruction was imminent. The artifacts discovered as accumulations around the rear door of the farmstead were all modern in nature, suggesting that the level of site cleanliness may have diminished given the pending loss of the farmstead.

The remaining three patterns suggest a transition over time in the ways in which sanitation was perceived and trash disposed. Of these, rear sheet midden accumulation appears to have been the earliest to occur. Sheet middens appear on late-eighteenth- and antebellum nineteenth-century farmsteads and reflect a system of sanitation which recognized the need to remove trash from the area of the immediate household (perhaps because of the malodorous conditions of such refuse), although not entirely disposing of such remains. Trash burning appears to have become prominent during the second half of the nineteenth century, most likely in response to the Sanitarian movement and concerns with trash disposal and public health. Trash burning was reported to have been C. C. L. Finch's preferred method of trash disposal and was noted archaeologically through the recovery of accumulations of ash and cinder containing burnt fragments of ceramic and glass. Finally, the piedmont Pattern of Refuse Disposal is regarded to represent a late-nineteenth- and twentieth-century phenomenon. At Finch Farm this pattern was revealed by a trash dump located at the head of a small gully. This dump largely contained intact and fragmentary early-twentieth-century bottles. Indeed, bottles are the most noted characteristic of the piedmont Refuse Disposal Pattern, and it is suggested here that the piedmont Pattern arose as a direct response to changes in material culture manufacture. By the late nineteenth century, mass-produced bottles were replacing a variety of traditional storage containers, most of which were reusable and had been reused. However, bottle glass was so prevalent and inexpensive that there was no need to reuse such items. Bottle glass, however, was not susceptible to reduction through fire, at least not through the kinds of fires normally used to burn trash on piedmont farmsteads. The piedmont Pattern thus offered one means of disposing of such refuse: by throwing it into unusable portions of the piedmont landscape. It is possible that trash burning and the piedmont Pattern may have coexisted, with nonbottle glass trash being burned and bottle glass being thrown into gullys and ravines.

In their study of piedmont farmsteads, historical archaeologists have frequently lamented the ravaged conditions of such sites and, in particular, the loss of closed-context cultural features containing data concerning socioeconomics, subsistence, and other current research domains. The work at Finch Farm suggests that indeed these features have been lost in those areas which were employed agriculturally subsequent to their historic inhabitation. However, this research also demonstrates the potential for preserved subsurface remains in the areas surrounding standing historic structures. This study further demonstrates the landscape potential of historic farmsteads, a potential which can be exploited even on those farmsteads which have suffered the scourge of erosion.

In its use of the land, in its placement of structures, in its gardens and orchards, Finch Farm provides eloquent testimony of the influence of progressive farming within the region and of the changes in farmstead ideology witnessed during the late nineteenth century. It suggests that such changes were monumental in scope and further indicates that the progressive ideology was responsible for a transformation within the historic landscape marked by a greater degree of permanency and elaboration within late-nineteenth-century farmsteads. Archaeologists working in the Deep South should recognize the imprint of agricultural reform on late-nineteenth-century farmsteads and should also seek to understand the landscape correlates of progressive farming, as revealed both within the Deep South and in the Mid-Atlantic and New England regions at an earlier point in the nineteenth century.[13] The archaeology of Finch Farm also emphasizes the need for more detailed study of pre-progressive farmsteads, for a greater consideration of that "dull area of yawning gullies and rotting cabins." As we turn our attention away from the substantial plantations of the South Carolina coast and toward the raggle taggle of small cabins dotting the gullied hillsides of the piedmont, we encounter a different agrarian world. Its study will provide us with a greater understanding of the meaning of life in agrarian South Carolina.

NOTES

1. For examples of piedmont farmstead studies from North Carolina and Georgia, see, in particular, Otteson and Riordan 1986; Stine 1989a; Wheaton 1987.
2. Glassie 1975:144.
3. Stine 1989a; Stine 1989b; see also Stine 1992c.
4. Adams 1987.
5. Socioeconomic indexing of nineteenth-century historical ceramics was established by Miller 1980 and Miller 1991.
6. Drucker, Meizner, and Legg 1982.

7. McAlester and McAlester 1984:309.
8. Ames 1986:255.
9. South 1977.
10. Lewis 1976:56.
11. South 1979.
12. For the archaeology of refuse disposal, see South 1977, 1979; Ann Otteson and Timothy Riordan's work (1986) at the Rocky Mountain site; Moir 1982; Jurney, Lebo, and Green 1988; and Drucker, Meizner, and Legg 1982.
13. See, in particular, Grettler 1990 and Grettler 1991.

WORKS CITED

Adams, Jane Helen
1987   *The Transformation of Rural Social Life in Union County, Illinois, in the Twentieth Century.* Ph.D. diss., Dept. of History, Univ. of Illinois, Urbana-Champaign.

Ames, Kenneth
1986   Meaning in Artifacts: Hall Furnishings in Victorian America. In *Common Places, Readings in American Vernacular Architecture,* edited by Dell Upton and John Michael Vlach, pp. 240–60. Univ. of Georgia Press, Athens.

Drucker, Lesley M., Woody C. Meizner, and James B. Legg
1982   *The Bannister Allen Plantation (38Ab102) and Thomas B. Clinkscales Farm (38Ab221): Data Recovery in the Richard B. Russell Multiple Resource Area, Abbeville County, South Carolina.* Russell Papers. Submitted to the National Park Service, Carolina Archaeological Services, Columbia.

Glassie, Henry
1975   *Folk Housing in Middle Virginia; Structural Analysis of Historic Artifacts.* Univ. of Tennessee Press, Knoxville.

Grettler, David J.
1990   *The Landscape of Reform: Society, Environment, and Agricultural Reform in Central Delaware, 1790–1840.* Ph.D. diss., Dept. of History, Univ. of Delaware, Newark.
1991   Farmer Snug and Farmer Slack: The Archaeology of Agricultural Reform in Delaware, 1780–1920. Paper presented at the 1992 Annual Meeting of the Society for Historical Archaeology, Kingston, Jamaica.

Jurney, David H., Susan A. Lebo, and Melissa M. Green
1988   *Historic Farming on the Hogwallow Prairies, Ethnoarchaeological Investigations of the Mountain Creek Area, North Central Texas.* Report submitted to the U.S. Army Corps of Engineers, Fort Worth District. Archaeology Research Program, Southern Methodist Univ., Dallas.

Lewis, Kenneth E.
1976   *Camden: A Frontier Town in 18th Century South Carolina.* Anthropological Studies 2, South Carolina Institute of Archaeology and Anthropology, Columbia.

Miller, George
1980   Classification and Economic Scaling of 19th Century Ceramics. *Historical Archaeology* 14:1–40.
1991   A Revised Set of CC Index Values for Classification and Economic Scaling of English Ceramics from 1787 to 1880. *Historical Archaeology* 25(1):1–25.

McAlester, Virginia, and Lee McAlester
1984   *A Field Guide to American Houses.* Albert A. Knopf, New York.

Moir, Randall W.
1982   Sheet Refuse: An Indicator of Past Lifeways. In *Settlement of the Prairie Margin: Archaeology of the Richland Creek Reservoir, Navarro and Freestone Counties, Texas, 1980–1981: A Research Synopsis,* edited by Mark L. Raab, pp. 139–52. Archaeological Monographs 1. Archaeology Research Laboratory, Southern Methodist Univ., Dallas.

Ottosen, Ann I., and Timothy B. Riordan
1986   *Report on Investigations Phase I Research and Recovery Program for Historic Resources Cultural Resource Effects Mitigation Plan, Rocky Mountain Pumped Storage, Floyd County, Georgia.* Submitted to the Georgia Power Company, Atlanta.

South, Stanley
1977   *Method and Theory in Historical Archaeology.* Academic Press, New York.
1979   Historic Site Content, Structure, and Function. *American Antiquity* 44(2):213–36.

Stine, Linda France
1989b   Twentieth Century Gender Roles: Perceptions from the Farm. Paper presented at the 22nd Annual Chacmool Conference, Calgary, Canada.

1992a   *Revealing Historic Landscapes in Charleston County: Archaeological Inventory, Contexts, and Management.* Submitted to the Charleston County Planning Dept. South Carolina Institute of Archaeology and Anthropology.
1992c   Social Differentiation Down on the Farm. In *Exploring Gender Through Archaeology: Selected Papers from the 1991 Boone Conference,* edited by Cheryl Claassen, pp. 103–9. Monographs in World Archaeology No. 11. Prehistory Press, Madison.

Wheaton, Thomas R., Jr.
1987   *Archaeological and Historical Investigations of the Barrow Farmstead, Fayette County, North Carolina.* Report submitted to Waste Management by Garrow and Associates, Atlanta.

10. "Burning Brick and Making a Large Fortune at It Too": Landscape Archaeology and Lowcountry Brickmaking

Lucy B. Wayne

This study uses the research approach of landscape archaeology to examine and document the role of brickmaking within the Wando River basin of South Carolina during the period between 1740 and 1860. Landscape archaeology is an approach which looks not only at why humans occupy a specific site or region, but also at how they modify the landscape to fit their own cultural patterns and, in turn, how these modifications affect the landscape through time.

The European colonists perceived the New World in terms of commodities.[1] They began almost immediately to catalog and devise ways to exploit the available resources. Because there was a perception that the land was vast and resources limitless, little concern was given to the effects of environmental exploitation. The land was something to be mastered and altered to suit a cultural mind-set.[2]

The process of adaptation was influenced by both environmental and historical factors. The impetus for the development of the brickmaking industry in the lowcountry was proximity to the urban center of Charleston and that city's demand for fireproof construction materials.

Between 1740 and 1860, there were at least 79 brickmakers operating in the Charleston vicinity, almost half of them on the Wando River or its tributaries (map 10.1). Each brickmaker produced thousands of marketable bricks per year, most of which went to the city for construction of houses, churches, commercial buildings, and fortifications. In Christ Church Parish on the Wando River this production represented a third or more of the yearly income of the plantations, surpassing the lowcountry cash crop staple of rice.

The Wando River Basin

The drainage basin extends 20 miles northeast of Charleston through portions of two counties or historic parishes (map 10.1). The 10-mile-wide peninsula between the Wando River and the Atlantic Ocean in Charleston County, known as Wando Neck, was historically Christ Church Parish. Unlike much of the lowcountry, the Wando Neck could not readily support the cash crops of indigo, rice, and cotton. The soils are poorly drained and frequently wet, and the river itself too saline to support rice cultivation, except at the extreme upper reaches of its tributaries. A similar situation exists along the northern and western shorelines in the neighboring parish of St. Thomas and St. Denis in Berkeley County.

This river basin did have assets. The first was

MAP 10.1. Brickyards
identified in the
Wando River
Basin, S.C.

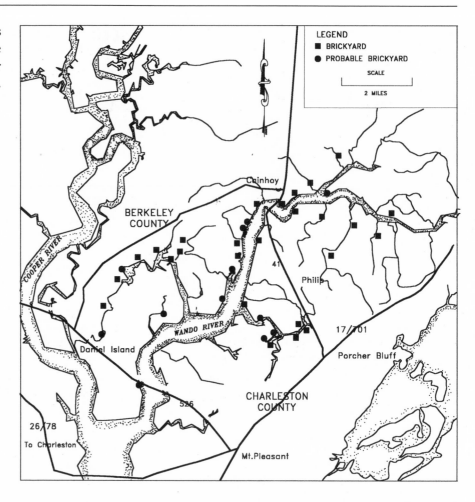

proximity to Charleston and the second was water transportation. This led to development of the region as a production center for the urban market. Area agriculture centered on produce and livestock, supplemented by income from firewood, timber, naval stores, and bricks.[3]

Brickmaking has four basic requirements: suitable clay, sand to temper the clay, fuel to fire the kilns, and labor. The Wando River basin had an abundance of all of these items, with labor provided by plantation slaves. In order to develop beyond the on-site usage level, one more item was required— transportation. The navigable river flowing to Charleston provided market access, which turned brickmaking into a thriving industry in this region.

A property advertisement which appeared in 1747 demonstrates the early recognition of the

attributes present along the Wando River: "To be Sold ... the Plantation where the Subscriber now lives, convenient to a good Landing on Wando River ... also great conveniency for Brick Works, there being excellent Clay close to the Landing with Plenty of Wood at Hand for burning ... William Bruce."[4]

Historical Development

Brickmaking has a long history, dating back to the ancient Middle East where it began with sun-dried bricks.[5] The craft was well developed in the low countries of northern Europe, particularly the Netherlands, by the fifteenth century. From there it was introduced to southeastern England where it was actively adopted because of a lack of local building stone.[6]

Since the largest single group of early European settlers in North America came from this area of England, it is likely that they brought the technique of brickmaking and masonry with them to the New World. Immigrants from the Netherlands and France also contributed to the establishment of the industry; in fact, the principal early period of brick building in the colonies in the late seventeenth century corresponds to the influx of French Huguenot settlers.[7] A large group of these Huguenots settled in the South Carolina lowcountry, particularly in the parish of St. Thomas and St. Denis.

Bricks were made in the lowcountry from the beginning of its settlement, but not on a large scale. By 1682, Thomas Newe's letters from South Carolina stated that "here is excellent Brick made, but little of it."[8] The industry received a major impetus from a series of disastrous fires in Charleston. In 1713, an act of the Assembly required all buildings within the fortified portion of Charleston to be of brick or stone construction. This act was repealed in 1715 as a result of complaints about the scarcity and expense of brick.[9]

Another fire in November 1740 destroyed much of the center of the city and the Assembly again acted, requiring that "all the Outside of all Buildings hereafter to be erected or built in Charles Town to be henceforth made of Brick or Stone, . . . and be covered with Tile, Slate, Stone or Bricks."[10] The act also set the price of bricks for the next ten years at six pounds per thousand for English brick, five pounds per thousand for Carolina brick, and three pounds, ten shillings per thousand for the less desirable (and smaller) New England bricks.[11] This act was probably instrumental in promoting the establishment of thriving brickyards in the region surrounding Charleston.

Evidence of how important these products were to the plantations within the Wando River basin rests in the ledgers and diaries of the antebellum period. Ledgers of Dr. Anthony Toomer, owner of a plantation on Toomer Creek, list numerous sales of cords of wood, turkeys, corn, butter, cabbages, carrots, chickens, eggs, spinach, asparagus, calves, artichokes, peas, rice, hay, ducks, and building materials such as brick, lime, and lumber. Bricks were the second-largest category in terms of income; firewood was the largest.[12] While similar records have not been located for other properties within the study area, their outputs were probably much the same.

Dr. Toomer's shipping records also provide a clue as to the volume of bricks being produced; in a three-year period, he listed shipments of 195,900 bricks to Charleston from a single kiln.[13] The adjacent Lexington plantation to the northwest had a pair of kilns with an associated brickmaking complex (map 10.2). Elm Grove plantation to the east had two brickyards,[14] and similar brickyards are recorded for many of the properties along the Wando and its tributaries.[15]

This manufacturing enterprise was sufficiently valuable to the plantations that, in his post–Revolutionary War claims for losses to the British, Arnoldus Vanderhorst of Lexington included his building "200 feet long by 30 for Sheltering Bricks" valued at 1,000 pounds. This is half the value claimed for his dwelling on the Vanderhorst Kiawah Island cotton plantation.[16]

The importance of this industry is also reflected in plantation settlement patterns, in which slaves, the means of production, were often located in proximity to the kilns rather than to the owner or the agricultural fields (map 10.2).

Brickmaking was often a winter and spring occupation.[17] Resource scheduling complemented the region's truck and grain farming and livestock production. The combination of available resources, a ready market, and a suitable labor force (slaves), led the majority of the plantations in the area to develop brick yards and landings along major streams. As one writer said of the Cooper River brickmaking industry: "The extensive brickmaking on Cooper River was sometimes a very profitable second string to rice. One old lady, said to have been Mrs. Frost, advised by three successive dreams, turned to it as an industry, and like [John] Gordon, made a fortune."[18] This statement applies to the planters along the Wando River.

The plantations of the Wando River basin also

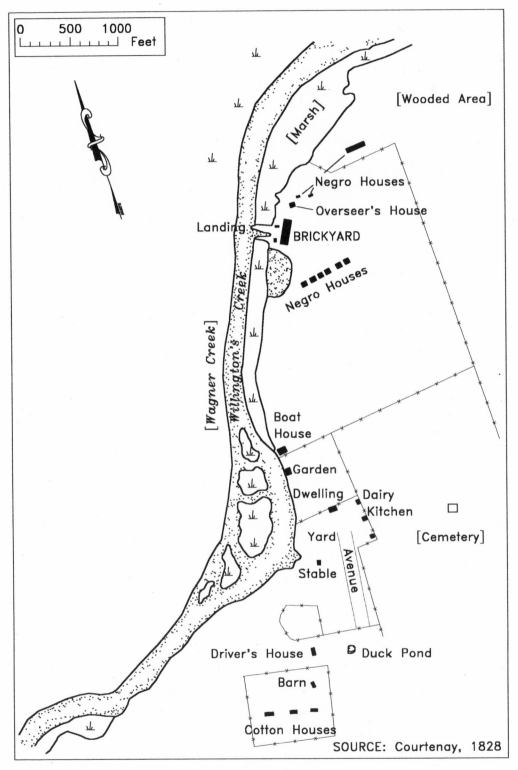

MAP 10.2. Lexington kiln site, Charleston County, S.C.

provided a convenient location for Charleston businessmen who wished to acquire the financial investment and status of planter without much distance between themselves and their major source of income in Charleston. At the same time, proximity to Charleston allowed planters to invest in Charleston businesses which complemented their plantation activities, such as factorages, shipping, and brickmasonry.

An example of this interrelationship can be seen at Lexington Plantation. The Vanderhorsts, primarily planters, also owned wharves and stores in Charleston. The next owner of this property was A. S. Willington, who was primarily a Charleston businessman and newspaper publisher. The third owner, Effingham Wagner, was also involved in Charleston commercial activities. All of these owners of Lexington owned homes in Charleston.[19] Their neighbors were equally involved in Charleston commerce. Anthony Toomer of Richmond Plantation, southeast of Lexington, and the Horlbecks of Boone Hall were brickmasons in Charleston.[20] William Hopton, owner of the property northwest of Lexington, was a merchant and public official.[21]

It is important to note, however, that although the planters and businessmen may have listed themselves as brickmakers, it is highly unlikely that they actually were personally involved in the manual labor of making brick. As Eaton points out, "During the eighteenth century and to a lesser extent in the ante-bellum period, household industries were carried on by slaves, who were employed on the large plantations to weave cloth, to make bricks, staves, and barrels, to manufacture nails, to boil soap, to do blacksmith work, and even to make artistic furniture."[22] Thus, the role of the named "brickmaker" in the lowcountry was essentially that of the supervisor and instructor. Often, the "brickmaker" was, in fact, merely the property owner, and an unnamed overseer actually directed the brickmaking. For example, in 1770, John Moore, identified as a brickmaker in St. Thomas and St. Denis Parish, advertised for an overseer who understood brickmaking.[23]

Little documentary evidence exists for the unnamed slaves and overseers who provided the labor and skill for brickmaking. There is an occasional advertisement such as that for an 1849 slave sale which listed four female slaves as "brick stowers."[24] This same advertisement provides evidence of the importance of this skill in its heading, which lists "Several Brickmakers" as the first skill for those being sold.[25] As a result of this lack of documentary information, discussion of brickmakers necessarily focuses on those property owners who were identified in the written record as practitioners of this trade.

This study identified 79 people as brickmakers in the lowcountry between 1745 and 1830; 38 brickyard locations near Charleston were matched to this list. There were probably others who could not be identified due to gaps in the written record, as well as the nature of that record. Information on eighteenth-century brickmakers was gathered primarily from newspaper advertisements and records of transactions for building materials.[26] The later antebellum information was based largely on map references, city directories, and census records.[27] It is interesting to note that in a male-dominated society several women were listed as brickmakers. At least two, Hannah Goodbe and Mrs. Frost, were actively engaged in providing bricks to the market.[28]

It is rather difficult to estimate the total brick production in the Wando basin prior to 1850. Some idea of scale can be drawn from references to the amounts of brick ordered for specific projects. A single structure, the 1745 Pinckney house in Charleston, required a total of 275,800 bricks ordered from three makers. During this same period, Zachariah Villepontoux provided almost 417,000 bricks for St. Michael's Church.[29] Hollings stated that it had taken about 100,000 bricks for a two-story, 45-foot square house.[30] After the Revolutionary War, Arnoldus Vanderhorst of Lexington Plantation claimed losses of materials for construction of a "3 story brick house in Charleston" at a value of 2,500 pounds, which could represent over 400,000 bricks at the going rate.[31] The many Charleston area fortifications continually required bricks; Villepontoux and Goodbe provided 94,000 between 1757 and 1758, while two other brickmakers provided an additional 68,600 during the same period.[32] Between 1775 and 1776, the Second Council of Safety purchased 40,500 bricks for Dorrels Fort from three different brickmakers.[33]

Based on the available comparative data, it seems likely that a brickmaking complex like that at Lexington Plantation on Wagners Creek could have been producing several hundred thousand bricks each season.[34] This could translate into more than $2,000 per year income for the planter, without the investment in seed or stock required for agricultural activities, or the risks of crop failure or insect damage. As evidenced by the settlement pattern, this brickyard was obviously an important part of the plantation (map 10.2). In addition to two kilns and numerous claypits, the complex included the plantation overseer's house and the only slave cabins within the property, consisting of three groups of dwellings. One of these dwellings was a 200-foot-long, 10-room quarters structure which may have been used for slaves brought in seasonally to make bricks.[35]

Total annual production figures were located for three antebellum brickmakers prior to the 1850 census: Anthony Toomer of Richmond, Peter Gaillard Stoney of Medway, and the Horlbecks of Boone Hall. Toomer's brick production for the three year-period between 1783 and 1785 totalled 195,900 bricks.[36] Stoney's Medway plantation shipped 594,000 bricks in the ten-month period from 1852 to 1853,[37] while the Horlbecks shipped 158,150 bricks during a single week in 1847.[38] In fact, during the ten years between 1850 and 1860, Boone Hall produced over 24 million bricks valued at more than $170,000.[39] Examination of the 1850 census records (table 10.1) shows that the nine brickmakers listed in these two parishes were producing over nine million bricks in 1849 (year of data collection), valued at $64,000. This production relied on a relatively small labor force of 288 slaves.[40]

Stoney's Medway plantation day book for 1852 provides an indication of the level of effort involved in a major brickmaking operation. This book listed

a maximum of 18 hands a day in the brickyard. Usually the record indicated either 6 or 12 hands supporting 1 or 2 molding tables. Maximum production from these 2 tables appears to have been 10,000 bricks per day. Activities listed including molding, stowing the case (kiln), hauling wood, carting clay, and unloading the kiln.[41]

Thus, brickmaking, while labor intensive, could be conducted at a high level of production using a limited number of slaves, probably on a seasonal basis at most brickyards. The value of the end product compared favorably to that of plantation cash crops in the lowcountry. For example, in 1850 rice sold at an average price of 3.4 cents per pound.[42] This places the value of rice production in Christ Church Parish at $32,803 in that year, compared to $34,160 for bricks.[43] In St. Thomas and St. Denis Parish, which produced a greater volume of rice, the value of the rice production in 1850 would have been $119,041, while brick value was estimated at $29,960.[44]

The low level of technology, lack of mechanization, and heavy reliance on manual labor were important factors in the demise of brickmaking in the lowcountry. Brickmaking was conducted by slaves. The Civil War not only brought financial ruin and physical devastation to this region, it ended slave-based labor. Without this cheap labor source and without mechanization, brickmakers could not compete with brickmaking operations using machine molding and continuous kilns. Railroads even supplanted low-cost water transportation. After 1865, brickmaking was essentially abandoned in this region, shifting to the piedmont region of the state with its abundant, high-quality clay resources.

Brickmaking Process

The craft of brickmaking as practiced before the Industrial Revolution began in the fall with digging the clay, which was allowed to weather over the winter.[45] The actual brickmaking generally began in late winter or early spring—a schedule which complemented that of agriculture. As Stoney remarks, planters in the brickmaking areas of the

TABLE 10.1
BRICKMAKERS LISTED IN THE CHARLESTON DISTRICT CENSUS OF 1850

Name	Capital Invested	Raw Materials			Hands Employed		Average Monthly Cost of Labor		Quantities	Value
		Kind	Qty.	Value	Male	Female	Male	Female		
CHRIST CHURCH PARISH										
Daniel Legare	$7,000	pine	70[a]	$135	7	7 (about 2 months)	$7	$5	70,000	$560
John Horlbeck	$75,000	wood	3,500[b]	$5,250	50	35	$50	$75	4,000,000	$28,000
		coal	200[a]	$1,400	—	—	—	—	—	—
T. H. I. White	$17,500	wood	600[a]	$900	13	17	$91	$60	700,000	$5,600
ST. THOMAS & ST. DENIS PARISH					(6 months)					
John Sanders	$28,000	—	—	—	15	15	$105	$75	700,000	$4,900
John L. O'Hear	$20,000	—	—	—	11	11	$77	$55	580,000	$4,060
John Marshall	$45,000	—	—	—	30	20	$210	$100	1,500,000	$10,500
J. B. Gordon	$30,000	—	—	—	15	12	$105	$60	600,000	$4,200
J. Venning	$30,000	—	—	—	13	10	$91	$50	600,000	$4,200
G. Thompson	$10,000	—	—	—	7	—	$49	—	300,000	$2,100
Totals	$262,500				161	127	$785	$480	9,050,000	$64,120

NOTES: [a]Unit of measure: cords. [b]Unit of measure: tons.
SOURCE: U.S. Census 1850.

lowcountry "enjoyed a sound economic mixture of agriculture and industry by making rice while the weather was hot and brick when it was cold."[46]

The weathered clay was mixed with sand and water to the desired consistency.[47] It was then carried to the molding table where the master brickmaker—in the lowcountry a slave—threw a large handful of clay into the sanded wood mold. Excess clay was scraped off and the filled mold was carried to the drying area where the bricks were removed from the mold.[48] A good brickmaker and his three or four helpers could mold as many as 5,000 bricks per day.[49]

After initial drying was completed, the bricks were stacked for further drying in a shed.[50] When sufficient bricks were accumulated, a kiln or clamp was constructed on a previously prepared surface, often consisting of a semipermanent brick floor and outer walls. The clamp was built up to form a series of arched firing chambers running the length of the kiln. The bricks in the kiln were carefully placed to allow space for the heat to pass between them and out the top of the clamp. After stacking, the kiln was sealed on the outside with clay and firing began.[51]

Firing lasted several days depending on the color of the kiln smoke. When the smoke changed from white to black, the kiln was fired for approximately 24 more hours. After firing was completed, the kiln was allowed to cool and was then disassembled.[52] The fired bricks were sorted by quality, based on color and hardness, and shipped to market.[53]

The most detailed contemporary description of an eighteenth-century brickyard is in an advertisement for the 1748 sale of the James and Deborah Fisher property:

> To be Sold, a Plantation on Wando-River, near Cainhoy, containing 500 Acres of Land, proper for Corn, Rice and Indigo, with a Dwelling House, Barn and Out Houses, and at the Landing a Good Brick Yard (with 2 large Houses, near 100 feet in Length, and about 30 in Breadth each) and a good Brick case for burning them. About 45 feet in Length, near 20 in Breadth, and 9 in Height, with 12 arches, and a Division in the Middle, a large quantity of Wood near at Hand, with other conveniences. Likewise a number of slaves, among whom are very good Coopers, several Sawyers and Brick Moulders; and also Household Furniture. . . .[54]

Brickyards and Landscape Archaeology

Landscape archaeology looks at why a site is occupied, how it is modified, and how these modifications affect the landscape. We have already determined why the brickyard sites were selected. Now we will examine the archaeological evidence to see how the landscape was modified to fit the brickmaker's goals and cultural patterns. This evidence of brickmaking consists of the kiln or its remains, clay pits, landings, clay and sand piles, and worker housing. As Noël Hume once pointed out, however, excavation of such sites may yield very few artifacts since they are primarily production sites, not occupation locations.[55]

Only a few brickyards have been documented archaeologically. The most useful information can be obtained from Harrington's Jamestown, Virginia, excavations and those of Atkinson and Elliott at the Nance's Ferry site in Alabama.[56] These excavations clearly indicate that the primary archaeological feature at a brickyard site is the kiln itself. This feature normally contains an unmortared outer wall built on a prepared surface, a series of firing chambers—perhaps with the ash remains of the last firing, and the remains of benches used to support the green bricks. In some cases, kilns may contain poorly fired bricks abandoned by the operators after the last firing.

So far, 26 brickyards have been identified along the Wando and its tributaries; others probably exist but have not been confirmed by field examination (map 10.1). In most cases, the archaeological study at these sites has been limited to survey level data. These surveys have identified brickyards at Parker's Island,[57] Guerin and Old House Creeks in the Francis Marion Forest,[58] Boone Hall,[59] Darrell Creek,[60] Palmetto Grove (or Longpoint),[61] and four brickyards within the Dunes West development.[62] Data recovery has been completed at Palmetto Grove,[63] the Lexington Kiln and Starvegut Hall sites at Dunes West,[64] and Boone Hall.[65] Other lowcountry brickyards have been recorded, but since they are not within the Wando River basin, they will not be addressed in this study.[66]

Although the remains excavated at the Jimmie Green site in Berkeley County, South Carolina, were interpreted as being those of a lime kiln,[67] examination of the plans indicates a strong resemblance to the brick kilns recorded at Jamestown and Nance's Ferry. Since this plantation also contained a documented brickyard, it is probable that this kiln represents reuse of a former brick kiln for lime burning, such as that which South found at Brunswick Town.[68] As the authors themselves note, the kiln's configuration is unlike that of other documented lime-making operations.[69]

The typical brickyard site examined in the Wando River basin consists of a brick rubble-covered shoreline or landing, one or more overgrown kiln mounds—sometimes with visible arches—sand or clay piles, and a series of extensive clay pits.[70] At least one site on Parker's Island contained an intact brick chimney, indicating the possible presence of a more sophisticated Cassel or updraft kiln.[71] Soak pits were tentatively identified at a brickyard site on Toomer Creek.[72]

As stated, 26 brickyard sites have been identified within the Wando River basin (map 10.1). Another dozen probably exist, based on examination of aerial photographs and topographic maps. On the aerial photographs, the primary site indicator is the regular-shaped, clustered wetlands which result from clay extraction. In at least two cases, at Boone Hall and at Nelliefield Creek, these clay pits have become large tidal lakes. A secondary indicator, not present at all sites, is shoreline modifications, particularly those which produced a pier or shoreline projection into the navigable stream.[73]

Identification of brickyard sites on topographic maps and from a boat relies on a similar set of signatures. In both cases, the key indicator is an area where the uplands meet navigable water with little or no intervening marsh. Vegetation in such areas consists of upland species such as palms, oaks, pines, and particularly cedars. At low tide these areas are readily identifiable by the brick rubble along the shore. At least one site also contains timber shoreline stabilization.[74]

Location of sites by land is hampered by relatively thick vegetation and lack of road access in most locations. When a site is encountered, however, there is little doubt about its nature, due to the extensive brick rubble. Presently the kilns appear as mounds up to five or six feet in height and of varying outer dimensions. Close examination of these mounds sometimes reveals arched openings or outer walls. Areas adjacent to the mounds sometimes have flat, brick-covered work surfaces.[75]

Site location seems to be correlated with deep water access, clay or loam soils, and ground which is higher than the marshes. It should be noted, however, that some of the kiln sites are on land which would not normally be considered desirable due to relative elevation. As a result, brickyards probably had networks of drainage ditches, in addition to the brick rubble used as fill. The distribution of brickyard sites appears to stop at the point at which the Wando River was able to support large-scale rice cultivation (map 10.1). This may indicate that where rice was profitable on the Wando, it was not necessary to diversify, although the nearby Cooper River brickyards coexisted with rice plantations.

The occurrence of all of the identified brickyard sites on deep water with shoreline modifications underscores the importance of being able to ship the product to a market. If these kilns had been established to provide bricks solely for the individual plantations, proximity to the planned structures would have been the major criteria, not proximity to water. In addition, these sites are much too large to have been used on a one-time basis. Examination of existing plantation structures or remains of previous structures indicates that the majority were not built of brick, except for the foundations. In fact, many of these foundations consist of broken or waster bricks, further evidence that the best products were sold rather than being used on site.

Historic maps (map 10.2) and surveys of six sites indicate that many brickyard complexes encompassed associated slave and/or overseer housing.[76] At least at Lexington Plantation, the long period of brickyard operation resulted in the encroachment of clay pits on two of these structures.[77] This complex also included the unusual 10-room structure which may have been used for temporary laborers at the brickyard.

The final issue to be considered is the effect of brickmaking on the natural landscape. Change began with clay extraction. The natural forest was cut down and clay and sand were excavated. This extraction resulted in large, steep-sided pits, often many feet in depth. In this low-lying land, the pits soon filled with water, forming lakes or ponds. Over time, natural succession vegetated these water bodies. If there is sufficient connection to a tidal river, the vegetation is typical of natural tidal marshes within the basin. More often, there is little or no connection to the river, and the wetlands support freshwater vegetation.

As brickmaking progressed, additional deforestation probably occurred to provide fuel for the kiln. This deforestation no doubt altered the natural vegetation patterns for long periods of time, although this cannot be documented from literature or from observation of existing sites.

In addition to deforestation, the topography was altered by the deposition of clay and sand piles and the construction of drainage ditches, as well as the kiln itself. These deposits are readily observable at most of the existing brickyard sites in the form of tree-covered mounds.

Once the bricks were made, the land was further changed through deposition of waster bricks and brick rubble as fill or surfacing. At this point, shoreline changes were made to facilitate shipping. These changes may have been limited to deposition of bricks along the natural shoreline, as at Boone Hall and along Darrell Creek, or they may have been more elaborate, including construction of wood, clay, and brick rubble landings, such as those at the Lexington and Toomer kiln sites. All of these shoreline changes affected the natural vegetation and altered the topography. In some cases, channel dredging may have been undertaken to insure continued access to deep water. This was particularly true along the smaller creeks, such as Old House and Fogerty Creeks in Berkeley County.

After the brickyards were abandoned, alterations to the landscape remained as essentially permanent features. Although the kilns may have been leveled by later occupants, the brick surfacing or fill was often a foot or more thick. This deposit was rarely removed in its entirety, nor were the shoreline alterations changed. As Deetz would argue, this cultural landscape provides a statement of cultural identity for those who transformed the environment.[78] The brickmakers saw the land as a resource to be exploited and reshaped for profit. The extent of these alterations defines their level of success in these manufacturing ventures.

Future Research Considerations

The clock is running for a large proportion of the brickyard sites in the South Carolina lowcountry. Growth and development in the Charleston area are increasing. The recently opened Mark Clark Expressway provides access to portions of Berkeley County which have been relatively inaccessible until now. Wando Neck in Charleston County is already experiencing rapid growth.

Although wetlands are the most pervasive feature of brickyard sites they are also the best protected. From an archaeological perspective, the adjacent uplands, which may contain industrial and domestic sites, are the most sensitive and threatened areas. Although I do not advocate broad-scale preservation of brickyards, certain protective steps should be taken.

First, an effort should be made to locate and record brickyards within the basin through an intensive archaeological survey. Second, these sites should be evaluated as a group in terms of significance and eligibility for the National Register of Historic Places. At that point, it may be appropriate to select a sample of the best-preserved sites for excavation in order to: 1) determine the types of kiln and other processes utilized; 2) determine the size of the kiln in order to estimate production volume; 3) identify details of the operation such as type of wood used for firing, and the nature of associated structures; and 4) obtain sufficient and appropriate samples to use for technological analyses of the bricks in order to address questions concerning trade network patterns and brick sources for specific buildings.

The final objective centers on interpretation. Brickmaking was an important and vital industry in the lowcountry. Today it is a little-known industry. It would be appropriate to use a well-preserved brickyard site as an interpretative tool to inform the public about this industry's role in the region, as well as the role of the African Americans who actually produced the thousands of bricks. In addition, Charleston is a major center for historic tourism; the presence of a historic industrial site near the city could provide a source of funding for long-term management of the resource.

Development of an interpretative site would require archaeological study of the site as well as possible reconstruction of the facilities, particularly the kiln. Colonial Williamsburg has very successfully established a demonstration brickyard as one of its interpretative features.[79] Such a living history demonstration is appropriate and could be very effective at a historic brickyard site in the Wando region.

The historical brickyards of the Wando River basin are an excellent example of a regional response to market demand. They reflect the diversity of the southern plantation system and provide strong evidence of close ties between the planters of this region and the nearby city of Charleston. They also provide an example of a culture's adaptive response to the environment and the effects of this adaptation on the landscape itself. They form a regional historical resource which should not be ignored or lost without being recorded, sampled, and selectively preserved.

NOTES

The quotation that forms the title of this essay is derived from a journalist with the Union army, 1864, cited in Perkerson 1952:101.

1. Cronon 1983:166.
2. Cronon 1983:169.
3. Scardaville 1985: 35–42; Wayne 1992:45.
4. *South Carolina Gazette* 1747.
5. Graham and Emery 1945:1.1,547.
6. Trindell 1968:486.
7. Trindell 1968:486.
8. Salley 1911:181.
9. Simons 1934:4,
10. *South Carolina Gazette* 1740.
11. Stoney and Staats n.d.:4.
12. Toomer 1783–85.
13. Toomer 1783–85; Wayne and Dickinson 1989:5-17 to 5-18.
14. Payne 1857.
15. Jones 1844; Diamond 1823.
16. Vanderhorst 1780.
17. Gurcke 1987:5; Graves 1854–55; Stoney 1938:48.
18. Irving 1932:23.
19. Wayne and Dickinson 1990:3-20 to 3-21.
20. Hollings 1978:89, 91.
21. Gregorie 1950:604.
22. Eaton 1966:372.
23. *South Carolina Gazette* 1770.
24. Capers and Huger 1849.
25. Capers and Huger 1849.
26. *South Carolina Gazette* 1741–78; Commissioners of Fortifications 1755–70; Council of Safety 1903:18–23; Hollings 1978; Simons n.d.; Simons 1934; Stoney and Staats n.d.; Hilligan 1790; McElligott 1989; Porcher 1944:160–64; Horlbeck Brothers 1770; Rauschenberg 1991:105, 110; Wayne and Dickinson 1989: 3-27 to 3-29.
27. Irving 1932:23; Huger 1812; Simons n.d.; Simons 1934; Stoney and Staats n.d.; Ravenel 1835; Mears and Turnbull 1859; U.S. Census 1850; Trinkley 1987b:23–28; Wayne and Dickinson 1989:3–27–3–29.
28. Irving 1932:23; Simons n.d.
29. Simons 1934:9.
30. Hollings 1978:12.

31. Vanderhorst 1780.
32. Simons 1934:8; Commissioners of Fortifications 1755–70.
33. Council of Safety Papers 1903:21–23.
34. Wayne and Dickinson 1990:6-10 to 6-11.
35. Wayne and Dickinson 1990:7-18 to 7-19.
36. Toomer 1783–85.
37. Stoney 1852.
38. Espenshade and Grunden 1991:16.
39. Espenshade and Grunden 1991:17.
40. United States Census, 1850.
41. Stoney 1852.
42. Smith 1985:215.
43. United States Census, 1850; Scardaville 1985:37.
44. United States Census, 1850; Scardaville 1985:37.
45. Dobson 1850:97.
46. Stoney 1938:48.
47. Lloyd 1925: 34.
48. Lloyd 1925: 31.
49. Gurcke 1987:19.
50. Gurcke 1987:26.
51. Neve 1726:50; Gurcke 1987:32.
52. Neve 1726:49; Weldon 1990a:24.
53. Hollings 1978:9; Neve 1726:51.
54. *South Carolina Gazette* 1748.
55. Noël Hume 1975:174.
56. Harrington 1950; Atkinson and Elliott 1978.
57. Southerlin, Espenshade, and Brockington 1988.
58. Zierden 1981; Watts 1979.
59. Espenshade and Grunden 1991.
60. Paul Brockington, Jr., President, Brockington and Associates, personal communication 1991.
61. Trinkley 1987.
62. Wayne and Dickinson 1989.
63. Brockington, personal communication 1991.
64. Wayne and Dickinson 1990.
65. Brockington personal communication 1991.
66. See, for example, Herold and Scruggs 1976; Trinkley, Mallin, and Wright 1979; and Bianchi 1974.
67. Wheaton, Reed, and Gantt 1987:113.
68. South 1963:3.
69. Wheaton, Reed, and Gantt 1987:159–63.
70. Wayne 1992:101.
71. Southerlin, Espenshade, and Brockington 1988:28.
72. Wayne 1989.
73. Wayne and Dickinson 1990:8–5; Beard 1990:6.
74. Wayne 1992:106.
75. Wayne 1992:106.
76. Southerlin, Espenshade, and Brockington 1988:28; Espenshade and Grunden 1991:37; Wayne and Dickinson 1989:5–6, 5–8, 5–18.
77. Wayne and Dickinson 1990:8–1.
78. Deetz 1990:2.
79. Weldon 1990a; Weldon 1990b.

Works Cited

Atkinson, James R., and Jack D. Elliott Jr.
1978   *Nance's Ferry: A 19th Century Brick and Lime Making Site.* Dept. of Anthropology, Mississippi State Univ., Starkville.

Beard, David V.
1990   Reconnaissance Survey Report: Underwater Archaeological Investigations of the Lexington Plantation Kiln Site Causeway in Wagner Creek, Charleston County, South Carolina. Ms. on file, South Carolina Coastal Council, Charleston.

Bianchi, Travis L.
1974   *Archaeological Investigations of South Carolina Highway Department's Proposed Connector from Port Royal to Ladies Island.* Research Manuscript Series 59. South Carolina Institute of Archaeology and Anthropology, Univ. of South Carolina, Columbia.

Capers and Huger
1849   List of 72 Rice Field Negroes. William Ravenel Papers, South Carolina Historical Society, Charleston.

Commissioners of Fortifications
1755   Journal of the Commissioners of Fortifications.
–70   Cited in research notes of Harriet Stoney Simons. Ms. on file, South Carolina Historical Society, Charleston.

Council of Safety
1903   Papers of the Second Council of Safety of the Revolutionary Party in South Carolina, November 1775–March 1776. *South Carolina Historical and Genealogical Magazine* 4(1):13–25.

Courtenay, James
1828   Lexington, the Property of A. S. Willington, Esq. McCrady Plat Map Collection no. 6137. Charles-

ton County Register of Mesne Conveyance, Charleston.

Cronon, William
1983   *Changes in the Land: Indians, Colonists, and the Ecology of New England.* Hill and Wang, New York.

Deetz, James
1990   Prologue: Landscapes as Cultural Statements. In *Earth Patterns: Essays in Landscape Archaeology,* edited by William M. Kelso and Rachel Most, pp. 1–4. Univ. Press of Virginia, Charlottesville.

Diamond, John
1823   The Plat of 500 Acres of High Land in St. Thomas Parish, Formerly Called Addison's Ferry. McCrady Plat Map Collection no. 4353. Charleston County Register of Mesne Conveyance, Charleston, South Carolina.

Dobson, Edward
1850   A Rudimentary Treatise on the Manufacture of Bricks and Tiles; Containing an Outline of the Principles of Brickmaking, and Detailed Accounts of the Various Processes Employed in the Making of Bricks and Tiles in Different Parts of England. 1971 reprint edited by Francis Celoria. *Journal of Ceramic History* 5.

Eaton, Clement
1966   *A History of the Old South.* The MacMillan Company, New York.

Espenshade, Christopher T., and Ramona Grunden
1991   *Archaeological Survey of the Brickyard Plantation Tract, Charleston County, South Carolina.* Brockington and Associates, Inc., Atlanta, Georgia.

Graham, Frank D., and Thomas J. Emery
1945   *Audel's Masons and Builders Guide #1.* Theo. Audel, New York.

Graves, Charles
1854   Plantation Diary. Planter, Prince William
–55   Parish, Granville County, South Carolina. Ms. on file, South Carolina Historical Society, Charleston.

Gregorie, Anne King (editor)
1950   *Records of the Court of Chancery of South Carolina, 1671–1729.* The American Historical Association, Washington, D.C.

Gurcke, Karl
1987   *Bricks and Brickmaking.* Univ. of Idaho Press, Moscow.

Harrington, J. C.
1950   Seventeenth Century Brickmaking and Tilemaking at Jamestown, Virginia. *The Virginia Magazine of History and Biography* 58(1):16–39.

Herold, Elaine B., and Kay R. Scruggs
1976   *An Archaeological and Historical Survey of the Grove and Flagg Plantations.* The Charleston Museum, Charleston, South Carolina.

Hilligan, Jacob C.
1790   *The Charleston Directory and Revenue System.* T. B. Bowen, Charleston, South Carolina.

Hollings, Marie F.
1978   *Brickwork of Charleston to 1780.* Master's thesis, Dept. of History, Univ. of South Carolina, Columbia.

Horlbeck Brothers
1770   Papers. Cited in Research Notes of Harriet Stoney Simons. Collections of the South Carolina Historical Society, Charleston.

Huger, Sarah E.
1812   Letter to Mrs. Daniel Horry. Pinckney-Lowndes Papers, South Carolina Historical Society, Charleston.

Irving, John B., M.D.
1932   *A Day on the Cooper River.* 1969 reprint, R. L. Bryn Co., Columbia, South Carolina.

Jones, Thomas
1844   Survey map of Parkers Island. Microfilm on file, South Carolina Department of Archives and History, Columbia.

Lloyd, Nathaniel
1925   *A History of English Brickwork.* H. Greville Montgomery, London, England.

McElligott, Carroll Ainsworth
1989   *Charleston Residents 1782–1794.* Heritage Books, Bowie, Maryland.

Mears and Turnbull (compilers)
1859   *The Charleston Directory.* Walker Evans and Co., Charleston, South Carolina.

Neve, Richard
1726   *The City and County Purchaser's and Builder's Dictionary: or the Complete Builder's Guide.* 1969 reprint, Augustus M. Kelley, Publishers, New York.

Noël Hume, Ivor
1975   *Historical Archaeology.* W. W. Norton and Co., New York.

Payne, Robert
1857   Plan of a Part of Elm Grove Plantation Situate on the South Side of Wando River, Christ Church Parish. Deed Book A, Page 145, Charleston County Records of Mesne Conveyance, Charleston, South Carolina.

Perkerson, Medora Field
1952   *White Columns of Georgia.* Rinehart, New York.

Porcher, Anne Allston (editor)
1944   Minutes of the Vestry of St. Stephen's Parish, South Carolina. *The South Carolina Historical and Genealogical Magazine* 45:157–72.

Rauschenberg, Bradford L.
1991   Brick and Tile Manufacturing in the South Carolina Low Country, 1750–1800. *Journal of Southern Decorative Arts* 17(2):103–13.

Ravenel, Edmund
1835   Notes Relating to the Purchase of Grove Plantation in St. Thomas's from Col. John Gordon, Feb. 1835. William Ravenel Papers, South Carolina Historical Society, Charleston.

Salley, A. S., Jr.
1911   Letters of Thomas Newe, 1682. *Narratives of Early Carolina.* C. Scribner's Sons, New York.

Scardaville, Michael
1985   Historical Background. In *Rural Settlement in the Charleston Bay Area: Eighteenth and Nineteenth Century Sites in the Mark Clark Expressway Corridor,* Paul Brockington, Michael Scardaville, Patrick H. Garrow, David Singer, Linda France, and Cheryl Holt, pp. 24–78. Submitted to the South Carolina Dept. of Highways and Public Transportation by Garrow and Associates, Atlanta, Georgia.

Simons, Harriett Stoney
n.d.   Research notes. Ms. on file, South Carolina Historical Society, Charleston.
1934   Brick in Provincial South Carolina, with Particular Reference to the Period 1740–1750. Ms. on file, South Carolina Historical Society, Charleston.

Smith, Julia Floyd
1985   *Slavery and Rice Culture in Low Country Georgia, 1750–1860.* Univ. of Tennessee Press, Knoxville.

South Carolina Gazette
1740   Notice. Act of Assembly. On file Charleston County Library, Charleston, South Carolina.
1747   Advertisement for sale of lands. Property of William Bruce, Mar. 2, 1747. On file Charleston County Library, Charleston.
1748   Advertisement for sale of lands. Property of Deborah Fisher, Nov. 21, 1748. On file Charleston County Library, Charleston.
1770   Advertisement for overseer. John Moore, Aug. 14, 1770. On file, Charleston County Library, Charleston.

South, Stanley
1963   Exploratory Excavation of a Brick Kiln at Town Creek, Brunswick County, N.C. Ms. on file, North Carolina State Dept. of Archives and History, Raleigh.

Southerlin, B. G., Christopher T. Espenshade, and Paul E. Brockington Jr.
1988   *Archaeological Survey of Parker Island, Charleston County, South Carolina.* Report on file, Brockington and Associates, Atlanta.

Stoney, John
1852   Overseer's Day Book for Medway Plantation, Berkeley County. Stoney Family Papers, South Carolina Historical Society, Charleston.

Stoney, Samuel Gaillard
1938   *Plantations of the Carolina Low Country.* Carolina Art Association, Charleston, South Carolina.

Stoney, Samuel Gaillard, and Henry P. Staats
n.d.   Comments on Old Charleston Brickwork. Ms. Submitted to Historic Charleston Foundation and the Southern Brick and Tile Manufacturers Association. Ms. on file, Historic Charleston Foundation, Charleston, South Carolina.

Toomer, Anthony
1783   Plantation Accounts of Anthony Toomer, Esq.
–85   Vanderhorst Collections, South Carolina Historical Society, Charleston.

Trindell, Roger T.
1968   Building in Brick in Early America. *The Geographical Review* 58(3):484–87.

Trinkley, Michael
1987   *An Archaeological Survey of Longpoint Development: Charleston County, South Carolina: Palmetto Grove Plantation.* Chicora Foundation Research Series 8. Columbia, South Carolina.

Trinkley, Michael, Elizabeth F. Mallin, and Newell O. Wright
1979   *Archaeological Investigations of Brickyard Landing, Colleton County, S.C.* South Carolina Dept. of Highways and Public Transportation, Columbia.

United States Census

1850   Products of Industry in the County of Charleston. Census of Manufactures Schedule 5. Microfilm on file, South Carolina Archives, Columbia.

Vanderhorst, Arnoldus

1780   Losses of Arnoldus Vanderhorst by the British. Vanderhorst Collections, South Carolina Historical Society, Charleston.

Watts, J.

1979   Site survey records, Francis Marion National Forest. Forms on file, U.S. Dept. of Agriculture, Forest Service, McClellanville, South Carolina.

Wayne, Lucy B.

1989   Field notes, archaeological survey, Dunes West, Charleston County, South Carolina. Ms. on file, SouthArc, Gainesville, Florida.

1992   *Burning Brick: A Study of a Lowcountry Industry.* Ph.D. diss., College of Architecture, Univ. of Florida, Gainesville.

Wayne, Lucy B., and Martin F. Dickinson

1989   *Archaeological Survey, Dunes West Development, Charleston County South Carolina.* Submitted to Dunes West Development, Mount Pleasant, South Carolina by Environmental Services and Permitting, Inc., Gainesville, Florida.

1990   *Four Men's Ramble: Archaeology in the Wando Neck, Charleston County, South Carolina.* Submitted to Dunes West Development Corporation, Mount Pleasant, South Carolina, by SouthArc, Inc., Gainesville, Florida.

Weldon, Bill

1990a   The Brickmaker's Year. *The Colonial Williamsburg Historic Trades Annual* 2:1–40.

1990b   The Arts and Mysteries of the Colonial Brickmaker. *Colonial Williamsburg, The Journal of the Colonial Williamsburg Foundation* 12(4): 7–15.

Wheaton, Thomas R., Jr., Mary Beth Reed, and Mary Elizabeth Gantt

1987   *The Jimmie Green Lime Kiln Site, Berkeley County, South Carolina.* Submitted to the South Carolina Dept. of Highways and Public Transportation, Columbia by Garrow and Associates, Atlanta.

Zierden, Martha

1981   Preliminary Management Report: Archaeological Survey of Compartment 117, Francis Marion National Forest. Ms. on file, U.S. Dept. of Agriculture, Forest Service, Columbia, South Carolina.

11. Iron Plantations and the Eighteenth- and Nineteenth-Century Landscape of the Northwestern South Carolina Piedmont

Terry A. Ferguson and Thomas A. Cowan

This chapter will outline our current understanding of the landscape of the piedmont South Carolina iron industry in the eighteenth and nineteenth centuries.[1] Particular attention will be paid to four of the most successful plantation-based iron-manufacturing complexes: William Hill's Ironworks, the Kings Mountain Company, the South Carolina Manufacturing Company, and the Nesbitt Manufacturing

Company (map 11.1). These industrial complexes illustrate the relationship of the charcoal iron industry to the natural environment and to the social and economic contexts of the piedmont region of South Carolina. The major goals of this essay are to briefly summarize and synthesize what is currently known about early iron production in South Carolina and to more precisely define the context, scale, and direction of future research into the archaeological record of the iron industry.

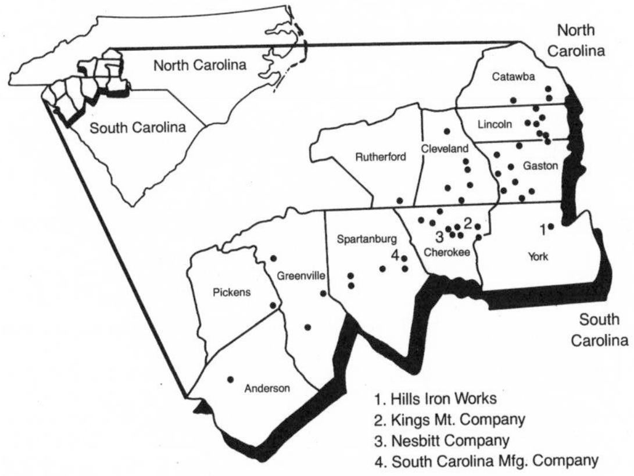

The Natural Environmental Situation of the Carolina Piedmont

The iron industry developed in the northwestern piedmont of South Carolina and adjacent south-central North Carolina (see map 11.1) in the late eighteenth and early nineteenth centuries because this region contained five resources essential for iron production. In decreasing order of importance, these were as follows: iron ore, extensive hardwood forests, fast-flowing streams and rivers with numerous rapids and waterfalls, marble (metamorphosed limestone), and metamorphic crystalline rocks suitable for use as building stone.

MAP 11.1. Documented iron-manufacturing sites in the piedmont of North Carolina and South Carolina. *Courtesy of Olencki Graphics.*

1. *Iron ore*—The presence of iron ore in the region is of obvious importance. Three principal varieties of iron: magnetite, hematite, and limonite, occur within the northeast to southwest trending crystalline rocks of the Inner Piedmont, King's Mountain, and Charlotte belts of the region. These ores were intensively exploited by eighteenth- and nineteenth-century ironworks.[2]

2. *Hardwood forests*—Abundant forests of predominately hardwoods present in the region in the late eighteenth and early nineteenth centuries supplied charcoal for use as the principal fuel supply. The species composition of the regional forests can be seen in a description of Hill's Ironworks in York County: "The high lands in general produce oak, pine, hickory, and some chestnut; the low lands generally mulberry, swamp oak, walnut, sycamore, &c. &c.; ..."[3]

3. *Rapids and waterfalls*—Numerous rapids and waterfalls throughout the upper piedmont of South Carolina provided locations at which the power of falling water could be harnessed and used during the iron-manufacturing process. Before the introduction of steam power in the 1850s water was the principal source of power for all phases of the iron-manufacturing process. Dams and sluiceways were constructed to control the water power needed to turn large waterwheels, which in turn supplied power to various pieces of iron-production equipment such as bellows and hammers. The bellows were quite large and blew air into the base of the furnace to increase the rate of combustion so that the iron ore and limestone would get hot enough to melt. The use of these bellows led to the term "blast furnace." Some of the furnaces in South Carolina, such as one at Hill's ironworks, did not use bellows but harnessed water power through the use of a water blast or trompe.[4]

4. *Marble*—Marble, or metamorphosed limestone, was important as a fluxing agent, a key ingredient that, when melted along with the iron ore, created a chemical reaction in which unwanted impurities were removed from the iron. Lenticular deposits of marble trend northeast to southwest and are restricted to the King's Mountain Belt.[5]

5. *Crystalline rocks*—Finally, local crystalline rocks suitable for use as building stone were necessary for construction of furnaces, forges, and factory buildings. Like the iron ore these metamorphic crystalline rocks occur within the Inner Piedmont, King's Mountain, and Charlotte belts of the region. The character of the rocks selected for use as hearthstones was of particular importance. This can be seen in reference to the stones used at Hill's ironworks:

Formerly the hearth stones were procured 25 miles distance from the works; they were of a yellow colour, hard quality, and flood the fire well. The longest blast ever yet made was 8 months, then blowed out from causes not owing to failure of the stones. The stones now in use were lately discovered; within one mile of the works there is a large bed of them; there are yellow mixed with red, of a coarse grit, resembling a coarse grindstone; they dress easy; how long they will stand cannot be told, but they promise well. The inwalls are made of the same kind of stone last mentioned ... April 29, 1795, by information of Mr. Hill, the foregoing remarks may be corrected, viz. The hearth stones which at the time had not been proved, have since been sufficiently tried, and prove very good.[6]

The Development of the Northwestern South Carolina Iron Industry: Late Eighteenth and Early Nineteenth Century

A general understanding of the historical development of the iron industry, particularly its social and economic aspects, is a prerequisite for understanding how iron manufacturing relates to the landscape. Accordingly, this and the following two sections will attempt to summarize three distinct periods of iron manufacturing in the piedmont of

South Carolina. This section will trace the development of the South Carolina iron industry from its origin in the mid-1770s to the mid-1820s.

Most studies of late colonial and antebellum South Carolina have focused on agriculture and the textile industry. The early charcoal iron industry, an important part of the economic development of South Carolina, has received very little attention, probably due to the iron industry's development in a restricted part of the state. Also, industrialization of the South has been viewed as a primarily post-reconstruction phenomenon, and the charcoal iron industry did not survive the reconstruction era.

South Carolina's attempts to develop an iron industry in the piedmont during the late 1700s and the first half of the 1800s were significant in that they represented the coming of the Industrial Revolution to the South. In his comprehensive study of the southern charcoal iron industry, Smith suggests that "[t]he early iron industry played an important role in rural and urban development . . . it supplied agriculture with necessary tools and implements, provided materials for the military, and contributed to the growth of a modern urban industrial society."[7]

Successful iron manufacturing began in the colonies as early as the 1640s in eastern Massachusetts. By the beginning of the eighteenth century it had spread to Pennsylvania and Virginia, and by the mid-eighteenth century the expanding industry began to pose a threat to producers of finished iron products in England and Wales.[8] In 1750 Parliament passed the Iron Act, allowing for the continuation of production of pig and bar iron, but prohibiting manufacture of finished products. Many colonials, however, ignored the Iron Act. In many cases colonial officials had no means of enforcement since early ironworks were commonly located in isolated areas far from provincial cities, making it difficult to monitor and control them.

It is possible that the Iron Act of 1750 deterred South Carolinians interested in developing iron industry until relations with Great Britain began to erode in the early 1770s. In February 1752, South Carolina Governor James Glen wrote to his superiors in England that "there never were ironworks of any sort in this Province, neither of Pig of Bar Iron nor any Mill, Engine, Forge or Furnace whatsoever and if any such should be erected I shall cause the same to be abated."[9] By the beginning of the American Revolution at least 82 furnaces and 175 forges were in operation in the colonies of Connecticut, Pennsylvania, Maryland, Massachusetts, New Jersey, New York, North Carolina, Rhode Island, and Virginia. In comparison, in 1788 there were about 77 furnaces in all of England and Wales. Average yearly output of both the colonial and English companies varied between 150 and 300 tons.[10]

The first sizable populations of Europeans to settle in the Carolina piedmont were primarily immigrants of Scotch-Irish and German descent who moved into the area from the North, particularly Pennsylvania, Virginia, and North Carolina, beginning in the mid-1750s.[11] It was not until the mid-1770s that the development of any iron manufacturing began.

As positive colonial sentiment toward Great Britain declined in 1774 and 1775, colonial assemblies began to pass legislation encouraging the manufacture of pig and bar iron. This government support appears to have been primarily in response to rising tensions between the colonial government and Great Britain. In 1775 members of the South Carolina Provincial Congress felt it desirable to encourage industries beneficial to a war effort. On November 28, 1775, the Provincial Congress issued a proclamation: "Resolved, That a premium of one thousand Pounds currency be given to the person who shall erect a Bloomery in this Colony, that shall first produce manufactured thereat, one ton of good Bar Iron; a premium of eight hundred Pounds to the person erecting another bloomery . . . and a premium of seven hundred Pounds to the person erecting a third such work. . . . These premiums over and above the common prices of such iron."[12] The Provincial Congress also passed resolutions for the production of bar steel and nail rods. Legislation similar to that of South Carolina was enacted during 1775 and 1776 by Maryland, North Carolina, Pennsylvania, and Virginia.[13]

Individual interest in developing ironworks probably influenced the government's role in supporting the initial development of an iron industry in South Carolina between 1775 and 1780. The South Carolina Assembly concluded that the best way to encourage iron manufacture was through loans to individual entrepreneurs desiring to establish ironworks.

In the summer of 1775, William Henry Drayton, William Tennent, and Oliver Hart made a "mission" to the backcountry of South Carolina to win settlers to the Whig cause. On August 20, 1775, Tennent wrote a letter to the Council of Safety in Charleston reporting on the progress of the trip. He noted that "Mr. Drayton is gone up to his ironworks and to the people about Lawson's Fork where he will do something."[14]

Apparently William Henry Drayton was considering development of an ironworks. Furthermore, Drayton had obtained a grant on July 21, 1775, for 500 acres of land in the Ninety-Six District on a branch of Lawson's Fork called Brown's Branch. Drayton's 500 acres were bounded on the north by the land of William Wofford. Drayton was apparently never able to develop an ironworks, and died by 1780, but by 1776 either Joseph Buffington or William Wofford had begun to develop an iron furnace on his property along Lawson's Fork Creek. From the middle to the late 1770s the South Carolina Assembly lent £6,382 to John Buffington "for the Ironworks," and £4,148 to William Wofford for the same activity. With these loans either Buffington or Wofford developed an ironworks during the 1770s on Lawson's Fork Creek, in present-day Spartanburg County.[15]

On March 6, 1776, the South Carolina Assembly loaned William Hill of the Ninety-Six District £1,000 for development of an ironworks on Allison's Creek, a branch of the Catawba River in present-day York County. The next day a committee was assigned to "consider and report the most proper places for erecting an ironworks in this Colony, and what encouragement from the public, in their opinion, may be most effectual to promote the establishment of such works, and the manufactur-

ing of Iron."[16] Between May and August of l777 the South Carolina Assembly lent at least an addition £7,000 to William Hill "to erect an ironwork." In August of l777 the commissioners of the state treasury agreed to give William Hill 10 years before he had to repay his loan.[17]

State loans for iron manufacture ceased with the end of the Revolution. Government support was replaced by private investment on the part of wealthy merchants and planters. Financial gain thus became the impetus for continued investment in ironworks. The combined need for skills and capital in iron-manufacturing operations in South Carolina led to a pattern of partnerships. For example, in March of l778 William Hill entered a partnership with Isaac Hayne, in which Hill was responsible for the construction of the furnace, the forge, and the necessary buildings. Hill was also to act as the manager, hire an overseer, a clerk, and the skilled artisans or "taskable fellows," as well as provide the ore and timber. Hayne, in turn, was to supply 40 slaves. Both partners were to share the cost of maintaining the labor force and operating a farm to furnish food for the laborers. Four of the seven eighteenth-century ironworks reported by John Drayton in 1802 were based on similar partnerships. In most cases one of the developers or investors was a wealthy planter or merchant.[18]

At least eight ironworks were established in the piedmont of South Carolina between 1775 and 1802, within the boundaries of the present-day counties of Anderson, Greenville, Pickens, Spartanburg, and York. These included William Hill's works on Allison's Creek in the York District; William Wofford's and Joseph Buffington's on Lawson's Fork Creek, along with those of William Hill's sons, Solimon and William Hill, on the Tyger River in Spartanburg District; those of Henry and Joshua Benson on the Reedy River; Adam Carruth and Lemuel J. Alston on the Saluda River; and Elias Earle on the north fork of the Saluda River in Greenville District; and those of Jesse Murphy on George's Creek and Robert Tate on Twenty-Six Mile Creek in Pendleton District.[19]

Most of the ironworks established in the late

1700s and early 1800s appear to have been of a type which Douglas defines as isolated country furnace and/or forge. These ironworks had limited production schedules and output, developed in relatively isolated rural areas, and primarily served local markets.[20]

Another type of ironworks defined by Douglas was the iron plantation that produced and sold a surplus of iron and ironware to distant markets, generally reached by nearby water transportation.[21] The only late-eighteenth- to early-nineteenth-century ironworks in South Carolina that is currently known to fit this second type was Hill's Ironworks, which operated from 1778 to around 1810 within present-day York County. This is currently the largest and best documented ironworks of the late eighteenth century in South Carolina.

William Hill's Iron Plantation

Construction of Hill's Ironworks (maps 11.2 and 11.3) was completed by November of 1779,[22] when Isaac Hayne advertised in Charleston *Gazette of the State of South Carolina,* that the Aera Furnace, "the first and only one ever erected in the State of South Carolina, . . . is now in blast. . . . Salt Pans, Pots of all sizes, Kettles . . . Skellets, Dutch Ovens . . . Stoves . . . and 2, 3, or 4 Pounders with Balls to suit . . . or any other castings in Iron, . . . may be had by Wholesale or retail."[23] Drayton indicates that Hill's Ironworks also produced cannon and "articles . . . which the daily wants of the inhabitants, of that part of the state require, . . . consisting of, chimney backs, gudgeons, cranks, pots, kettles, skillets, hammers for forges, and boxes for cart and wagon wheels; and other castings for machinery."[24]

Charleston in 1784 was an important market for the iron goods produced at Hill's Ironworks. For example, Daniel Bourdeaux advertised in the *City Gazette and Daily Advertiser* that his store at 48 Bay Street offered such items as bar iron, anvils, and assorted nails.[25] In August of 1789, Bourdeaux placed the following advertisement, "A Compleat set of Machinery Iron for a wind saw mill, weighing about two tons, cast at the Area Foundary, by particular order, but arriving too late for the purpose of the person who ordered it, is now for sale at Mr. Lamotte's wharf, and may be informed of the price, by applying to Daniel Bourdeaux."[26] Charles Graves of Charleston ran an advertisement in June of 1800 in the *City Gazette and Daily Advertiser* for "20 Neat Chimney Backs and a few sets of cast iron ginboxes, from the Aera and Aetna Iron Works."[27]

Hill not only distributed his goods locally and in Charleston but also at other locations along the fall line in South Carolina and Georgia. Some of the individuals and localities marketing Hill's products

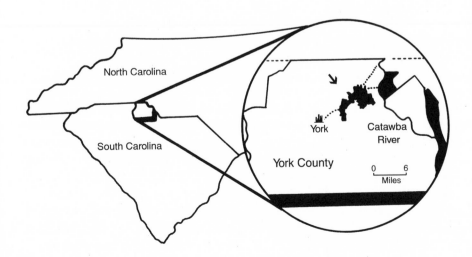

MAP 11.2. Location of Hills Ironworks within South Carolina and York County. *Courtesy of Olencki Graphics.*

MAP 11.3. Detail of the landholdings of Hills Ironworks showing location and associa-tion of natural and cultural features. *Courtesy of Olencki Graphics.*

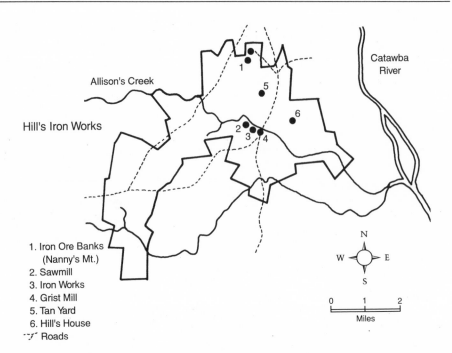

Allison's Creek

Catawba River

Hill's Iron Works

1. Iron Ore Banks
   (Nanny's Mt.)
2. Sawmill
3. Iron Works
4. Grist Mill
5. Tan Yard
6. Hill's House
-⁀- Roads

N
W — E
S

0   1   2
Miles

in 1806 were Isaac Hayne in Charleston, John Schultz & Co. in Columbia, Willie Vaugh in Camden, and Thomas Barret in Augusta.[28]

During the Revolutionary War, Hill received at least £20,000 from the state for the production of war materials. These war materials included such articles as "One hundred and Six tons Castings of Cannon Balls, Shells, Camp Kettles, and Other Utensils for the army."[29]

Although Hill was successful in establishing and operating his ironworks with Hayne's financial backing, and disbursements from the state between 1775 and 1780, he encountered several problems in 1780 and 1781. In June of 1780 the British sent a detachment of soldiers to burn Hill's works and confiscate almost 90 slave laborers. In August of 1781 Hill's partner, Isaac Hayne, was convicted for breaking parole and hung by a British military court in Charleston.[30]

Hill was not able to rebuild the works until 1786, when Daniel Bourdeaux, Joseph Atkinson, and Pierce Butler advanced Hill £4,105, each receiving one-quarter interest in the ironworks. Bourdeaux was a merchant and planter who lived in Charleston and was co-owner of at least three

trading vessels, five slave ships, and several sawmills in the lower piedmont. The new investors were also involved in backcountry land speculation. In 1779 Bourdeaux joined Joseph Atkinson and Pierce Butler in the speculative firm of Joseph Atkinson and Company. The three partners were probably still together in 1786 when they advanced William Hill £4,000.[31]

From the mid-1780s to the mid-1790s, Hill's Ironworks appears to have prospered. The Aera furnace at the works was rebuilt in 1787. Another furnace, the Aetna furnace, was built in 1788. In 1793 Hill and his partners purchased additional ironworks, Washington Furnace, Lincolnton Forge, and various tracts of land in North Carolina approximately 20 miles northwest of Hill's Iron-works. These structures had been originally con-structed by John Sloan between 1786 and 1788.[32]

Hill also prospered during this time. For example, in March 1785 William Hill was appointed one of several justices of the peace for the York District, and in 1789 he was appointed commis-sioner for the inspection and exportation of tobacco near the Catawba River. In 1786 the general assembly had passed an ordinance directing the establishment of a tobacco inspection warehouse at or near Hill's Ironworks on Allison's Creek.[33]

Hill also became vitally interested in water transportation. Even though his ironworks on Allison's Creek were only two miles from the Catawba River, the nearest navigable point on the Catawba was the town of Camden, some 70 miles away. It required the hiring of six days of labor to transport products there. Thus, Hill became a charter member of the Santee Canal Company in 1786 and then the Catawba and Wateree Company in 1787. Furthermore, he was appointed commissioner to contract for and superintend the opening of the Broad and Pacolet Rivers in 1801, and commissioner to superintend and contract for the opening of the navigation of the Broad River in 1805.[34]

Hill's Ironworks suffered several major financial setbacks in the mid-1790s. In 1791, Hill began a long series of exchanges with state treasury officials, the general assembly, and at least two South Carolina governors, including William Moultrie and Charles Pinckney, over his failure to repay his 1777 loan and the mortgage that the state held as collateral. Hill argued that he should be exonerated from the whole of his debt for several reasons, including depreciation of the loan's original value, the burning of the works, execution of his original partner during the war, and contributions to supplying the war effort. When these appeals failed, he sought alternative means to settle his accounts by supplying the state arsenal with arms. In 1793 the works lost the backing of Bourdeaux and Butler when the two had to relinquish 100,000 acres of piedmont land that they had purchased for speculation. Bourdeaux also experienced other business failures and defaulted on several debts.[35]

In June of 1796 William Edward Hayne, a merchant of Charleston and the youngest son of Hill's first partner, advanced £5,000 to Hill that he had collected from 25 wealthy Charleston backers, at least five of whom were merchants and several other state legislators. Hayne built a house near the works and in 1798 entered into a partnership with Hill. The terms of this partnership indicated that Hill was to supervise, conduct, and manage the works while Hayne was to control all monies and attend to record keeping.[36]

Hill and Hayne kept the ironworks in operation until around 1810 when operations apparently ended. During this time Hill continued to unsuccessfully pursue resolution of his debt with the state. When Hill died in 1816 he left a total estate of 5,000 acres, 20 slaves, and other assets valued at $5,910.[37]

One of the primary reasons for the ironworks closing may have been recognized by Robert Mills as early as 1826: "Hill's works were in operation about 30 years, but the ore was not considered productive enough, and the work was discontinued."[38] Geologist Oscar Lieber suggested that the works ceased because of "an inferiority of the iron as bloom iron, occasioned by the same hardness which rendered it particularly suitable for certain castings, a greatly decreased quantity of timber for fuel in the neighborhood, and the expense of transportation."[39]

Other Eighteenth- and Early-Nineteenth-Century Ironworks

As indicated above, several contemporaries of Hill had similar ironworks that were in operation from the late eighteenth through the early nineteenth century within the boundaries of present-day Spartanburg and Cherokee Counties.[40] The owners and operators of two of these ironworks, Adam Carruth and Elias Earle, had gun factories in addition to their ironworks. For example, in 1816 Earle secured a federal government contract for 10,000 stands of arms, at a rate of $15 per stand, which he was to deliver within five years. Due to his re-election to Congress, Earle was unable to fulfill his contract obligations. Carruth expanded his ironworks, begun in 1801, into a large armory during the War of 1812, and thus was able to assume responsibility for the contract in 1816. Unfortunately, Earle had owed the federal government over $12,000, which was imposed on Carruth as a condition of the contract. Carruth experienced additional financial difficulties when federal inspections were delayed and a $20,000 backlog of arms accumulated. These additional difficulties forced Carruth to petition and obtain $10,000 from the South Carolina General Assembly.[41]

Carruth continued to have problems with the Ordnance Department, but was able to obtain three indulgences from the state general assembly. In 1822, not long after he was able to postpone payment of his debt to the state for the third time, his other creditors brought suit and forced him into bankruptcy.[42]

Another of Earle's iron-related activities is of particular note. Between 1807 and 1815, through personal explorations and negotiations with the United States Government and the Cherokee Nation, he attempted to establish an ironworks on Cherokee lands. The following is a summary of his activities:

> In the early part of the year 1807, Col. Elias Earle, of South Carolina, proposed to the Secretary of War the establishment of iron works, with suitable shops, in the Cherokee Nation, on substantially the following conditions, viz.: That a suitable place should be looked out and selected where sufficient quantities of good iron ore could be found, in the vicinity of proper water privileges, for such an establishment; that the Indians should be induced to make a cession of a tract of land, not less than 6 miles square, which should embrace the ore bed and water privilege; that so much of the land so ceded as the President of the United States should deem proper should be conveyed to him (Earle), including the ore and water facilities, whereon he should be authorized to erect iron works, smith shops, and so forth. Earle, on his part, engaged to erect such iron works and shops as to enable him to furnish such quantities of iron and implements of husbandry as should be sufficient for the use of the various Indian tribes in that part of the country, including those on the west side of the Ohio and Mississippi Rivers; also to deliver annually to the order of the Government of the United States such quantities of iron and implements as should be needed for the Indian

service, and on such reasonable terms as should be mutually agreed upon. The Secretary of War referred the propositions of Colonel Earle to the President of the United States, who gave them his sanction, and accordingly Agent Meigs, of the Cherokees, was instructed to endeavor to procure from the Cherokees such a cession as was proposed, so soon as Colonel Earle should have explored the country and selected a suitable place for the proposed establishment. Colonel Earle made the necessary explorations, and found a place at the mouth of Chickamauga Creek which seemed to meet the requirements of the case.[43]

Although Earle was successful in negotiating a treaty with the Cherokees for a six-mile-square tract of land, Tennessee blocked congressional action. The ironworks treaty and Earle's plan failed.

As Hill's and other early eighteenth-century ironworks ended operations in the early nineteenth century, new ironworks were being established along the Broad River and its tributaries within the present-day borders of Cherokee and York Counties. These included two operations on Cherokee Creek in Spartanburg District: Wilson Nesbitt's Furnace, established around 1811, and what was to later become the Cowpen's Furnace, established in 1807.[44] In 1815 an ironworks was established by Jacob Stroup and Edward Fewell on King's Creek in what was then Union District. In 1815, Fewell and Stroup entered a partnership and purchased 500 acres of land, "lying on both sides of King's Creek ... [at] Dulin's old mill seat]," which included iron ore beds and a standing grist mill and saw mill, for $2,000.[45]

Their partnership is more consistent with the pattern of ownership evident throughout this period than with the pattern of corporate organization that was to develop in the second quarter of the nineteenth century. Fewell was a native of Lincoln County, North Carolina, an important area of iron manufacture during the late eighteenth and early nineteenth centuries, where he probably learned the art of iron smelting. He apparently moved to South Carolina to become partners with Stroup, and thus played a role in transmitting the technology of iron manufacture to the South Carolina piedmont. He was primarily responsible for the construction and operation of the iron furnace.

Stroup was responsible for building and operating a forge at the site of Fewell's furnace. Both partners, however, shared the acquisition and use of ore and timberlands, as well as the expense of maintaining dams and roads on the property. Fewell agreed to furnish Stroup annually with 125 tons of pig iron at $25 per ton, which Stroup could then turn into bar iron in his forge. Stroup, in return, agreed to provide Fewell with as much bar iron as he might need, provided that both could produce such quantities of pig and bar iron. "Misunderstandings or disputes" were to be settled by a group of "four or six disinterested men chosen by the parties." The decision of the group was to be final.[46] In 1822, Fewell died and the works was destroyed by a major flood, following which the assets of the company were sold at a public sheriff's auction.[47] Stroup married his partner's widow and rebuilt the iron-works on King's Creek.

In 1825 a group of New York investors headed by Duncan P. Campbell bought the King's Creek furnace from Stroup for $12,235. Campbell hoped to develop the works to serve a northern market. After Stroup sold the King's Creek Ironworks he began to construct another ironworks a few miles away on the east bank of the Broad River at the mouth of Doolittle Creek. He named his new company the Cherokee Ironworks. By l830 the Cherokee Ironworks had grown to include a central tract of 2,434 acres upon which were located a furnace and forge, a blacksmith's shop, grist and sawmills, and a number of worker and slave quarters. The property also contained several ore banks and two limestone quarries. The Cherokee Iron-works holdings also included two additional tracts of ore and timberland consisting of 391 and 442 acres. Also, by 1830, Stroup had bought a mill seat and grist mill on a 220-acre tract of land across the river from the Cherokee Ironworks. By 1830, the Cherokee Ironworks controlled almost 3,500 acres.[48]

It was not uncommon for the iron workers of this period to migrate from one iron-producing region to another, generally in a north-south direction. Jacob Stroup exemplified this pattern. He apparently migrated into the Carolina piedmont from the north, eventually left the area, and continued south, where in the 1830s and 1840s he established three ironworks in northern Georgia before his death in 1846.[49]

The Florescence of the Iron Industry of Northwestern South Carolina: Early to the Mid-Nineteenth Century

The Social and Economic Situation of the Early to Mid-Nineteenth Century

This section will briefly trace the development of the iron industry from the mid-1820s to the early 1860s. This period can be considered the florescence of the iron industry in the South Carolina piedmont. The ironworks of this period were no longer as isolated as were those in the earlier period, and they served expanded regional markets. The scale of operations, in terms of capital and production, was also greater. The greater capital required to support these companies required an expanded base of investments. Many influential people were involved in the formation of formal, incorporated operations. Out-of-state and foreign investment and market speculation also increased at this time.

These trends were part of a larger pattern involving the gradual evolution of the iron industry from rural plantations in the late eighteenth and early nineteenth centuries toward more complex urban industrial businesses associated with industrialism in the post–Civil War period. The consolidation and incorporation of some of the South Carolina ironworks were simply attempts to improve management and marketing. These advances were not followed by significant technological improvements.

By the 1830s the iron-manufacturing activities in northwestern South Carolina focused almost entirely on three operations: the South Carolina Manufacturing Company, which ultimately controlled approximately 25,000 acres within Spartanburg County adjacent to the Pacolet River and western Cherokee County; the King's Mountain Iron Company, located on approximately 10,000 acres on the east side of the Broad River in eastern Cherokee County and western York County; and the Nesbitt Iron Manufacturing Company, located on approximately 10,000 acres in Cherokee County on the west side of the Broad River. By the 1840s, when iron manufacturing was reaching its peak in the piedmont region, these three operations controlled a total of approximately 45,000 acres of land, had a capital base of around $500,000, and produced as much as 4,000 tons of iron a year.[50]

The South Carolina Manufacturing Company

The South Carolina Manufacturing Company started as a partnership in 1826 between Abner Benson, Andrew B. Moore, and Wilson Nesbitt. Even though it was incorporated in 1826, it apparently did not start development until 1834 when Simpson Bobo, Gabriel Cannon, William Clark, and Vardy McBee became investors. In 1834 the South Carolina Manufacturing Company purchased and rebuilt the Cowpens Furnace along Cherokee Creek, which had originally been built around 1807. At this time the South Carolina Manufacturing Company also began to purchase large tracts of land in the northern portion of present-day Spartanburg County and southern Cherokee County.

Also in 1834, they built the Hurricane Iron-works at Hurricane Shoals on the Pacolet River, which included the Hurricane Cold-Blast Furnace and the Hurricane Rolling Mill and Nail Works. The rolling mill and nailworks consisted of five heating furnaces, one train of rolls, three nail machines, and one water-driven hammer. In addition the company also maintained blacksmith and machine shops. In 1841 the company charter was amended to increase its capital stock to $301,000, but it appears that the stock never exceeded $100,000. The South Carolina

Manufacturing Company existed until the 1880s, when deed records indicate that the majority of land held by the company was sold.[51]

The King's Mountain Iron Company

The King's Mountain Iron Company was formed in the 1830s from the consolidation of operations established by Jacob Stroup between 1815 and 1830 in present-day eastern Cherokee and western York Counties. Before the Cherokee Ironworks on the east bank of the Broad river was completed by Stroup, it was sold between 1826 and 1830 for $17,000 to Emor Graham and Company. This partnership incorporated and received a charter as the South Carolina Iron Manufacturing Company, allowing a capital stock of $100,000. Also, in 1832, the company purchased for $6,000 the furnace Stroup had built on King's Creek and sold in 1825 to a group of New York investors headed by Duncan P. Campbell. In 1836, the company secured a new charter as the King's Mountain Iron Company, due in part to the similarity of the previous name to the already extant South Carolina Manufacturing Company. It was allowed to increase its stock to $200,000. Eventually, a large group of powerful and influential investors was involved with this operation, including George McDuffie, Emor Graham, James A. Black, David Johnson, Jacob Deal, John Bryce, William McGill, John B. Davis, John McEloree, and P. R. Brice.[52]

By 1839 the King's Mountain Iron Company's timber and ore lands had grown to over 9,000 acres. At the height of production, the King's Mountain Company was composed of the Cherokee Iron-works, which included the Cherokee Furnace, a forge, a blacksmith's shop, grist mills, sawmills, a number of buildings for housing laborers, two outlying furnaces along King's Creek, and a rolling mill on the west bank of the Broad River.[53]

Sketchy production records for 1839 reveal levels of production similar to charcoal-fueled ironworks in other regions during the period. Throughout the last two decades of the antebellum period, annual production of pig and bar iron would stay at about 400 tons. Between 1839 and l860, the company's capital stock remained at just under $100,000, and average annual sales remained between $30,000 and $35,000.[54]

On February 24, l859, a short article about the King's Mountain Iron Company in the *Yorkville Enquirer* noted:

> The affairs of this [company] we are pleased to learn are in prosperous condition. For the last year it has declared a dividend of six percent and seven percent for each of the preceding years. It was the first rolling mill established in this state its existence dating back some thirty years. The demand for their manufacture is altogether local. Beyond that, it cannot compete with the production of foreign forge. The capital stock of the company amounts to about $100,000—not quite large enough to induce us to league with the Pennsylvanians. Under the superintendence of Swann and Montgomery; their company has been doing a prosperous business for years, and while other companies have barely maintained an existence it has proved for the stockholders a handsome investment. The King's Mountain Iron is now famed throughout this and the adjoining States, and the real struggle for the company has been to supply the demand.[55]

The Nesbitt Iron Manufacturing Company

The Nesbitt Iron Manufacturing Company (maps 11.4 and 11.5), chartered in 1835, was the largest iron company to exist in South Carolina. In 1836 the charter was amended, increasing the capital stock from $100,000 to $300,000 and shortening the name to the Nesbitt Manufacturing Company. Stockholders consisted mainly of wealthy planters and merchants, most with influential political positions. Original investors included Thomas Cooper, Pierce Butler, Franklin H. Elmore, Benjamin T. Elmore, Baylis J. Earle, Wade Hampton II, and Wilson Nesbitt. The total number of investors later reached 16, with the addition of Sammuel N. Earle, John G. Brown, James M. Taylor, E. W. Harrison, Moses Stroup, William Clark, Joseph Shelton, W. E. Martin, and James E. Nott.[56]

The property of the Nesbitt Iron Manufacturing was described by Thomas Cooper in 1837. In his letter to Nicholas Biddle, president of the U.S. Bank, Cooper writes, "There is about 2000 acres of Iron ore qualities from 20 to 60 per cent, in solid hills and abundant in veins, with two furnaces and another in contemplation immediately in the midst of this body of ore. Limestone in inexhaustible abundance is every where contiguous to it. Eight thousand acres of woodland furnish fuel. We have a dam substantially built 300 yards long giving us command of the whole Broad river. A race on which we hope to have a furnace, a rolling and slitting mill, in less than a twelve month. We own 5 to 600 acres of corn land; horses, mules, and 135 Negro Servants."[57]

Major construction occurred during the late 1830s, and by 1843 the company consisted of four furnaces: Susan Furnace on Peoples Creek, Ellen Furnace on a tributary of Peoples Creek called

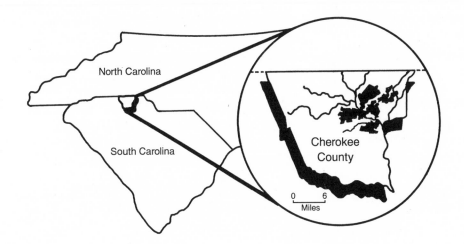

MAP 11.4. Location of the Nesbitt and Kings Mountain companies within South Carolina and Cherokee County. *Courtesy of Olencki Graphics.*

MAP 11.5. The Land-
holdings of the Nesbitt
and Kings Mountain
companies showing
location of primary site
features. *Courtesy of
Olencki Graphics.*

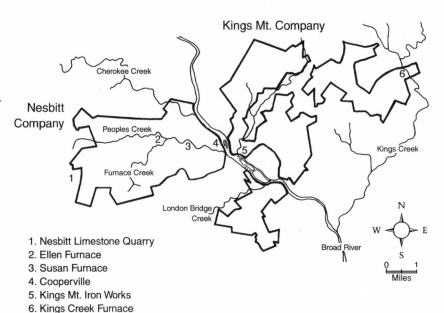

1. Nesbitt Limestone Quarry
2. Ellen Furnace
3. Susan Furnace
4. Cooperville
5. Kings Mt. Iron Works
6. Kings Creek Furnace

Furnace Creek, and the North and South Twin Furnaces at Cooperville on the Broad River. Other features at Cooperville included a dam, a canal, a puddling furnace, rolling mill, foundry, machine shop, nail factory, reheating ovens, ore stamper, and blacksmith, carpenter, and wheelwright shops, in addition to a grist and flour mill, sawmill, post office, store, and dwellings for superintendents and slaves.[58]

The Nesbitt Manufacturing Company had financial difficulties during the whole period of time it was in operation. Of particular note are the debts it owed to the Bank of the State of South Carolina. Lesesne discusses these dealings at length, focusing on the activities of Franklin H. Elmore, who was both the president of the bank as well as a principal shareholder in the Nesbitt Manufacturing Company.[59]

In the late 1840s the Nesbitt Manufacturing Company was dissolved. In 1850, the Swedish Iron Manufacturing Company of South Carolina was chartered and took over the old Nesbitt Manufacturing Company works. Investors consisted primarily of a group of Swedes and Germans, along with Charleston investors.[60] In 1853, the *Charleston Courier* included an advertisement for the sale of the Cooperville Ironworks that noted: "The machinery is driven by water power, obtained by means of a large dam across the river. Among the Buildings are Hot Blast Bloomery, (3 fires,) Blast Houses, Rolling Mill, Hammer, Nail Factory, Machine Shop, Blacksmith's Shop, Foundry, Saw Mill, Flour Mill, Store, Store House for Irnn [Iron], Hotel, Dwelling House, Cottages, &c.&c."[61] The advertisement also notes that the company owned "upwards of 10,000 acres and has abundant bodies of iron ore and limestone."[62] The ironworks was still in operation, but on a limited scale in 1862 when it received a new charter as the Magnetic Iron Company of South Carolina.[63]

The Decline and Demise of the Iron Industry in Northwestern South Carolina: Middle to Late Nineteenth Century

The Social and Economic Situation of the Middle to Late Nineteenth Century

The decline and ultimate demise of the charcoal iron industry in South Carolina can be attributed to many factors, such as 1) the inability to compete

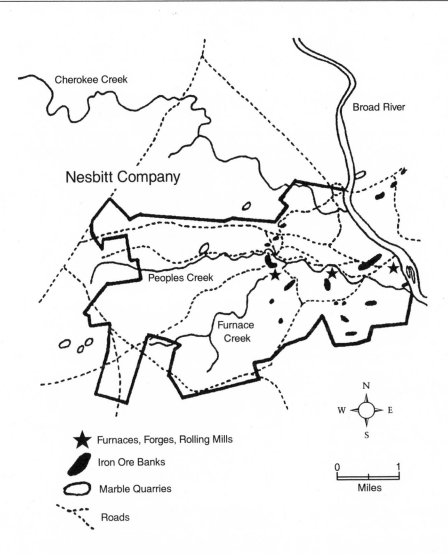

MAP 11.6. Detail of the Nesbitt Company landholdings showing location and association of natural and cultural features. *Courtesy of Olencki Graphics.*

with ironworks in other regions, 2) resource depletion, 3) labor problems, and 4) general economic trends. This decline was not unique, for the same factors led to the decline of the entire charcoal-fueled portion of the iron industry in the whole eastern United States. Between 1860 and 1880 literally hundreds of rural furnaces and forges closed down.

The demise of the South Carolina iron industry was part of a larger pattern in the evolution of the American iron industry from individually owned, rural ironworks to the highly complex and consolidated companies that had developed by the turn of the twentieth century.[64] The methods employed by charcoal-fueled iron makers of the Carolina piedmont had essentially been perfected by the early nineteenth century. The principal way iron producers could increase production was to increase the furnace size. However, furnaces in South Carolina were generally built to the largest dimensions attainable for charcoal-fueled furnaces. If furnaces were made larger, the charcoal in them would be crushed, greatly reducing the efficiency of the burning process.

Coal-fueled furnaces, however, could be made much larger and were thus much more efficient.

Larger coal-fueled furnaces were, furthermore, better at retaining the tremendous amounts of heat needed for iron smelting. Thus, South Carolina manufacturers could not match the production of iron makers in areas where there were coal resources. These factors would become paramount after the Civil War when South Carolina producers, using an essentially eighteenth-century technology, found they could no longer compete with the larger, more modern industry that had developed in the North.[65]

The demise of large iron-manufacturing operations in the Carolinas after the Civil War can be tied, in large part, to a change in the quality of transportation in other regions and to the fact that charcoal-fueled operations were costlier than those fueled by coal.[66] By the late 1860s improved transportation and changes in production methods beyond the capabilities of South Carolina operations had turned the prosperity of the companies into an inability to compete. These factors, coupled with resource depletion and the loss of the slave-based labor structure, led to an inability to remain economically competitive.

Smith concludes that competition in the iron trade was the overriding factor in the decline of the industry over the whole eastern United States. He believes that its eventual demise can be largely explained by the inability of ironmasters to compete for markets. Though he does not consider resource depletion—particularly that of timber for charcoal production—a universal factor, Smith does agree with Lander that resource depletion was a major factor in the Carolina piedmont. Finally, Smith concludes that the success of the southern charcoal iron industry from the late 1700s through the mid-1800s over most of the southeastern United States was in part due to its compatibility with the agricultural regime.[67]

By whatever combination of factors, the iron industry in the Carolinas collapsed by the turn of the twentieth century. The King's Mountain Company provides a good example of the economic woes that preceded the end. In l867, staving off creditors was the only information recorded in the stockholders minute book of the King's Mountain Company.[68] The company soon ceased operations, as did the other iron companies in the piedmont.

The Archaeological Record of Characteristics and Activities on Iron Plantations in Piedmont South Carolina

In defining iron plantations, Smith establishes the following criteria: 1) a large land holding; 2) distinctive settlement form and spatial organization reflecting centralized control by the owner(s); 3) a specialized industrial production; and 4) a distinct division of labor and management functions with management in the hands of the ironmasters.[69] This section will discuss how the iron plantations of the South Carolina piedmont satisfy these criteria.

Land Holdings and the Spatial Organization of Land Use

All currently documented iron plantations in piedmont South Carolina controlled large tracts of land. These lands, once cleared and plowed, provided food to support the operation, in addition to providing adequate supplies of iron ore and timber for charcoal production. Hill's Ironworks controlled around 15,000 acres. The description in the 1795 sale announcement for Hill's Ironworks in the *City Gazette and Daily Advertiser* gives some indication of the scope of the company's land holdings: "IRONWORKS Called Aera and Aetna, Situated in York county within two miles of the Catawba in the said state, together with about 15,000 acres of land lying contiguous to, and attached to the said Ironworks, and on which are about twenty-five improved farms . . . 5500 acres of land were originally purchased with the works in 1785, but near 10,000 acres been rod and purchased since."[70] By 1798, Hill's Ironworks owned and controlled some 62 tracts containing over 17,500 acres of land. A series of plats from the early 1800s show approximately 8,000 acres of land associated with one of Hill's furnaces (see maps 11.2 and 11.3).[71] Beginning in the 1830s, the South Carolina Manufacturing Company controlled as much as 25,000 acres, while the King's Mountain Iron Company and the Nesbitt Iron Manufacturing Company owned around 10,000 acres each by the end of the 1830s (see maps 11.4, 11.5, and 11.6).[72]

The lands of the Swedish Iron Manufacturing Company, formerly the Nesbitt Iron Manufacturing Company, were described around 1855 by the company's superintendent, A. M. Latham, in the following manner:

Lands, etc.—The number of acres belonging to the Company altogether amounts to about 10,000, the greater portion of which has been denuded of timber, and that many years ago. A young growth is, however, rapidly coming on, and in the course of few years a part of the old coaling grounds will again be ready for cutting over. Judicious thinning would very much facilitate the growth of the young timber, and would, in my opinion, pay well for such an outlay. There are still about 1,500 acres of Company's lands, having the original growth, situated principally on the opposite side of the river, and this I have deemed it proper to hold as a reserve, to meet any emergency that might occur. For agricultural purposes, I view the lands belonging to the Company as particularly valuable—the soil being generally of a most productive character, and highly susceptible of improvement. There is, however, but little improvement yet observable in this section of country—the method universally adopted being that of wasting or wearing out the lands, and then removing to another country, to follow the same ruinous course. About 100 acres are under fence in the immediate vicinity of the works, parts of which have been very much improved by draining, deep cultivation, and manuring; and the result has been far beyond what I could have expected under the circumstances. The average yield of wheat in this section of the country might be set down at 5 to 10 bushels per acre, whilst on some lands cultivated last year by the Company, under rather unfavorable circumstances, being visited

with frosts of a severe nature late in April, the return was 25 bushels per acre, the seed necessary for each acre being only one bushel. Farther improvements having been effected during the past year, the prospect for an abundant crop is now very fine, the yield expected to be at least 40 bushels per acre, and that with only one bushel seed! Corn seems to take equally well with good treatment, and gives an average of 30 to 50 bushels per acre on our best cultivated lands. Oats, also, seem to do very well, when properly cultivated; but I do not consider the climate so suitable for this crop as for some other cereals, such as wheat, rye, barley, etc. Sweet potatoes, beet, and turnips, are esculents which the climate and soil are admirably suited to; but these crops the agriculturists of this country altogether neglect, or at least cultivate them in small patches, without bestowing on the soil any preparation farther than stirring it with what is called the bull-tongue plough, when a little manure may be administered on the top surface, and the crop left to its fate. On a patch of 2½ acres of turnips, I last year grew 1,200 bushels, and at same time had a very fair crop of wheat from the land previous to sowing in turnips. Such might be calculated on with considerable certainty every season, and the yield doubled under more favorable circumstances; that is to say, with better implements, a more liberal supply of manure, and deeper tillage. There are about 400 acres of land of excellent quality, and situated very conveniently to the works already cleared, but under no fence. If these lands were enclosed and properly treated, I do not hesitate to say that they might be made a source of great profit to such an establishment, as the provisions necessary for supplying the laborers might be raised in abundance thereon, and a large quantity to spare.[73]

Ore Bodies and Iron Mining

The principal resource contained with the tracts of land associated with an ironworks was the iron ore. The procurement of iron ore involved the mining by hand of surface or near-surface deposits. In 1795 the

City Gazette and Daily Advertiser described the nature and location of ore bodies located on present-day Nanny Mountain and the mining activities associated with Hill's Ironworks as follows:

> The distance of the ore from the Aera furnace is 1¾ from the Aetna furnace 1¼ mile; the ore appears to the inexhaustible. The ore works easily and well in the furnace; the metal is good for hammer, gudgeons, or any kind of machinery and hollow ware, and will make good bar iron. Some trial has been made of it in steel, and it promises well; nothing is necessary for preparing the ore for use but burning. The ore is generally raised by monthly wages at 300 lbs. of iron per month, and one good miner can keep one furnace in blast. A team can draw four loads of ore per day, at the price above mentioned for a team.
>
> The ore consists of large rocks above the surface, the depth not yet known; in cavities between the rocks lie an oker and feed ore. There will be no occasion to sink shafts or drive levels for 50 years to come.[74]

The lands controlled by the Nesbitt Company and later by the Swedish Iron Manufacturing Company contain the most extensive outcropping of iron in the area (see map 11.4). Eight distinct ore banks—Field's, Sweet Spring, Gibson's, Houge, Jackson's, Red, Creits', and Blocky Mine—are discussed at length, as they were in 1855 by Jones.[75]

To date, iron mining has been archaeologically documented at three sites: Nanny Mountain ore bank (38YK216), Creits' ore bank (38CK2), and Thicketty Mountain ore bank (38CK74).[76] The Nanny Mountain Mine, associated with Hill's Ironworks, is located in York County. It was first described and illustrated (see map 11.3) by Lieber, and characterized under the general heading of gossan.[77] More recently, Butler describes the locality as follows: "Pits and trenches still exist on the north end of the mountain even though there is no record of being mined for the last 140 years. The ore is mainly vuggy limonite and hematite in a body as much as six feet thick that parallels the bedding of the quartzite, which has an orientation of N 10° E,

86° SE. Fresh country rock in the vicinity of the iron ore contains disseminated pyrite. The ore body is probably the oxidized near-surface portion of a pyrite deposit."[78]

The Thicketty Mountain Iron ore bank was first used by ironworks which developed along Cherokee Creek in the early 1800s, such as Nesbitt's Furnace (38CK72) and the Cowpens Furnace (38CK73).[79] From the 1830s to the late 1800s these deposits, along with others in western Cherokee County, were owned or controlled by the South Carolina Manufacturing Company. This mining locality consists of ore pits and prospects scattered over several acres of wooded area north of Thicketty Mountain in Cherokee County. Evidence of mining once covered a larger area around Thicketty Mountain, but agricultural activities over the past 100 years have filled in many of the excavations. The pits still visible in the area generally range from 5 to 10 meters across and 2 to 3 meters deep. The iron ore, known in the 1800s as Brown ore, occurs within the Carolina Gneiss of that portion of Cherokee County and is described by Keith and Sterrett in the following manner:

> Brown iron ore, consisting of limonite and some intermixed hematite, has been mined several miles west and northwest of Gaffney. The deposits are scattered over an area a few miles square. The ore was smelted near the mines, in a furnace on Cherokee Creek. The deposits occur in the highly crumpled varieties of the garnet and kyanite schists of the Carolina gneiss and fill fissures and cracks in the gneiss. Some of the deposits appear to have replaced or to have resulted from the original sulphides and others to have been simply deposited from solutions that circulated through fractured rocks. Most of these deposits are in the form of scoriaceous rusty-looking masses. Where the inclosing [*sic*] rocks have weathered away the ore is left in large and small fragments scattered through the surface soils.[80]

Forested Areas and Charcoal Production

The major portion of the land controlled by an ironworks was required for the production of charcoal, the principal fuel supply for all stages of the iron-manufacturing process. Large numbers of trees were cut to produce an adequate supply. Production figures at Hill's Ironworks give an idea of the number of trees required. Up to 500 bushels of charcoal were required to produce a single ton of iron. The Aera furnace at Hill's Ironworks generally produced up to 18 tons per week.[81] Therefore, up to 7,500 bushels of charcoal were required per week, or approximately 190,000 bushels for a typical 6-month blast. Stated another way, on average a cord of wood produces approximately 40 bushels of charcoal and an acre generally produces 35 cords.[82] At 1,400 bushels per acre, the Aera furnace required 170 cords or approximately 5 acres of timber per week, which converts to cutting 125 acres every 6 months.

The iron industry's thirst for fuel led to the deforestation of large areas of countryside surrounding furnaces and forges. These denuded areas became known as "coaling grounds" and often covered several square miles. Portions of these coaling grounds were still observable in recent years, when more areas of this region were still under cultivation.[83] Moss remembers, as a boy, seeing charcoal-production areas on lands once controlled by the King's Mountain Iron Company.[84] He describes these areas as dark stains approximately 30 to 40 feet in diameter, generally in clusters of four to five. To date, none of these coaling grounds have been documented archaeologically for the iron plantations in the South Carolina piedmont.

Intensive labor was required by woodcutters and colliers to produce adequate quantities of charcoal. The average ironworks often employed two dozen men just for chopping wood.[85] Colliers converted the cut timber into charcoal by stacking it into large piles and covering it with a layer of soil while it slowly burned. The burning process took from one to three weeks to complete and required attention round the clock. If the timber burned too fast it would not turn into charcoal, only ashes. To prevent this colliers would cover the pile with more soil or plug the small air holes left in the soil layer.[86] The production of charcoal at Hill's Ironworks in 1795 is described in the *City Gazette and Daily Advertiser* as follows:

> The works lie central to the lands, in so much that from 4 to 6 loads of coal [charcoal] may be hauled per day; before there will be any occasion to go to an Improper distance for coal, the woods will bear a second cutting. The farmers at present are willing to give their wood gratis where they are clearing, it being to their benefit to get it off their land, reserving fencing. The hearths contain from 35 to 40 cords, and are generally filled 3 to 4 times (saw logs and saplings excluded) from an acre; horses are usually worked, though oxen would be preferable. A cord of wood is of the following dimensions; 4 feet long, 4 feet 4 inches high, 8 feet broad; the wood, may be floated to the works, but heretofore it has been hauled. Six pounds of iron are usually given to the wood-cutters for every cord cut, they finding themselves. The wood is generally coaled by colliers hired by the month; the wages commonly given to colliers are 400 lbs. of iron pre month to the master collier, 250 lbs. to the under colliers, and much less to the green hands. Twenty pounds of iron or castings are usually given to a team for carting coal per day, they finding forage and driver. The coaling ground is in general level and free from stone and gravel; the hearths are made at a small expense. There is no store now established to furnish a regular supply to the work people; if a store of goods well laid in, was established, the hands would be better satisfied to take goods for payment at 125 percent advance, than they are now with the present mode of payment, which is either in bar iron or castings, according to their respective branches.[87]

Marble Quarrying and Lime Production

Little is known about the actual quarrying of marble during the iron-manufacturing period. Jones, in discussing the Black Rock and Spark's Quarries located on the lands of the Swedish Iron Manufacturing Company, indicates that the seam containing both is 30 to 40 yards across and was only quarried to a depth of a few feet below the ground surface.[88]

To date, a series of outcrops have been identified in the field that correspond to the quarries documented by Toumey and Keith and Sterrett.[89] No archaeological remains associated with the iron-manufacturing period have been observed. These outcrops are contained within the King's Mountain Belt in virtually continuous seams of Gaffney Marble, which extends from the vicinity of Limestone College in a northeast direction across the state line to eastern Catawba County, North Carolina.[90]

The 80-foot-deep marble quarry on the campus of Limestone College (38CK69) in Gaffney, South Carolina, is one of the largest quarries used during the period of iron manufacturing.[91] This quarry at Limestone Springs and other quarries in the area not only provided the fluxing agent used during iron production, but also supplied lime kilns where marble was burned and turned into lime. The lime was used primarily for agricultural purposes.

Lime was produced at the kilns during the iron-manufacturing period, but production did not begin on a large scale until the 1880s, when continuous-process kilns were introduced.[92] There were five such kilns in operation in 1907 at Limestone Springs, producing 540 barrels of lime per day.[93] The quarry at Limestone College was in operation until at least the 1930s.[94] Other quarries in the area were closed even later, into the 1970s, or are still in operation today for the production of crushed rock. Due to the intensive lime-production activities and the more recent procurement of crushed rock, the chances of finding intact archaeological remains of nineteenth-century activities at any but the smallest marble quarries is unlikely.

Road Systems and Local and Regional Transportation Networks

Complex systems of roads and tram roads existed within and between the ironwork's various land holdings (see maps 11.3 and 11.6). The purpose of this network was to provide an adequate means of transportation for workers, iron ore, charcoal, and marble to the furnace, forge, and later production sites. Deed records in 1830 indicate that, in addition to a stock of sheep and cattle, the Cherokee Iron-

works maintained four teams of workhorses and nine yoke of oxen, as well as four ore and coal wagons, a pair of log wheels, and an additional wagon for use on the road system.[95]

Preserved portions of roadway are visible today around the localities of several ironworks in both North Carolina and South Carolina. Baker and Hall describe a particularly well-preserved section of tram road in North Carolina where they identified the locations of wooden ties.[96] Preserved portions of old roads and tram roads are particularly common on lands once controlled by the Nesbitt Company and later the Swedish Iron Manufacturing Company.

Ironworks were in most cases located in close proximity to major regional roads to expedite overland movement of goods to market centers. For example, Hill's Ironworks was located on the main road linking Camden and Charleston with the northwestern piedmont (see map 11.3), as well as with the southern spur of the "great wagon road."[97]

Structural Features and Settlement Patterning

The lands associated with an ironworks contained a variety of structural features associated with various stages of the manufacturing process and the general operation of the plantation. For example, "On the settlement of the Ironworks [of William Hill] are a good two story brick house, 40 by 35 feet, with cellars, and other necessary buildings, together with four grist mills and two saw mills."[98] The preceding quotation identifies a distinctive aspect of the settlement patterning of early iron plantations, the spatial association of furnaces with grist and saw mills (see map 11.3). This pattern can be seen at other early ironworks. For example, Ancrum in 1810 documents the co-occurrence of a forge, sawmill, and wheat mill at one of Earle's ironworks on the Rocky River.[99]

Latham around 1855 describes the structural features associated with the Swedish Iron Manufacturing Company in the following manner:

> Ironworks, Buildings, etc.—These consist of two blast furnaces, forge, attached to which are four hot-blast, blooming (Catalan) fires, one refining fire, one puddling furnace, shingling

hammer, rolling mill, nail factory (with six cutting-machines), foundry, machine shop, pattern shop (with a large stock of patterns), blacksmiths' and wagon shops, with the full complement of tools required in such establishments, grist and saw mills, a large and commodious mansion house, boarding house, store, a sufficient number of dwellings for workmen, and other outside buildings necessary. These, it may be mentioned, are all in a state of excellent repair, with the exception of the rolling mill roof, which was destroyed by fire some time ago, and sufficient spare time has not been had for its re-erection. . . . The two blast-furnaces now in repair (two more not worked) are built of brick, the height 36 feet, and 9½ feet across the boshes. They are considered the best furnaces in this section of country, and cost, when new, $25,000. . . . The foundry contains two large reverberatory furnaces, with an ample supply of patterns of every description required in the country, and pattern and machine shops, having the necessary lathes, drills, and other machinery for finishing and fitting up all the different descriptions of casting—all on a large and complete scale, and erected with the view of doing a very extensive foundry business. When on the subject of buildings, I may also mention the grist-mill as one of great importance to the works. It contains two flour and two corn-mills, the rocks the best that could be had, whilst the machinery and accommodation are amply sufficient for the largest establishment. . . . The water-power being of so continuous a character, must also much enhance the value of such an establishment, especially in a climate where droughts are frequent, and often of long duration. In connexion with this, I may mention, the river is upward of three hundred yards wide at this point; that the dam stretches across the river; that it was renewed in a great measure last year, and resting on a foundation of rock as it does, there is little danger to be anticipated from floods in the river.[100]

The ironworks described by Latham is archaeologically the best preserved and most extensive nineteenth-century iron-manufacturing operation in northwest South Carolina (see maps 11.5 and 11.6). Features associated with this ironworks are located within the archaeological sites of Cooperville, South Carolina (38CK2), also known as the Cherokee Ford Ironworks; Susan Furnace (38CK67); Ellen Furnace (38CK68); and Nesbitt's, or Gaffney, Limestone Quarry (38CK69). The factory complex at the site of Cooperville on the west bank of the Broad River at Cherokee Ford is at present the only known iron factory complex still in existence in the piedmont of North Carolina or South Carolina. The outlying furnaces—Susan, located along People's Creek upstream from the company's main factory complex on the Broad River, and Ellen, located along Furnace Creek, a tributary of People's Creek about a mile upstream from Susan—both exhibit partially collapsed but well-preserved furnaces and associated features.

In terms of distinctive settlement patterning, the site of Cooperville exhibits the same pattern discussed above in association with Hill's Ironworks, the association of furnaces and forges with grain and sawmills. The site of Cooperville also exhibits a spatial pattern once shared by the now destroyed factory sites of the South Carolina Manufacturing Company and the King's Mountain Company, the association of bloomery forge, rolling mill, and cutting mill in close proximity to one another. The importance of this patterning, particularly at these three sites, is supported by Cooper, who states, "It is not common in England to erect ironworks without making a bloomery, a slitting mill, and a rolling mill, parts of the establishment. It ought to be so every where, but is seldom so in this country."[101]

Another distinctive spatial pattern is the location of the furnaces in the immediate vicinity of the ore bodies (see map 11.6). At most of the furnace sites there appears to have been an attempt to maximize the exploitation of the iron ore over the other necessary resources.

Iron Furnaces and Initial Stages of the Iron-Manufacturing Process

One of the most prominent features associated with iron-manufacturing localities is the iron furnace (see map 11.6). In addition to Susan Furnace

(38CK67) and Ellen Furnace (38CK68), two other furnaces are still visible above ground: King's Creek Furnace (38CK71) and Cowpens Furnace (38CK73). The Cowpens Furnace (38CK73) is the best-preserved furnace known in South Carolina.

Iron furnaces served essentially as crucibles in which the iron ore, charcoal, and marble were combined and melted down. All South Carolina furnaces observed to date appear to have been constructed in a style similar to the Pennsylvanian furnace type used elsewhere in the Upper South and Middle Atlantic states. All appear to have been constructed of locally quarried stone and were approximately the same size and shape, about 25 to 30 feet square at the base and originally tapered inward slightly to a height of about 25 to 35 feet. Lower arched openings were about eight feet across at the widest point and lined with brick or stone. Small square openings were also contained in the stonework, which once contained structural timbers of buildings and sheds originally attached to the furnace stack. The interiors of the furnaces were chimney- to egg-shaped with the widest interior dimension near the base, or bosh, at around 7 to 8 feet. Interior heights ranged from approximately 20 to 30 feet. For example, the dimensions of the Cowpens Furnace and the daily charge it took to fill it were reported by Tuomey as follows: height, 28 feet; width at boshes, 7 feet, 6 inches; hearth, 1 foot, 10 inches; and charge of ore (brown hematite), 12,000 pounds; charcoal, 600 bushels; limestone, 1,500 pounds. He stated that the yield was about 5,000 pounds of iron.[102]

The interior dimensions of these furnaces are particularly important because they are the largest dimensions attainable in charcoal-fueled furnaces. If furnaces were built larger, the charcoal would be crushed, preventing efficient burning. Therefore, iron makers could not increase the size of their furnaces to increase production. As a result, management and labor coordination became key factors for success in early iron production.

Furnaces were typically built next to steep banks so that ramps could be erected from the bank to the top of the furnace to help load the furnace.

Iron ore, limestone, and charcoal were carried over these ramps and fed into openings in the top of the furnace. As the charcoal in the furnace burned, fanned to high temperatures through the used of large water-powered bellows, the iron ore and marble melted. The molten limestone chemically drew off unwanted minerals—principally quartz—from the iron, producing a molten calcium glass with a relatively low density. The molten iron was of much higher density than the calcium glass and would settle to the bottom of the furnace's interior.[103]

Molten iron and the calcium glass settled into distinct layers at the base of the furnace, with calcium glass on top and iron on the bottom. These molten layers were channeled out of the furnace separately. The calcium glass was skimmed off to produce a waste product called slag. Pieces of this slag are the most ubiquitous artifactual remains associated with the iron-manufacturing sites. The molten iron was then run off into sand-paved castings beds. As the iron ore, limestone, and charcoal burned down, additional quantities were added. This kept the furnace constantly filled and in operation for as long as five or six months, usually until stores of iron ore and charcoal were depleted or until the furnace's interior stone lining needed repair.[104]

Forges, Foundries, Rolling Mills, and Secondary Stages of the Iron-Manufacturing Process

When the molten iron was removed from the furnace it was allowed to cool into puddled masses called "pig iron," that could then be easily transported and later reheated and refined through a process of repeated hammering or forging. Pig iron was generally cast into pieces weighing approximately 100 pounds, and transported by wagon from furnace sites to foundries, bloomeries, or forges.

Forging of pig iron created bar iron, also known as billets or blooms. Forging was used to produce wrought nails, guns, and most iron or metal components for agricultural, trade, and industrial tools. Foundries were locations where pig iron was remelted into patterns or molds to form products such as wood stoves, hollowware, or cooking vessels, cannons and shot, and even grist, rice, and sawmill machinery. Rolling mills rolled bar iron into sheets for processing into cut nails and other iron items which could be stamped out rapidly at a cutting or slitting mill.

Forge hammers and rolling mill rollers weighed hundreds of pounds and, like furnace bellows, were dependent upon water power for their operation. Many ironworks combined a furnace, forge or bloomery, rolling mills, and cutting mills at one or more locations so that the same dam and sluice system could power several different water wheels and pieces of machinery. The term "ironworks" normally describe this broad multicomponent type of operation. The average ironworks also included other components, such as houses, storage buildings, and other associated structures and related site features.[105]

Division of Labor and Management

As indicated above, white wage labor was used in the production of charcoal and other iron production–related activities. Iron production required a variety of skilled and unskilled labor. Workers were usually hired from the farms surrounding an ironworks to cut timber, make charcoal, mine ores and limestone, and transport these materials as well as finished products to and from the furnace or forge site. Skilled iron makers, pattern makers, and forgemen often moved from other iron-producing regions like piedmont North Carolina, Virginia, Pennsylvania, and even central Europe to work at South Carolina ironworks. A receipt book for one of Hill's furnaces dated from April 1798 to 1803 contains a list of 36 people who either provided the works with agricultural goods or some service.[106] These workers were sometimes paid in cash; more frequently they were paid in iron products, a common practice at that time. Table 11.1 gives the iron value of various activities performed at Hill's Ironworks.

Even though white wage labor was utilized on the iron plantations, much of the labor was pro-

vided by slaves. Usually a relatively large number of slaves were required. For example, Hill's Ironworks in 1795 required these laborers: "There are upwards of ninety negros attached to the works, between 70 and 80 of whom are grown, the rest are children. Most of those negros have been employed for a considerable time at the works, and are useful and valuable as forgemen, blacksmiths, founders, miners, and various other occupations."[107]

The number of slaves owned by the works is of particular importance for economic and social reasons. Though not necessarily large by coastal plain plantation standards, this number of slaves was large for the piedmont at this time and represented a significant investment of capital. For example, in 1790, 75 percent of the households in York County owned no slaves, while an additional 12 percent owned 3 or fewer. Only 14 persons in York County owned more than 10; a total of 26 was the largest number, other than Hill's Ironworks, with 82 slaves.[108] In all, Hill's Ironworks accounted for 9 percent of the 908 slaves in York County. Many of the slaves owned by Hill's Ironworks held positions which were critical to the operation of the works. These positions included miner, collier, wagoner, blacksmith, forgeman, filler, gutterman, and keeper of the furnace.[109]

Lander indicates that all three of the major antebellum companies followed labor patterns similar to that of Hill's Ironworks: a heavy reliance on slaves supplemented by a few local or northern whites in skilled and managerial positions.[110] For example, throughout the period between 1839 and 1860, the King's Mountain Company maintained a labor force of about 90 men. Of these, between 11 and 30 were company-owned slaves. The remainder of the workforce was hired from the surrounding countryside. Some worked by the job, others by the month or year. A portion of those hired were probably slaves owned by local farmers who hired them out to supplement their own incomes or as an investment in the iron company, as measured by the slave's value. Several local whites worked as colliers and wagoners, while the most skilled tasks, like pattern making and the master iron maker's

TABLE 11.1

VALUE IN IRON OF VARIOUS IRON-MANUFACTURING ACTIVITIES

Occupation	Payment in Iron Goods
woodcutter	6 lbs. iron per cord "they finding [the timber] themselves"
master colliers	400 lbs. per month
under colliers	250 lbs. per month "much less for green hands"
wagoners	20 lbs. iron or castings per team for hauling charcoal or ore per day
miners	300 lbs. per month
founders	1,250 lbs. castings per month "he finds himself and pays his keepers wages."
fillers	154 lbs. castings per month
laborers	100 to 130 lbs. per month
wheelwrights	250 lbs. per month
carpenters and blacksmiths	175 lbs. per month "they find themselves"
hammermen *or forgemen*	150 lbs. iron for drawing 2000 lbs. "plus 2 1/2 dollars per cent [for each 100 lbs.?]"
finers	200 lbs. bar iron for 2,240 lbs. anchonies drawn [the intermediate step between pig and bar iron]
wagoners to Camden	20 lbs. per day for 6 day round trip to carry 2,300 lbs.

SOURCE: *City Gazette and Daily Advertiser* 1795

TABLE 11.2
VALUE IN IRON OF VARIOUS FOODSTUFFS

Foodstuffs	Payment in Iron Goods
Beef	30 lbs. iron "per l00 net"
Pork	35 to 40 lbs. "per l00 net"
Wheat	8 lbs. iron per bushel
Corn	4 lbs. "per bushel"
Oats	2 l/2 lbs. "per bushel"
West Indian Rum	114 to 112 dollars

SOURCE: *City Gazette and Daily Advertiser* 1795.

position, were filled by artisans who had moved from other early iron-producing regions like New Hampshire and Virginia. The use of skilled artisans trained in other regions seems to have been a common pattern in South Carolina's early iron companies. This pattern was not unique to the iron industry; it was prevalent among several other trades practiced in the region in the last two decades before the Civil War.[111]

The Nesbitt company paid northern laborers from one to two dollars a day plus room and board. It paid its superintendents from $1,500 to $2,000 a year. The Nesbitt Company, which sold 187 Negroes in 1854, owned several enslaved laborers valued at up to $2,500 each, prices considered by Lander to be unusually high for a slave in the 1830s and 1840s.[112] The South Carolina Manufacturing Company's labor force of 80 in 1840 also consisted mainly of slaves. Lander goes on to indicate that the Nesbitt Company occasionally hired African Americans from neighboring farmers for $10 a month plus board.

The life of one black ironworker was described in the 1930s by his son, who was around five years old at the outbreak of the Civil War:

I was born on June 20th and I remember when the war broke out, for I was about five years old. We lived in Spartanburg County not far from old Cherokee Ford. My father was Emanuel Elmore, and he lived, to be about 90 years old.

My master was called by everybody, Col. Elmore, and that is all that I can remember about his name. When he went to the war I wanted to go with him, but I was too little. He joined the Spartanburg Sharp Shooters. They had a drill ground near the Falls. My pa took me to see them drill, and they were calling him Col. Elmore then. When I got home I tried to do like him and everybody laughed at me. That is about all that I remember about the war. In those days, children did not know things like they do now, and grown folks did not know as much either.

I used to go and watch my father work. He was a moulder in the Cherokee Ironworks, way back there when everything was done by hand. He moulded everything, from knives and forks to skillets and wash pots. If you could have seen pa's hammer, you would have seen something worth looking at. It was so big that it jarred the whole earth when it struck a lick. Of course it was a forge hammer, driven by water power. They called the hammer 'Big Henry'. The butt end was as big as an ordinary telephone pole.

The water wheel had fifteen or twenty spokes in it, but when it was running it looked like it was solid. I used to like to sit and watch that old wheel. The water ran over it and the more water came over, the more power the wheel gave out.

At the ironworks they made everything by hand that was used in a hardware store, like nails, horse shoes and rims for all kinds of wheels, like wagon and buggy wheels. There were moulds for everything no matter how large or small the thing to be made was. Pa could almost pick up the right mould in the dark, he was so used to doing it. The patterns for the pots and kettles of different sizes were all in rows, each row being a different size. In my mind I can still see them.

Hot molten iron from the vats was dipped with spoons which were handled by two men. Both spoons had long handles, with a man at each handle. The spoons would hold from four to five gallons of hot iron that poured just like water does. As quick as the man poured the hot iron in the mould, another man came along behind them and closed the mould. The large moulds had doors and the small moulds had lids. They had small pans and small spoons for little things, like nails, knives and forks. When the mould had set until cold, the piece was prized out.

Pa had a turn for making covered skillets and fire dogs. He made them so pretty that white ladies would come and give an order for a 'pair of dogs' and tell him how they wanted them to look. He would take his hammer and beat them to look just that way. Rollers pressed out the hot iron for machines and for special lengths and things that had to be flat. Railroad ties were pressed out in these rollers. Once the man that handled the hot iron to be pressed through these rollers got fastened in them himself. He was a big man. The blood flew out of him as his bones were crushed, and he was rolled into a mass about the thickness and width of my hand. Each roller weighed about 2,000 pounds.

The man who got killed was named Alex Golightly. He taught the boys my age how to swim, fish and hunt. His death was the worst thing that had happened in the community. The man who worked at the foundry made Alex a coffin. It had to be made long and thin because he was mashed up so bad. In those days coffins were nothing but boxes anyway, but Alex's coffin was the most terrible thing that I have ever seen. I reckon if they had pretty coffins then like they do now folks would have bought them to sleep in.

Hundreds went to Alex's funeral, white and black, to see that long narrow coffin and the grave which was dug to fit it. On the way to the graveyard, negroes sang songs, for Alex was a good man. They carried him to the Cherokee graveyard on the old Smith Ford Road, and there they buried him. My father helped to build the coffin and he helped haul him to the graveyard. Pa worked at the Iron Foundry until he was very old. He worked there before I was ever born.

My father was sold four times—during slavery. When he was brought to Virginia he was put on the block and auctioned off for $4,000. He said that the last time he was sold he only brought $1,500.[113]

The management of ironworks by the ironmaster not only involved coordinating iron production, but also involved the integration of agricultural activities. Southern ironmasters commonly put their furnaces in blast during November and December and continued production into May and June. During the summer and into the fall most of the slave labor force was involved in planting and harvesting cash crops, especially cotton. This pattern is supported by evidence of the seasonal operation of ironworks in south-central North Carolina. In an unsigned note an ironmaster recorded the dates in November and the chain of events associated with the blasting off of a furnace: "[O]n Monday night put the Fiar [*sic*] in the Furnace, on Sunday morning the 14th put up ore, Monday night the 15th put the blast on. Wednesday Morning the 17th let out mettle. Saturday the 20th made pots."[114]

Olmsted noted the seasonal routine of iron manufacture in North Carolina, when he wrote that "[m]ost of the Iron Works of the west [the region around Vesuvius Furnace] are kept in operation only in the fall and winter months, the remaining seasons of the year are devoted to agriculture."[115] That ironworks slaves were shifted from the ironworks to farming in the spring and summer is supported by a letter William A. Graham Jr. wrote from Vesuvius Furnace on May 23, 1839, in which he noted, "[t]he Furnace blowed out 5 or 6 weeks since making a blow of 6 months since that time I have been busily engaged in clear land planting [illegible] will plant nearly 200 acres in Corn at the place and father rebuilding the little mill. 100 acres Cotton on the River and wheat . . . I sold a load of cotton to Eli Smith 29 miles from Hillsboro . . . sent three small backs [cast-iron chimney backs] for chimneys."[116] A letter William A. Graham Jr. wrote to his father on February 25, 1835, concerns the same practice at Vesuvius. The letter also provides insights into the nature of ironworks management:

We are beginning to get the plantation in reasonable order[.] We commenced making Iron on new year Day have made about 30,000 lbs. since though so far it has taken most all to defray expenses, the Iron having to pay the Hands at both places [Vesuvius Furnace and Springhill Forge] and buy Provisions for both[.] The Furnace has been in Blast since the middle of December. Jesse Mangate and a man by the name of McGiniss [*sic*] are the superintendents[.] Wingate manages very well[.] In fact we could not get on without him[.] They have made a good many Castings. John and myself, had a talk about the payments lately[,] We have concluded . . . that you may take away 5 or 6 tons as soon as you can with convenience as they are getting in the way.[117]

The preceding quotations are indicative of another important social aspect of the both the North Carolina and South Carolina ironworks; that is, the kinship ties that existed in both ownership and management. At least eight furnaces and an equal number of forges were established in Lincoln, Gaston, and Catawba Counties during the last decade of the eighteenth century and the first quarter of the nineteenth century. In his analysis of the early North Carolina iron industry, Cappon stresses that Lincoln County and the surrounding region contained the most active iron industry in North Carolina during the antebellum period.[118] He also noted that the area's iron industry was controlled by five closely interrelated families throughout much of the period from 1795 to 1860. As indicated previously, there were many family ties, as well as business ties, which crossed between the North Carolina and South Carolina ironworks. For example, Hill's partner, William Edward Hayne, was married to Eloisa Davidson Brevard, the daughter of Joseph Brevard, co-owner of Vesuvius furnace and Brevard's forge.[119]

Future Archaeological Research into the Iron Industry of Piedmont South Carolina

To date, a total of 25 distinct iron-manufacturing operations have been documented in the South Carolina counties of Anderson, Cherokee, Greenville, Pickens, Spartanburg, and York. Archaeological evidence of the early iron industry of the piedmont in South Carolina is observable in at least four of these counties and has been identified in the field at 12 archaeological sites, 10 of which were deemed significant enough to be placed on the National Register of Historic Places in 1987.[120] In adjacent North Carolina, 28 more locations have been documented in the counties of Catawba, Cleveland, Gaston, Lincoln, and Rutherford. Archaeological evidence has been identified in the field at 13 sites in 3 of these counties.[121]

The archaeological resources of the Carolina piedmont exhibit a broad range of variability covering various aspects of early iron manufacture. They have the potential to yield information about early southern industrial activity, the role of iron in southern material culture, rural and industrial settlement patterning, and early industrial slave lifeways.

One specific research problem for which the archaeological remains of this region are particularly suited is the comparative investigation of furnace style and construction, and determination of the range of variability present in the area. This includes the study of the inclusion or exclusion of technological features developed in other regions. Four furnaces in South Carolina—Susan (38CK67), Ellen (38CK68), King's Creek (38CK71), and Cowpens (38CK73)—and five furnaces in North Carolina—Vesuvius (31LN60), Rehobeth-Reinhardt (38LN61), Stonewall (38LN63), Madison (31LN64), and Washington Furnace (31GS147)—retain sufficient integrity to be significant objects of study from the perspective of industrial engineering.[122]

Other research problems in industrial engineering include the delineation and comparison of mining and quarrying technologies, particularly between eighteenth- and nineteenth-century operations. Another research problem for which the archaeological resources are suited is the definition of the types of iron products manufactured in this region. The definition of temporal types as well as functional types should be possible.

The archaeological resources of this region also have the potential to yield information about both intersite and intrasite patterning. Questions such as how furnace sites were spatially organized and how they were located relative to necessary resources might be addressed. The spatial organization of the Cooperville (38CK2) complex should provide valuable as well as unique information about the simultaneous management of both agricultural and manufacturing activities. A particularly important problem for which Cooperville is well suited is the study of slave house patterning, since very little is known about the lives of slaves on iron-manufacturing plantations. Finally, the question of how these ironworks fit in with the rural way of life that was developing at the same time also requires further investigation, since it is another area of study which is poorly understood.

No matter which of these or other research problems is studied in the future, it is vital that they be studied using a landscape perspective. As this chapter demonstrates, a landscape perspective requires that content and context be considered at both the site and situational levels and at local and regional scales. For example, a furnace site, such as either Susan (38CK67) or Ellen (38CK68), cannot be fully understood unless it is viewed in relationship to all the relevant features of the landscape contained on the more than 10,000 acres of land controlled by the Nesbitt Company.

At an even broader scale, one can see how fully understanding the operation of the Nesbitt Company requires an understanding of its control of resources and production relative to other iron-manufacturing operations, as well as the social, political, and economic situation of the period when the company operated. An important implication of using a landscape perspective is the need to rethink how basic ideas and concepts, such as site and situation, are used in research and the management of cultural resources. For example, should the individual locations of furnaces, mines, quarries, and coaling grounds be considered as discrete sites or would it be more appropriate to consider the whole land holding of the plantation the site, with individual locations seen as features of the site? The answers to such questions will require much thought and discussion relative to specific research problems and management needs.

The archaeological record of the iron industry documents the earliest large-scale industry of the Carolinas. This essay has shown that at least four of the ironworks that exist in the northwest piedmont of South Carolina during the eighteenth and nineteenth centuries should be considered *iron plantations*. The four ironworks on which this chapter has focused adequately meet all the criteria set forth by Smith to be considered plantations: 1) a large land holding, 2) distinctive settlement form and spatial organization reflecting centralized control by the owner(s), 3) a specialized industrial production, and 4) a distinct division of labor and management functions with management in the hands of the ironmasters.[123] For example, these ironworks all controlled at least 10,000 acres of timber land, and consumed over 500,000 bushels of charcoal annually. They exhibited a complex settlement patterning reflecting the procurement of a variety of resources, farming, and manufacturing stages. They typically employed over 100 workers, most of whom were slaves, and annually produced between 100 and 300 tons of iron products.

Early iron-manufacturing ventures in the Carolina piedmont represented the coming of the industrial revolution to the South. The scope of these ventures was not matched until the rise of the textile industry after the Civil War. The role of this industry in defining the piedmont landscape cannot and should not be ignored.

NOTES

1. Landscape, as it is used here, is in keeping with geographer Carl Sauer's idea that the way people live makes a distinctive imprint on the surface of the earth, a landscape. Sauer felt that the introduction of a different cultural pattern into a region by a new group of people, or the adoption of different technologies, significantly affected the natural environment and created an observable cultural landscape (Kovacik and Winberry 1989:1–2). Landscape, as defined by Sauer, is a function of settlement activity. According to Donna Roper, "[T]he process of establishing settlements over the landscape is an adaptation to two sets of conditions, 'site,' and 'situation'" (1979:10–12). The concepts of site and situation, as used here, were originally developed in geography by Ullman 1954. Based on Ullman, Berry (1964:4) defines site as a unit of analysis, characterized by local man-land relations and by form and morphology. Berry (1964:4) defines situation as a horizontal as well as functional unit of analysis that refers to regional interdependencies and connections between places, or to what Ullman 1954 calls spatial interaction. Eschman and Marcus define site as "the features of the local environment on which settlements are established and over which they grow" (1972:28). "Situation" is further defined by Eschman and Marcus as "both . . . the physical conditions relative to the site that extend over a wider area than the actual settlement occupies and to man's cultural characteristics with and around the [settlement]" (1972:28). In keeping with these concepts, the two principal sources of information for defining the landscape discussed in this essay are the historical record and patterning exhibited by the archaeological record at the local or site scale and the regional or situation scale.
2. Tuomey 1848; Lieber 1856; Lieber 1858; Shepard and Jones 1866; Sloan 1908; Keith and Sterrett 1931; Butler 1966; Butler 1981; Horton and Butler 1981.
3. *City Gazette and Daily Advertiser* 1795.
4. Drayton 1802:251–52.
5. Tuomey 1848; Lieber 1856, 1858; Shepard and Jones 1866; Sloan 1908; Keith and Sterrett 1931; Butler 1981.
6. *City Gazette and Daily Advertiser* 1795.
7. Smith 1982:1.
8. McCuster and Menard 1985.
9. Records on the British Public Records Office 1752, 25:34–35.
10. McCuster and Menard 1985.
11. Moss 1981:110.
12. Force 1840:72.
13. Force 1840:72; Cecil Binning 1933.
14. Chestnutt 1985:337–38.
15. Chestnutt 1985:337–38; South Carolina Treasury Ledger 1775–77:115, 133, 151, 156, 184, 202, 288; Cooper and McCord 1874:404–5; Landrum 1900:153–57.
16. Force 1840:590
17. South Carolina Treasury Ledger 1775–77:5, 15, 20.
18. Lander 1954:339–50; Brevard Papers 1778; Drayton 1802:150–52.
19. Drayton 1802:149–53; Lander 1954:337.
20. Douglas 1971:261–64.
21. Douglas 1971:261–64.
22. Thomas Cowan 1987.
23. *Gazette of the State of South Carolina* 1779.
24. Drayton 1802.
25. *City Gazette and Daily Advertiser* 1784.
26. *City Gazette and Daily Advertiser* 1789.
27. *City Gazette and Daily Advertiser* 1800.
28. *South Carolina State Gazette and Columbia Advertiser* 1806.
29. South Carolina Treasury Ledger 1778–80:305, 320; Stevens 1985:133–35.
30. Lander 1954:39.
31. York County Deeds B:152–193; Bailey and Cooper 1983, 3:79–81.
32. Lincoln County Deeds, 17:26, 32; 19:78.
33. Bailey and Cooper 1983, 3:339–41.
34. Bailey and Cooper 1983, 3:339–41.
35. Bailey and Cooper 1983:79–81; Cowan 1987:14–18.
36. York County Deeds E:132–51.
37. Will and Estate Papers of William Hill; Cowan 1987.
38. Mills 1826:781.
39. Lieber 1858:84–85.
40. Drayton 1802.
41. Lander 1954:338,340; Gardner 1963:56.
42. Lander 1954:341.

43. Powell 1887:199–201; Birnie 1974:63–64.

44. Lesley 1859.

45. York County Deeds H:13–14.

46. York County Deeds H:13–14, 39–41.

47. Bobby Moss 1972:309.

48. York County Deeds K:350–56; L:345–52.

49. Ledbetter et al. 1987:294–95.

50. Lander 1954:354.

51. Lander 1954:342; Lesley 1859; Spartanburg County Cross Index of Deeds 1795–1919:187.

52. Lander 1954:342; Moss 1972:309.

53. South Carolina State Plats 8:6, 29; Book 11:18; Moss 1972:309.

54. King's Mountain Iron Company Minute Book 1837–67.

55. *Yorkville Enquirer* 1859.

56. Lander 1954:343; Lander 1953:183.

57. Lander 1953:183.

58. Moss 1970.

59. Lander 1953, 1954; Lesesne 1961; Lesene 1970.

60. Lander 1954:348.

61. *Charleston Daily Courier* 1853.

62. *Charleston Daily Courier* 1853.

63. Lander 1954; Lesesne 1970.

64. Ransom 1966; Walker 1966.

65. Paskoff 1983.

66. Paskoff 1983.

67. Smith 1982; Lander 1954.

68. King's Mountain Iron Company Minute Book 1837–1867.

69. Smith 1982:28.

70. *City Gazette and Daily Advertiser* 1795.

71. York County Plats 1:449, 451, 453.

72. York County Plats 1:449, 451, 453.

73. Shepard and Jones 1866:20–21.

74. *City Gazette and Daily Advertiser* 1795.

75. Shepard and Jones 1866. These ore banks are also described and mapped by Tuomey 1848, Lieber 1858, Sloan 1908, and Keith and Sterrett 1931.

76. Ferguson and Cowan 1986.

77. Lieber 1856:84.

78. Butler 1966:43.

79. Ferguson and Cowan 1986.

80. Keith and Sterrett 1931:9.

81. *City Gazette and Daily Advertiser* 1795.

82. Smith 1982:220.

83. Moss 1970.

84. Moss, personal communication 1992.

85. Smith 1982:37–41.

86. Cutbush 1814.

87. *City Gazette and Daily Advertiser* 1795.

88. Shepard and Jones 1866.

89. Tuomey 1848; Keith and Sterrett 1931.

90. Horton and Butler 1981.

91. Ferguson and Cowan 1986.

92. Horton and Butler 1981; See Tuomey 1848 for a discussion of the lime production process.

93. Sloan 1908.

94. Moss 1972.

95. York County Deeds L:345–52.

96. Baker and Hall 1985.

97. Cowan 1987.

98. *City Gazette and Daily Advertiser* 1795.

99. William Ancrum 1810.

100. Shepard and Jones 1866:17.

101. Cooper 1815:19.

102. Tuomey 1848:278.

103. Cutbush 1814; Clarke 1968.

104. Cutbush 1814; Cooper 1815; Smith 1982.

105. Cutbush 1814; Cooper 1815; Smith 1982.

106. Receipt Book 1798–1803.

107. *City Gazette and Daily Advertiser* 1795.

108. York County Census 1790.

109. York County Deeds 4:147–148.

110. Lander 1954:350.

111. See King's Mountain Iron Company Minute Book:51–52; Elmore Papers 1839–1840; Union County Census 1850; York County Census 1850.

112. Lander 1954:350.

113. WPA Folklore Writers Project 1937.

114. Brevard Papers 1817.

115. Olmsted 1827:119–20.

116. Graham Papers, Letter of William Alexander Graham Jr. from Vesuvius Furnace, May 23, 1839.

117. Graham Papers 1835, Letter of William Alexander Graham, Spring Hill Forge, to William A. Graham, Hillsboro, N.C., Feb. 25, 1835.

118. Cappon 1932:337, "Iron Making—a Forgotten Industry of North America."

119. *Charleston Daily Courier* 1806; Cowan 1987:23.

120. Ferguson and Cowan 1986.

121. Ferguson and Cowan 1987.

122. Ferguson and Cowan 1987.

123. Smith 1982:28.

Works Cited

Ancrum, William
1810   Journal of William Ancrum July 4, 1810–Aug. 5, 1810. Ms. on file, South Caroliniana Library, Univ. of South Carolina, Columbia.

Bailey, Louise, and Elizabeth Cooper
1983   *Biographical Directory of the South Carolina House of Representatives, 1775–1790*, 3:339–41. Univ. of South Carolina Press, Columbia.

Baker, C. Michael, and Linda Hall
1985   An Archaeological Evaluation of Three Proposed Alternate Sites for the Gastonia Municipal Airport. Ms. on file, Delta Associates P. E., Richmond, Virginia.

Berry, Brian
1964   Approaches to Regional Analysis: A Synthesis. *Annals of the Association of American Geographers* 54:2–11.

Birnie, Joseph
1974   *The Earles and the Birnies*. Whittet and Shepperson, Richmond, Virginia.

Brevard Papers
1778   Partnership agreement, Mar. 3, 1778, of Isaac Hayne and William Hill. Brevard Papers, North Carolina State Dept. of Archives and History, Raleigh.

Butler, J. Robert
1966   Geology and Mineral Resources of York County, South Carolina. *South Carolina Division of Geology Bulletin* 33. Columbia.
1981   Geology of the Blacksburg South Quadrangle, South Carolina. In Geological *Investigations of the Kings Mountain Belt and Adjacent Areas in the Carolinas*, edited by J. W. Horton, Jr., J. R. Butler, and David M. Milton, pp. 65–71. Carolina Geological Society Field Trip Guidebook. Columbia.

Cappon, Lester
1932   Iron Making—a Forgotten Industry of North Carolina. *North Carolina Historical Review* 9:331–48.

Charleston Daily Courier
1853   *Charleston Daily Courier,* Feb. 19, 1853.

Chestnutt, David (editor)
1985   *The Papers of Henry Laurens*, vol. 10, pp. 337–38. Univ. of South Carolina Press, Columbia.

City Gazette and Daily Advertiser
1784   *City Gazette and Daily Advertiser,* July 19, 1784. Charleston.
1795   *City Gazette and Daily Advertiser,* May 12, 1795. Charleston.
1800   *City Gazette and Daily Advertiser,* June 16, 1800. Charleston.

Clarke, Mary
1968   *Pioneer Iron Works*. Chilton Book, New York.

Cooper, Thomas
1815   *The Emporium of Arts and Sciences, New Series*, vol. 1. Kimber and Richardson, Philadelphia (June 1813) 1(1):5–444.

Cooper, Thomas, and Lousi McCord
1874   *Statutes at Large of South Carolina*. On file, Univ. of South Carolina, Columbia.

Cowan, Thomas
1987   William Hill and the Aera Ironworks. *The Journal of Early Southern Decorative Art* 13(2):1–31.

Cutbush, James
1814   *The American Artist's Manual: or, Dictionary of Practical Knowledge in the Application of Philosophy to the Arts and Manufactures*. Johnson and Warner, Philadelphia.

Douglas, Elisha
1971   *The Coming of Age of American Business: Three Centuries of Enterprise 1600–1700*. Univ. of North Carolina Press, Chapel Hill.

Drayton, John
1802   *A View of South Carolina, as Respects Her Natural and Physical Concerns*. W. P. Young, Charleston.

Eschman, D., and M. Marcus
1972   The Geologic and Topographic Setting of Cities. In *Urbanization and Environment*, edited by T. Detwyler, and M. Marcus et al. Duxburg Press, Belmont, California.

Ferguson, Terry, and Thomas Cowan
1986   *The Early Ironworks of Northwest South Carolina: A Final Report of Investigations Conducted from 1985–1986*. Submitted to the South Carolina Dept. of Archives and History, State Historic Preservation Office, Columbia.
1987   *Investigations into the Ironworks of South-Central North Carolina: A Final Report of Investigations Conducted from 1986–1987*. Submitted to the

North Carolina Division of Archives and History, State Historic Preservation Office, Raleigh.

Force, Peter
1840   *American Archives: Fourth Series* 1–6. M. St. Clair Clarke and Peter Force, Washington.

Gardner, Robert
1963   *Small Armsmaker.* New York.

Gazette of the State of South Carolina
1779   *Gazette of the State of South Carolina,* Nov. 24, 1779. Charleston.

Graham Papers
1835   Letter of William Alexander Graham Jr. to William Alexander Graham Sr., Feb. 25, 1835. PC 61. North Carolina Archives and History, Raleigh.
1839   Letter of William Alexander Graham Jr. from Vesuvius Furnace, May 23, 1839. PC 61. North Carolina Archives and History, Raleigh.

Horton, J. Wright, and J. Robert Butler
1981   Geology and Mining History of the Kings Mountain Belt in the Carolinas—A Summary and Status Report. In *Geological Investigations of the Kings Mountain Belt and Adjacent Areas in the Carolinas,* edited by J. W. Horton Jr., J. R. Butler, and David M. Milton, pp. 194–207. A Carolina Geological Society Field Trip Guidebook. South Carolina Geological Survey, Columbia.

Keith, Authur, and D. B. Sterrett
1931   Gaffney–Kings Mountain Folio: U.S. Geological Survey Folio, No. 222, 13 pages.

King's Mountain Iron Company Minute Book
1837– Minute Book of the Stock Holders of the King's
67   Mountain Iron Company. South Carolina, Dept. of Archive and History, Columbia.

Kovacik, Charles F., and John J. Winberry
1989   *South Carolina: The Making of a Landscape.* Univ. of South Carolina Press, Columbia. Originally published in 1987 as *South Carolina: A Geography.* Westview Press, Boulder and London.

Lander, Ernest M., Jr.
1953   Thomas Cooper's Views in Retirement. *The South Carolina Historical and Genealogical Magazine* 54(1):173–84.
1954   The Iron Industry in Ante-Bellum South Carolina. *Journal of Southern History* 20(3):337–55.

Landrum, John
1900   *The History of Spartanburg County.* Franklin Printing and Publishing, Atlanta.

Ledbetter, Jerald, and Dean Wood, Karen Wood, Robbie Ethridge, Chad Braley
1987   *Cultural Resources Survey of Allatoona Lake Area 1.* Submitted to the U.S. Army Corps of Engineers, Mobile.

Lesene, Joab
1961   The Nesbitt Manufacturing Company's Debt to the Bank of the State of South Carolina. *The Proceedings of the South Carolina Historical Association,* 15–22. Columbia.
1970   *The Bank of the State of South Carolina: A General and Political History.* Univ. of South Carolina Press, Columbia.

Lesley, John
1859   *Iron Manufacturer's Guide to the Furnaces, Forge's, and Rolling Mills of the United States.* John Wiley, New York.

Lieber, Oscar
1856   *Report on the Survey of South Carolina: Being the First Annual Report to the General Assembly of South Carolina, Embracing the Progress of the Survey During the Year 1856.* R. W. Gibbes, Columbia.
1858   *Report on the Survey of South Carolina: Being the Second Annual Report to the General Assembly of South Carolina, Embracing the Progress of the Survey During the Year 1858.* R. W. Gibbes, Columbia.

Lincoln County Deeds
1786   Book 17:26, 32. Lincoln County Courthouse, Lincolnton.

McCuster, John, and Russell Menard
1985   *The Economy of British America, 1607–1789.* Univ. of North Carolina Press, Chapel Hill.

Mills, Robert
1972   *Statistics of South Carolina.* Originally published 1826. Reprint, Hurlbut and Lloyd, Charleston.

Moss, Bobby
1970   Cooperville: Iron Capital of South Carolina. *South Carolina History Illustrated* 1 (2):32–35, 64–65.
1972   *The Old Iron District: A Study of the Development of Cherokee County—1750–1897.* Jacobs Press, Clinton, South Carolina.
1981   The Old Iron District—a Legacy of Iron Mining and Manufacturing in South Carolina. In: *Geological Investigations of the Kings Mountain Belt and Adjacent Areas in the Carolinas,* edited by J. W. Horton Jr., J. R. Butler, and David M.

Milton. Carolina Geological Society Field Trip Guidebook. South Carolina Geological Survey, Columbia.

Olmsted, Denison
1827   *Papers on Agricultural Subjects and Professor Olmsteads [sic] Report on the Geology of North Carolina Part 2.* J. Galfs and Son, Raleigh.

Paskoff, Paul
1980   Labor Productivity and Managerial Efficiency against a Static Technology: The Pennsylvania Iron Industry, 1750–1800. *Journal of Economic History* 15:129–35.
1983   *Industrial Evolution: Organization, Structure, and Growth of the Pennsylvania Iron Industry, 1750–1860.* Johns Hopkins Univ. Press, Baltimore.

Powell, John
1887   *Fifth Annual Report of the Bureau of American Ethnology for 1883–1884.* United States Government Printing Office, Washington, D.C. Pp. 199–201.

Ransom, James
1966   *Vanishing Iron Works of the Rampos: The Story of the Forges, Furnaces, and Mines of the New Jersey–New York Border Area.* Rutgers Univ. Press, New Brunswick.

Receipt Book
1798– Receipt Book, Hill and Hayne Ironworks, 1
1803   798–1803 (part of Sheriff's Receipt Book, 1803–1812, William Edward Hayne), South Carolina Dept. of Archives and History, Columbia.

Records on the British Public Records Office
1752   *Records on the British Public Records Office Relating to South Carolina,* vol. 25, 34–35. South Carolina Archives and History, Columbia.

Roper, Donna
1979   *Archaeological Survey and Settlement Pattern Models In Central Illinois.* Scientific Paper 14. Illinois State Museum, Springfield.

Shepard, Charles, and E. F. Jones
1866   *Report Upon The Property of the Magnetic Iron Company of South Carolina, (Formerly the Swedish Iron Manufacturing Company,) situated in the districts of York, Union, and Spartanburg.* Courier Job Press, Charleston.

Sloan, Earle
1908   *Catalogue of the Mineral Localities of South Carolina.* South Carolina Geological Survey, Columbia.

Smith, James
1982   *Historical Geography of the Southern Charcoal Iron Industry, 1800–1860.* Ph.D. diss., Dept. of Geography, Univ. of Tennessee, Knoxville.

South Carolina State Gazette and Columbian Advertiser
1806   *State Gazette and Columbia Advertiser,* Dec. 20, 1806. Columbia.

South Carolina State Plats
1839   State Plats of South Carolina, Columbia Series, Dept. of Archives and History, Columbia.

South Carolina Treasury Ledger
1778– South Carolina Treasury Ledger, 1778–80:305,
80   320. Dept. of Archives and History, Columbia.

Spartanburg County Cross Index of Deeds
1795– Lands Granted by the South Carolina Manufac-
1919   turing Company. South Carolina Provincial Congress. Spartanburg County Courthouse, Spartanburg.

Stevens, Michael (compiler)
1985   *Journal of the House of Representatives 1791.* Univ. of South Carolina Press, Columbia.

Tuomey, Michael
1848   *Report of the Geology of South Carolina.* A. H. Johnson, Columbia.

Ullman, E.
1954   Geography as Spatial Interaction. In *Proceedings of the Western Committee on Regional Economic Analysis,* edited by D. Revzan and E. Englebert. Univ. of California Press, Berkeley.

Union County Census
1850   Union District Census. Dept. of Archives and History, Columbia.

Walker, Joseph
1966   *Hopewell Village: A Social and Economic History of an Iron Making Community.* Univ. of Pennsylvania Press, Philadelphia.

Will and Estate Papers of William Hill
1817   Will and Estate Papers of William Hill. On file Dept. of Archives and History, Columbia.

WPA Folklore Writers Project
1937   Ex-slaves Account Dec. 23, 1937 (Project 1885—Folklore), Elmer Turnage editor. Spartanburg District 4, Work Project Administration Writers Program, United States Archives, Washington.

York County Census
1790   York District, First Federal Census. Dept. of Archives and History, Columbia.
1850   York District Census, Dept. of Archives and History, Columbia.

York County Deeds

1786   Book B:52–193; 152–155, 167–171, 177–193. Dept. of Archives and History, Columbia.

1798   Book E:32–151. Dept. of Archives and History, Columbia.

1815   Book H:3–14, 39–41. Dept. of Archives and History, Columbia.

1825   Book K:50–356. Dept. of Archives and History, Columbia.

1830   Book L:45–352. Dept. of Archives and History, Columbia.

York County Plats

1798   Book 1:449–53. Dept. of Archives and History, Columbia.

Yorkville Enquirer

1859   *Yorkville Enquirer,* Feb. 24, 1859. Yorkville.

12. The Archaeological Record of Tar and Pitch Production in Coastal Carolina

Michael A. Harmon and Rodney J. Snedeker

Tar kilns dot the landscape as a visible byproduct of the naval stores industry. This industry was important to the economic development of the southeastern coastal states from the eighteenth through the early twentieth centuries. Although tar kilns are numerous, land management activities have resulted in the destruction of countless examples. This destruction, combined with a small amount of previous archaeological research, justifies the need to study the remaining kilns as valuable indicators of past lifeways.

The naval stores industry was a primary part of the economic base for historic exploitation of the coastal plain from Virginia to Florida and the Gulf Coast. This industry depended primarily on the longleaf pine tree for the production of tar, pitch, turpentine, and lumber. None of these products were used exclusively by the naval industry. They are called naval stores because of their early association with naval use and the significance of their role in worldwide shipping.[1]

Naval stores consisted of gum and wood products.[2] Gum is present in the outer layer of pine trees and protects tree tissue from injury. *Gum naval stores* were obtained by "boxing" trees to obtain gum (oleoresin), which was distilled to produce turpentine. Rosin was a refined residue of distillation.

These products were used in the manufacture of soap, paint, varnish, lacquer, rubber, and ink. *Wood naval stores* consisted of lumber, tar, and pitch. White pines, primarily from New England, were used as ship masts and the southern live oak was favored for planking and curved ship timbers.[3] Tar was produced by firing dead pine wood (lightwood) in an earth-covered kiln. Pitch was tar that had been refined by boiling. Charcoal was produced by the same technique used for manufacturing tar, but hardwood was the preferred fuel. Blacksmiths used charcoal to fire their forges.

Tar kilns were constructed in a similar manner in the coastal plain and piedmont, although piedmont kilns used a slightly different system and were placed on sloping ground to promote tar flow.[4] Tar production in the foothills and mountains tended to be small scale and generally involved burning lightwood in an inverted iron kettle placed on a rock outcrop.[5]

Tar was used as a waterproofing material to protect ship riggings from decay. Pitch was used to seal caulking on both the inside and outside of ship hulls.[6] Nonmarine uses included general waterproofing, wheel lubrication, and medicine for livestock and humans.[7]

Historical Background

Colonial Production 1608–1783

Naval stores were produced in many areas of eastern North America following initial settlement. North American production of naval stores began in Nova Scotia. Early production centers included Virginia, following the 1608 settlement of Jamestown, and New England, after the 1620 settlement of Plymouth. The history of naval stores production in South Carolina has been summarized.[8] In South Carolina, naval stores were produced and exported to England shortly after settlement in 1670. The Carolinas rapidly surpassed New England in tar production because of their more abundant pine trees and the presence of the longleaf pine *(Pinus palustris)*, which contained a greater amount of gum than the northern pitch pine *(Pinus rigida)*. Southern pine trees produced larger quantities of sap and gum because gum production is directly related to growing season length.[9]

Tar and pitch production prior to 1705 was relatively small scale. The naval stores bounty led to accelerated production and the establishment of naval stores as a major colonial industry. The bounty was prompted by England's war with France and Sweden's war with Russia. Traditionally, Sweden provided the British government with naval stores. Because of continued warfare with Russia, the cost of Swedish tar rose and the supply dwindled. The British government believed that a bounty would encourage the American colonies to abandon their efforts at manufacturing, which would allow the British to maintain their monopoly on the export of manufactured goods.

South Carolina exports totaled 2,037 barrels of tar and 4,580 barrels of pitch in 1712, but increased to 40,000 barrels of both products combined by 1720. The bounty of 10 shillings prompted accelerated production of naval stores. The British sold tar and pitch to other countries for cash, which aided continued development of the British navy. Colonial production peaked by the 1730s because

of overproduction, expiration of the bounty, and regained access to European suppliers.[10]

Guidelines were established in 1715 because American tar and pitch were generally inferior to that produced by the Swedes. Tar production in America was usually a supplementary income source for planters or entrepreneurs. In Sweden it was practiced as forestry, with certain trees selected, cut, allowed to cure, and then fired. The Swedes took greater care in kiln construction than the Americans, who tended to use all parts of the pine tree for tar production.[11] Throughout the colonial period regulations were passed to improve tar quality, but with limited success. Barrel quantity was established at 31 and ½ gallons with standards for tar and pitch production and shipping. The English maintained the naval stores bounty (with several lapses) until 1774, when it was allowed to expire. Limited production occurred during the American Revolution.

Antebellum Production 1783–1865

Tar and pitch continued to be major products after the American Revolution. The overall importance of naval stores declined with the emergence of rice agriculture and the plantation system. Forests were cleared and placed in agriculture. After 1720 rice agriculture became the agricultural staple of the plantation system. Production of naval stores and timber continued as supplementary income sources.[12]

The quality of tar and pitch improved when producers realized that a higher-quality product would bring a better price. Sharrer maintains that two important changes occurred in naval stores production following the end of the War of 1812.[13] Tar and pitch production declined relative to turpentine production. New York and North Carolina surpassed New England in manufacture of this product. The shift to frame structures and increased use of paints and varnishes created new demands for turpentine. By the 1840s turpentine production was more important economically than that of tar and pitch.[14] During the 1840s and 1850s, the turpentine industry began moving southward from the nearly depleted North Carolina forests.[15] Prior to 1838, turpentiners believed that trees located south of the Cape Fear River would not flow sap sufficiently for production.[16]

Production was disrupted by the Civil War. The war required large amounts of timber and wood and also resulted in railroad and bridge destruction. Many pine forests were burned either accidentally or intentionally. In Barrett's words, "The territory between the Pee Dee and Cape Fear river was one, vast, extensive pine forest, and on nearly every stream there was a factory for the making of turpentine, rosin, and tar. Seldom would the soldiers pass up an opportunity to fire these factories because burning rosin and tar created a spectacle of flame and smoke that surpassed in grandeur anything they had ever seen."[17]

Postbellum Production 1865–1900

The industry recovered after the end of the Civil War. Free black and white laborers replaced the slave labor used before the war. Tar and pitch production required minimal cash to begin production. Once production began, profits arrived quickly. Northern investors also began to control a large portion of the business. During the 1880s, South Carolina and Georgia took the lead in production because of the depletion of pine stands in North Carolina. In the early twentieth century, Georgia and Florida became the major producers. The need for large amounts of tar and pitch became smaller as the shipbuilding industry shifted to steel rather than wooden vessels during the 1880s.[18] Production dropped steadily during the late nineteenth century and came to a virtual standstill in the early twentieth century with increased use of the welding beam and the appearance of the automobile.[19]

Tar Kilns

The tar- and pitch-making process has been described in various historical accounts.[20] These sources refer primarily to the Carolinas, but also to Florida and Louisiana.[21] The references are primary accounts with generally similar descriptions.[22] The tar-making process can be divided into seven steps on the basis of these references (fig. 12.1).

1. *Selection and procurement of fuel*—Dead and seasoned resinous pine wood (lightwood or fat wood) was the preferred fuel. Although several sources referred to this tree as the pitch pine, it is apparently the southern longleaf pine. The pieces were sawed, cut, and split for easier stacking. Usually waste wood, such as stumps, knots, and limbs, was used for kiln fuel. Schoepf is the only reference that mentions a preference for green tar that was produced from turpentine trees, rather than dead tar from dead trees.[23]
2. *Kiln foundation preparation*—A circular kiln floor was cleared with or without a prepared clay surface. Generally it was basin shaped with a gentle slope toward the center. Robin differs from this description, stating that a square basin was excavated with iron bars placed across the opening. This variation may be characteristic of French tar production.[24]
3. *Trench construction*—All of the sources mentioned either a trench or trench containing a pipe which extended outward from the kiln center. This drain extended past the kiln edge. All of the earlier references (1722–61) recorded a single trench. The two later references (1788, 1807) both referred to multiple drains. This difference between single and multiple trenches may be a dating key.
4. *Fuel wood placement*—There was usually limited detail concerning this stage of kiln preparation. The references noted that the wood was either piled or placed. Robin mentioned a pyramid-shaped stack, while Catesby (1754) noted the kiln looked like a haystack, with 13- to 14-foot-high sides and the center two feet higher.[25] The kiln top was four to five feet wider than the base.
5. *Kiln covering*—The lightwood pile was then covered with earth or turf and, in one case,[26] with a pole framework to keep the turf in place. Covering the kiln allowed the wood to

produce more tar before it was consumed, kept tar from catching fire, and nearly eliminated ash which contaminated tar.[27]

6. *Ignition and burning*—There was a general consensus in the sources concerning the method of kiln firing. The kiln was set on fire at the top. When the fire had caught, the top was covered with earth to prevent combustion. Long poles were used to stick holes in the kiln sides to "temper the heat" with the openings beginning at the top and proceeding downward as the lightwood burned. Tar making was a smoky, dirty, and often hazardous occupation. If the burn proceeded too slowly, there was danger that the kiln could explode and hurt the operators. If the fire flared up, tar would be wasted.

7. *Tar collection*—Catesby gives the greatest detail concerning tar collection.[28] Tar began to flow on the second day after firing and usually continued to run for four to five days. The holes in the kiln sides and top were plugged with earth to put out the fire, which preserved the charcoal in the kiln for later collection. The references contain some insight into what might be temporal variation. Coxe notes that the tar drained into an open pit.[29] References from 1741 to 1807 stated tar drained into barrels (or casks). The 1788 and 1807 references mention the presence of multiple catchments.[30]

Nineteenth-century references that describe the tar-making process are generally unavailable. Perry maintains that the process remained largely unchanged, but notes that by the 1920s some burners were making rectangular kilns.[31]

The following account of tar burning in Moore County, North Carolina, reflects both continuity and limited change in kiln construction in the early twentieth century.[32] A slight hollow (20 feet diameter) was excavated into clay soil that had a trench running from the center to a pit (six feet deep) just outside the hollow. Twelve to fifteen cords of lightwood were split into rails and stacked with the ends oriented toward the center. Knots, stumps, and roots were placed in the kiln center. The seven-foot-high kiln was topped with a roof of rails. The kiln was then "flagged," or covered with pine boughs. Green logs were stacked layer upon layer up the kiln sides resulting in an octagonal enclosure. A six-inch-thick layer of sand and clay was laid over the framework. A hole was cleared in the roof in the late afternoon and a fire was started which was allowed to burn all night. Early the next morning the hole in the roof was covered to smolder the kiln. Tar began to run by mid-afternoon. A bucket on a long pole was used to scoop the tar into a wooden trough which flowed into a barrel. The kiln was tended day and night until the tar flow stopped. A yield of one

Fig. 12.1. Tar kiln cross section. *After Combes 1974:10.*

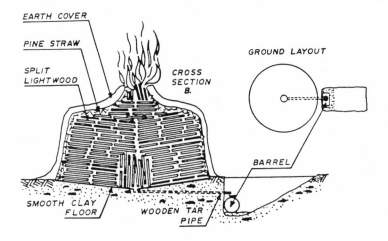

FLATLAND TAR KILN

EARTH COVER

PINE STRAW

SPLIT LIGHTWOOD

CROSS SECTION B.

GROUND LAYOUT

BARREL

SMOOTH CLAY FLOOR

WOODEN TAR PIPE

barrel per cord of wood was considered a good yield.

This example is interesting because it is similar in many respects to accounts from more than a century earlier. The description is detailed and complemented by photographs of the operation. The earlier references lack information concerning log cribs around kiln perimeters, suggesting this is a more recent technique. Additionally, it is noted that women and children helped construct the kiln. The eighteenth- and nineteenth-century accounts imply this work was accomplished entirely by men. Unlike earlier production, which depended mainly on slave labor, this kiln was burned using the sharecropper system. The property owner provided the pine wood and barrels. The workers gathered the wood, built the kiln, and delivered the tar to the railroad for shipment. Profits were generally split in half.

Pitch Production

The resulting tar could be either sold and shipped or reduced into pitch, which was a refined and less caustic pine product. Pitch production references are available only from the eighteenth and nineteenth centuries. Pitch was manufactured by boiling, either in iron kettles or more commonly in pits. Robin (1807) is the only source that mentions the use of heated iron balls to boil the tar rather than an open fire.[33] Pitch pit dimensions are given by Catesby (1754) as five to six feet in diameter and three feet deep, and by Schoepf (1788) as four and a half feet in diameter and six feet deep.[34] Pitch pits are generally described as being lined with clay unless such soil was naturally occurring. The pitch was stirred while boiling, the hole was covered to smother the fire, and the pitch was dipped into barrels before cooling. Three barrels of tar produced two barrels of pitch.

Archaeological Background, Methods, and Results

The earliest recorded tar kiln excavation was conducted by Stanley South at Charles Towne

Landing.[35] Several years later, two charcoal kilns in the piedmont were tested and compared to tar kilns.[36] These landscape features were generally ignored by archaeologists until the middle 1980s. Some archaeologists still consider tar kilns unworthy of being given archaeological site designations.

The South and North Carolina coastal plain National Forests provide an excellent data base for the study of tar kilns. They are large expanses of contiguous land that have been studied with relatively consistent survey methods and comparable intensity. The Francis Marion National Forest in South Carolina covers approximately 250,000 acres. It lies north of Charleston and south of Georgetown. The Santee, Cooper, and Wando Rivers border the forest.[37] The Croatan National Forest in North Carolina, which lies south of New Bern, consists of 157,000 acres of public land. The Croatan is bordered by the Neuse, Trent, and White Oak Rivers, which drain into the Atlantic Ocean inside the Outer Banks.

A total of 101 kilns has been recorded on the Croatan National Forest since 1984. Kilns or kiln clusters are recorded as archaeological sites on state site forms. Multiple kilns that are less than 100 meters apart and which occur on the same landform are usually recorded as single sites. Kiln elements are measured and mapped. Three-quarter-inch diameter cores are taken from kiln elements to examine soil and charcoal stratigraphy.

Over 100 tar kiln sites have also been recorded on the Francis Marion National Forest.[38] Tar kilns are recorded in a manner similar to that used on the Croatan.

Kiln Element Variation

Historical documents generally lack terms to describe the archaeological remains of tar kilns. Exceptions are the containments for flowing tar and boiling pitch, both referred to as pits. Kilns have been altered by erosion and frequently by fallen trees and burned-out stump holes, which may make identification of kiln elements difficult. Kilns must be recorded in a consistent manner to ensure comparability. Adequate recording of kiln remains will aid in determining whether they are eligible for listing on the National Register. In this report, the terms "mound," "central depression," "ring trench," and "collection pit" (fig. 12.2) are suggested as standard labels for kiln elements.

Kiln mounds are composed primarily of soil, with lesser amounts of charcoal and charred wood which formed during kiln firing. Auger tests reveal layers of mixed soil and charcoal and also thick, solid layers of charcoal. Excavations have resulted in the exposure of woodpile remains. In the Charles Towne and Francis Marion excavations, lightwood log sections were found in a pattern radiating outward from the kiln center. The piled lightwood angled downward toward the middle of the kiln along the basin-shaped kiln floor.[39]

Kiln mounds range from three to twenty-two meters in diameter, with circular mounds the most common. Oval shapes are less common and

rectangular mounds are very infrequent. Historical sources indicate rectangular mounds are the most recent.[40] It is also possible that different shapes reflect preferences by kiln constructors and/or variable rates of soil erosion. Keyhole-shaped mounds have been recorded on the Croatan in recent years. These mounds have an elongated earthen platform around the collection pit. The platform may encircle the pit or be in the form of ramps on each side of the collection pit. Ramps are not recorded in historical documents but would have allowed easier loading and may have been necessary for tar removal in seasonally wet areas. On the basis of oral history informants, the keyhole configuration denotes the latest kiln design.[41]

Historical sources mention prepared clay floors which have not been revealed through excavation. Auger testing indicates most clay floors were not intentionally manufactured, but were byproducts of natural soil conditions (such as shallow topsoil).

Two circular kilns have been recorded with tin floors. Tin floors aided post-firing cleaning and more efficient tar removal. One oval, brick-lined kiln was recorded at this same site. This kiln represents an attempt to improve efficiency. Repeated firings proved the bricks were not durable enough for their intended use. These kilns date to the late nineteenth and early twentieth centuries and are the only known examples in which tin floors were employed. The kilns were used for industrial production and were reused for multiple firings. Use of tin floors and brick walls was cost-prohibitive except in industrial situations.[42]

Kilns are usually assumed to represent single-firing episodes. Excavations on the Francis Marion have revealed a double-firing kiln.[43] In North Carolina, kilns have been recorded with double mounds, which indicates multiple firings. Auger tests at apparent single-firing kilns have shown that they are, in actuality, double-firing kilns.

Multiple-firing kilns are not recorded in historical documents. Such kilns may have resulted from incomplete firing, and the kiln would have had to have been opened and rebuilt for a second firing. A kiln may have been reused because of a favorable

TAR KILN ELEMENTS

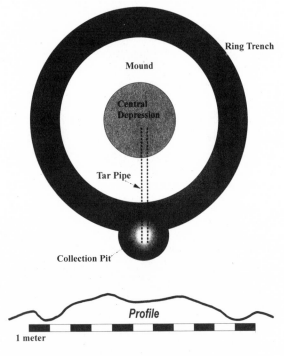

FIG. 12.2. Plan view of tar kiln elements.

location close to additional lightwood fuel sources and transportation routes. Reuse of one kiln in the same location would raise the kiln level higher above ground level. Groundwater tends to be relatively high in much of the coastal plain. Raising the kiln would result in easier kiln operation.

Kiln mound profiles may be flat in cross-section, but usually they have *central depressions,* which are low spots in the center of kiln mounds. Central depressions have a diameter range of 1 to 11 meters and a depth range of 15 to 60 centimeters. Circular, oval, and rectangular depressions have been recorded in North Carolina. Smith recorded three different profiles on the Francis Marion that include shallow central depressions, deep central depressions, and central depressions with a deep center and central high spot.[44] These differences probably reflect differential soil settling and/or kiln covering after firing.

Presence of the central depression may be explained in several ways. The kiln center was covered with dirt after ignition. If this layer was not as thick as the layer covering the remainder of the kiln, the resultant settling could have formed this depression. fire temperature was probably greatest in the kiln center, which would have produced a "cleaner" burn with greater settling after tar removal. Charcoal could have been collected from kiln centers. Collection was a secondary rather than primary function of tar kilns. Central high spots may have resulted when the kiln center was covered with dirt to stop combustion and the surrounding area was not covered, resulting in a raised center.[45]

The *ring trench* commonly found surrounding mound perimeters is recorded in only one historical document. A manuscript by Thomas Gamble that dates from the early twentieth century is the only documented record of trench construction.[46] This evidence, although limited, suggests trenches are a relatively late kiln feature. The large number of recorded kilns with ring trenches, however, suggests this was an earlier practice. Trenches may have been kiln features that were not documented because of their common occurrence.

Trench width ranges from 75 to 100 centime-ters, with a depth range of 35 to 65 centimeters. Many kilns which lack ring trenches may have had trenches which have been filled or covered by kiln mound slopewash. Trenches may have been used for water drainage, but the fact that most trenches drain directly into tar-collection pits seems to make this unlikely. (The ring trench could serve as the easiest and most readily available dirt source for kiln covering during all phases of the firing process.) Trench floors are either level and U-shaped in cross section or undulating with alternating high and low spots. Undulating trench floors may have resulted from the practice of opening and closing holes in the kiln sides to promote even burning and prevent complete oxidation.

Tar pipes and troughs were used to allow liquid tar to flow into collection pits. Some kilns have been excavated that only had an unlined ditch to promote tar flow.[47] Excavation of a collection pit on the Croatan National Forest revealed a circular stain (20 centimeters [8 inches] in diameter) which repre-sents the decayed remains of a drain pipe. The 1994 excavation of a kiln (31CV160) on the same forest located and recorded the remains of a four-foot-long section of a wooden tar collection pipe. A one-foot-wide trench had been excavated and the eight-inch diameter hollowed or sectioned log was then put in place. The pipe is thought to be hardwood, but analysis is not yet complete.[48] The remains of these features have also been uncovered in South Carolina.[49] Remains of a log that had been split longitudinally and hollowed were recovered in one of the three kilns at the South Carolina site. Apparently clay had been placed over the trough as a hood to protect the tar from contamination. This type of drainage pipe was not recorded in available historical references. The pipe was apparently in two sections, and the outer section was removed after firing, presumably for use in another kiln. Pipe reuse may have been a common practice. A pipe would become fire hardened and coated on the inside with tar, which would make it useful in other kilns. Pipe removal (after firing) may be the expla-nation for slumping that is frequently observed near the kiln mound/collection pit interface.

Collection pits were designed to contain tar draining from the kiln. They range from one to two meters in diameter and from 30 to 60 centimeters in depth. Their absence apparently indicates kiln firing for charcoal production rather than for tar.[50] Sometimes it is difficult to distinguish collection pits from burned or rotted tree stumps. Collection pits tend to be more shallow and more regular in cross section and located next to kiln mounds.

Both single and multiple catchments are recorded in the historical record. Single collection pits are recorded from 1722 to 1761 and in the late nineteenth century.[51] Multiple collection pits are recorded in the late eighteenth and early nineteenth centuries (1788 and 1807). This evidence seems to indicate the use of single collection pits in the early and recent historical periods.

The use of multiple collection pits seems plausible when considering the large quantity of tar that flowed from the average kiln. The use of dual or multiple collection pits would have promoted more efficient retrieval of tar. If one outlet became blocked or clogged, the other outlet would have allowed tar retrieval.

Collection pits have been recorded that are circular, oval, and rectangular. Pit placement may be parallel or perpendicular to the kiln mound.[52] Reasons for these variations and their implications are uncertain. Collection pits are usually unlined, but may be lined with clay or tar residue. Available references suggest that open pits were used prior to 1741 and in the late nineteenth century and that barrels were used from ca. 1741 to 1807. There may be some validity to this pattern, although it is likely that the use of barrels or open pits for tar collection was primarily a matter of personal choice.

Pitch Production

Evidence of pitch processing is sparse in the Francis Marion and Croatan National Forests. Tar could be fired in iron kettles over hearths near the tar kiln or fired in a pitch pit. Evidence for the use of iron kettles is lacking, probably because of the limited evidence for such an activity.

Six pitch pits were recorded during a study on the Francis Marion.[53] One of these pits was excavated. It was circular, with a clay-lined, flat base and rounded sides. Four clay-lined pitch pits have been recorded on the Croatan National Forest. One pit is known locally as the "Indian Cookpot." The four pits are shaped like iron kettles and range from one to two meters in diameter. Two other probable (unlined) pitch pits have been recorded. These pits are conical in shape and are three to four meters in diameter.[54] There is some question that these two pits were used for processing pitch because they lacked tar or pitch residue.

Storage and Reduction Facilities

A small number of structures have been recorded that were used for the storage and reduction of tar and pitch. More facilities surely exist that have not been located or which have not been correctly identified.

A structure with a mean ceramic date of pre-1771 was recorded on the Curriboo plantation site. It measured 11 feet by 37 feet, and had a smaller cellar. A layer of hardened pine tar covered the cellar bottom. The structure had overall low artifact density with very few pottery sherds and a high density of only nails. This evidence suggests the structure was used for the storage and/or processing of tar.[55]

One site on the Croatan National Forest (31CV102), which is known locally as the "old tar plant," has been recorded. This site dates from the late nineteenth and early twentieth centuries. Archaeological remains of this steam-powered plant include the foundation for a steam boiler, a flywheel pit, and processing pits. It is apparently a turpentine distillery.[56] Tar and pitch may have been processed here, as suggested by the nearby presence of tar kilns and concentrations of tar residue in several areas of the plant.

Artifact Assemblage

Tar kiln sites have yielded a very small quantity of artifacts. Various researchers have commented on the ephemeral nature of associated occupations and the limited potential for artifact recovery.[57] Charcoal and charred wood, however, are easily recovered and are amenable to species identification. Augering, which is used to study kiln stratigraphy, has resulted in the recovery of this kind of artifact but no others. Wrought nails and a creamware sherd were recovered at Charles Towne, indicating a late-eighteenth-century kiln construction.[58] Two machine-cut nails (dating roughly from 1790 to 1870) were recovered by excavations in the Francis Marion Forest.[59] Eighteenth-century flat buttons associated with a tar kiln in Colleton County were found by use of a metal detector.[60]

Interestingly, a stub-clay tobacco pipe was recovered from the bottom of the collection pit at kiln 31CV160, Croatan National Forest, North Carolina. The pipe is unglazed and has a fluted stem and bowl. The pipe is very similar in size and form to the third decorated type identified by Stanley South.[61] South excavated the pottery and kiln waster dump of Gottfried Aust, a Moravian potter who ran a shop in Betharbara, North Carolina, from 1755 until 1771.

While few in number, these pipes, buttons, nails, and ceramic artifacts are proof that portable objects can be found at these types of industrial sites. A relatively small number of kilns have been excavated, which has limited the potential for material recovery. Although tar kiln sites exhibit low artifact density, additional kiln testing and testing around kilns should prove productive.

Tar kiln sites recorded during recent surveys on the Francis Marion were tested with screened shovel tests (30- to 60-meter intervals) with only charcoal recovered. These results are not promising and may indicate larger units are needed or tests need to be placed near kilns at closer intervals. Surface collections at kiln sites after timber harvest and vegetation clearing may result in the location of previously buried artifacts.

Metal detectors have been used by some researchers in an effort to increase artifact recovery. Use of metal detectors is a labor-efficient technique biased toward the recovery of metal artifacts but with the potential for helping to date kilns and associated areas.

Historical accounts indicate kiln preparation and firing required one to two weeks of relatively constant attention. Laborers had to camp overnight while the kiln was being fired, and temporary shelters would be constructed. Kiln tenders were primarily black males during the eighteenth century and most of the nineteenth century. The advent of sharecropping resulted in women and children also being involved.

Artifacts are expected from these camps but in very low density. They may be difficult to identify as related to kiln operation. Material culture associated with kilns, such as tools and draft animal hardware, could also reflect farming or logging. Subsistence-related debris would not be easily distinguished from that associated with home sites or trash dumping.

Any perishable objects, such as wood shelters, would have deteriorated or been destroyed by natural or human-induced fire. Fires might also distort any hearths, making them unnoticeable. Additional testing may result in the recovery of habitation refuse, such as fragments of containers (dishes, jars, glasses) that were broken and/or discarded during kiln use. Personal and clothing items and hardware associated with draft animals and wagons may be present. Recovery of additional artifacts from kiln sites could provide information about kiln operation and data concerning time periods and cultural affiliations.

Kiln Distribution

The probability of tar kiln location is based on several factors: landform, relative elevation, and present vegetation. The proximity of previously recorded kilns indicates additional tar kilns may be present.[62]

Kilns are frequently located on low ridges or knolls which are not recorded on USGS maps. These sites can be located only by pedestrian coverage of areas that normally lack other kinds of archeological sites. Elevation differences are minimal in the relatively flat coastal plain. Kiln landforms also tend to border seasonal drains. Kilns were placed on ridges and other high spots to aid kiln operation and promote water drainage.

Present vegetation is not always an accurate indicator of past vegetation; however, areas that now have longleaf pine trees have usually had this same vegetation type for several hundred years. The longleaf pine range has decreased because this kind of pine does not regenerate easily without planting.[63] It also tends to be relatively slow growing, and many areas have been replanted with loblolly and other fast-growing species.

The presence of nearby recorded tar kilns indicates a likelihood for additional kilns. Frequently, kilns are found in clusters in North Carolina, so the presence of one recorded kiln increases the potential for other kilns being present. Tar kilns are not usually associated with domestic or agricultural sites. Wood buildings would have been endangered by fire from kiln burning.

Overall kiln distribution patterns are biased by several factors. Historical occupation of the coastal plain for the last 300 years has affected the integrity of naval stores sites by habitation (and associated construction), agricultural practices, and the timber industry.[64] Rapid commercial development of the Carolina coastal plain has resulted in the destruction of countless kilns in recent years. National Forest land has not been subjected to this kind of destruction.

Agriculture is an important economic pursuit throughout the coastal plain. Kilns have been recorded with plow furrows in them that probably date from the eighteenth through early twentieth centuries. Cultivation damaged but did not remove these kilns. They can still be identified. Development of heavy equipment in the late nineteenth century allowed more areas to be placed into agricultural production. Mechanization resulted in more frequent kiln destruction through kiln leveling and soil removal.

Timber management, such as bedding for pine tree planting, has destroyed kilns in many areas both on and off the National Forests. Logging has depleted longleaf pine stands and modified water drainage patterns. Artificially drained areas now supporting longleaf pine populations may have originally grown hardwoods and more water-tolerant pines (such as loblolly and pond pine). The construction of tramways, roads, log landings, and tree removal have destroyed countless kilns.

The rising sea level, especially in the last 50 years, has covered and eroded kilns located near the shoreline. We believe that kilns near ocean and river shorelines tend to be earlier than those further inland. Kiln distribution patterning is consistent with the historic settlement pattern. Initial settlement relied on waterways as the main transportation arteries, but development of roads and railroads allowed settlement and exploitation of forest resources in more remote areas. Project-specific historical research is necessary to determine the temporal relationship of kilns to transportation routes.

Historical maps are useful indicators of tar kiln presence primarily for large landholdings. Traditionally, a relatively large percentage of the coastal plain has been owned by a comparatively small number of people. Such landowners or companies generally produced maps of their holdings which do not show individual kilns, but which do show naval stores areas likely to contain kilns. Historical timber stand maps (more than 50 years old), such as the Interstate Cooperage Company timber map, are useful tools for kiln prediction. This company owned 50,420 acres in Jones, Craven, and Carteret Counties, an area which comprises roughly one-third of present-day Croatan National Forest. Areas marked by hatched lines are described as "merchantable longleaf turpentine areas of unmerchantable sawtimber." The same kind of tree preferred by turpentiners was also preferred for tar production; therefore, these areas are consistent predictors of tar kiln locations.

Kiln Density

As of 1992, 6,005 acres have been surveyed on the Croatan National Forest. A total of 101 kilns has been recorded, for an average density of one kiln per 44.8 acres surveyed. The 1989 Francis Marion survey of 3,779 acres resulted in the location of only 33 kilns. This total translates to an average of one kiln for every 115 acres surveyed. Kiln density on the Croatan appears to be roughly 2.5 times that of the Francis Marion. The results of a recent 30,000-acre survey are not yet complete but support this lower kiln density.[65]

Explanations for this apparent difference are uncertain. Survey intensity may be a factor, but coverage on both forests has been roughly comparable. The totals are probably accurate and may merely reflect North Carolina's leadership in naval stores production during most of the eighteenth and nineteenth centuries. South Carolina had more intensive agricultural use than North Carolina. Kilns may have been fired and leveled before an area was cultivated, thereby resulting in a lower kiln total.

Kiln clustering also appears to have been more common on the Croatan. Of the 62 sites, 27 (or 43 percent) represent multiple kilns (or kiln clusters). On the Francis Marion, only 5 (22 percent) of the 23 sites had multiple kilns. These data suggest that kiln clustering is twice as common on the North Carolina coastal plain as on the South Carolina coastal plain. This pattern of lower kiln clustering in South Carolina is also reflected on the Francis Marion by recent surveys.[66] This is a valid difference, because the location of one kiln prompts the search for additional kilns.

The need for continued study of tar kilns and pitch pits is apparent because examination of the available data base has shown numerous problem areas exist. Problem areas examined in this chapter include tar kiln variation in construction and firing, artifact assemblages, kiln density, distribution, and temporal change.

The naval stores industry was important to the economic development of the Carolinas. Tar kilns and pitch pits are visible archeological remains with potential for contributing to our understanding of the industry. The significance of naval stores sites can be addressed under criteria (a) and (d) of the National Register of Historic Places guidelines (36 CFR 60.4). Criterion (a) includes sites that "are associated with events that have made a significant contribution to the broad patterns of our history" and criterion (d) lists sites that "have yielded, or may be likely to yield, information important in prehistory and history."[67]

These sites are also important because of their value to the general public. Archaeologists have been criticized because of the esoteric nature of their profession. Preservation and interpretation of naval stores sites (fig. 12.3) can ensure a connection with the past and instill the general public with an appreciation of forest products and their role in the development of the United States.

Recent archaeological surveys in the coastal plain have recorded a larger number of tar kilns than earlier surveys. This is an encouraging development, but researchers continue to rate these sites as insignificant and not worthy of study beyond their initial recording. Statements that kilns are common and others have been preserved or excavated are seen in the literature. There is also the belief that further investigations would provide only a limited amount of valuable information.[68] We agree that kiln preservation should be selective, but further study of kilns and other naval stores production sites is warranted because of a number of unresolved problem areas.

It has been argued that the tar-making process was largely unchanged throughout its development. The potential of dendrochronology as a dating technique has not been examined in detail, but may be a viable method. Some authors believe that most North Carolina (and presumably South Carolina) tar kilns predate the Civil War.[69] The need for tar was constant during the nineteenth and early twentieth centuries. Tar products were used by all households. Relatively poor transportation networks and the development of crossroad communities ensured the need for tar production at the local level. Although tar and pitch production were less important to the national economy, they maintained importance at the local and regional levels.

The problem of assigning dates to individual tar kilns remains largely unsolved. Dating can be accomplished through reconstruction of historic contexts and determining a kiln's relationship to archaeological sites.[70] Kiln access routes appear to be a general dating key. Kilns are usually located near roadways or waterways. Kilns near navigable streams and rivers tend to be older than kilns near roads. The historical pattern of coastal plain settlement consisted of moving inward along the rivers and navigable streams, with the development of roads and railroads following afterward.

Kiln sites exhibit low artifact density but continued study has yielded dateable artifacts, including the ca. 1755–71 pipe recovered at site 31CV160. Historical research can provide temporal information concerning tar production at specific sites. Although historical records have the potential for providing information about naval stores operations, we must remember the sources of such accounts. These records were produced by land-owners and travelers who recorded what they saw. None of these accounts were by the actual operators. The kiln operator's presence is related "firsthand" only through the archaeological record.

The reliability of tar kiln physical attributes as temporal indicators is an area that is presently ambiguous, but which warrants further study. If the six historical references spanning the eighteenth and early nineteenth centuries (1722–1807) are compared, certain changes in kiln operation may be inferred and test implications developed. Multiple drains and collection pits are mentioned in the late eighteenth and early nineteenth centuries. Prior to this time, single drains and collection pits were recorded. Prior to 1741, tar was recorded as draining directly into collection pits rather than into barrels as related in the later accounts.

Rectangular and "keyhole"-shaped kilns appear to be more recent, with rectangular kilns being a twentieth-century development. There is a gap in the historical records for much of the nineteenth century, so changes in kiln form, if present, were not recorded. The late-nineteenth-century account described previously is from the interior coastal plain, where kiln construction may have varied from that employed in the coastal plain closer to the ocean.[71] The significance of these implications depends on further study.

The naval stores industry was a regional

FIG. 12.3. Interpretive kiln firing at Charles Towne Landing 1670. *Janson L. Cox, photographer.*

industry associated with coastal plain development. Studies of the naval stores industry need also to include the turpentine industry and its relationship to the production of tar and pitch. Emphasis in this essay has been placed on tar and pitch production because this industry has received less attention than the turpentine industry.[72]

Information concerning tar kiln and pitch pit locations is readily available for South Carolina and North Carolina. Once the data from the recent large-scale survey on the Francis Marion National Forest is available in written and Geographic Information System (GIS) format it should be useful for distributional studies. Comparative data is needed from other portions of the Atlantic and Gulf coastal areas. This information could be incorporated into regional distribution models.

Kiln distribution also needs to be examined at the site level. Kiln clusters are more common in North Carolina than South Carolina. The relationship of kilns at a single site warrants examination. Multiple kilns of the same time period may represent a large-scale industrial or plantation-related operation. Single kilns may represent smaller-scale operations or just areas with a lower density of longleaf pine.

Kiln location across different environments is an area of potential study. Kilns have been recorded on high, dry longleaf pine ridges and along hardwood cove edges. Those kilns situated near hardwoods may have been fired mainly for hardwood charcoal production. Such kilns should be tested and charcoal samples gathered for species identification. Combes has suggested attributes for the identification of charcoal kilns which deserve testing once the wood content of kilns has been determined.[73]

Tar kilns and pitch pits are landscape features that can be interpreted for the general public. The Tarpit picnic area on the Francis Marion National Forest consists of a tar kiln near U.S. Highway 17A with an interpretive sign. An interpretive tar kiln site is being developed for the Pine Cliff Picnic Area on the Croatan. An experimental kiln firing at Charles Towne Landing has been developed into an interpretive display. The Tarheel Trail at Moores Creek Battlefield near Wilmington has a signed trail with illustrations depicting aspects of naval stores production. The Bladen Lakes Educational State Forest near Elizabethtown has exhibits on forest management and a well-developed naval stores exhibit which includes a reconstructed tar kiln and a turpentine mill.

Tar and pitch production was an integral aspect of the naval stores industry and the changing landscape of South Carolina. Continued research should produce a better understanding of the industry and its importance to the history of the lowcountry.

Notes

1. The reader is referred to Perry 1947 for a detailed treatise on naval store production.
2. Robinson 1988:3–8.
3. Sharrer 1981:243, 253.
4. Combes 1974.
5. Wigginton 1979:252–56; Hockensmith 1986.
6. Sharrer 1981:243.
7. Wigginton 1979:252.
8. Hart 1986:5–9.
9. Sharrer 1981:243.
10. Kovacik and Winberry 1989:70–71.
11. Sharrer 1981:248.
12. Williams, Cable, and Reed 1992:38–40.
13. Sharrer 1981:253–254.
14. Perry 1947:147.
15. Robinson 1988:11–13.
16. USDA 1915 in Loftfield 1991:17.
17. Barrett 1987:299.
18. Sharrer 1981:269.
19. Cross 1973:22.
20. Catesby 1977; Coxe 1976; Glen 1761; Oldmixon 1969; Robin 1966; Schoepf 1968.
21. Robin 1966.
22. Catesby 1977 is the most detailed and Robin 1966 is the least similar to the other references listed in n. 20 above.
23. Schoepf 1968.
24. Robin 1966.

25. Robin 1966.
26. Catesby 1754.
27. Hart 1986:12.
28. Catesby 1977.
29. Coxe 1976.
30. Catesby 1977; Glen 1761; Oldmixon 1969; Robin 1966; Schoepf 1968.
31. Perry 1947:66–70.
32. Haynes 1916 in Linder 1982.
33. Robin 1966.
34. Catesby 1977; Schoepf 1968.
35. South 1971.
36. Combes 1974.
37. Anderson and Logan 1981.
38. Robert Wise, personal communication 1991.
39. Hart 1986:19; South 1971:181.
40. Perry 1947:66–70.
41. Harry Warren, personal communication, cited in Loftfield 1991:20.
42. Robinson 1991:97–106.
43. Hart 1986:19–20.
44. Smith 1989:108.
45. Smith 1989:108.
46. As cited in L. Hart 1986:11, Thomas Gamble n.d.:1.
47. South 1971.
48. Harmon, Snedeker, and Ashcraft 1995.
49. Hart 1986:18.
50. Combes 1974:9.
51. Linder 1982.

52. Smith 1989:108.
53. Hart 1986:20.
54. Loftfield 1991:10.
55. Wheaton, Garrow, and Friedlander 1983:190–92.
56. Robinson, personal communication 1992.
57. Harmon and Snedeker 1988; Robinson 1988; Hargrove 1987.
58. South 1971:182–83.
59. Hart 1986:18, 22.
60. Chris Espenshade, personal communication 1992.
61. South 1963.
62. Harmon and Snedeker 1988.
63. Merrens 1964:86.
64. Wheaton 1992:9–11.
65. Ishmael Williams, personal communication 1992.
66. Williams, personal communication 1992.
67. National Register of Historic Places guidelines (36 CFR 60.4). The National Historic Preservation Act P.L. 89-665, 16 U.S.C. 470–470t (1966) authorizes the NRHP and sets up criteria for evaluation (C.F.R. 60).
68. Allan and Espenshade 1990; Williams et al. 1992.
69. Hargrove 1987; Robinson 1988:15.
70. Robinson 1988:15.
71. Linder 1982.
72. For example, Bond 1987; Forney 1984; Robinson 1991.
73. Combes 1974.

Works Cited

Allan, Linda K., and Christopher T. Espenshade
1990   *Archeological Resources Survey of Selected Portions of the Wambaw and Witherbee Districts, Francis Marion National Forest, Berkeley County, South Carolina.* Submitted to the United States Forest Service, Francis Marion National Forest, South Carolina. Brockington and Associates, Atlanta.

Anderson, David G., and Patricia A. Logan
1981   *Francis Marion National Forest Cultural Resources Overview.* United States Forest Service, Dept. of Agriculture, Columbia.

Barrett, John G.
1987   *The Civil War in North Carolina.* Univ. of North Carolina Press, Chapel Hill.

Bond, Stanley C., Jr.
1987   The Development of the Naval Stores Industry in St. Johns County, Florida. *The Florida Anthropologist* 40(3):187–202.

Catesby, Mark
1977   The Natural History of Carolina, Florida, and the Bahama Islands; Containing the figures of Birds, Beasts, Fishes, Serpents, Insects, and Plants . . . [Originally published 1754]. In *The Colonial South Carolina Scene, Contemporary Views, 1697–1774,* edited by H. Roy Merrens, pp. 87–109. Tricentennial Edition. Univ. of South Carolina Press.

Combes, John D.
1974   Charcoal Kilns and Cemetery at Parris Mountain State Park. Univ. of South Carolina, S.C. Institute of Archeology and Anthropology. *Notebook* 6(1):3–17.

Coxe, Daniel, Esq.

1976 *A Description of the English Province of Carolina, by the Spainards call'd Florida, and by the French La Louisiane.* Originally published 1772. Reprint, Univ. Presses of Florida, Gainesville.

Cross, John K.

1973 Tar Burning, A Forgotten Art? *Forests and People* 23(2):21–23.

Forney, Sandra J.

1984 Chronological Placement of Materials Associated with the Naval Stores Industry within the National Forests in Florida. Paper presented at the annual meeting of the Society for Historical Archeology, Williamsburg.

Glen, James

1761 Naval stores. Handout prepared for the Berkeley County Historical Society. Ms. on file, United States Dept. of Agriculture, National Forests in North Carolina, Asheville.

Hargrove, Thomas H. (editor)

1987 *A Cultural Resource Survey at the U.S. Marine Corps Air Station, Cherry Point, N.C.* Archeological Research Consultants, Chapel Hill.

Harmon, Michael A., and Rodney J. Snedeker

1988 Tar Kiln Variability and Significance. Paper presented at the Southeastern Archeological Conference, New Orleans.

Harmon, Michael A., and Rodney J. Snedeker, and A. Scott Ashcraft

1995 *Archaeological Investigation of 31CV160: A Coastal Plain Tar Kiln.* Croatan National Forest, Craven County, North Carolina, USDA National Forests in North Carolina, Asheville.

Hart, Linda F.

1986 Excavations at the Limerick Tar Kiln Site— 38BK472. Ms. on file, U.S. Forest Service, Francis Marion National Forest, McClellanville.

Hockensmith, Charles D.

1986 Euro-American Petroglyphs Associated with Pine Tar Kilns and Lye Leaching Devices in Kentucky. *Tennessee Anthropologist* 11(2):100–31.

Kovacik, Charles F., and John J. Winberry

1989 *South Carolina: The Making of a Landscape.* Univ. of South Carolina Press, Columbia. Originally published in 1987 as *South Carolina: A Geography.* Westview Press, Boulder and London.

Linder, Suzanne L.

1982 *They Came by Train and Chose to Remain: The Importance of Moore County Railroads, 1850–1900.* Richmond Technical College, Hamlet.

Loftfield, Thomas C.

1991 *Archeological/Historical Reconnaissance of Three Soil Compaction Study Plots near Pinecliff in Croatan National Forest, Craven County, North Carolina.* Dept. of Anthropology, Univ. of North Carolina at Wilmington. Submitted to the U.S. Dept. of Agriculture, National Forests in North Carolina, Croatan National Forest, Asheville.

Merrens, Harry R.

1964 *Colonial North Carolina in the Eighteenth Century: A Study in Historical Geography.* Univ. of North Carolina Press, Chapel Hill.

Oldmixon, John

1969 *The British Empire in America Containing the History of the Discovery, Settlement, Progress and State of the British colonies on the Continent and Islands of America.* Originally published 1741. Reprint, Economic Classics, New York.

Perry, Percival

1947 *The Naval Stores Industry in the Ante-Bellum South: 1789–1861.* Ph.D. diss., Dept. of History, Duke Univ.

Robin, C. C.

1966 *Voyage to Louisiana by C. C. Robin, 1803–1805.* Originally published 1807. Reprint, Pelican Publishing Company, New Orleans.

Robinson, Kenneth N.

1988 Archeology and the North Carolina Naval Stores Industry: A Prospectus. Ms. on file, Office of State Archeology, Raleigh.

1991 Archeological Data Recovery at Weed's Lightwood Plant: An Early Twentieth Century Naval Stores Distillery, Cumberland County, North Carolina. Submitted to the North Carolina Dept. of Transportation, Raleigh.

Schoepf, Johann D.

1968 *Travels in the Confederation 1783–1784.* Originally published 1788. Reprint, Burt Franklin Publisher, New York.

Sharrer, G. Terry

1981 Naval stores, 1781–1881. In *Material Culture of the Wooden Age,* edited by Brooke Hindle, pp. 241–361. Sleepy Hollow Press, Tarrytown, New York.

Smith, Charlotte A.

1989 *Cultural Resources Survey of Fiscal Year 1991*

Timber Sales, Francis Marion National Forest.
Report on file, U.S. Forest Service, McClellanville.

South, Stanley

1963   Exploratory Excavation of a Brick Kiln at Town
Creek, Brunswick County, N.C. Ms. on file,
North Carolina State Dept. of Archives and
History, Raleigh.

1971   *Archeology at the Charles Towne Site (38CH1) on
Albemarle Point in South Carolina.* 2 vols.
Research Manuscript Series 10. South Carolina
Institute of Archeology and Anthropology,
Columbia.

Wheaton, Thomas R., Jr.

1992   *An Archaeological Survey of 2,012 Acres in the
Wambaw District, Francis Marion National Forest.*
Submitted to the U.S. Forest Service, New South,
Stone Mountain, Georgia.

Wheaton, Thomas, R., Jr., Amy Friedlander, and
Patrick H. Garrow

1983   *Yaughan and Curriboo Plantations: Studies in
Afro-American Archaeology.* Soil Systems,
Marietta, Georgia.

Wigginton, Eliot

1979   *Foxfire 4.* Anchor Press, Garden City.

Williams, G. Ishmael, John S. Cable, and Mary Beth Reed.

1992   *An Archeological Survey of 2,195 Acres in the
Cainhoy Area, Wambaw and Witherbee Districts,
Francis Marion National Forest. Francis Marion
National Forest Indefinite Services Survey Report 1.*
New South Associates Technical Report 66.
Submitted to the U.S. Dept. of Agriculture, Forest
Service. New South Associates, Stone Mountain,
Georgia.

13. The Urban Landscape in South Carolina

Martha Zierden

The study of urban history and urban archaeology are relatively recent develop ments. Barely twenty years old, urban archaeology currently features varied approaches to the data base. Many scholars have begun to organize their data and interpretations within the framework of landscape studies.

The Archaeological Study of Urban Sites

Although the definitions of *urban* and *urban archaeology* are as diverse as the practitioners of the discipline, the definitions proposed by Staski will be used here: Urban archaeology is the study of relationships between material culture, human behavior, and cognition in an urban setting. An urban setting is defined as a permanent location in which the density of settlement and the amount of human energy expended per unit of land are considerably greater than in the surrounding region. An urban center, or city, is a sociopolitical entity that exhibits the characteristics of an urban setting. Further, John Stilgoe has implied that an urban setting is a planned population center, deliberately designed to serve commerce rather than

agriculture. Central to his discussion is a planned network of streets and lots, relatively expensive real estate, and thus small lots, a concentration of citizens involved in mercantile endeavors, and recognizable boundaries between the mercantile center and the agricultural hinterland.[1]

When North America was first being occupied by immigrants from Europe in the sixteenth, seventeenth, and eighteenth centuries, these people brought with them the traditions of an urban-based society. Colonial proprietors encouraged the development of urban centers for protection, community, and commerce.[2] Although their efforts met with mixed success—commercially profitable towns and cities were more prevalent in northern colonies than in southern—urban centers played a pivotal role in the development of American life.

Many colonial towns served as important social, political, and commercial centers for abbre- viated hinterlands, but were not large enough, dense enough, nor complex enough to be considered "cities." Nonetheless, it was in the study of such settlements as Williamsburg, Virginia, St. Mary's City, Maryland, and St. Augustine, Florida, that the theory and techniques of urban archaeology developed.[3] It was also through programs in these cities that the discipline began to be "archaeology *of* the city" rather than "archaeology *in* the city."[4] Research in these areas began to address problems of urban development such as social and ethnic stratification and urban spatial patterning.[5] These projects were also the origin of many techniques for dealing with some of the practical and logistical problems of studying urban sites.[6]

The 1970s saw an increase in the number of archaeological studies in large urban centers, such as New York and Atlanta, primarily as the result of federally funded development and urban renewal. Many of these mitigation projects were site-specific in focus. Researchers in Alexandria, Virginia, were the first to recognize the entire city as the logical unit of research and to implement a long-term research program. Dubbed the "city-site approach" by Cressey and others, the program involves historical research, archaeological testing, data recovery, and extensive public involvement. The Alexandria program was unique in many ways, and it continues to serve as a model for research programs in other cities. Such municipally sponsored and supported programs are rare, however, and isolated mitigation projects are still prevalent. These two trends are evident in the 1983 volume on urban archaeology edited by Roy Dickens.[7] In many ways, this publication can be viewed as the culmination of the "emergence" period of urban archaeology, and its publication heralded the integration of the field into the mainstream of historical archaeology.

During the 1980s, urban archaeology evolved into a mature subdiscipline, developing a particular set of methods and applying a variety of research questions to urban sites, including those particular to an urban situation as well as those shared by other areas of historical archaeology. Urban archaeologists, including the present author, have begun to approach cities through the concept of landscape. Landscape—the natural environment modified for permanent human occupation—embraces technomic, social, and ideological ideas within shared spaces.[8] Landscape archaeology requires a broader scale than most archaeological studies encompass. Archaeologists usually focus incremen-

tally on the excavation unit, the house, or the community. Landscape requires consideration of the spaces between these units. The various components of the city—public and private buildings, outbuildings, fences, gardens, streets, public places, stretches of woods and water—are ideally suited to research through the landscape approach.

Urban Archaeology in South Carolina

Urban archaeology in South Carolina parallels many of these national trends. In most cases, South Carolina's urban centers are living sites, occupied from their founding through the present day. They contain archaeological evidence for the continuum of human behavior in that location. In this state, urban centers can be small villages such as Cainhoy, or large cities such as Charleston. In some ways, lumping these various villages, towns, and cities masks major differences among them. However, some overarching theoretical, methodological, and logistical considerations are common to all, in contrast to the more numerous rural sites of the last three centuries.

Urban archaeology in South Carolina began not in its biggest cities, but within the small late-eighteenth-century town of Camden. In his pioneering study, Kenneth Lewis examined spatial patterning and site activities within the town proper. He observed that in contrast to comparable towns in Britain, Camden exhibited a markedly more dispersed settlement pattern, smaller population, larger land use units, a greater proportion of nondomestic activities on town lots, and a relatively large proportion of high-status residents. Lewis suggested that these characteristics reflect Camden's role as a frontier town, serving as a locus of "those activities associated with the collection and redistribution of goods and commodities passing into and out of the area of colonization."[9] Lewis later expanded his ideas into a regional study of frontier development, using South Carolina as a model. The rise of urban centers is an integral aspect of this important research.[10] Lewis's study encompasses concepts of urbanization and landscape evolution and remains highly relevant today.

Since Lewis's work, Camden and Charleston remain the only two urban centers to be studied archaeologically in any great detail. The remainder of this chapter will be concerned with work in Charleston, but other urban projects in South Carolina should be mentioned. Stanley South conducted excavations at the original site of Charles Towne (1670–80, now Charles Town Landing, a state park), beginning in 1968. These excavations were extensive, and many were of an emergency nature, conducted just prior to construction. Much of the work focused on the military aspect of the site, not the daily life of town residents.[11] Dan Elliott of the LAMAR Institute has been researching "lost" colonial towns along the Savannah River in Georgia and South Carolina.[12] He has also recently surveyed the site of Jamestown in Berkeley County. Kenneth Lewis has examined a few sites in downtown Columbia, using a landscape approach.[13] Larry Lepionka has investigated two sites in downtown Beaufort.[14] MAAR Associates conducted excavations in Laurens.[15] The South Carolina Department of Highways and Public Transportation has surveyed a number of corridors in small towns and cities throughout the state.[16]

Archaeology in Charleston

Archaeological research was initiated in Charleston at the same time as Lewis's work in Camden. The late John Miller excavated a number of sites in Charleston in the 1960s, including the Exchange building basement. None of these projects have been published. Stanley South and Richard Polhemus excavated a concentration of delft pottery near the Charleston waterfront in the 1970s. Concerted efforts to study Charleston archaeologically were initiated by Elaine Herold of The Charleston Museum in the late 1970s. She excavated a number of sites, particularly the Heyward-Washington house. This four-year excavation at a museum-owned historic site was conducted on a volunteer

basis. Tens of thousands of artifacts were recovered, and Dr. Herold continues to work on the report. The Heyward-Washington house remains the largest urban domestic project in South Carolina.[17]

The late 1970s and early 1980s also witnessed a period of federally funded urban renewal projects in downtown Charleston which required archaeological mitigation. Elaine Herold conducted several of these surveys in the late 1970s,[18] and Zierden worked on additional sites in the early 1980s.[19] Other archaeological firms have subsequently worked on federally funded projects in Charleston. Gilbert/Commonwealth of Michigan worked at the site of the Post Office/Courthouse annex. Garrow and Associates surveyed a portion of peninsular Charleston north of the early-nineteenth-century suburbs which would be affected by construction of a new Cooper River bridge. New South Associates excavated the 1792 Courthouse.[20] The largest project to date has been the Charleston Place site, an entire city block surveyed by Cosans and Henry and tested by Honerkamp. This was followed by extensive monitoring and salvage during site demolition.[21]

All of the federally funded projects were located within the historic commercial core of Charleston, an area used intensively for both domestic and commercial activities. Research at these sites included identification of the processes responsible for the formation of the archaeological record, definition of the temporal parameters of site occupation, dietary studies, and study of site function and socioeconomic status. The projects demonstrated that urban sites in Charleston are deep, highly varied in terms of quantity and types of deposits, and incredibly complex. They also showed that the bulk of deposits reflect only the domestic activities at the site. These studies laid the groundwork for the study of adaptation to the urban environment, a study initiated in 1984.[22]

In 1980, Elaine Herold initiated the preparation of a citywide archival study. This project, conducted and completed by Zierden and Calhoun, followed the example of Cressey and Stephens and used archival records as a source of surveying the archaeological resources of the city and suggesting questions for long-term study.[23] Following the example of Deagan,[24] relevant documents are those that give insights into the formation of adaptive patterns, the ways in which they are manifested in the community, and the ways in which they are reflected in the ground. More specifically, research concentrated on those aspects which had a particular relevance to proposed research questions. These included:

1. Information relevant to an understanding of social variability in the city. This includes population demography, occupation, income ranges, social and ethnic classes.
2. Information relevant to the material world and economy of Charleston. This includes studies of Charleston's economic system, her position in the world economy, range of activities in the commercial sector of Charleston's population, descriptions of the range of imports available to Charleston's citizens, local production of goods, and the mechanisms and manifestations of distribution and exchange in the city.
3. Information relevant to the physical formation of the archaeological record. This includes information on the physical landscape of Charleston, patterns of growth and development, location of different activity areas, and the nature of the physical environment prior to intense utilization. This also includes such physical contributions as architectural styles and building construction methods, cultural and natural disasters, spatial distribution of features, disposal and sanitation practices, and public works.

The four-part survey was completed in 1984.[25] This initial study focused on the portion of the city occupied in the eighteenth century and on the city's economic activities. Research topics proposed in the study and investigated at subsequently excavated sites included site-formation processes, site function, status variability, urban subsistence strategy, the archaeological signature of urban slavery and the free black population, spatial patterning, the development of socially definable neighborhoods, and rural/urban contrasts.[26]

This study was amended in 1987.[27] The second study focused on physical changes to the city in the nineteenth century, development of residential suburban areas in the late eighteenth to late nineteenth century, and the city's African American and European immigrant populations. Many of the originally proposed research questions were amended, based on new archival and archaeological data, and new ones were proposed. One major step was the reformulation of the questions into an investigation of the urban landscape.

The Urban Landscape

The past decade of archaeological research in Charleston has produced a data base of 19 sites. The sites vary widely, but can be grouped into two categories: residential and residential-commercial. The latter are located in that portion of the city that has been intensely utilized for commercial activity from at least the early eighteenth century through the present day. The nine dual sites include retail, craft, and residential areas (Charleston Place, First Trident, Lodge Alley, 38 State Street, Visitor's Center), the Beef Market, two public waterfront dump/wharf areas (Atlantic Wharf, Exchange Building), and a tavern (McCrady's Longroom).[28]

The 10 residential sites are, with two exceptions, located in what were suburban areas of the late eighteenth or early nineteenth century and contain standing structures dating from the initial occupation of the site. Their continuous use as residential properties into the present facilitates study of the domestic evolution of these sites. Those double houses (homes of the gentry) that were built in the eighteenth– and nineteenth–century suburbs include those of William Gibbes (1772), Miles Brewton (1769), John Rutledge (1763), Thomas Heyward (1772), Joseph Manigault (1803), and William Aiken (1817). The Rutledge and Heyward lots were occupied in the early eighteenth century, prior to construction of the present houses. The remainder were among the first in their respective neighborhoods. The four middle-class sites include 66 and 40 Society Streets, rebuilt on Ansonborough lots after the 1838 fire, and 70 Nassau Street, built in the Charleston Neck in the 1840s. President Street was located on the west side of the Neck, and developed as a middle-class neighborhood in the nineteenth century. These projects were the first that were amenable to the interdisciplinary study of architectural and archaeological components; previous sites were razed lots.[29]

The double house sites, occupied by Charleston's elite, provided most of the data from which the following interpretations were derived. For the purposes of this and other Charleston studies, "elite" or "gentry" Charlestonians were wealthy enough to own their townhouse and at least one plantation; the wealth was controlled primarily by men. Furthermore, these Charlestonians main-

tained at least eight slaves in the city, as well as a larger number on their plantation(s), and the men held public office at some point in their adult life. They used their wealth to purchase goods and acquire manners that displayed their gentry status—elaborate dwellings and gardens, appropriate furnishings and clothing, elaborate tea and tablewares for entertaining. In physical terms, the elites are those with houses in excess of 7,000 square feet and urban lots larger than 18,000 square feet. In contrast, the middle-class artisans and professional men lived in houses averaging 4,600 square feet on lots of 6,000 square feet. These men often rented these properties and earned a living elsewhere in the city.

More extensive and more recent archaeological work has been conducted at the residential sites, and these data have formed the core of information on

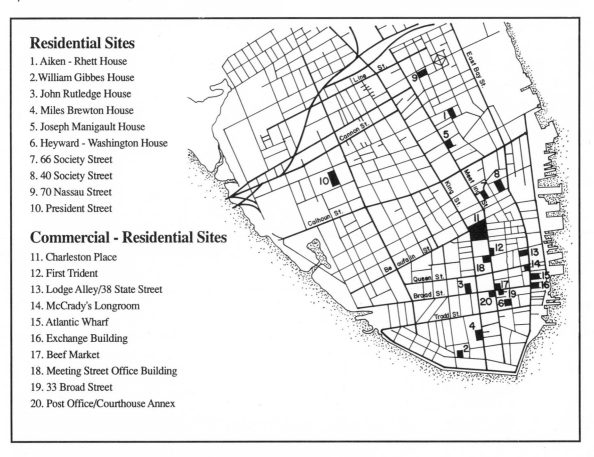

Residential Sites

1. Aiken - Rhett House
2. William Gibbes House
3. John Rutledge House
4. Miles Brewton House
5. Joseph Manigault House
6. Heyward - Washington House
7. 66 Society Street
8. 40 Society Street
9. 70 Nassau Street
10. President Street

Commercial - Residential Sites

11. Charleston Place
12. First Trident
13. Lodge Alley/38 State Street
14. McCrady's Longroom
15. Atlantic Wharf
16. Exchange Building
17. Beef Market
18. Meeting Street Office Building
19. 33 Broad Street
20. Post Office/Courthouse Annex

MAP 13.1. Residential and commercial-residential sites, Charleston.

the Charleston landscape. However, the commercial sites have also informed the interpretations summarized below. Each of the phenomena discussed have been observed at multiple sites.

Investigations of the urban landscape have utilized three sources of data: standing structures, archaeological deposits, and documentary sources. The study has been interdisciplinary and has built upon the research of historians, architectural historians, zooarchaeologists, ethnobotanists, and palynologists, as well as field archaeologists. Landscape studies have focused on both the buildings, public and private, and the spaces between them—work yards, gardens, fences, streets, and public areas. While the interpretations have been citywide, the unit of study has been the urban compound. While such sites are highly varied, they contain basic components essential to daily life.

Urban lots were deep and narrow to maximize the available street frontage. Houses fronted directly on the street, with the narrow end facing the road. By the mid-eighteenth century, two house styles dominated Charleston architecture: the single house and the double house. The Charleston single house was one-room wide and usually two deep; the narrow end fronted the street, while the south or west side contained porches (or piazzas) facing the yard. A variety of antecedents have been suggested as the source of the style: West Indian, African, and English. The single house has been interpreted as a response to both the scarcity of urban space and the humid subtropical climate. Most recently Bernard Herman has suggested that "the single house stands as a solution accommodating two very different architectural agendas: the commercial needs of urban ports and market towns, and the cultivated manners and affectations of elite white lowcountry plantation culture."[30]

Typically, the gable end fronted the street, and entrance was through a false front door onto the piazza. The true entrance was located in the center of the long wall and opened onto a central hall. A variation of this style featured an entrance on the north side of the house, resulting in a suite of rooms along the south side.[31]

The double house, as its name implies, contained four rooms to a floor, with a central hall. It was often more elaborate than the single house. The larger Charleston houses, particularly double houses, were often elevated with an above-ground basement; the second floor was then the first living floor. This cooled the house, gave protection from flooding, and provided social distance from the public streets. This sense of distance was further enhanced by the presence of forbidding brick walls and wrought-iron fences that often stood between the houses and the streets.[32]

Behind the main house, auxiliary structures were arranged within a fenced compound and often included slave quarters, kitchen, stables, and privies. The presence of livestock or gardens might require additional structures. In addition to privies, features related to urban sanitation included wells, drain systems, and work yards that were often segregated and paved. While there was some variation in the size, content, and arrangement of these structures, they were considered basic functional components of urban life and were present in some form. The urban compounds of the wealthy often contained substantial brick structures for all of these activities. The properties of less affluent residents might contain less substantial structures or fewer outbuildings; such residents owned fewer horses and fewer, if any, slaves, for example. More than one household might share privies, wells, and passageways.[33] The support structures were often aligned along one or both walls to the rear of the house. The Aiken-Rhett yard, which never contained a formal garden, suggests the deliberate location of livestock facilities and privies away from the main house, while the Gibbes and Miles Brewton yards, with support structures along one side, reflect attempts to segregate the working yard, the domain of slaves, from the formal garden, the domain of owners.

These seemingly spacious yards thus quickly became cramped as an owner's family, as many as 20 slaves, and a variety of livestock—horses, cows, and assorted fowl—lived and worked within a restricted area. As the nineteenth century progressed, Charlestonians became seriously concerned with the health and sanitation problems resulting from such population pressure, and they worked to offset the dangers inherent in these conditions. Cisterns to collect rainwater and brick drains to remove waste water are tangible archaeological evidence of attempts to make the yards more livable.

This fairly static pattern can serve as a basic outline of lot element patterning in Charleston, but ongoing research suggests that this pattern evolved through the eighteenth and nineteenth centuries. The Miles Brewton house, for example, contained fewer outbuildings and a less formal arrangement of lot elements during the eighteenth century. In particular, the existing brick walls which surround the property and separate the formal garden from the working yard, as well as many of the outbuildings, appear to be nineteenth-century additions. Refuse disposal was initially concentrated near the outbuildings, but these areas were later paved in an attempt to keep them clean.

As discussed above, the author's examination of Charleston's physical development using a landscape approach incorporates and builds upon individual research topics originally proposed for the city. The questions posed by Honerkamp and his colleagues at the Charleston Place site—diet, urban spatial patterning and lot layout, potable water supply, and sanitation—have been expanded

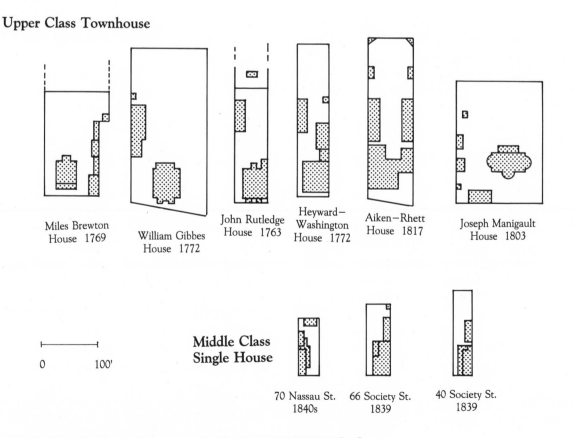

Upper Class Townhouse

Miles Brewton House 1769

William Gibbes House 1772

John Rutledge House 1763

Heyward–Washington House 1772

Aiken–Rhett House 1817

Joseph Manigault House 1803

0   100'

Middle Class Single House

70 Nassau St. 1840s

66 Society St. 1839

40 Society St. 1839

Fig. 13.1. Relative lot size and structure distribution, 1750–1850, Charleston.

through examination of other commercial properties and later through the study of the residential lots. These new interpretations of the Charleston landscape are summarized as follows:

1. Dramatic deforestation of the Charleston area occurred between ca. 1760 and ca. 1800. Palynological and ethnobotanical analysis suggest this was accompanied by the filling of low-lying areas and a reduction in mesic (wetland) plants. This deforestation was suggested in the documentary record through the dramatic rise in the price of firewood. This development was also reflected in the ethnobotanical record by increased use of coal during these years.[34]

2. An increasing desire for privacy, and a desire to separate and clearly define different activity areas were reflected in the construction of solid brick walls around and within the urban compounds in the second quarter of the nineteenth century. This was also reflective of increasing white paranoia toward the slave population as the antebellum period progressed. Some archaeological evidence suggested that these barriers replaced more open boundaries, often post-and-rail fences.[35]

3. Yards were refuse-laden throughout the eighteenth and nineteenth centuries. The elite site residents attempted to offset this by isolating the work yard from the formal yard. The archaeological record suggests that, by the second quarter of the nineteenth century, they were also paving these work yards and moving refuse disposal farther to the rear of the lot or depositing refuse off-site. Elaborate drainage systems were also constructed. By the 1850s, cisterns to collect rainwater were becoming common; urban density and the proximity of wells to privies had resulted in groundwater contamination.[36]

4. The faunal assemblages of urban sites contained a larger percentage of commensal (or vermin) species compared to rural sites, reflecting the congestion of urban life and the greater tendency for these pests to live in close proximity to humans; however, the elite townhouse sites exhibited a smaller percentage of commensals than other urban sites, suggesting that their efforts to clean up their yards were at least partially successful.[37]

5. Analysis of faunal material has demonstrated that a sizable portion of the beef consumed on Charleston sites came from on-site butcheries. This was particularly true for elite sites. In contrast, it appears that sites associated with public meals and entertainment, such as taverns and clubs, obtained their meat from the market. The architectural and documentary records hinted at livestock maintenance on site; the archaeological record suggested that it was very common.[38]

6. The faunal record clearly demonstrated a dependence on domestic mammals by Charlestonians, more so than rural peoples. The faunal assemblages of upper, middle, and lower classes were remarkable in their similarity, with only subtle differences among them. It appears that elite Charlestonians enjoyed a more diverse diet, and this diversity was supplied by wild birds, reptiles, and fish.[39]

Public Archaeology and Urban Sites

As living sites occupied by citizens who are descendants of those being studied, cities are an important setting for archaeological projects that involve the public. The operation of the urban archaeology program under the auspices of The Charleston Museum has provided direct opportunities for public consumption of archaeological data, ranging from display of archaeological artifacts to interpretation of site-specific archaeology at the museum's historic houses. The museum has produced traditional public products such as popular booklets and site-specific displays. In Charleston, a number of these are located in new or newly renovated public buildings on the dig site.[40]

The museum has also developed some more integrated approaches to public archaeology. Archaeological artifacts are integral to both permanent and special exhibition. In both cases, archaeological materials are exhibited with documents and decorative arts objects when they are used to interpret the same concepts. Special exhibits on topics ranging from foodways to African American labor have utilized archaeological interpretations as well as artifacts.

The summarized interpretive ideas presented in this chapter have been incorporated into the recently revised interpretation of The Charleston Museum's historic houses, which also includes emphasis on the resident enslaved African Americans, placement of the properties within the larger social and temporal context of the region, and the gritty reality of daily life at the outbuildings. The meeting point between these ideas and the traditional emphasis on fine furniture and political accomplishments has been the suggestion that the grim hardships of daily life in colonial and antebellum cities made the elegant lifestyles of the elite all the more notable.

Finally, many of the projects in Charleston, particularly those focusing on African-American history, have involved the public in planning and interpretation. To be truly "interdisciplinary," urban archaeology must be sensitive to the interests and knowledge claims of descendant groups and must be able to combine archaeological approaches, concepts, and results with those from more traditional disciplines. At the same time, archaeologists must emphasize the unique and nonrenewable nature of the archaeological record, stressing that it is an integral element of a historic property, requiring special care and handling to preserve it and revise ongoing interpretations.[41]

Future Directions

This discussion suggests that utilizing the landscape approach in the archaeological study of urban development is fruitful. It also suggests that much more work can be done. The Charleston data base currently consists of 19 sites out of possibly hundreds. Further, the percentage of excavated area to total site area is small; on some sites it consists of fewer than five test pits. As Dee Dee Joyce has pointed out (this volume), sites occupied by people other than successful white merchant/planter families are seriously underrepresented. Numerous problems have been encountered in identifying the sites of free black Charlestonians (70 Nassau being the exception) and poor white laborers, primarily German and Irish immigrants. Further, archaeologists have not yet developed a reliable method of separating the refuse of the enslaved from that of their masters on the large urban compounds; this may in fact be impossible to do. Although some data have been collected (from Charleston Place, 70 Nassau, and President Street), little research has been conducted on the post-1870 landscape. Clearly, more work is warranted.

Charleston is famous for its historic architecture—the structural landscape—and these resources have been surveyed, protected, restored, reused, and placed on the National Register of Historic Places. Rarely do National Register nominations for buildings, singly or in groups, mention an associated archaeological component. Yet, each historic structure in South Carolina, whether urban or rural, contains an archaeological component amenable to research (e.g., Stine and Stine, this volume; Joseph, this volume). The combined survey and study of above- and below-ground resources is a fruitful avenue of research.

Many, if not all, of the other towns and cities in South Carolina are amenable to archaeological research, but outside of Charleston little has been done. These few projects suggest that there are endless opportunities for archaeological investigation of South Carolina's urban landscape.

NOTES

1. Staski 1982:97; Stilgoe 1982:88–99.
2. Brownell and Goldfield 1977; Mohl and Betten 1970.
3. Noël Hume 1963; Miller 1983; Deagan 1983.
4. Staski 1982.
5. Deagan 1974; see also Deagan 1983.

6. Deagan 1981; Dickens and Bowen 1980; Honerkamp, Council, and Will 1982; Miller 1988; also Miller 1983; Rubertone and Gallagher 1981; Schuyler 1982.

7. Cressey et al. 1982.

8. Kelso and Most 1990; also Deetz 1990.

9. Lewis 1976.

10. Lewis 1984.

11. South 1971; South 1989.

12. Elliott 1990a; Elliott 1990b.

13. Lewis 1989b; Grimes 1985.

14. Lepionka 1985; Lepionka 1989; Lepionka 1990.

15. Payne 1986; Payne and Hulan 1986.

16. Olga M. Caballero, personal communication 1991.

17. Herold 1981b; Polhemus n.d.; Herold 1978.

18. Herold 1981a; Herold 1984; as well as Herold and Thomas 1981a; Herold and Thomas 1981b.

19. Zierden, Calhoun, and Paysinger 1983; Zierden, Calhoun, and Pinckney 1983; Zierden, Calhoun, and Reitz n.d.

20. Bastain 1987; Cassedy et al. 1992; Cobb, Holland, and Burr 1990; Reed et al. 1989; Joseph and Elliott 1995.

21. Cosans and Henry 1978; Herold and Thomas 1981a; Honerkamp, Council, and Will 1982; Zierden and Hacker 1987.

22. Zierden 1984; Honerkamp and Council 1984.

23. Zierden and Calhoun 1984; Cressey and Stephens 1982.

24. Deagan 1983.

25. Zierden and Calhoun 1982; and Zierden and Calhoun 1984; Calhoun and Zierden 1984; Calhoun, Paysinger, and Zierden 1982.

26. Honerkamp 1987; Honerkamp and Zierden 1989; Zierden and Calhoun 1986; and Zierden and Calhoun 1990.

27. Rosengarten et al. 1987.

28. Honerkamp, Council, and Will 1982; Zierden and Hacker 1987; Zierden, Calhoun, and Paysinger 1983; Zierden, Calhoun, and Pinckney 1983; Grimes and Zierden 1988; Calhoun, Reitz, Trinkley, and Zierden 1984; Zierden n.d.; Zierden and Debi Hacker 1986b; Zierden et al. 1982; Lewis 1983: 2–3.

29. Zierden et al. 1987; Zierden n.d.; Zierden 1990; Martha Zierden 1996 [in press]; Zierden and Grimes 1989; Zierden 1993; Herold 1978; Zierden and Hacker 1986a; Zierden, Calhoun, and Hacker 1986; Zierden et al. 1988; Zierden and Raynor 1988.

30. Herman 1989; see also Lounsbury 1994; Severens 1988.

31. Zierden and Herman 1996; Rogers 1980.

32. Zierden and Herman 1996; Peter Coclanis 1985; Coclanis 1989; Weir 1983.

33. Zierden and Hacker 1987:99.

34. Reinhard 1989; Reinhard 1990; Trinkley 1983a; Weir 1983.

35. Zierden and Herman 1996.

36. Honerkamp and Council 1984; Zierden and Herman 1996.

37. Reitz 1986a; Reitz 1986b; Reitz 1987.

38. Reitz and Zierden 1991.

39. Reitz 1986a; Reitz 1986b.

40. Honerkamp and Zierden 1989; Grimes et al. 1987; Calhoun, Zierden, and Drucker 1986.

41. Honerkamp and Zierden 1997.

WORKS CITED

Bastian, Beverly
1987   Historical and Archaeological Investigations at the United States Post Office/Courthouse Annex, Charleston, South Carolina. Ms. on file, United States Dept. of the Interior, National Park Service, Atlanta.

Brownell, Blaine, and David Goldfield
1977   *The City in Southern History.* Kennikat Press, Port Washington, New York.

Calhoun, Jeanne, and Martha Zierden
1984   *Charleston's Commercial Landscape, 1803–1860.* Archaeological Contributions 7. The Charleston Museum, Charleston.

Calhoun, Jeanne, Elizabeth Paysinger, and Martha Zierden
1982   *A Survey of Economic Activity in Charleston, 1732–1770.* Archaeological Contributions 2, The Charleston Museum, Charleston.

Calhoun, Jeanne, Elizabeth Reitz, Michael Trinkley, and Martha Zierden
1984   *Meat in Due Season: Preliminary Investigations of Marketing Practices in Colonial Charleston.* Archaeological Contribution 9, The Charleston Museum, Charleston.

Calhoun, Jeanne, Martha Zierden, and Lesley Drucker
1987   Home Upriver: Rural Life on Daniels Island,

Berkeley County, South Carolina. Booklet on file, South Carolina Dept. of Highways and Public Transportation, Columbia.

Cassedy, Daniel, Patrick Garrow, Jeffrey Holland, and Edward Turber

1992   Additional Archaeological and Architectural Investigation for the Grace Memorial Bridge Replacement, Charleston, South Carolina. Ms. on file, Garrow and Associates, Raleigh, North Carolina.

Cobb, Charles, Jeffrey Holland, and Eugene Burr

1990   *Final Report: Phase II Archaeological, Historical, and Architectural Investigations in the Grace and New Market Alignments: Grace Memorial Bridge Replacement, Charleston, South Carolina.* Submitted to the South Carolina Dept. of Highways and Public Transportation by Garrow and Associates, Atlanta.

Coclanis, Peter A.

1985   The Sociology of Architecture in Colonial Charleston: Pattern and Process in an 18th Century Southern City. *Journal of Southern History* 18:607–23.

1989   *The Shadow of a Dream: Economic Life and Death in the South Carolina Lowcountry 1670–1920.* Oxford Univ. Press, New York.

Cosans, Betty, and Susan Henry

1978   *Archaeological Assessment of the Charleston Center Project Area, Charleston, South Carolina.* Ms. on file, Government Offices, City of Charleston.

Cressey, Pamela, and John F. Stephens

1982   The City Site Approach to Urban Archaeology. In *Archaeology of Urban America,* edited by Roy Dickens, pp. 41–62. Academic Press, New York.

Cressey, Pamela, John F. Stephens, Steven Shephard, and Barbara Magid

1982   The Core-Periphery Relationship and the Archaeological Record in Alexandria, Virginia. In *Archaeology of Urban America,* edited by Roy Dickens, pp. 143–74. Academic Press, New York.

Deagan, Kathleen

1974   *Sex, Status and Role in the Mestizaje of Spanish Colonial Florida.* Ph.D. diss., Dept. of Anthropology, Univ. of Florida, Gainesville.

1981   Downtown Survey: The Discovery of 16th Century St. Augustine in an Urban Area. *American Antiquity* 46:626–33.

1983   *Spanish St. Augustine: the Archaeology of a Colonial Creole Community.* Academic Press, New York.

Deetz, James

1990   Prologue: Landscapes as Cultural Statements. In *Earth Patterns,* edited by William Kelso and Rachel Most, pp. 1–4. Univ. Press of Virginia, Charlottesville.

Dickens, Roy, and William Bowen

1980   Problems and Promises in Urban Historical Archaeology: The MARTA Project. *Historical Archaeology* 14:42–57.

Elliott, Daniel

1990a   Lost City Survey. *LAMAR Briefs* 15, Lamar Institute, Athens.

1990b   *The Lost City Survey: Archaeological Reconnaissance of Nine Eighteenth Century Settlements in Chatham and Effingham Counties.* Lamar Institute Publications, Athens.

Grimes, Kimberly

1985   A Site History of 1927, 1919 Pickens Street. *Notebook,* South Carolina Institute of Archaeology and Anthropology, Columbia.

Grimes, Kimberly, and Martha Zierden

1988   *A Hub of Human Activity: Archaeological Investigations of the Visitor's Reception and Transportation Center.* Archaeological Contributions 19, The Charleston Museum, Charleston.

Grimes, Kimberly, Dale Rosengarten, Martha Zierden, and Elizabeth Alston

1987   *Between the Tracks: The Heritage of Charleston's East Side Community.* Leaflet no. 30, The Charleston Museum, Charleston.

Herman, Bernard L.

1989   Rethinking the Charleston Single House. Paper presented to the Vernacular Architecture Forum, St. Louis, Missouri.

Herold, Elaine

1978   *Preliminary Report on the Research at the Heyward-Washington House.* On file, The Charleston Museum, Charleston.

1981a   Historical Archaeological Report on the Meeting Street Office Building Site. Ms. on file, The Charleston Museum, Charleston.

1981b   *Archaeological Research at the Exchange Building, Charleston, S.C.: 1979–1980.* Ms. on file, The Charleston Museum, Charleston.

1984   Archaeological and Historical Research at 33 Broad Street, Charleston, S.C. Ms. on file, The

Charleston Museum, Charleston.

Herold, Elaine B., and Elizabeth Thomas

1981a   History of the Charleston Center Area. Ms. on file, The Charleston Museum, Charleston.

1981b   Historical Archaeological Survey of the First Citizens Bank and Trust Project on South Market Street, Charleston, SC. Ms. on file, The Charleston Museum, Charleston.

Honerkamp, Nicholas

1987   Household or Neighborhoods: Finding Appropriate Levels of Research in Urban Archaeology. Paper presented at the 1987 Meetings of the Society for Historical Archaeology, Savannah.

Honerkamp, Nicholas, and Martha Zierden

1989   *Charleston Place: The Archaeology of Urban Life.* The Charleston Museum Leaflet no. 31, Charleston.

1997   The Evolution of Interpretation at Charleston Place. In *Presenting Archaeology to the Public: Digging for Truths,* edited by John Jameson, pp. 130–43. Alta Mira Press, Walnut Creek, California.

Honerkamp, Nicholas, and R. Bruce Council

1984   Individual versus Corporate Adaptation in Urban Contexts. *Tennessee Anthropologist* IX(1):22–31.

Honerkamp, Nicholas, R. Bruce Council, and M. Elizabeth Will

1982   *An Archaeological Investigation of the Charleston Convention Center Site, Charleston, South Carolina.* Ms. on file, U.S. Department of the Interior, National Park Service, Atlanta.

Joseph, J. W., and Rita Elliott

1995   *Restoration Archaeology at the Charleston County Courthouse site, (38Ch1498), Charleston, South Carolina.* Ms. on file, County of Charleston.

Kelso, William, and Rachel Most (editors)

1990   *Earth Patterns: Essays in Landscape Archaeology.* Univ. Press of Virginia, Charlottesville.

Lepionka, Larry

1985   Habersham House Excavations: First Phase. Ms. on file, Historic Beaufort Foundation, Beaufort.

1989   Excavations at 926 Bay Street, Beaufort, South Carolina: A Report on Preliminary Investigations. Ms. on file, South Carolina Institute of Archaeology and Anthropology, Columbia.

1990   Excavations at 926 Bay Street: Preliminary Report on Skeletal Remains. Ms. on file, South Carolina Institute of Archaeology and Anthropology, Columbia.

Lewis, Kenneth E.

1976   *Camden: A Frontier Town in 18th Century South Carolina.* Anthropological Studies 2, South Carolina Institute of Archaeology and Anthropology, Columbia.

1983   Archaeological Investigations in the Interior of McCrady's Longroom, 38Ch559, Charleston, S.C. *Notebook* 15(3–4), South Carolina Institute of Archaeology and Anthropology, Columbia.

1984   *The American Frontier: An Archaeological Study of Settlement Pattern and Process.* Academic Press, New York.

1989b   Settlement Function and Archaeological Patterning in a Historic Urban Context: the Woodrow Wilson House in Columbia, S.C. In *Studies in South Carolina Archaeology,* edited by Albert Goodyear and Glen Hanson, pp. 225–52. Anthropological Studies 9, South Carolina Institute of Archaeology and Anthropology, Columbia.

Lounsbury, Carl

1994   *An Illustrated Glossary of Early Southern Architecture and Landscape.* Oxford Univ. Press, New York.

Miller, Henry

1983   *A Search for the "Citty of Saint Maries."* St. Mary's City Archaeological Series 1, St. Mary's City, Maryland.

1988   Baroque Cities in the Wilderness: Archaeology and Urban Development in the Colonial Chesapeake. *Historical Archaeology* 22(2):57–73.

Mohl, Raymond, and Neil Betten

1970   *Urban America in Historical Perspective.* Weybright and Talley, New York.

Noël Hume, Ivor

1963   *Here Lies Virginia.* Alfred A. Knopf, New York.

Payne, Ted M.

1986   The Early Industrial Period in Laurens, South Carolina: An Historical and Archaeological Study for the Relocation of Highway US 221. Ms. on file, South Carolina Dept. of Highways and Public Transportation, Columbia.

Payne, Ted M., and Richard H. Hulan

1986   US 221 Relocation, City of Laurens, Laurens County, South Carolina. Ms. on file, South Carolina Dept. of Highways and Public Transportation, Columbia.

Polhemus, Richard

n.d.   Gillon Street Delft Site (38Ch70). Ms. on file,

Information Management Division, South Carolina Institute of Archaeology and Anthropology, Columbia.

Reed, Mary Beth, Patrick Garrow, Gordon Watts, and J. W. Joseph

1989   *Final Report: An Architectural, Archaeological, and Historical Survey of Selected Portions of Charleston and Mount Pleasant: Grace Memorial Bridge Replacement, Charleston, South Carolina.* Submitted to Parsons, Brinckerhoff, Quade, and Douglas. Report on file, Garrow and Associates, Atlanta.

Reinhard, Karl

1989   Parasitological and Palynological Study of Soil Samples from the John Rutledge House. In *Investigating Elite Lifeways through Archaeology,* edited by Martha Zierden and Kimberly Grimes, pp. 166–74. Archaeological Contributions 21, The Charleston Museum, Charleston.

1990   Pollen Analysis of the Miles Brewton House, Charleston, South Carolina. Ms. on file, The Charleston Museum, Charleston.

Reitz, Elizabeth

1986a   Urban/Rural Contrasts in the Vertebrate Fauna from the Southern Coastal Plain. *Historical Archaeology* 20(2):47–58.

1986b   Urban Site Formation Processes and the Faunal Record. Paper presented at the 43d annual Southeastern Archaeological Conference, Nashville.

1987   Vertebrate Fauna and Socioeconomic Status. In *Consumer Choices in Historical Archaeology,* edited by Suzanne Spencer-Wood, pp. 101–19, Plenum Press, New York.

Reitz, Elizabeth, and Martha Zierden

1991   Cattle Bones and Status from Charleston, South Carolina. In *Perspectives in Zooarchaeology: Essays in Honor of P. W. Parmalee,* edited by Bonnie Styles, James Purdue, and Walter Klippel, pp. 395–408. Illinois State Museum Publications, Springfield.

Rogers, George C.

1980   *Charleston in the Age of the Pinckneys.* Univ. of South Carolina Press, Columbia.

Rosengarten, Dale, Martha Zierden, Kimberly Grimes, Ziyadah Owusu, Elizabeth Alston, and Will Williams III

1987   *Between the Tracks: Charleston's East Side During the Nineteenth Century.* Archaeological Contribu-

tions 17, The Charleston Museum, Charleston.

Rubertone, Patricia, and Joan M. Gallagher

1981   *Archaeological Site Examination: A Case Study in Urban Archaeology.* Atlanta Russell Papers 1988. Ms. on file, U.S. Dept. of the Interior, National Park Service, Washington, D.C.

Schuyler, Robert (editor)

1982   Urban Archaeology in America. *North American Archaeologist* 3(3).

Severens, Kenneth

1988   *Charleston: Antebellum Architecture and Civic Destiny.* Univ. of Tennessee Press, Knoxville.

South, Stanley

1971   *Archeology at the Charles Towne Site (38CH1) on Albemarle Point in South Carolina.* 2 vols. Research Manuscript Series 10. South Carolina Institute of Archeology and Anthropology, Columbia.

1989   From Archaeology to Interpretation at Charles Towne. In *Studies in South Carolina Archaeology: Essays in Honor of Robert L. Stephensen,* edited by Albert Goodyear III and Glen T. Hanson, pp. 157–68. Anthropological Studies 9, South Carolina Institute of Archaeology and Anthropology, Univ. of South Carolina, Columbia.

Staski, Edward

1982   Advances in Urban Archaeology. In *Advances in Archaeological Method and Theory,* vol. 5, edited by Michael Schiffer, pp. 97–150. Academic Press, New York.

Stilgoe, John R.

1982   *Common Landscape of America, 1580–1845.* Yale Univ. Press, New Haven.

Trinkley, Michael

1983a   Analysis of Ethnobotanical Remains. In *An Archaeological Study of the First Trident Site,* edited by Martha Zierden, Jeanne Calhoun, and Elizabeth Pinckney, pp. 88–96. Archaeological Contributions 6, The Charleston Museum, Charleston.

Weir, Robert M.

1983   *Colonial South Carolina: A History.* KTO Press, Millwood, New York.

Zierden, Martha

n.d.   Archaeological Excavations at the Miles Brewton house. Ms. in preparation, The Charleston Museum.

1984   The Urban Environment: 18th Century Charleston. Paper presented at the 17th annual meeting

of the Society for Historical Archaeology,
Williamsburg.

1990a   The Past and the Present: Urban Archaeology in
Charleston, South Carolina. In *Cultural Heritage
Conservation in the American South,* edited by
Benita J. Howell. Southern Anthropological
Society Proceedings 23, Univ. of Georgia Press,
Athens.

1993   *Archaeological Testing at the Stable Building of the
Heyward–Washington House.* Archaeological
Contributions 23, The Charleston Museum,
Charleston.

1996   The Urban Landscape, the Work Yard, and
Archaeological Site Formation Processes in
Charleston, South Carolina. In *Historical
Archaeology and the Study of American Culture,*
edited by Bernard Herman and Lu Ann De
Cunzo, Winterthur Museum Publications.

Zierden, Martha, and Bernard L. Herman

1996   Charleston Townhouses: Archaeology, Architec-
ture, and the Urban Landscape, 1750–1850. In
*Landscape Archaeology: Reading and Interpreting
the American Historical Landscape,* edited by
Rebecca Yamin and Karen Bescherer Metheny.
Univ. of Tennessee Press, Knoxville.

Zierden, Martha, and Debi Hacker

1986a   *Exploration of the North Entrance of the Joseph
Manigault House.* Archaeological Contributions
15, The Charleston Museum, Charleston.

1986b   *Examination of Construction Sequence at the
Exchange Building.* Archaeological Contributions
14, The Charleston Museum, Charleston.

1987   *Charleston Place: Archaeological Investigations of
the Commercial Landscape.* Archaeological
Contributions 16, The Charleston Museum,
Charleston.

Zierden, Martha A., and Jeanne A. Calhoun

1982   *Preliminary Report: An Archaeological Preservation Plan for Charleston, South Carolina.* Archaeological Contributions 1, The Charleston
Museum, Charleston

1984   *An Archaeological Preservation Plan for Charleston, South Carolina.* Archaeological Contributions 8, The Charleston Museum, Charleston.

1986   Urban Adaptation in Charleston, South Carolina,
1730–1820. *Historical Archaeology* 20(1):29–43.

1990   An Archaeological Interpretation of Elite
Townhouse Sites in Charleston, South Carolina,
1770–1850. *Southeastern Archaeology* 9(2):79–92.

Zierden, Martha, and Kimberly Grimes

1989   *Investigating Elite Lifeways through Archaeology:
The John Rutledge House.* Archaeological
Contributions 21, The Charleston Museum,
Charleston.

Zierden, Martha, and Robert Raynor

1988   *The President Street Site: An Experiment in Public
Archaeology.* Archaeological Contributions 18,
The Charleston Museum, Charleston.

Zierden, Martha, Elizabeth Reitz, Michael Trinkley, and
Elizabeth Paysinger

1982   *Archaeological Excavations at McCrady's
Longroom.* Archaeological Contributions 3,
The Charleston Museum, Charleston.

Zierden, Martha, Jeanne Calhoun, and Elizabeth
Paysinger

1983a   *Archaeological Investigations at Lodge Alley.*
Archaeological Contributions 5, The Charleston
Museum, Charleston.

Zierden, Martha, Jeanne Calhoun, and Debi Hacker

1986   *Outside of Town: Preliminary Investigation of the
Aiken-Rhett House.* Archaeological Contributions
11, The Charleston Museum, Charleston.

Zierden, Martha, Jeanne Calhoun, and Elizabeth
Pinckney

1983   *An Archaeological Study of the First Trident Site.*
Archaeological Contributions 6, The Charleston
Museum, Charleston.

Zierden, Martha, Jeanne Calhoun, and Elizabeth Reitz

n.d.   Archaeological Investigations of the Charleston
Waterfront. Notes on file, The Charleston
Museum, Charleston.

Zierden, Martha, Jeanne Calhoun, Suzanne Buckley, and
Debi Hacker

1987   *Georgian Opulence: Archaeological Investigation of
the Gibbes House.* Archaeological Contributions
12, The Charleston Museum, Charleston.

Zierden, Martha, Kimberly Grimes, David Hudgens, and
Cherie Black

1988   *Charleston's First Suburb: Excavations at 66
Society Street.* Archaeological Contributions 20,
The Charleston Museum, Charleston.

14. The Charleston Landscape on the Eve of the Civil War: Race, Class, and Ethnic Relations in Ward Five

DEE DEE JOYCE

In this chapter, I use a landscape approach to investigate race, class, and ethnic relations in Charleston, South Carolina, on the eve of the Civil War. I argue that these social relations are encoded on the landscape through the production of shared and divided social space. An examination of the city's landscape reveals social boundaries, power struggles, and social group formation.

Social scientists use landscape as a theoretical framework in which to analyze the complex and dynamic relationship of humans to space.[1] Following the work of French sociologist Henri Lefebvre,[2] I see landscape and the production of space as a rudimentary element of social relations. Social relations are not only reflected in the landscape; the expressed landscape actively shapes those relations. It is the *process* by which a landscape is produced and encoded that is of critical importance for understanding past social relations.

To discern past social relations, it is necessary to "read space" by deciphering the social–spatial relations encoded on the landscape. Due to the population density of an urban environment, the landscape code may be difficult to perceive unless it is analyzed on a micro-, street–by–street, level. The density of social relations not only poses problems for current researchers but also posed problems of boundary maintenance for past social groups. In a social landscape that provides many opportunities for contact, it is critical for social groups to maintain and defend their boundaries and social position in everyday life. A landscape approach not only provides a way to examine past social relations, but also provides a method for examining how social groups are formed and maintained though the use of space and material culture.

Social groups are formed when individuals perceive a commonality among themselves and a difference between themselves and others. Social relations are the interactions between members of society based on their perceived membership in a particular social group. Groups may be formed on a sense of shared gender, race, class, ethnicity, religion, etc. Each type of relation is fundamentally different from the others and must be analyzed accordingly, i.e., an analysis of class must refer to relations of production, and race to an ideology of biological difference.

Each type of social relation varies independently of the others.[3] In this way, an upper-class white male may consider it improper for a woman of the same race and class to perform physical labor and whip a pregnant slave if she fails to carry his bags; conversely, a white male of a lower class may expect his pregnant wife to help pull the plow. Likewise, a white slave owner may find it appropriate for a slave to dress in cast–off finery, but a white member of a lower class may take great offense when a slave is better attired than a free person. With regard to personal space, a white mistress may command a slave to sleep at the foot of her bed, but a lower-class white may not want to live on the same street as a slave.

The composition, form, relationship, and importance of specific social groups varies in time and place depending on the particular historical period or context. In this investigation I attempt to decode the landscape of Charleston, South Carolina, on the eve of the Civil War in order to understand the social relations that produced that distinctive landscape.

In 1861 Charleston was home to over 48,000 residents and, for the first time in its history, contained a white majority.[4] The racial shift was due to the forced westward migration of slaves to the Cotton Belt and the simultaneous influx of German and Irish immigrants via northeastern cities. Charleston was also home to one of the largest free black populations outside of New Orleans.[5]

Although Charleston was a leading social, political, and cultural center of the South, its economic power began to wane throughout the early nineteenth century due to a decline in rice production. The elite responded to the slump through diversification; the main economic base became commercial shipping and small-scale manufacturing. Charleston's budding industrial base included rice and lumber mills, shipping and rail firms, an iron foundry, and tanneries. By mid-century, Charleston became the third largest manufacturing center in the South. The ramifications of the economic shift from staple crop production to a more diversified economy were evident in social relations as slavery was transformed and immigrant populations swelled.[6]

Charleston's labor force consisted of a diversity of groups, from slaves to native–born whites. Many manufacturing firms purchased large numbers of male slaves and housed them in barracks nearby.

The South Carolina Railroad Company, which owned over 100 slaves under the age of 40, constructed large barracks and tenements in Charleston's upper wards.[7] Many employers hired slaves from other owners for short–term and long–term periods. Although it was illegal, some slaves hired themselves out and paid a portion of their wages to their owners or even hired other slaves to do their work.[8] Free blacks and immigrants were also part of Charleston's labor force. In the 1850s, increasing numbers of destitute Irish families migrated to Charleston in search of employment. These poor immigrants joined the ranks of the underemployed in direct competition with free blacks, hired–out slaves, and unskilled native born whites.

The manufacturing center of the city was located in the newly incorporated suburbs, called "The Neck," where land was cheap and homes were affordable. Most of Charleston's working force lived on "The Neck" or "Upper Wards." The Neck was divided into four wards when the city was incorporated in 1851. Ward 5 was chosen for this investigation due to its diverse population and blend of residential and industrial sites. According to the 1861 Census, Ward 5 contained nearly 6,000 inhabitants: 48 percent white, 37 percent slave, and 15 percent free black, the largest percentage of free blacks of any city ward. Of the 2,739 whites, 456 were Irish and 194 were German immigrants.[9]

The focus of the landscape analysis was an eight-square-block area in the center of Ward 5 where wealthy planters, free blacks, immigrants, and slaves crowded together along broad, tree–lined avenues and dank, swampy alleyways. A composite map of the research area delineating structures, lots, and streets was constructed by updating an 1852 Bridgens and Allen insurance map[10] with deed maps for new construction, the 1853 Ward books,[11] and the 1888 Sanborn Insurance Map.[12] City Directories for 1859 and 1860[13] were used in conjunction with the 1861 City Census[14] to correlate households with particular street addresses. The U.S. Population Schedule of 1860 was used to assign race, ethnicity, and social class,[15] and the 1860 U.S. Slave Schedule was used to trace slave ownership.[16] The 1861 City Census was used to locate slave houses, and finally the 1860 State Free Negro Capitation Tax Book was used to locate free blacks who were not listed in the city directories.[17] Even with all these sources, many residents could not be definitely linked with specific houses. In those cases, all known associations were made and the gaps were filled in by tracing the probable route of the census taker.

In order to make sense of the Charleston landscape, it is necessary to examine the race, class, and ethnic composition of the city and the conflicts inherent in those relations. In 1860, nearly 1,500 slaves lived in Ward 5, roughly equally divided between males and females, with the majority of slaves under 30 years old.[18] Due to economic diversification and the labor demands of an urban environment, many of Charleston's slaves were "hired–out." This hybrid system was very lucrative for slave owners and was jealously guarded by them. For women slave owners who received slaves as part of their inheritance, the hire system was a means of obtaining personal income. An owner could expect to see annual returns of 10–25 percent on her capital.[19]

The usual term of hire was for one year and the second party was responsible for the care and upkeep of the slave. Slaves could also live off the owner's property and hire out their own time, paying the owner a set amount per week or month and keeping the remainder for personal use. The slave made his or her own housing arrangements.[20] Many lived in hastily constructed shanties and tenements built by owners and developers in the Neck or lived with free blacks. These tenements were so common in the upper wards that whites expressed fear of these densely settled areas of "unsupervised Negroes."[21] It is difficult to estimate the number of slaves who were hired–out and thus were in direct competition with free workers. An indication of the large number can be inferred from the $26,000 profit the City of Charleston realized in 1859 from slave badges. Badges, most of which cost less then $2.00, had to be worn by hired–out slaves.[22]

White artisans and mechanics vigorously opposed the hire system.[23] They could not compete with the lower wages paid to blacks and resented the legal restriction of blacks to working-class professions. The competition was felt not only by men but also by women. In Charleston, 90 percent of female slaves worked in domestic labor. The choice of which additional domestics to hire was made by the head domestic, and, as one white worker complained, "it universally happens that those domestics prefer men [and women] of their own color."[24]

At the opposite end of the class scale from slaves was the owner class. The owner class was subdivided into three categories in relation to the means of production: bourgeois owner, professional owner, and petit bourgeois owner.[25] The bourgeois owners were wealthy planters and factors who employed others and often owned numerous slaves. They were predominately native-born whites, although two members of this elite class were wealthy, slaveholding mulattos. Just below this group was the professional owner class, which was comprised of physicians, clergymen, and master craftsmen who owned the means of production and often employed a small number of workers. The members of this group were almost exclusively native-born whites.[26]

A large number of the petit bourgeois owner class comprised German immigrants. Germans held almost exclusive control of the wholesale and retail grocery business and were also bakers, tavern keepers, manufacturers, and clerks. The Germans, who made up 27 percent of Ward 5's immigrant population, were second only to South Carolina–born whites in the amount of wealth controlled. Of the 194 Germans in the Ward, less than 10 listed unskilled professions.[27]

Charleston's working-class population is of particular interest because of its diversity along race and ethnic lines. The worker class was divided into the following subcategories based on the relationship to the means of production: professional worker, skilled worker, and unskilled worker.[28] The professional class was made up of clerks, service workers, and the police. Membership in this social class provided a means to move up the social ladder.

Free blacks were legally barred from many professional working positions, thereby negating free black competition found in other working-class situations. Germans in the professional working class were almost exclusively clerks, and the Irish were most commonly members of the police force. In fact, by 1860 one–third of the police force was Irish.[29]

Members of the skilled working class, such as machinists, wheelwrights, and carpenters, owned the means of production. In 1860, the number of male skilled workers was nearly equally divided among free blacks, whites, and immigrants, even though free blacks made up a much smaller percentage of the total population. The control of skilled working positions by free blacks is most evident in the comparison of free blacks to Irish skilled laborers. Even though the number of free black and Irish males was approximately equal in Ward 5, free black males dominated the skilled trades. For the most part, German immigrants found skilled professions—many became bakers, for instance—where they did not face competition from free blacks or Irishmen. The exception was the competition of German and free black machinists.[30]

The competition between Irish and free blacks is also evident in the unskilled worker category. Although the population numbers of free black males and Irish males in Ward 5 was approximately equal, the Irish comprised approximately 80 percent of the unskilled labor force. The most common listing for Irish unskilled workers was laborer, far surpassing Germans and free blacks. The second most common position for Irishmen was drayman.[31]

The class, race, and ethnic structure in the early nineteenth century was not as competitive as it was on the eve of the Civil War. In the early antebellum period, free blacks dominated the skilled labor positions with limited competition from native whites. Several free blacks became immensely wealthy within the artisan fields, and they formed exclusive organizations reserved for wealthy mulattos.[32] They formed close ties with the white elite and had little to do with native-born, working-class whites, poor free blacks, or slaves.[33]

The preexisting social order and working-class system became strained with the shrinking southern economy and mass migration of Irish immigrants in the late 1840s and 1850s. Fleeing joblessness and poverty in the Northeast, the Irish hoped for a better life in southern urban centers such as Charleston and Savannah.[34] Instead, they found their upward mobility blocked by a powerful free black community of skilled artisans. Even unskilled positions were difficult to obtain due to the hiring-out system. The owner class, which found the hiring-out arrangement very profitable, was not sympathetic to the pleas of poor Irish for restricted use of hired–out slave labor.[35]

The late 1850s was a desperate time for Charleston's poor. After reaching its industrial and economic peak in 1856, the economy began a downward spiral.[36] Yellow fever epidemics in 1856 and 1858 devastated the immigrant community and the numbers of inmates in the Poor House and Orphanage rose.[37] As the sectional crisis became more heated, competition among Charleston's working population escalated. The Irish, along with other working-class whites, chose to defend their right to labor by attacking the hiring–out system and free blacks. The ace in the white working-man's pocket was his right to vote in the midst of a sectional crisis in which his support was necessary. Even though the upper classes considered the white working class a "worthless, unprincipled class . . . [and] enemies to our peculiar institution,"[38] they also realized a united working class was a powerful social force. The Irish and Germans formed workers' unions and elected working men's representatives from the upper wards who attacked the rights of free blacks, hired–out slaves, and their white protectors. These working-class representatives even proposed enslaving all free blacks and confiscating their property by January 1862.[39]

As in most cases involving working-class struggles, the members of the class were divided along race and ethnic lines. Rather than rising together against the owner class, they competed against each other or, in the case of the free black elite, sought assurances of protection from the owner class. The separateness of these groups can be seen in their separation in the landscape and in the boundaries drawn in material culture.

Members of the bourgeois owner class held the reins of power politically, economically, and socially. They purchased large corner lots on high ground in the 1830s and 1840s and built walled compounds, the urban equivalent of the rural plantation. A typical compound contained a variety of structures: a main house facing the street front and a separate kitchen building, stables, privy, and sheds to the rear away from the street. The size and conspicuous location of their corner lot homes reinforced and legitimated their right to rule.

The highest social class shared an intimate social space with the lowest social class—slaves. This intimacy of space could only exist where social supremacy was a "basic social premise."[40] The upper-class conviction of superiority was so deep–seated that profound intimacy in social space was regarded with casual indifference. Social space between owner and slave was closely shared but at the same time separate. Slave women often slept at the foot of their mistress's bed, but, as one Charles-tonian recalled, "it was considered rather uncivi-lized for the servants to sleep under the same roof with 'the family'."[41] Slaves were hidden from casual street view by placing the quarters to the rear of the main house and by placing the main house windows so a direct view of the quarters was obstructed.[42]

View and direction of view were important aspects of landscape. The front view was critical in maintaining social group ties; the rear was invisible. Like a giant pair of blinders, the street front perspec-tive maintained order in the midst of denial. The importance of front view was evident with the professional owner class. While bourgeois owners lived on the corner lots of wide residential streets, the professional owners lived along the interior of these same residential avenues facing members of the same social class or fronting parks. Their "country club" pattern of residential separateness reinforced their shared social bond and their distinctiveness from those living on narrower residential streets and alleys. The bucolic setting

of their residences not only separated them from the poverty and filth of the city but also may have naturalized and romanticized their social station.

Approximately one–third of the petit bourgeois owner class comprised German grocers, tavern keepers, or druggists. Most of these immigrant owners resided above their shops on the corners of densely populated residential streets.[43] The shops were conveniently located to serve a diversity of customers—white, free black, and slave. Grocers also doubled as grog shops, so they became a point of contact and possible conflict for these diverse groups. German grocers often lived next door to free blacks, and German families occasionally shared tenements with free blacks. In contrast, no Irish families listed in a multifamily dwelling in Ward 5 shared a building with free blacks.[44]

The German residence pattern was a function of their occupation as well as their social class. As grocers, they needed to reside in an accessible location near their customers. As members of the petit bourgeoisie, they were not in conflict with free blacks who made up the skilled labor force or the unskilled labor force. The Germans were in a unique social position to profit from a close contact with all social groups in Charleston. By providing grocery items, liquor, pharmaceutical, and bakery products, the Germans furnished a service that was unique and noncompetitive.

The greatest class conflict centered on the skilled and unskilled working class, and this was the arena in which boundaries were most clearly drawn. Free black artisans lived primarily along the main industrial thoroughfare which connected the two rivers or clustered along a few narrow residential streets. Free black artisans were usually designated as mulatto in the census records and were often property owners.[45] Several historians have docu-mented the color barrier between light- and dark-skinned free blacks, and preliminary study indicates that the barrier was also found on the landscape.[46]

The larger city blocks in Ward 5 were frequently divided in the center by dead–end alleys. These alleys, called courts, were lined with shanties and tenements built by investors for quick profits. The shoddily constructed units were often built in marshy areas where mosquitoes were rampant. Houses lacked clean well water and proper sewage disposal and were centers of disease. In one Irish court, 39 individuals lived in 8 houses, each shanty measuring only 10 by 20 feet.[47]

These crowded, disease-infested courts were home to Charleston's poor whites, free blacks and slaves. They also became the most segregated parts of the cities. Although the residents shared a common lower-class position, they clearly marked their separateness on the landscape by maintaining a segregated social space. On one marsh–filled court, Thompson's Court, 29 free blacks lived with 10 slaves. No whites occupied the court. On nearby Heyward Court, 37 of the 48 inhabitants were Irish or Scottish and three were slaves. Only 8 free blacks were listed as living at the court. In contrast, 20 slaves and 5 free blacks lived on Dereef's Court, but no whites resided there.[48]

Charleston's mid-nineteenth-century landscape was similar to Philadelphia's landscape during the same period. In Philadelphia, large homes were placed on major streets, with cheaper homes and tenements located behind them on alleys and courts. Like Charleston, these courts and alleys were home to the immigrant Irish. The effect of the residential pattern was to "segregate the city's classes into visibly and comprehensively distinct residential spaces."[49]

In Philadelphia, as in Charleston, street frontage or view was critical. For all residents, the view from the front of the structure was crucial and the view toward the rear less important. People of the same economic class and race usually faced each other. Social space was very circumscribed in courts and alleys; therefore, residents maintained their boundaries by exclusion. On streets with a mixed class or mixed racial composition, a structure or lot was often left vacant to form a boundary.

The social position of higher classes presented a clearly defined boundary in and of itself. However, the boundary between members of the skilled and unskilled working classes was not as distinct; or, in the case of the Irish, the social reality was opposite

to the way they perceived a racially just world should be. Because the lines were not clearly defined or not acceptable as they stood, it became necessary to establish, reinforce, and constantly maintain boundaries. The most clearly defined spatial boundaries were in the courts where members of the unskilled working class attempted to maintain their separateness along race and ethnic lines.

Boundaries were not only drawn on the landscape but in personal attire and possessions. The white working class perpetrated attacks on free blacks and slaves for "rising above their station."[50] The exclusive right to certain attire was an issue of the working man's movement in the 1859 mayoral election. One voter suggested a "return to the 'good old times'" when black women did not shade their faces to maintain a lighter complexion or wear "rich brocades and silks." The writer also longed for the days when the dandy barber and tailor-boy (both free black trades) "did not sport his 'puppy switch' or perfume the air with his fragrant weed." In August 1860, a fifty-year-old free black man was attacked in the public market by a crowd of angry whites for wearing a watch and chain. Another free black man was beaten for carrying a cane, the sign of a gentleman, and several southern cities attempted to enact laws prohibiting blacks from smoking pipes.[51]

Elite women viewed dress as a sign of class and used it to remind the lower class of its proper station.[52] Conversely, upper-class women often handed down clothing to their slaves, confident in the power of their social relations. Middle- and lower-class whites did not feel this same confidence in light of a growing middle-class black population in urban areas. In 1828, the *Philadelphia Monthly Magazine* published a five-page satire, complete with illustrations, on a middle-class black subscription ball. Tension centered on the attire of the participants and the "proper" relations of blacks and whites. Complaints were voiced over "white coachmen and *white footmen*" [emphasis in the original] and concern was expressed for the time when "masters and servants change places." Most significantly, the greatest outcry came from lower-class whites who "assaulted women as they stepped from coaches, insulting them, tearing their gowns, and throwing some guests into the gutter."[53]

The targets of these displays were also conscious of their intent. After emancipation, a middle-class black seamstress explained that whites would hire other workers if they found black seamstresses and tailors wearing the same style of clothing as their white employers. Affluent blacks avoided conflict with poor whites by ordering from catalogs so "the poor buckrah wouldn't know what you had in your house."[54]

Conclusions and Suggestions for Additional Research

A landscape approach provides a dynamic theoretical framework in which to investigate past social relations. In contrast to a static settlement-pattern approach which studies things in space, a landscape approach focuses on the process by which a particular landscape is produced. It is in the actual *production* of the landscape that information on social relations, power struggles, and boundary maintenance can be discerned.

The landscape produced in Ward 5 reflects past class, ethnic, and race relations on the eve of the Civil War and demonstrates how material components of everyday life were actively used to maintain social relations. Through their position on the landscape, the most powerful members of the elite prominently displayed their social prestige and power by controlling the corner lots on wide residential streets. The only other group to share these prominent corners were also members of an unquestioned elite—the churches (Citadel Square Baptist, Second Presbyterian, and St. Luke's Episcopal).

German grocers, who monopolized the grocery business, occupied the corners of narrower residential streets and commercial thoroughfares. As part grocery store and part grog shop, these businesses were centers of interaction for a diverse clientele. Their strategic position on the landscape, close to free black, slaves, and middle-class whites, is a reflection of German grocers' position in the social network. German immigrants, unlike the Irish to follow, established their class position as skilled workers and members of the petite bourgeoisie. Their racial classification was indisputably white. Within their secure race/class position, German immigrants were able to maintain a distinct spatial pattern that allowed for a close association with other social groups, including free blacks and slaves.

Free blacks were also divided socially and spatially. Within the free black community, class and race were important factors in social position (the vast majority of free blacks were considered "mulatto"). Like elite whites, elite free blacks held street corner positions. Middle-class free blacks did not feel the same power in spatial positioning and resided in clusters along narrower residential streets and along the main industrial thoroughfare. Lower-class free blacks, whose free position was under constant attack, also resided in clusters along particular residential streets and narrow courts.

The spatial position of slaves is difficult to determine due to the indeterminate numbers of slaves who lived-out. Slaves who lived with their masters usually lived in the rear of the main house in special slave quarters, kitchen buildings, carriage houses, or outbuildings. Since the master controlled the spatial positioning of slaves within the lot, the spatial position reflected the master's view of slaves' social position. As chattel, slaves were housed with livestock; as humans of inferior biological and social standing, slaves were concealed from public view in the rear of the lot. Industrial slaves lived in large barracks and tenements near their workplace. Slaves who lived-out had greater control of residence location, but like all residents, had to live within the confines of an already established social/spatial world. Slaves, as members of the lowest racial and class group, lived in crowded courts that dissected residential blocks.

The mass migration of Irish immigrants in the 1850s disrupted pre-existing social relations. As members of an unskilled workforce, they were in direct competition with free blacks and hired-out slaves. Their racial heritage was also questioned during the 1850s Know Nothings movement in the North.[55] Therefore, the ambiguous class/race situation of the immigrant Irish made boundary maintenance essential. The boundaries were formed along race lines through the formation of segregated social space. Poverty forced Irish immigrants to live in boarding houses and courts; their decision to live on highly segregated courts with other Irish or in boarding houses with other Irish families was based on a decision to form a boundary between themselves and nonwhites, especially free blacks.

Like space, clothing and personal possessions are used to maintain social boundaries. As public reflections of social group affiliation, material possessions can be arenas of conflict concerning social group membership. For instance, the social position of the elite vis-à-vis slaves was so beyond question that the elite gave slaves their cast-off garments However, for the white working class, the attire of free blacks and slaves was of critical concern. Aware of the ideological rhetoric that placed whites above nonwhites, the white working class found material reality in conflict with ideology. Consequently, white workers petitioned for sumptuary laws that would restrict slave and free black use of carriages, smoking, and fashionable attire.

This investigation is an attempt to demonstrate the importance of landscape and material culture for the study of past social relations. Through the study of landscape and material remains it is possible to examine the diversity of actors that are a part of Charleston's history. In the past, archaeological investigations of Charleston's landscape have centered on elite sites.[56] These sites provide important information on the intimate use of space and race relations among slaveholders and their slaves. In its preservation plan,[57] The Charleston Museum has made a commitment to the investigation of non–elite sites and, following through on its pledge, several middle-class white sites and one free black site have been tested.[58] However, acquiring additional archaeological information from free black sites, immigrant laborer sites, and industrial and hired–out slave sites is critical.

Although a diverse and dynamic population resided in nineteenth–century Charleston, most of its members are unrepresented in archaeological investigations. Archaeologists in Charleston have declared this history as significant and worthy of investigation, but now it is necessary for the greater community to also understand and appreciate Charleston's diverse history. The need for a more inclusive history and preservation plan goes beyond the need for a more accurate picture of the past. When people are left out of a social past, they do not form a sense of cultural belonging or cultural citizenship.[59] Even if that past is bitter or filled with conflict, it is central to realize that it is based on a shared time within a shared territory. Archaeologists, preservationists, planners, and citizens have a responsibility to nurture a "shared public memory,"[60] a memory that includes all people who were a part of Charleston's past.

NOTES

1. Bender 1992; Borchert 1980; Gregory and Urry 1985; Hirsh and O'Hanlon 1995; Pred 1990; Harvey 1990.
2. Lefebvre 1991.
3. Fields 1982; Fields 1990.
4. Ford 1861.
5. Powers 1994; Wade 1964.
6. Coclanis 1989.
7. Rosengarten et al. 1987.
8. Wade 1964.
9. Ford 1861.
10. Bridgens and Allen 1852.
11. *Charleston City Ward Book,* Ward 5, 1853.
12. Sanborn Insurance Company 1888.
13. Charleston City Directory 1859 and 1860.
14. Ford 1861.
15. Eighth Census of United States, 1860, Population Schedule, Ward 5.
16. U.S. Slave Population Schedule, Ward 5.
17. South Carolina State Free Negro Capitation Tax Books, Charleston, South Carolina, 1860.
18. U.S. Slave Population Schedule, 1860.

19. Pease and Pease 1990.
20. Smith 1950; Wade 1964.
21. Rosengarten et al. 1987; Wade 1964.
22. Singleton 1984.
23. Petition of Mechanics and Workingmen of the City of Charleston . . . Their Own Time 1858.
24. Fraser 1989.
25. Resnick and Wolff 1981.
26. 1860 U.S. Population Schedule, Ward 5.
27. 1860 U.S. Population Schedule, Ward 5.
28. Resnick and Wolff 1981.
29. Fraser 1989.
30. 1860 U.S. Population Schedule, Ward 5.
31. 1860 U.S. Population Schedule, Ward 5.
32. Johnson and Roark 1984a, 1984b.
33. Johnson and Roark 1984a, 1984b.
34. Fraser 1989; Shoemaker 1990.
35. Powers 1994; Silver 1979.
36. Coclanis 1989.
37. Pease and Pease 1990; Bellows 1993.
38. Johnson and Roark 1984a, 1984b.
39. Johnson and Roark 1984a, 1984b.
40. Radford 1974.
41. Rosengarten et al. 1987.
42. Zierden, personal communication 1995.
43. Rosengarten et al. 1987.
44. 1860 U.S. Population Schedule, Ward 5.
45. 1860 U.S. Population Schedule, Ward 5.
46. Drago 1990; Johnson and Roark 1984b:48; Powers 1994.
47. Rosengarten et al. 1987.
48. Ford 1861.
49. Blumin 1989:167.
50. Johnson and Roark 1984a, 1984b.
51. Johnson and Roark 1984a, 1984b.
52. Fox–Genovese 1988.
53. Nash 1988:254.
54. Fields and Fields 1983:73.
55. Lewis 1985; Reitz 1987; Zierden and Calhoun 1990; Zierden, Calhoun, and Hacker 1986; Zierden and Grimes 1989.
56. Anbinder 1992.
57. Zierden and Calhoun 1982; Zierden and Calhoun 1984; Zierden and Calhoun 1990.
58. Zierden 1990a, 1990b.
59. Kuo Wei Tchen as quoted in Hayden 1995:8.
60. Hayden 1995:9.

Works Cited

Anbinder, Tyler
1992   *Nativism and Slavery: The Northern Know Nothings and the Politics of the 1850s.* Oxford Univ. Press, New York.

Bellows, Barbara
1993   *Benevolence among Slaveholders: Assisting the Poor in Charleston, 1670–1860.* Louisiana State Univ. Press, Baton Rouge.

Bender, Barbara
1992   Theorising Landscapes, and the Prehistoric Landscapes of Stonehenge. In *Man* 27:735–55.

Blumin, Stuart
1989   *The Emergence of the Middle Class: Social Experience in the American City, 1760–1900.* Cambridge Univ. Press, Cambridge, England.

Borchert, James
1980   *Alley Life in Washington: Family, Community, Religion, and Folklife in the City, 1850–1970.* Univ. of Illinois Press, Urbana.

Bridgens and Allen Insurance Map
1852   An Original Map of the City of Charleston. Map on file, the South Carolina Historical Society, Charleston.

Calhoun, Jeanne, and Martha Zierden
1984   *Charleston's Commercial Landscape, 1803–1860.* Archaeological Contributions 7. The Charleston Museum, Charleston.

Carchedi, Guglielmo
1977   *On the Economic Identification of Social Classes.* Routledge and Kegan Paul, London.

Charleston City Directories
1859   *The Charleston Directory.* Means and Turnbull, compilers. Evans and Cogswell, Charleston. On file at the South Carolina Historical Society, Charleston.
1860   *Directory of the City of Charleston, 1860.* Eugene Ferslew, compiler. Evans and Cogswell, Charleston. Microfilm copy available at the South Carolina Historical Society, Charleston.

Charleston City Ward Book
1853   Microfilm copy available from Charleston City Archives.

Coclanis, Peter A.
1989   *The Shadow of a Dream: Economic Life and Death in the South Carolina Lowcountry 1670–1920.* Oxford Univ. Press, New York.

Drago, Edmund
1990   *Initiative, Paternalism, and Race Relations.* Univ. of Georgia Press, Athens.

Eighth Census
1860   Microfilm available from Charleston Public Library.

Fields, Barbara
1982   Ideology and Race in American History. In *Region, Race, and Reconstruction,* edited by J. Morgan Kousser and James M. McPherson, pp. 143–77. Oxford Univ. Press, New York.
1990   Slavery, Race and Ideology in the United States of America. *New Left Review* 181:95–118.

Fields, Mamie Garvin, and Karen Fields
1983   *Lemon Swamp and Other Places.* The Free Press, New York.

Ford, Frederick A. (compiler)
1861   *Census of the City of Charleston, South Carolina, for the Year 1861.* Evans and Cogswell, Charleston. On file at the Charleston Library Society, Charleston.

Fox-Genovese, Elizabeth
1988   *Within the Plantation Household: Black and White Women of the Old South.* Univ. of North Carolina Press, Chapel Hill.

Fraser, Walter J., Jr.
1989   *Charleston! Charleston!.* Univ. of South Carolina Press, Columbia.

Gregory, Derek, and John Urry (editors)
1985   *Social Relations and Spatial Structures.* St. Martin's Press, New York.

Harvey, David
1990   Between Space and Time: Reflections on the Geographical Imagination. In *Annals of the Association of American Geographers* 80:418–34.

Hayden, Dolores
1995   *The Power of Place: Urban Landscapes as Public History.* MIT Press, Cambridge, Massachusetts.

Hirsh, Eric, and Michael O'Hanlon (editors)
1995   *The Anthropology of Landscape: Perspectives on Place and Space.* Clarendon Press, Oxford.

Johnson, Michael P., and James L. Roark
1984a   *No Chariot Let Down.* W. W. Norton, New York.
1984b   *Black Masters.* W. W. Norton, New York.

Lefebvre, Henri
1991   *The Production of Space,* translated by Donald Nicholson–Smith. Basil Blackwell, Cambridge.

Lewis, Lynne
1985   The Planter Class: The Archaeological Record at Drayton Hall. In *The Archaeology of Slavery and Plantation Life,* edited by Theresa A. Singleton, pp. 121–40. Academic Press, Orlando.

Nash, Gary
1988   *Forging Freedom: The Formation of Philadelphia's Black Community, 1720–1840.* Harvard Univ. Press, Cambridge, Massachusetts.

Pease, Jane H., and William H. Pease
1990   *Ladies, Women, and Wenches: Choice and Constraint in Antebellum Charleston and Boston.* Univ. of North Carolina Press, Chapel Hill.

Petition of Mechanics and Workingmen of the City of Charleston Praying more effectual Legislation for the prevention of slaves hiring out of their own time and other purposes.
1858   Slavery Petitions, General Assembly, South Carolina Dept. of Archives and History.

Powers, Bernard
1994   *Black Charlestonians: A Social History, 1822–1885.* Univ. of Arkansas Press, Fayetteville.

Pred, Allan
1990   *Making Histories and Constructing Human Geographies: The Local Transformation of Practice, Power Relations, and Consciousness.* Westview Press, Boulder.

Radford, John Price
1974   *Culture, Economy and Urban Structure in Charleston, 1860–1880.* Ph.D. diss., Clark University. Univ. Microfilms, Ann Arbor.

Reitz, Elizabeth
1987   Vertebrate Fauna and Socioeconomic Status. In *Consumer Choices in Historical Archaeology,* edited by Suzanne Spencer-Wood, pp. 101–19, Plenum Press, New York.

Resnick, Stephen and Richard Wolff
1981   Classes in Marxian Theory. *Review of Radical Political Economy.* 13:1–18.

Rosengarten, Dale, Martha Zierden, Kimberly Grimes, Ziyadah Owusu, Elizabeth Alston, and Will Williams III
1987   *Between the Tracks: Charleston's East Side During the Nineteenth Century.* Archaeological Contributions 17, The Charleston Museum, Charleston.

Sanborn Insurance Company
1888   Sanborn Fire Insurance Company Map of the City of Charleston. On file at the South Carolina Historical Society, Charleston.

Shoemaker, Edward
1990   *Strangers and Citizens: The Irish Immigrant Community of Savannah, 1837–1861.* Ph.D. diss., Dept. of History, Emory Univ., Atlanta.

Silver, Christopher
1979   A New Look at Old South Urbanization: The Irish Worker in Charleston South Carolina, 1840–1860. In *South Atlantic Urban Studies,* vol. 3, edited by Samuel M. Hines and George W. Hopkins, pp. 141–72. Univ. of South Carolina Press, Columbia.

Singleton, Theresa A.
1984   The Slave Tag: An Artifact of Urban Slavery. *South Carolina Antiquities* 16:41–68.

Smith, D. E. Huger
1950   *A Charlestonian's Recollections, 1846–1913.* Carolina Art Association, Charleston.

South Carolina State Free Negro Capitation Tax Books
1860   Microfilm available from Avery Research Center, Charleston.

Wade, Richard C.
1964   *Slavery in the Cities.* Oxford Univ. Press, London.

Zierden, Martha
1990b Archaeological Excavations at 70 Nassau Street. Notes on file, The Charleston Museum, Charleston.
1990c Management Summary: Test Excavations at 40 Society Street, The Charleston Museum, Charleston.

Zierden, Martha A., and Jeanne A. Calhoun
1982   *Preliminary Report: An Archaeological Preservation Plan for Charleston, South Carolina.* Archaeological Contributions 1, The Charleston Museum, Charleston
1984   *An Archaeological Preservation Plan for Charleston, South Carolina.* Archaeological Contributions 8, The Charleston Museum, Charleston.
1990   An Archaeological Interpretation of Elite Townhouse Sites in Charleston, South Carolina, 1770–1850. *Southeastern Archaeology* 9(2):79–92.

Zierden, Martha, and Kimberly Grimes
1989   *Investigating Elite Lifeways through Archaeology: The John Rutledge House.* Archaeological Contributions 21, The Charleston Museum, Charleston.

Zierden, Martha, Jeanne Calhoun, and Debi Hacker
1986   *Outside of Town: Preliminary Investigation of the Aiken-Rhett House.* Archaeological Contributions 11, The Charleston Museum, Charleston.

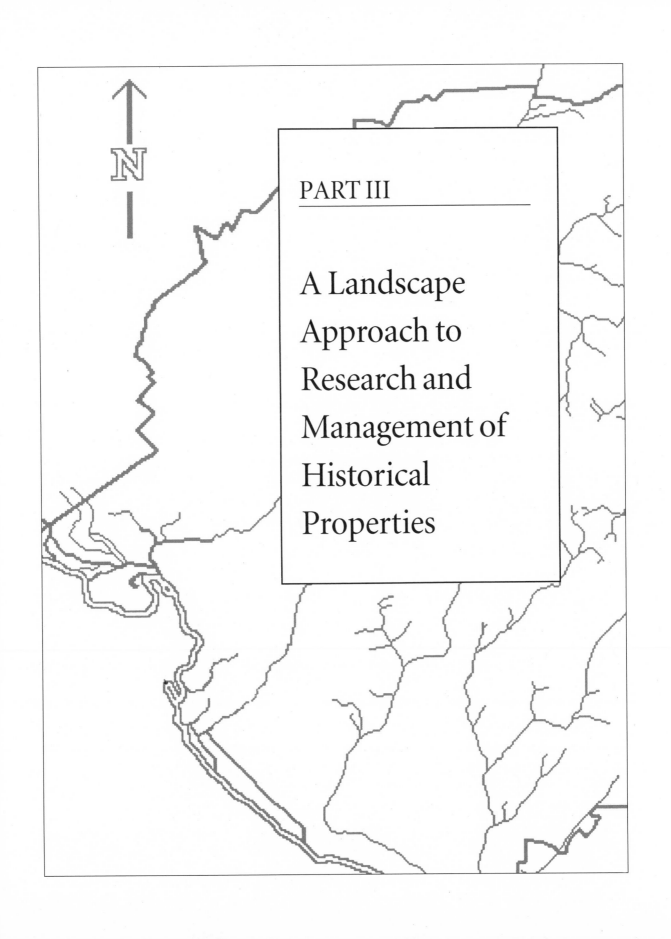

N

PART III

A Landscape
Approach to
Research and
Management of
Historical
Properties

15. South Carolina's Landscapes: Innovative Research and Cultural Resource Management Perspectives

LINDA F. STINE AND ROY S. STINE

South Carolina is graced by aboriginal shell rings, mounds, and villages from diverse cultures and time periods. Myriad colonists have left forts, plantations, farms, old towns, and some of the earliest settlements in the country. This has created a rich blend of cultures, each making its mark upon the land. The result is a unique landscape that influences modern settlement, agriculture, and business.[1] South Carolina's objects, buildings, sites, districts, and specific landscapes, as defined by the National Register of Historic Places (NRHP), are some of the most interesting in the nation.[2] This special landscape has to be recorded, evaluated, and managed. A landscape approach helps in these tasks by contributing to archaeological theory, method, data base construction, and interpretation.

As defined in this volume's introduction, landscape archaeology is part of the integrative study of how people are shaped and shaped by the land in dynamic cultural and natural contexts. A landscape approach in preservation guides interdisciplinary research and evaluation of historical properties. Scholars, whether architects, historians, geographers, or archaeologists, participate in initial planning meetings. Early participation fosters a regional perspective for evaluating and managing a project's historic properties.

Too often, South Carolina's private, state, and federal archaeologists find themselves simply reacting to certain crises. The preservation community's energy is spent putting out brushfires because Civil War batteries, African American cemeteries, brick kilns, and other historic properties are discovered by a bulldozer operator. It is difficult to evaluate, record, and manage these threatened sites quickly. A hasty call may save an endangered site, but at high cost after great compromise. Such simple site-by-site assessment is time consuming and can yield inconsistent results. A landscape approach allows investigators to focus on the relational ties between regional and site-specific landscape data. Managers using this perspective refine their awareness of the potential importance of specific sites within their jurisdiction. Such knowledge helps a cultural resource manager to become proactive, not simply reactive.

A landscape approach also alleviates problems with management of cultural resources on private lands. Developers include the costs of cultural resource assessment and management, but only if the regulations of the preservation community are equally enforced. Their request for standardization is important, because the majority of recorded archaeological sites have been discovered during contract projects.[3] Many private developers do not need state or federal agency permits until the development is under construction. In this manner archaeological sites are destroyed before permitting begins and the preservation community is notified. Some archaeologists are ameliorating this in early planning meetings with contractors. These preservationists are using a landscape approach to educate developers by illustrating how cultural resource planning enhances the aesthetic and historic value of a development .[4]

Defining a Landscape Approach to Cultural Resource Management

Landscape theory provides cultural resource managers with a powerful set of tools. In this book, scholars have explored how diverse groups of South Carolinians changed and were changed by their interaction with the land. A central concept includes the idea that landscape is "comprehensive and cultural" as well as historic.[5] Such an approach is holistic, interdisciplinary, multiscalar, and dynamic.[6]

The concept of landscape is not new. Carl Sauer, writing in the 1920s, adapted European anthropological, historical, and geographical notions of the landscape to formulate his own working definition. Sauer writes that people live and work within the landscape, "we are part of it, live with it, are limited by it, and modify it."[7] Members of cultures interact with the natural environment. Certain material forms result, leaving a definitive mark or cultural landscape. Building on the work of Sauer, scholars have shown how landscape theory allows archaeologists to shift the scale of study as needed. Archaeologists find that landscape theory is versatile and helps them to integrate diverse data. These data can incorporate site-specific, regional, social, and natural factors.[8]

To use more familiar archaeological terminology, a landscape perspective easily lends itself to researching both structure and process over expanding and contracting space and throughout various time periods. This approach builds on more traditional studies of intra- and intersite settlement patterns. Archaeological investigations framed within an ecological and/or direct historical perspective can prove equally useful in landscape studies.[9] Landscape then serves as an over-arching approach, incorporating processual or post-processual studies by archaeologists connected to universities, contracting firms, foundations, or avocational societies. By focusing on the relations between the natural and cultural worlds, landscape alters our perspective to reach beyond description. Landscape theory seeks to make connections between material remains, social institutions, natural resources, and human perceptions. Concomitant landscape methods are used to acquire data to test assumptions about those connections.

Interdisciplinary landscape methods must allow for shifting the research scale or perspective among artifacts, sites, and regions.[10] In fact, landscape investigators may find it beneficial to start by taking a nonsite approach. Focusing on the landscape, scholars begin by asking why certain areas were inhabited while others were not. Questions about the differing intensity of artifact concentrations are researched. This is one way for archaeologists to try to recapture a sense of past people's differential use of resources, pointing to perceptions of the land. Those using a nonsite approach still collect categorical data. These include specific types of sites, isolated occurrences, and unused areas. Site numbers can be assigned and resources managed after consultation with site file managers and environmental review specialists.[11]

Whether taking a nonsite ("distributional") or traditional site-oriented approach, a landscape perspective leads to a holistic investigation. By focusing on the social and natural landscape, archaeologists are forced to reevaluate simple culture histories based on tool and settlement types. Cultural ecological studies can be examined in conjunction with studies of social relations. Substantive questions can be asked, shedding new light on old data and leading to the collection of new types of information.

History of South Carolina Landscape Studies

A landscape perspective is used in various South Carolina studies of historic properties. One initial, ground-breaking project is that of South and Hartley (1980). The authors' investigation of the natural and social factors affecting seventeenth-century settlement pattern in lower Charleston County falls within the scope of landscape studies. It is a classic discussion of the importance of natural and cultural variables and their influence on early settlement patterns. They discovered that habitation sites tend to be found on high ground along the navigable rivers west of Charleston.[12] This work has been incorporated in research designs and more formal predictive models of area settlement strategies.

South and Hartley's studies guided recent research describing Charleston County's historic landscapes.[13] The Charleston report contains a preliminary inventory of recorded archaeological sites and discussion of probable site locations. This work is integrated with the results of a standing structures survey.[14] Together they show patterns of shifting settlement over time and space. A landscape perspective interrelates culture history, the lowcountry environment, and the present landscape to help county planners manage cultural resources.

The Yamasee Project conducted by Chester DePratter, William Green, and David McKivergan is, in part, a landscape study.[15] They have been investigating the origins and migrations of the Yamasee Indians from the late seventeenth through the early nineteenth centuries across the coastal plain of South Carolina. Green has provided an ethnohistorical context for these migrations. The sociocultural ramifications of contact between the English, Spanish, Yamasee, and others are investigated. Included is a detailed description of archaeological research at Altamaha (38BU1206), the main village of the lower Yamasee. The work of Green and DePratter is continued by McKivergan. He takes a regional approach to Yamasee settlement, testing the high ground–navigable water hypothesis of South

and Hartley.[16] DePratter, McKivergan, and others have completed an initial archaeological reconnaissance of the region. The results indicate that the historic Yamasee also sought to settle along the higher elevations, close to navigable waters. This project is already yielding interesting results concerning early historic landscapes in South Carolina.

Recent plantation studies in South Carolina also include landscape concepts.[17] Interdisciplinary studies of the elaborate formal garden, slave quarters, and other areas of Crowfield Plantation in the Goose Creek area are underway. Colin Brooker and Michael Trinkley have been working on a number of plantations in the Beaufort area. Their explorations of tabby construction and plantation site structure are leading them to a landscape approach. They argue, for example, for the presence of a historic, picturesque landscape on Spring Island (38BU1) in Beaufort County. National Park Service survey and testing at Snee Farm, near Charleston, is, in part, a search for evidence of a past ornamental garden landscape. These types of studies fall under the rubric of landscape, but are more focused on formal perceptions of ornamental gardens and the seating of the main plantation house. Such understandings of the formal plantation landscape are important, especially if contrasted to studies of the "functional" portions of the plantation.

Zierden, Drucker, and Calhoun (1986) provide another example of the use of a landscape perspective to help evaluate and interpret agrarian resources.[18] In studying Lesesne and Fairbank plantations on Daniel's Island, Berkeley County, they evaluate approximately 50 acres deemed eligible for nomination to the National Register of Historic Places. Drawing on interdisciplinary expertise, these researchers interpret changing settlement patterns at the two plantations, spanning the seventeenth through twentieth centuries. They include a comparative discussion of urban settlement patterns and social relations in contradistinction to rural patterns. This was predicated primarily on the previous urban archaeological investigations of The Charleston Museum. Investigations continue, incorporating archaeological, architectural, and historical research studies of area landscapes.[19]

One result of their efforts is substantial documentation of a nucleated settlement pattern associated with colonial and antebellum cotton production. They contrast the pattern at the cotton plantation with a "more multi-nucleated rice plantation" pattern found in the area.[20] They suggest an economic model for settlement placement across the landscape. They conclude that certain patterns will be associated throughout a rice plantation landscape, as opposed to the landscape patterns found at cotton or other types of plantations.

Another ongoing study of plantations is that of Leland Ferguson and his students at the University of South Carolina, Columbia.[21] They are investigating eighteenth-century land use and settlement patterns along the East Branch of the Cooper River in Berkeley County, South Carolina. These researchers are isolating important social and natural variables in regional patterns. They are also investigating settlement patterns of African American villages, main plantation houses, and associated outbuildings. The importance of relative view or perspective toward understanding past landscapes is stressed in the East Cooper Project. An archaeologist examining intersite settlement in a slave quarter can demonstrate the communal nature of an African American village and its attendant positive social aspects. On the other hand, the archaeologist can also interpret this settlement pattern from the viewpoint of an owner/planter—as either a source of perceived control or lack thereof.[22]

A review of landscape studies shows that plantation settlement patterning in South Carolina is affected by a complex web of environmental and social interactions. Although there is some patterned regularity, no simple one-to-one correspondence between crops grown, time period, and arrangement of plantation activities and structures is found.[23] The arrangement of dependencies, slave villages, fields, landings, and the main house complex seems to be based on several factors. The shape and quality of the plantation lands set the stage for what types of crops could be grown, where structures could best stand, and how to best organize within that particular landscape. The social, ideological, and economic milieux of each time period also influences choice of crops grown, building types, and arrangement of activities.[24] Some owners lived year-round on their plantations, others lived there seasonally, and still others remained absentee owners; these residency variations also affect patterns. Idiosyncratic decisions about agricultural and labor management also lead to differences in settlement patterns. Variation in settlement processes and structures also stems from changing and differential social relations. These studies show that regional pattern variability is greater than previously thought.

Plantation research results demonstrate the importance and need for a landscape approach when interpreting and evaluating sites. A number of plantation sites are being investigated in the South Carolina lowcountry and are yielding intriguing results. Very few plantation sites are being explored in the piedmont region. By increasing our scope of research we can improve our understanding of plantation systems in South Carolina.

Working with the State Historic Preservation Office

Developing Historical Contexts

The recent fast pace of construction in South Carolina has affected our understanding of how best to manage cultural resources such as plantations and slave village sites. Contract archaeologists and managers are re-educating themselves about alternatives to excavation. Preservation plans incorporating greenspacing, passive parks, and interpretive walks are under review. Site significance is now evaluated in light of an increasing variety and number of recorded sites. New sites are recorded at an estimated rate of 800–1,000 per year.[25] Landscape studies can be adapted to guide development of South Carolina's historic contexts. Highlighting specific historic contexts will add consistency, help to point out lacunae in our present knowledge, and point to areas in need of survey and preservation.

As part of South Carolina's comprehensive planning process, historic contexts are presented as themes and culture histories. Pertinent themes and culture periods that relate to the development of South Carolina are identified.[26] These determinations are based on informal interaction among members of the preservation community. Discussion among architects, architectural historians, environmental review specialists, archivists, survey specialists, and archaeologists is often ad hoc. State preservationists share common goals, but often do not share a common professional language. The concepts and methods connected to "the landscape" serve as a good starting point for communication. This information is used to target possible types of cultural resources and to guide their evaluation.

This contextual approach is an outgrowth of the National Park Service's 1980s "Resource Protection Planning Process" (RP3). RP3's purpose was to help historians, architects, and archaeologists to integrate preservation plans using concepts from anthropology. A series of nested domains was created to provide a model for research and site assessment. Many preservationists, not always trained in social science, found it too technical and jargon-laden to be useful for preservation planning. Researchers also felt constrained, as RP3 was not based on region-specific models. By focusing on regional contexts, professionals with diverse training now share more common ground.

Landscape can be thematically oriented, it can be specific, and it can be generalized. Results enrich present historic contexts and help to develop additional ones. Historic contexts serve many purposes. Landscape studies suggest connections between different types of features, whether a standing structure, roadway, archaeological midden, or formal garden. Information from multiple sources highlight a specific theme. At another scale, interrelations between seemingly diverse historic properties can be discovered. These data can be incorporated into a statewide preservation plan for historical archaeology. One vital role is to help evaluate the significance of sites for the National Register of Historic Places (NRHP). Historic contexts provide a basis for judging how a particular object, building, site, landscape, or district might shed light on South Carolina history. They provide a framework for preservation planning, showing which research domains are relatively untapped and which are more fully developed. This helps cultural resource managers decide whether or not a particular site, building, or other property is significant and worthy of nomination to the NRHP. This is important, because eligibility to the register brings certain standardized preservation procedures into play.

National Register Evaluations

The NRHP criteria for evaluating the significance of historic properties are the cornerstones of many preservation and management activities. There are four specific criteria that have been implemented for determining significance (a-d). As archaeological sites tend to fall under one criterion, (d), this discussion will be limited to that criterion.

Criterion (d) states that a historic property must "yield, or prove likely to yield, information important to prehistory or history."[27] Archaeologists are responsible for proving site importance. They do this in part by showing how potential site data fit into a well-organized research design. As Butler and Hardesty so cogently discuss, significance must be assessed in light of the property's potential to add to the theoretical and substantive knowledge of the discipline of archaeology.[28] One way to determine site significance under this criterion is to place the site or sites within a theoretical framework, such as landscape. This helps focus the researcher's evaluations within a regional perspective, and forces consideration of both natural and cultural processes and their influence on landscape formation.

The National Park Service has published "Guidelines for Evaluation and Documenting Rural Historic Landscapes," adding historic landscapes to the list of objects, sites, districts, and buildings that can be nominated to the National Register of Historic Places. The authors define a rural historic landscape as a "geographical area that historically has been used by people, or shaped or modified by human activity, occupancy, or intervention, and that possesses a significant concentration, linkage, or continuity of areas of landuse, vegetation, buildings and structures, roads, and waterways, and natural features."[29] With the potential addition of significant landscapes to the National Register of Historic Places, it behooves researchers and managers to add landscape studies to their professional repertoires. In order to do so, preservationists must become familiar with landscape theory and methods.

Every standing structure must be assessed for its archaeological potential as well as structural significance. One must first recognize that the questions, goals, and methods of standing structures survey and archaeological survey are somewhat different. However, qualities of clarity, integrity, and redundancy are important in ascertaining the significance of both structures and below-ground sites.[30] The present state and federal management system for these types of cultural resources is divisive as presently structured, but can be circumnavigated by occasional interdepartmental meetings. The free exchange of ideas, expertise, and questions about landscape features enhances the ability of both archaeologists and architects to determine significance of historic properties. Participation in occasional multidisciplinary survey teams, for example, has opened lines of communication at the South Carolina State Historic Preservation Office.

A landscape perspective can integrate the results of architectural and archaeological survey. There already exist a number of landscape features, such as landings, earthworks, oak alleys, and roads that fall under management as both standing structures and as archaeological sites. The expertise of archaeologists, geographers, historians, landscape architects, and architectural historians is often needed during examination of a plantation's historic gardens, outbuildings, and both above- and below-ground cultural resources. These and similar landscape features serve as a starting point for discussion between standing structure surveyors and archaeologists. By working together, investigators can determine the relative research potential of a particular historic property.

Joint projects, such as Snee Farm (38CH917) in Charleston County, illustrate the power of a landscape perspective. When first acquired by preservationists, the interpretation of the property focused on the extant house, identified as Charles Pinckney's ca. 1754 home. While some consideration was given to the importance of the site's archaeological potential, significance was primarily judged on the house's association with a historic figure. Numerous studies of the structure have been undertaken.[31] Pinckney may not have occupied the existing building. The archaeological record, in contrast, revealed extensive evidence of Pinckney's presence. The standing house appears to date from the nineteenth-century occupation of the plantation. Archaeological excavations uncovered an associated, contemporaneous slave village. Archaeology continues to reveal diverse features, including remains from the Pinckney occupation.[32]

As the NRHP nomination stressed the qualities of the existing house and its association with Pinckney, the revised dating of the structure has called the significance evaluation into question. The site is arguably significant under criterion (d). Using a landscape approach, the distribution of structures and features within the existing setting are being studied. Excavations, historical research, and architectural studies show that data generated by study of Snee Farm can address substantive questions in historical archaeology.

The National Park Service has refocused its efforts at Snee Farm in order to interpret a succession of past landscapes to the public. After completing ongoing investigations, the National Park Service will be able to recreate, across the actual land or through drawings and models, the mid-eighteenth-century landscape related to Pinckney. They will also be able to recreate the early- to mid-nineteenth- and twentieth-centuries landscapes. In its present setting, the house faces a modern subdivision instead of the outbuildings and fields of the past. As a result, Snee Farm data also illustrate examples of broad, important social and economic changes that have occurred throughout the lowcountry's history. Using a diverse array of methods, and drawing on multiple sources, the National Park Service is using Snee Farm data to guide public understanding of the past. These data also are vital for future facilities planning on the property.

Geographic Information Systems (GIS) and Planning

Federal and state managers are creating large, computerized data bases. A Geographic Information System (GIS) serves as a good example of a spatial data base system. A GIS inherently mandates a landscape approach. A typical GIS can store a vast amount of data about a certain region. The data is derived from a multitude of sources. Among these are maps of differing degrees of accuracy and effective scales. Investigators have to record the lineage of data before they consider, integrate, and manipulate spatial data.[33] These data are used to create new maps for planning purposes.

A GIS consists of digital data that can reproduce spatial data in a series of maps called layers. These layers can include whatever data are needed: a map of hydrology, soil, elevation, archaeological site locations, or other related data. These maps can be overlaid using a precise series of instructions to produce new maps, providing researchers with important new spatial information. GIS users combine various software and hardware arrangements to produce these map layers. Researchers can use personal computers, work stations, or mainframe systems as funding permits. Creating a data base is relatively expensive and is used most often by large institutions.[34]

The scope of a GIS is dependent upon the needs of the agencies creating the data base. A GIS can shift scales, zooming in on a particular study area or out to cover a larger region. Thus, archaeological concentrations and isolated finds can be recorded and updated as needed. Maps detailing specific site resources, such as elevation of site and distance to water, can be created. Layer upon layer of different, mapped information is stored in the system. Each layer can be pulled out to help the researcher answer specific questions. Most important, new layers can also be created, distilled, or synthesized from previous layers. Certain key functions are used to help interpret and manage data. For example, most GIS's have a buffer function. One can encode commands so that the system will place a protective buffer of x feet around all coded wetlands and archaeological sites.[35] With these functions a GIS can be a powerful planning tool. Like any tool, it can be misused if misunderstood.

Many planners do not realize that much of South Carolina's cultural resources have yet to be discovered. Only Greenwood County has been systematically surveyed by archaeologists.[36] That particular survey was a basic reconnaissance survey. By its very nature, many sites were not discovered or recorded. Empty spots on a topographic map *do not* indicate that no archaeological sites are located in the area. They more likely illustrate those areas that need to be surveyed. Also, many of the sites that are recorded in the site files have not been professionally evaluated for potential eligibility for nomination to the NRHP.

Another problem with construction of an archaeological layer in a GIS for South Carolina concerns the National Register. Many NRHP sites, objects, districts, and buildings do not as yet have corresponding archaeological site file numbers. A layer constructed from site file data will have to be created independently from a layer containing recorded National Register sites (data housed at the South Carolina Department of Archives and History, Historic Preservation Division).

The present construction of an archaeology layer for South Carolina will be of great value for research and management of historic landscapes.[37] The archaeologists at the Francis Marion National Forest are also creating a data base for eventual implementation of a GIS. Archaeologists can use the power of a GIS to determine potential site locations, flagging specific attributes and features of the land. By working with land managers, archaeologists and other preservationists can help in the creation of interdisciplinary storehouses of knowledge. They can make sure that GIS users do not lose sight of the current limitations of the system, based on the current limits of the profession's data base. A good example in South Carolina is found in the ACE Basin Project (Ashley, Combahee, Edisto River drainage area). Many different state agencies have joined forces to help identify, evaluate, and protect both cultural and natural areas important to that region's heritage. This project proves that information can be fruitfully shared.[38]

Conservation and Preservation

Projects such as the ACE Basin or the evolving Ashley River Special Area Management Plan illustrate the interdisciplinary needs of modern preservation. A host of citizen groups and agencies at the local, state, and national levels are interested in preserving South Carolina's resources. Some are primarily concerned with conservation of natural areas, such as wetlands, or with preservation of a specific wildlife species, such as eagles. Some want to protect regional viewscapes. Others are concerned with preservation of human-made objects, such as buildings, cemeteries, and military fortifications. All are concerned with protecting and managing certain parts of the Carolina landscape. Sometimes these groups are at cross purposes, wasting money, time, and energy debating one another instead of presenting a unified front. A shared landscape perspective would focus their efforts.

Many of these agencies and private groups simply do not see a connection between the importance of protecting a tabby ruin as opposed to protecting a plant habitat or a viewscape. Conservation is seen as separate from preservation. This attitude must be changed through outreach programs. Mutual exchange of ideas, mutual respect

for heritage efforts, and sharing a communal focus on landscape will increase protection of all of the state's resources.

Case Study: Charleston's Civil War Sites

In 1992 the South Carolina Institute of Archaeology and Anthropology was involved in a grant with the Charleston Planning Office, identifying and mapping recorded archaeological resources.[39] Charleston has a multitude of historic properties and great local enthusiasm for preservation. For example, Charleston County has some of the best preserved Civil War fortifications in the state, if not the country. Huge forts, earthworks, and camps once protected the city from repeated Union attacks. The majority of the breastworks and forts are on James Island. These raised earthworks catch one's eye in the lowcountry. They still offer visitors a commanding view of rivers, road crossings, and the somewhat rural landscape of the island.

James Island was one of the few places South Carolinians actually kept the Union at bay. Many African American troops, fighting for the Union, camped, trained, fought, and died in this area. The Battle of Secessionville, for example, was one of the most important battlefield sites in South Carolina.[40] By placing the battle in its regional context, the entire line of landscape features and related encampments increase in importance.

In the past, pieces of this great system were only occasionally reported. Some breastworks and forts were recorded at the South Carolina Institute of Archaeology and Anthropology archaeological site files, on a few National Register nominations at the State Historic Preservation Office, and on local collectors' maps. Others were mentioned in requests for land-altering permits with the South Carolina Coastal Council and the Army Corps of Engineers. These data have not been correlated.

In terms of preservation, the significance of individual fragments of defensive lines are often judged not significant. At the scale of a single site, some consider these properties as redundant, offering little to further the theoretical and substantive knowledge of our discipline.[41] That helps to explain the destruction of Battery No. 2 on the James Island Siegeline; a water tower now stands in its place. Concerned citizens could not articulate why the battery was so important to the state's heritage. With a landscape perspective, group members could have shown how this battery was an important part of Charleston's defenses.

Inherently, a landscape approach forces one to evaluate a site from differing points of view and levels of analysis. This particular landscape feature should have been judged worthy or not worthy of nomination to the National Register (or of saving) based upon its relationship to the whole complex of similar sites. Significance could also be demonstrated by its potential for interpretation and education and by its particular qualities of integrity and clarity. Its particular contribution to our understanding of the Civil War in Charleston and environs may have been negligible or strong. It is gone. It is too late for such a determination for Battery No. 2, but not for other Civil War sites.

From metal-detecting collectors to state representatives, there is strong support for preservation of these sites. However, no single agency presently exists to serve as a clearinghouse for these various groups. No overarching, central plan exists for the management of these properties. A focus could be found by creating an entity to concentrate solely on the preservation of Charleston's Civil War landscapes. Again, a landscape perspective and a related preservation ethic can be shared by myriad agencies and individuals. Diverse, specific agendas can be conjoined by a new study of the area's Civil War landscape. National groups, such as the Conservation Fund and the Association for the Preservation of Civil War Sites are interested in aiding local efforts with match funds and expertise. Local groups, however, must spearhead the financial effort to save these resources. Federal and state agencies can provide data and assistance as well.

A landscape perspective may reveal that batteries, typical of archaeological features often viewed as redundant, are really linchpins in the whole siege line. Improved selection can be made of which landscape features are worthy of preservation, without expensive and redundant archaeological mapping and excavation of each particular portion of the line. Breastworks, batteries, and campsites can be incorporated into a passive park. These types of Civil War features are impressive and educational edifices. They also tend to cover a lot of ground. Protection of significant portions of these historic sites can be embedded in protection of the viewscape, as well as certain habitats. Some portions of the line can be developed for public enjoyment and interpretation. Development of a linear park, such as that found along Columbia's waterways, is one management option.

Agencies such as the South Carolina Coastal Council already have created a data base locating area wetlands, roads, and other topographic features from diverse maps. When these data are digitized, a protected GIS layer locating recorded archaeological sites should be incorporated. Historical plans and maps need to be entered into a separate layer. To obtain a regional and contextual perspective, the archaeological sites and landscape features related to the Civil War need to be identified. A preliminary inventory of these sites is available.[42] Site-specific archaeological information could be added and compared to locations and patterns based on historic accounts. GPS, or Global Positioning Satellite technology, could be used to map above-ground features quickly and accurately. The data can be incorporated into the GIS. Researchers would then be able to study the interaction of these landscape features. Models that investigate the effect of fort and breastwork destruction on wetland habitat could be created and tested.[43]

Conclusion: Landscape and Management of Cultural Resources

Landscape studies in South Carolina are relatively new. "Landscape" is providing a good focus for initial syntheses of the state's archaeology. Settlement studies and artifact patterns are more variable than previously assumed. However, as these and other studies have shown, cultural patterns can be recognized more readily at specific scales of analysis. A landscape approach helps pinpoint both variability and consistency in patterning. At the most minute level, all intact sites are intrinsically unique and potentially significant. However, certain common characteristics may be uncovered for particular site types at particular time periods. This information can help guide management of South Carolina's cultural resources.

Using landscape as an overarching perspective helps guide researchers and managers across the shoals of NRHP evaluations. Such interdisciplinary studies are easily adapted to developing mandated historic contexts. Landscape methods are particularly conducive to the needs of cultural resource managers. Methods can include development and implementation of regional data bases such as a Geographic Information System (GIS). New methods, such as increased use of interdisciplinary teams, is fostered by a landscape approach. Discussion of the best means to manage a particular property is facilitated by using a landscape approach. Communication between preservationists and conservationists is enhanced as managers visualize mutual areas of particular concern within the modern landscape.

Preservation projects are always underfinanced and usually understaffed. Employing a new landscape paradigm will help. Evoking a landscape perspective does not cost money; in fact, it may save duplication of effort and thus time and money. A landscape perspective will enrich the present understanding of the state's past. It fosters a proactive stance in South Carolina preservation, as opposed to a less expedient reactive stance. Preservation of the state's myriad historical properties is a slow, ongoing concern. By incorporating a landscape approach, and related new technologies such as GIS, cultural resource managers will improve their abilities to assess and protect South Carolina's heritage.

Many people are visually oriented, and landscape interpretations, such as those found at many national and state parks, offer public education and enjoyment. Alderson and Low state that historic "[i]nterpretation is an attempt to create understanding."[44] Landscape studies and subsequent interpretation will help foster public understanding of the importance of particular historic properties. This helps to generate awareness and support for a preservation ethic.

Citizens, old and new, deeply rooted or newly transplanted, are aware of their region's special qualities. Some may not consciously realize that historic properties form an integral part of that special landscape. The explosion of development in the last few decades is taking its toll on cultural resources.[45] Preservationists and managers can help to educate the public and ensure resource protection. South Carolinians are not alone in their interest in the state's diverse history. In a recent survey of visitors to the state, many listed historic sites as second only to beaches as a reason for visiting. For the Charleston area, historical sites rated a resounding No. 1.[46] Obviously, the public supports protection of cultural resources through laws, taxes, and volunteer labor. By protecting and interpreting landscapes, preservationists justify that support.

NOTES

1. Kovacik and Winberry 1989.
2. National Register of Historic Places (36CFR60, 36CFR800). The National Historic Preservation Act (NHPA), P.L. 89-665, 16 U.S.C. 470–470t (1966) authorizes the National Register of Historic Places (C.F.R. Part 60), which includes setting up criteria for evaluating properties for nomination. This law also creates the Advisory Council on Historic Preservation in 36 C.F.R. Part 800. It includes the Advisory Council regulations on how to implement Section 106 of the NHPA. Some major amendments to the NHPA are found in P.L. 95–515, which codifies Executive Order No. 11593, Protection and Enhancement of the Cultural Environment, May 13, 1971 (36 F.R. 8921).

3. Stine 1992a. Some builders are already incorporating archaeological surveys during planning, even before applying for various permits. Duncan Newkirk, personal communication 1990.

4. For example, Lucy Wayne and Martin Dickinson (SouthArc 1995) are taking this approach with Georgia Pacific's Dunes West Development near Charleston.

5. Meinig 1990:xv.

6. Conzen 1990; Crumley and Marquardt 1987; Crumley and Marquardt 1990; Roberts 1987; Stine 1992a.

7. Sauer 1963b:324–25; see Winberry, this volume, for a complete discussion of the theoretical development of landscape studies in geography.

8. Sauer 1963b:343; Kovacik and Winberry 1989:1; Butzer 1982; Crumley and Marquardt 1987, 1990.

9. American archaeologists use the term "landscape" to include both the geophysical setting and the built environment. In contrast, in Australia, "landscape" is more narrowly defined as the natural environment, juxtaposed against the "built environment." A landscape perspective incorporates study of these products and their interrelationships (Cremin 1992).

10. Such as Zierden, Drucker, and Calhoun 1986; Zierden and Herman 1996; and Crumley and Marquardt 1987, 1990.

11. Green, Stine, and Stine 1992.

12. South and Hartley 1980; South and Hartley 1985.

13. South and Hartley's studies (1980, 1985); Stine 1992a.

14. Fick 1992.

15. The work of William Green (1991) and Chester DePratter and William Green (1990) is continued by David McKivergan (1991).

16. South and Hartley 1980; McKivergan 1991; William Green, personal communication 1992.

17. Crowfield Plantation in the Goose Creek area investigations are underway. Beth Gantt, personal communication 1991; Spring Island is discussed by Brooker in Trinkley 1990a:147–49; Snee Farm landscape investigations were discussed with National Park Service archaeologist Bennie Keel, personal communication 1992.

18. Zierden, Drucker, and Calhoun 1986.

19. Zierden and Calhoun 1984; Zierden and Herman 1996; Zierden, this volume.

20. Zierden, Drucker, and Calhoun 1986:1–5.

21. Ferguson 1986; results described in Adams 1990; Affleck 1990; Anthony 1989; Babson 1987; Babson 1988; and Ferguson and Babson 1986. In 1995 Ferguson's Univ. of South Carolina archaeological fieldschool retested portions of Snee Farm, Wando area, for comparative data.

22. Babson 1987.

23. For example, Adams 1990; Adams 1992; Babson 1987; Dickinson and Wayne 1990; Lees 1980; Jay Mills 1988; Poplin 1989; Poplin and Scardaville 1991; Stine 1992b; Wheaton, Friedlander, and Garrow 1983; Zierden, Drucker, and Calhoun 1986.

24. Stine 1992a, 1992b; Joseph, this volume; Poplin 1992; Joyce, this volume.

25. Keith Derting, personal communication 1995. See also Derting and Leader 1995.

26. South Carolina State Historic Preservation Office 1990:Appendix G, 59–61; Appendix H, 63–76.

27. 36CFR60.4.

28. Butler 1987; Hardesty 1995.

29. McClelland et al. 1990:1–2.

30. See Hardesty 1995; Glassow 1977; Raab and Klinger 1977; Sharrock and Grayson 1979 for discussions on significance evaluations. See Sprinkle 1995 for working with above and below ground data and the NRHP.

31. For example, Brockington 1987; King 1991. During a visit to the Park in 1995, I confirmed that National Park Service archaeologists have maintained an ongoing archaeological program at Snee Farm. This program's immediate purpose is to mitigate adverse impacts to cultural resources at the site during utility, road, and other construction activities. The long-term result is and will be the addition of new knowledge about settlement patterns, feature types and distributions, and land use at the Park.

32. Stine 1987, 1992b; King 1991; Bennie Keel, personal communication 1992.

33. Lanter 1991.

34. Allen, Green, and Zubrow 1990.

35. Green, Stine, and Stine 1992.

36. Rodeffer and Holschlag 1979.

37. Derting and Leader 1995 and Scurry and Carlson 1995 describe ongoing research and development of an archaeological layer for the South Carolina statewide GIS.

38. Contact personnel at the South Carolina Division

of Water Resources, the South Carolina Coastal Council, the South Carolina Institute for Archaeology and Anthropology, and archaeologists at the Francis Marion National Forest for additional information. Nancy Brock (Archives and History), personal communication 1991; Keith Derting (SCIAA), personal communication 1995; Bob Morgan and Bob Wise (Francis Marion National Forest), personal communication 1991; Steve Snyder (South Carolina Coastal Council), personal communication 1991.

39. Stine 1992a.
40. Power 1991; Judge and Smith 1991; Stine 1993.
41. Butler 1987.
42. Stine 1992a.
43. Green, Stine, and Stine 1992; Stine 1992a.
44. Alderson and Low 1976:3. South 1989 offers an example of using this perspective for interpretations at Charles Towne Landing park.
45. Kovacik and Winberry 1989:1, 215.
46. South Carolina Dept. of Parks, Recreation, and Tourism 1990:2, 5, 17.

Works Cited

Adams, Natalie P.
1990   *Early African-American Domestic Architecture from Berkeley County, South Carolina.* Master's thesis, Dept. of Anthropology, Univ. of South Carolina, Columbia.
1992   Elite Ideology and African-American Resistance: Architectural Change at South Carolina Slave Settlements. Paper presented at the Society for Historical Archaeology Meetings, Kingston, Jamaica.

Affleck, Richard M.
1990   *Power and Space: Settlement Pattern Change at Middleburg Plantation, Berkeley County, South Carolina.* Master's thesis, Dept. of Anthropology, Univ. of South Carolina, Columbia.

Alderson, William T., and Shirley Payne Low
1976   *Interpretation of Historic Sites.* 4th ed., American Association for State and Local History, Nashville.

Allen, Kathleen, Stanton Green, and Ezra Zubrow
1990   *Interpreting Space: GIS and Archaeology.* Taylor and Francis, London and New York.

Anthony, Ronald W.
1989   *Cultural Diversity at Mid to Late 18th Century Lowcountry Plantation Slave Settlements.* Master's thesis, Dept. of Anthropology, Univ. of South Carolina, Columbia.

Babson, David W.
1987   Plantation Ideology and the Archaeology of Racism: Evidence from the Tanner Road Site (38BK416), Berkeley County, South Carolina. *South Carolina Antiquities* 19(1, 2):35–47.
1988   *The Tanner Road Settlement: The Archaeology of Racism on Limerick Plantation.* Volumes in Historical Archaeology, Conference on Historic Sites Archaeology, vol. 4, edited by Stanley South. South Carolina Institute of Archaeology and Anthropology, Columbia. Reprint of 1987 Master's thesis, Dept. of Anthropology, Univ. of South Carolina, Columbia.

Brockington, Paul E., Jr.
1987   *A Cultural Resource Survey at Snee Farm, 38CH917.* Ms. on file at Brockington and Associates, Atlanta.

Butler, William B.
1987   Forum: Significance and Other Frustrations in the CRM Process. *American Antiquity* 52(4):820–29.

Butzer, Karl
1982   *Archaeology as Human Ecology: Method and Theory for a Contextual Approach.* Cambridge Univ. Press, England.

Conzen, Michael P.
1990   Preface and Introduction. In the *Making of the American Landscape,* edited by Michael Conzen, pp. vii–ix and 1–3. Unwin Hyman, Boston.

Cremin, Aedeen
1992   Landscape Archaeology as a Central Paradigm in Historical Archaeology. Paper presented at the Society for Historical Archaeology Meetings, Kingston, Jamaica.

Crumley, Carole, and William Marquardt
1990   Landscape: A Unifying Concept in Regional Analysis. In *Interpreting Space: GIS and Archaeology,* edited by Kathleen Allen, Stanton Green, and Ezra Zubrow, pp. 73–79. Taylor and Francis, London.

Crumley, Carole, and William Marquardt (editors)
1987   *Regional Dynamics: Burgundian Landscapes in Historical Perspective.* Academic Press, New York and San Diego.
DePratter, Chester, and William Green
1990   Origins of the Yamasee. Paper presented at the Southeastern Archaeological Conference, Mobile.
Derting, Keith, and Jonathan Leader
1995   Information Management Within SCIAA: A South Carolina Perspective. In *Archaeological Site Management: A Southeastern Perspective,* edited by David G. Anderson and Virginia Horak, pp. 72–81. Readings in Archaeological Resource Protection Series No. 3. Interagency Archaeological Services Division, Atlanta, Georgia.
Dickinson, Martin, and Lucy Wayne
1990   *Four Men's Ramble: Archaeology in the Wando Neck, Charleston County, South Carolina.* Submitted to Dunes West Development of Charleston, SouthArc, Gainesville.
Ferguson, Leland G.
1986   Slave Settlement and Community Patterns Along the East Branch of the Cooper River: Plans for Research. *South Carolina Antiquities* 18(1, 2):25–32.
Ferguson, Leland, and David Babson
1986   *Survey of Plantation Sites along the East Branch of Cooper River: A Model for Predicting Archaeological Site Location.* Ms. on file, Dept. of Anthropology, Univ. of South Carolina, Columbia.
Fick, Sarah
1992   *Architectural and Archaeological Survey of Charleston County.* Submitted to the Charleston County Planning Office by Preservation Consultants, Charleston.
Glassow, Michael.
1977   Issues in Evaluating the Significance of Archaeological Resources. *American Antiquity* 42:413–20.
Green, Stanton, Roy Stine, and Linda Stine
1992   Infinite Landscapes: The Role of View in Landscape Archaeology. Paper presented at the Anthropology of Human Behavior Through Geographic Information and Analysis: An International Conference, Univ. of California, Santa Barbara.
Green, William
1991   *The Search for Altamaha: The Archaeology and Ethnohistory of an Early 18th Century Yamasee Indian Town.* Master's thesis, Dept. of Anthropology, Univ. of South Carolina, Columbia.
Hardesty, Donald L.
1995   Research Questions and Information. *CRM* 18(6) Supplement:4–8.
Judge, Christopher, and Steven D. Smith
1991   *Acquiring the Past for the Future: The South Carolina Heritage Trust Status Assessment of Cultural Resource Sites.* Research Manuscript Series 213, South Carolina Institute of Archaeology and Anthropology, Univ. of South Carolina, Columbia.
King, Julia A.
1991   *Recommendations for the Management of Archaeological Resources Historic Snee Farm.* Submitted to Friends of Historic Snee Farm, Charleston, South Carolina.
Kovacik, Charles F., and John J. Winberry
1989   *South Carolina: The Making of a Landscape.* Univ. of South Carolina Press, Columbia. Originally published in 1987 as *South Carolina: A Geography.* Westview Press, Boulder and London.
Lanter, David
1991   Design of a Lineage-Based Meta-Data Base for GIS. *Cartography and Geographic Information Systems* 18(4):255–61.
Lees, William B.
1980   *Limerick, Old and in the Way: Archaeological Investigations at the Limerick Plantation, Berkeley County, South Carolina.* Anthropological Studies 5. South Carolina Institute of Archaeology and Anthropology, Columbia.
McClelland, Linda F., J. Timothy Keller, Genevieve Keller, and Robert Melnick
1990   *Guidelines for Evaluating and Documenting Rural Historic Landscapes.* National Register Bulletin 30. Washington, D.C.
McKivergan, David, Jr.
1991   *Migration and Settlement Among the Yamasee of South Carolina.* Master's thesis, Dept. of Anthropology, Univ. of South Carolina, Columbia.
Meinig, Donald W.
1990   Foreword. In *The Making of the American Landscape,* edited by Michael Conzen, pp. xv–xvi. Unwin Hyman, Boston.
Mills, James O.
1988   Investigations at the Slave Settlement, Richmond Hill Plantation, Georgetown County, South

Carolina. In *The Search for Architectural Remains at the Planter's House and Slave Settlement, Richmond Hill Plantation, Georgetown County, South Carolina.* Research Manuscript Series 205, Part 2, South Carolina Institute of Archaeology and Anthropology, Univ. of South Carolina, Columbia.

Poplin, Eric
1989   *True Blue Plantation. Archaeological Data Recovery at a Waccamaw Neck Rice Plantation.* Submitted to Heritage Plantation by Brockington and Associates of Atlanta.
1992   Variations in Structure: A Comparison of Absentee and Principal Residence on Rice Plantations in the Low Country of South Carolina. Paper presented at the Society for Historical Archaeology Meetings, Kingston, Jamaica.

Poplin, Eric, and Michael Scardaville
1991   *Archaeological Data Recovery at Long Point Plantation (38CH321) Mark Clark Expressway (I-526), Charleston County, South Carolina.* Submitted to the South Carolina Dept. of Highways and Public Transportation by Brockington and Associates of Atlanta.

Power, Tracy, Jr.
1991   *"An Affair of Outposts, in Which the Subordinate Officers and the Troops on the Spot Did the Best They Could": The Battle of Secessionville, 16 June 1862.* Ms. on file, South Carolina State Historic Preservation Office, Dept. of Archives and History, Columbia.

Raab, L. M., and T. C. Klinger
1977   A Critical Appraisal of "Significance" in Contract Archaeology. *American Antiquity* 42:629–34.

Roberts, B. K.
1987   Landscape Archaeology. In *Landscape and Culture: Geographical and Archaeological Perspectives,* edited by J. M. Wagstaff, pp. 77–95. Basil Blackwell, New York, and T. J. Press Ltd., Padstow, Cornwall, Great Britain.

Rodeffer, Michael J., and Stephanie L. Holschlag
1979   *Greenwood County: An Archaeological Reconnaissance.* Lander College, Greenwood. Report on file, South Carolina Institute of Archaeology and Anthropology, Columbia.

Sauer, Carl Ortwin
1963b   The Morphology of Landscape. In *Land and Life:*

A Selection from the Writings of Carl Ortwin Sauer, edited by John Leighly, pp. 315–50. Univ. of California Press, Berkeley. Second printing 1965. Originally published in 1925 in Univ. of California Publications in Geography (vol. 2, no. 2):19–53.

Scurry, James D., and Ruth E. Carlson
1995   Improving Site Recording Accuracy in a GIS: A South Carolina Example. In *Archaeological Site File Management: A Southeastern Perspective,* edited by David G. Anderson and Virginia Horak, pp. 82–87. Readings in Archaeological Resource Protection Series No. 3. Interagency Archaeological Services Division.

Sharrock, F. W., and D. K. Grayson
1979   "Significance" in Contract Archaeology. *American Antiquity* 44:327–28.

South Carolina Dept. of Parks, Recreation, and Tourism
1990   *South Carolina Out-of-State Visitor Survey By Region, 1987–1988.* Report on file, Division of Engineering and Planning Research and Statistics Section, Columbia.

South, Stanley
1989   Secessionville. From Archaeology to Interpretation at CharlesTowne. In *Studies in South Carolina Archaeology: Essays in Honor of Robert L. Stephensen,* edited by Albert Goodyear III and Glen T. Hanson, pp. 157–68. Anthropological Studies 9, South Carolina Institute of Archaeology and Anthropology, Univ. of South Carolina, Columbia.

South, Stanley, and Michael Hartley
1980   *Deep Water and High Ground: Seventeenth Century Low Country Settlement.* South Carolina Institute of Archaeology and Anthropology Research Manuscript Series 166, Columbia.
1985   Deep Water and High Ground: Seventeenth-Century Settlement Patterns on the Carolina Coast. In *Structure and Process in Southeastern Archaeology,* edited by Roy S. Dickens and Trawick Ward, pp. 263–86. Univ. of Alabama Press, Tuscaloosa.

SouthArc, Inc.
1995   *Cultural Resource Management Plan, Dunes West Archaeological Sites, Charleston County, S.C.* Submitted to Dunes West, Georgia-Pacific Development Company. On file SouthArc offices, Gainesville.

Sprinkle, John H., Jr.

1995   A Site Form for Important Sites—Converting Archaeological Reports into National Register Nominations. *CRM* 18(6) Supplement:13–16.

Stine, Linda France

1992a   *Revealing Historic Landscapes in Charleston County: Archaeological Inventory, Contexts, and Management.* Submitted to the Charleston County Planning Dept. South Carolina Institute of Archaeology and Anthropology.

1992b   *Archaeological Data Recovery Seeking a Slave Settlement, Snee Farm, Charleston County, South Carolina.* Submitted to the National Park Service, Southeastern Division. Draft Ms. on file Brockington and Associates, Atlanta.

1993   Site Destruction or Park Construction: Charleston County's Civil War Sites. In *Site Destruction in Georgia and the Carolinas,* edited by David G. Anderson and Virginia Horak, pp. 49–58. Interagency Archeological Services Division, National Park Service, Atlanta, Georgia.

Trinkley, Michael (editor)

1990a   *The Second Phase of Archaeological Survey on Spring Island, Beaufort County, South Carolina: Investigations of Prehistoric and Historic Settle-ment Patterns on an Isolated Sea Island.* Chicora Foundation, Columbia.

Wheaton, Thomas, R., Jr., Amy Friedlander, and Patrick H. Garrow

1983   *Yaughan and Curriboo Plantations: Studies in Afro-American Archaeology.* Soil Systems, Marietta, Georgia.

Zierden, Martha, and Bernard L. Herman

1996   Charleston Townhouses: Archaeology, Architecture, and the Urban Landscape, 1750–1850. In *Landscape Archaeology: Reading and Interpreting the American Historical Landscape,* edited by Rebecca Yamin and Karen Bescherer Metheny. Univ. of Tennessee Press, Knoxville.

Zierden, Martha A., and Jeanne A. Calhoun

1984   *An Archaeological Preservation Plan for Charleston, South Carolina.* Archaeological Contributions 8, The Charleston Museum, Charleston.

Zierden, Martha A., Lesley M. Drucker, and Jeanne Calhoun

1986   *Home Upriver: Rural Life on Daniel's Island, Berkeley County, South Carolina.* Submitted to the South Carolina Dept. of Highways and Public Transportation. A Joint Venture of Carolina Archaeological Services/The Charleston Museum, Columbia and Charleston.

16. Waterscape Archaeology: Recognizing the Archaeological Significance of the Plantation Waterscape

JIM ERRANTE

In this chapter I present the concept of *waterscape archaeology* and argue for its use in situations that involve a waterfront context. I have developed this concept to fill a void in plantation archaeology. A large percentage of South Carolina and Georgia lowcountry plantations maintained an intimate relationship with navigable river systems; however, a failure to acknowledge this relationship is seen in most archaeological studies, especially in cultural resource management (CRM) projects. Those that do recognize the importance of waterways for understanding the plantation landscape discover that few techniques exist that unite underwater and terrestrial archaeology. In this essay, I discuss arguments and ideas for the development of waterscape archaeology, using an interdisciplinary approach that includes input from underwater, terrestrial, and landscape archaeology.

Definitions

Terrestrial archaeologists are beginning to focus their research in terms of the "landscape." In common usage, landscape is defined as a "picture of natural inland scenery."[1] This definition neglects both the interaction of humans and the presence of bodies of water. A holistic interpretation has been offered by geographers as "the assemblage of real world features—natural, semi-natural and wholly artificial—[that] give character and diversity to the earth's surface and form the physical framework within which human societies exist."[2] Although this allows for human participation in any earthly environment, this range of meaning is rarely exercised. It is unfortunate that the connotation of "landscape" rarely evokes images of a maritime environment. It is this situation that inspired the development of a descriptive term to call attention to the importance of the maritime environment in historical archaeology studies.

The term "waterscape" refers to a natural or artificial waterfront, an underwater and terrestrial area where water and land masses converge. "Waterscape archaeology" was developed to deal with cultural remains found at the waterscape and to heighten awareness and emphasize the significance of this context. This approach has been applied in the study of South Carolina's antebellum plantations, which were adjoined to lowcountry river systems and toward the archaeological remains associated with this connection.[3] Waterscape archaeology is by no means restricted to the southern plantation context. It may be adapted to other situations where a physical or cognitive connection exists between underwater and terrestrial archaeological remains.

Danish archaeologist Christer Westerdahl, during a maritime archaeological survey of Swedish Norrland, selected the phrase "the maritime cultural landscape" as a way to unify the remnants of maritime culture on land as well as underwater.[4] Westerdahl defines the maritime cultural landscape as "comprising the whole network of sailing routes, old as well as new, with ports and harbors along the coast, and its related constructions and remains of human activity, underwater as well as terrestrial."[5]

Westerdahl's definition is intended to include all types of sites associated with maritime cultures, whether archaeological (material) or cognitive (place-names). He argues that each maritime cultural landscape includes a terrestrial component, but not necessarily as a physical extension of the latter. This type of situation can be exemplified by ocean shipwreck sites. Sites of this nature do not have a physical link with the land, but may be connected by such elements as the cargo of a ship. The cargo may be traced to the terrestrial component of its origin.

The use of waterscape archaeology deals specifically with aspects of the archaeological maritime cultural landscape that share an immediate relationship between terrestrial and underwater components. This situation can be demonstrated by a boat landing and the submerged artifacts directly associated with the landing's use. These types of cultural resources should be considered when developing archaeological research designs.

As an integral part of developing a research design, archaeological investigation requires the selection of an effective scale. The selected scale should neither bias the data nor dilute the research by being too restrictive or too broad. Marquardt and Crumley define an effective scale as "any scale at which pattern may be recognized and meaning inferred."[6] No scale can be deemed inherently wrong so long as it facilitates the accomplishment of research goals. Interpreting site size prior to, during, and after investigation helps the researcher achieve

greater awareness of site components and decide whether they should be included or excluded from the chosen project scale.

Problems arise when components crucial to achieving the project goals are not recognized or are excluded from the study area, thereby biasing the research results. Such problems commonly result from the often spatially limited and unusually shaped nature of many CRM project areas. In this situation, the project size and shape are defined by designated impact areas. Associated archaeological components and landforms extending outside the project area are often overlooked. Goodyear, Raab, and Klinger contend that an allocation for researching such landforms be made at the research design stage.[7]

Site components extending outside the project area should be acknowledged and given reasonable consideration within the research design, whether or not any research will be conducted in these areas. In light of this, terrestrial projects should include the recognition of underwater components when there is a potential for their existence. The broader definition of landscape as "the physical framework within which human societies exist" provides researchers with a wider spectrum within which site scale can be defined. The waterscape is thus viewed as an extension of the landscape: it is connected, not separate.[8]

Another perspective from which a cultural environment can be viewed and site scale selected is the cognitive landscape. The human use of space does not always result in artifact deposition. A cognitive landscape denotes "the mapping and imprinting of the functional aspects of the surroundings in the human mind."[9] Some boat landings may contain minimal or no artifact deposits at their location. This may be related to the type or amount of usage or to the natural forces affecting site integrity. The presence or absence of artifacts and features alone should not determine the significance of the site. The significance of a site should also be judged on such criteria as its historical context, ownership, or associations with certain events.

Context of Plantation Waterscapes

Plantation waterscapes offer prodigious research potential. Many elements of technology and economy are found within the plantation waterscape, especially those relating to farming, manufacturing, and transport systems. Boat landings were transit points where a range of activities and cross-cultural interactions took place.

A variety of features and artifact patterns are extant within the waterscape. Many products were grown, processed, and transported within the plantation waterscape. Such features as boat landings, sunken vessels, causeways, milling stations, rice fields, and rice dikes, and their associated water control systems, are commonly found along the plantation waterfront. These features were often associated with refuse disposal and artifact loss.

Through time, South Carolina's plantations altered their focus and settlement attributes due to changes in agricultural practices, innovations in technology, changes in the legal and political structure, and wartime predicaments. Elements of these changes are reflected archaeologically in the plantation waterscape.

Plantation populations contained a variety of cultural groups—African, Native American, West Indian, and European. Interaction among these cultural groups in the plantation waterscape created a variety of archaeological features. These features carry an abundance of information about plantation systems and the lives of people operating within them. For example, slave populations made substantial contributions to every aspect of plantation life, and the plantation waterscape was no exception.

The author investigated the waterscape archaeology of Middleburg Plantation (38BK38) on the East Branch of the Cooper River, Berkeley County.[10] Fieldwork involved an underwater and terrestrial survey of the plantation's waterscape to locate and document associated boat landings. Additional research provided information about the types of activities people were engaged in at the water's edge on similar colonial and antebellum sites in the lowcountry. When combined with research efforts of more traditional terrestrial archaeologists, a more complete picture of life at Middleburg has been constructed.[11]

CRM and Waterscapes

Unlike the Middleburg investigations, very few cultural resource management projects in the southeastern United States have investigated both the underwater and terrestrial components of a single plantation site. Underwater and terrestrial surveys have been conducted at different times on the same plantations, but rarely in association with each other.

Most compliance projects rarely identify the underwater environment as a potential impact area. This problem may be a result of either ignorance of the possibility that underwater archaeological sites exist, or the assumption that underwater sites will not be disturbed by terrestrial development. When riverside property is developed, erosion-control devices, such as embankments or riprap, are often constructed, and usually involve moving soil with heavy machinery. Riverside properties selected for development today are often chosen for many of the same reasons people chose similar locations in the past (e.g., high ground, deep water). Riverside development today often includes the construction of docks and often results in damage or destruction of underwater archaeological deposits.

Underwater archaeologists have also been guilty of certain shortcomings. Until recently a variety of dilemmas have repressed the field's potential. Its history reflects a ponderous concentration on shipwrecks and searching for wrecks instead of surveying for cultural resources.[12] It has been repeatedly hampered by treasure hunters passing themselves off as archaeologists.

Recent developments have refocused the direction of archaeology underwater. These developments include moving away from particularistic goals and moving toward the research of a variety of events rather than focusing on major historical events, developing explicit research designs, using new approaches for systematic sampling and survey methods, selective or problem-oriented excavation, and experimental and ethnoarchaeological approaches. Efforts are being made toward improving conservation, the selective study of remains with the goal of understanding human behavior, in experimental archaeology, and in efforts to propose generalizations about past human behaviors and its affects on present human behavior.[13]

Underwater and terrestrial archaeology need to be theoretically and methodologically coordinated in situations where archaeological components include both underwater and terrestrial environments. To be studied appropriately, plantation waterscapes require a combination of both techniques.

The research potential of plantation waterscapes is high and provides opportunities for the application of creative approaches. Specific guidelines for defining plantation waterscapes remain to be established. A range of feature types remain to be discovered, documented, and interpreted. Artifact patterns are still open to discovery and interpretation. The application of waterscape data has only barely been tapped.

Population pressures and development are currently the greatest threat to the archaeological integrity of lowcountry plantations. There is little doubt that if archaeologists do not begin to acknowledge waterscapes as significant and vulnerable, few developers will think twice about destroying a partially or totally submerged site that is out of mind and out of view.

NOTES

1. Guralnik 1982.
2. Roberts 1987:79.
3. Errante 1989:74–78; Errante 1991:71–77; Errante 1993.
4. Westerdahl 1978; Westerdahl 1980a; Westerdahl 1980b; Westerdahl 1991; Westerdahl 1992.
5. Westerdahl 1992:6.
6. Marquardt and Crumley 1987:2.
7. Goodyear, Raab, and Klinger 1978:164–65.

8. Roberts 1987:79; see also discussions by Green, this volume, and Beard, this volume, on the importance of incorporating the waterscape into landscape studies.
9. Lofgren 1981; Westerdahl 1992:2.
10. Errante 1993.
11. Adams 1990; Affleck 1990; Errante 1993; Ferguson and Babson 1986.
12. Gould 1983:8–9.
13. Gould 1983:21–22.

WORKS CITED

Adams, Natalie P.
1990   *Early African-American Domestic Architecture from Berkeley County, South Carolina.* Master's thesis, Dept. of Anthropology, Univ. of South Carolina, Columbia.

Affleck, Richard M.
1990   *Power and Space: Settlement Pattern Change at Middleburg Plantation, Berkeley County, South Carolina.* Master's thesis, Dept. of Anthropology, Univ. of South Carolina, Columbia.

Errante, James R.
1989   The Significance of Waterscapes in the Context of South Carolina's Tidal Rice Growing Plantations. In *Critical Approaches to Archaeology and Anthropology, Annual Papers of the University of South Carolina Anthropology Students Association,* vol. 4, edited by Kathleen Bolen, Kathy Forbes, and Ruth Trocolli, pp. 74–78. Univ. of South Carolina, Columbia.

1991   Underwater Archaeological Sites. In *Acquiring the Past for the Future: The South Carolina Heritage Trust Statewide Assessment of Cultural Sites,* edited and authored by Christopher Judge and Steven Smith, with contributions by James R.

Errante, pp. 71–77. South Carolina Institute of Archaeology and Anthropology, Research Manuscript Series 213, Columbia.

1993 *Waterscape Archaeology: A Survey for 18th Century Boat Landings.* Master's thesis, Dept. of Anthropology, Univ. of South Carolina, Columbia.

Ferguson, Leland, and David Babson

1986 *Survey of Plantation Sites along the East Branch of Cooper River: A Model for Predicting Archaeological Site Location.* Ms. on file, Dept. of Anthropology, Univ. of South Carolina, Columbia.

Goodyear, Albert C., L. Mark Raab, and Timothy C. Klinger

1978 Archaeological Research Design. *American Antiquity* 43(2):159–73.

Gould, Richard A.

1983 Looking Below the Surface. In *Shipwreck Anthropology,* edited by Richard Gould, pp. 3–22. Univ. of New Mexico Press, Albuquerque.

Guralnik, David B.

1982 *Webster's New World Dictionary of the American Language.* Warner Books, New York.

Lofgren, O.

1981 Manniskan i landskapet-landsapet i manniskan. *Tradition och miljo,* edited by L. Honko and O. Lofgren, pp. 235–61. Lund.

Marquardt, William H., and Carole L. Crumley

1987 Theoretical Issues in the Analysis of Spatial Patterning. In *Regional Dynamics, Burgundian Landscapes in Historical Perspective,* edited by Carole L. Crumley and William H. Marquardt, pp. 1–18. Academic Press, San Diego.

Roberts, B. K.

1987 Landscape Archaeology. In *Landscape and Culture: Geographical and Archaeological Perspectives,* edited by J. M. Wagstaff, pp. 77–95. Basil Blackwell, New York, and T. J. Press Ltd., Padstow, Cornwall, Great Britain.

Westerdahl, C.

1978 *Marinarkeologisk inventering med utanqspunkt fran ettanorrlandskt exempel. C-uppstats arkeologi.* Graduation thesis, Univ. of Stockholm.

1980a On Oral Tradition and Place Names. *The International Journal of Nautical Archaeology* 9:311–29.

1980b Nagot om aldre maritim kultur. In *Meddelande XLI–XLII 1978–80. V sterbottens norra fornminnesforensing,* Skelleftea Museum, Skelleftea, pp. 7–12.

1991 Norrlandsleden: The Maritime Cultural Landscape of the Norrland Sailing Route. In *Aspects of Maritime Scandinavia a.d. 200–1200,* Proceedings for the Nordic Seminar on Maritime Aspects of Archaeology, Mar. 13–15, 1989. Edited by O. Crumlin Pederson, Roskilde.

1992 The Maritime Cultural Landscape. *The International Journal of Nautical Archaeology* 21(1):5–14. Published for the Nautical Archaeology Society by Academic Press, Boston.

17. Refocusing on Community Heritage: Historical Landscapes, Archaeology, and Heritage Tourism

LESLEY M. DRUCKER

Based on the historic preservation and management paradigms presented in this chapter, historical landscapes can be usefully viewed as cultural and geographical resources which allow us to trace and understand how human relationships with the land have evolved through time.[1] Historical landscapes embody and define themes, or historic contexts, that are the core of how a community sees and markets itself (National Historic Preservation Act, as amended; 36 CFR 800). They therefore illustrate cultural diversity.

In South Carolina this cultural diversity defines a complex heritage that combines African American, European American, and Native American roots. Because landscape history documents how people interact with their environment, a community's unique story is reflected in its visible landscapes, which contain untapped financial and educational resources. These cultural markers illustrate the community's settlement, commercial, agrarian, industrial, governmental, and religious history.

Heritage Tourism: The New Southern Economy

From coast to mountains, South Carolina is blessed with traditional communities and picturesque scenery. These open spaces and historical places provide its citizens with a vibrant diversity of culture and landscapes crucial to the state's character, sense of history, and economic growth. According to the American Automobile Association, 29 percent of car vacationers head for the Southeast, more than to any other region of the country.[2] Because the American public tends to view southern locales as charming, quiet places to live and visit, the uncluttered, small-town lifestyle of most southern communities appeals to families, retirees, and filmmakers.

For a poor southern state like South Carolina, heritage tourism is thus proving to be a valuable economic asset, ranking well ahead of many other recreational activities.[3] In one author's words, "Not every town or city in South Carolina has a beach. But they do have sites important to their local heritage and the very fabric of what makes them Southern. . . ."[4]

The Growth Dilemma

The effect of economic decay on southern communities is compounded by unplanned economic growth, which is swallowing up small towns and rural areas throughout South Carolina.[5] Folklorist

Doug DeNatale has said, "In communities across America there is a distinct sense of place developed by the people who live there. Many of these places are undergoing unprecedented change due to rapid growth. The public must address the need for balance among local culture and economic development."[6] For example, beach tourism employed 70,000 people and poured $6.3 billion into South Carolina's economy in 1990. Coastal land development also brings pollution, soaring land prices, higher property taxes, and "heated controversy and bitter feelings as residents struggle with dramatic changes to their homes and communities."[7]

Landscape change is causing many residents to reflect on how progress and decay have affected the health of their neighborhoods, commercial districts, and farmlands. "People living in cities should realize how much they rely on South Carolina's small towns . . . to get away . ., experience the countryside, . . . visit small places that reflect history and local culture. When a small town dies, we lose a piece of history."[8]

Like its neighbors, South Carolina is losing not only its small towns, but its other links with the past as well. In developing urban and coastal areas, archaeological sites fall a silent and often unrecognized victim to suburban sprawl, downtown rehabilitation, and profit-motivated relic hunters. Whether Native American village, Civil War earthwork, or tenant farmstead, South Carolina's historical landscapes are typically defined by above-ground structures and other built features, vegetation, and archaeological (buried) components. As often the only voice for the vanished and nearly forgotten lifestyles and settlements of the poor blacks, whites, and Indians who have shaped South Carolina history, archaeological sites are crucial to the recognition and appreciation of community character. These physical remnants of a diverse heritage are also an important source for discerning key trends in state and local history.

Although many people mistakenly associate the term "conservation" only with the natural environment and "historic preservation" only with buildings, cultural resource conservation and management require attention to more than just downtown America. Historic preservation encompasses a much broader perspective: one that includes landscapes, viewscapes, and archaeological sites.

While South Carolina programs like the Heritage Trust,[9] Lowcountry Open Land Trust, Historic Beaufort, and Historic Charleston are saving a sample of the state's buried heritage by buying land or accepting conservation easements, these efforts are often geographically and financially limited. Unless communities begin to assume responsibility for protecting their own heritage resources, the state's past will continue to disappear beneath pavement, houses, lakes, and shopping centers.

Landscapes Reflect Community Values

One preservationist has said, "[N]ational chain stores homogenize our landscape and disparage our sense of place."[10] Recognizing how historical landscapes reflect community values is a powerful perspective for redesigning the direction and scope of local change. In fact, conserving local landscapes provides an excellent vehicle for managed community growth.

Why? To begin with, landscapes and viewscapes are familiar friends. They form a visual and tactile connection between the South's agrarian heritage and its industrial-technological growth in the twentieth century. They give community residents a much-needed sense of reassurance, stability, and belonging—a priceless quality where so much of life is "artificial and impermanent."[11] Economic development plans that include long-term management of local historical and archaeological sites reinforce this sense of community tradition and continuity.

Preservation of historical landscapes has other benefits as well. Viewscapes are a source of civic pride, since they illustrate both South Carolina's place in the nation's history and the local community's distinctive flavor. As geographical anchors of community traditions, historical landscapes also embody and reinforce multicultural and ethnic identities that are unique to each community.

Finally, historical landscapes are important because they help us tell the authentic story of our state's past to those who are this nation's future—our children and grandchildren. As Ben Handy, a member of the National Trust for Historic Preservation, remarks, "It is not always a pretty story, especially from the viewpoint of America's minorities. Slavery, legal discrimination, and economic injustice are among the evils that, at one time or another, entire ethnic groups have suffered. Yet this further argues the importance of preserving historic ... sites because they tell these stories of our past more honestly and with more passion than any other kind of recorded history."[12]

Community Programs

Although historical landscapes often are framed in an urban context, rural landscapes play a growing role in national conservation programs. As one preservationist stated, "They can provide links to the past, lifestyle or psychic rewards in the present, and preservation of environmental resources needed for the future."[13] While no landscape is considered better than another, there is inherent value in having a diverse mix of landscapes across the nation.

If judicious blending of old and new landscapes contributes to urban revitalization and attracts business and industry to South Carolina, then communities that incorporate their local heritage into development planning create a powerful framework for counteracting both decay and unplanned growth. Southern landscape architects are now urging local leaders to "establish local land-use laws to stop abusive resort development" and to invest in long-term development rather than growth as a means of resisting unwanted changes to their environment.[14]

Land use planners also indirectly promote a landscape approach in their assessment of the

dynamic between community growth and traditional values. Ken Driggers, a South Carolina planner, says, "South Carolina communities are becoming more ... appreciative of the traditional community patterns, activities, and cultural features that are unique to each of them. By educating people about the importance of these cultural resources ..., preservationists hope to prevent the deterioration and/or loss of this identity due to mismanaged, rapid growth. Alternatives to growth must focus on designing more livable spaces within the framework of the traditional landscape."[15]

Local recognition of the economic benefits of preserving community character is one of the more encouraging growth industries across the nation, especially in southern states. The Fall 1995/Winter 1996 listing of titles in the National Trust for Historic Preservation's "Information" series includes three booklets that provide guidance about these economic benefits for community planners.

Within South Carolina, Palmetto Conservation Foundation, Palmetto Project, and South Carolina Coastal Conservation League are three grassroots organizations that help communities develop and market their assets through land use planning, education, and research. As one preservationist stated, "With all the benefits coming from tourism, we want to come up with an agenda where we can bring more people into prosperity."[16] Palmetto Pride Community Projects encourage community improvement through permanent preservation of some aspect of local history and heritage. While these agendas encourage small towns to regain prosperity and maintain local character, they do not link the two through a historical landscape perspective.

Landscape Conservation and Public Policy

Through programs such as the National Register of Historic Places, federal/state survey and planning grants, and the South Carolina Downtown Development Association, many cities and small towns have adopted downtown and neighborhood rehabilitation programs.[17] Communities are also investing in their past by encouraging heritage tourism and investing in bed-and-breakfast inns, local historical and maritime museums, historical theme parks, and recreational programs involving public (volunteer) archaeology.

Several sea islands off South Carolina's coast have begun to expand the scope of these programs by establishing protected greenways and historical or archaeological districts. These community facelifts provide direct financial benefits in the form of tax credits and tourist dollars, as well as indirect benefits, such as stabilization and improvement of property values, control over new industry siting, and a larger community tax base.

Despite a growing interest among coastal communities in protecting and managing historical resources, however, there remains a statewide lack of political or economic commitment to saving an illustrative sample of archaeological sites for the future. Probably the least recognized component of historical landscapes is archaeological sites, and for this reason, protection of South Carolina's buried heritage on private property is extremely haphazard, even accidental.

Unless preservation ordinances specifically address archaeological sites, they do little to deter archaeological losses.[18] Over 35 South Carolina communities, including 11 Certified Local Governments, have some type of municipal or county preservation ordinance on the books, but few enforce evaluation or protection of archaeological sites during design review for new construction.

The Secretary of the Interior's Standards for Rehabilitation,[19] however, clearly state the national intent toward archaeological sites, whether the setting is urban or rural. Item number 8 of the Standards states, "Significant archeological resources affected by a project shall be protected and preserved. If such resources must be disturbed, mitigation measures shall be undertaken." Despite having preservation ordinances on the books, then, most South Carolina communities do not meet national preservation goals for archaeological sites.

National policy over the past few years has brought about shifts in assigning environmental priorities. "While the risk of losing 'heritage' value is not a common measure of environmental quality and may not alone provide a rationale for special protection, the coincidence of heritage characteristics with environmental sensitivity may help identify priority targets."[20]

Achieving More Balanced Community Development

Adoption of a landscape perspective offers communities a tool for evaluating and managing locally important historical and archaeological sites, even if there is insufficient current revenue to protect them under an existing design review process. Conservation of archaeological sites follows quite naturally from a viewpoint that seeks to recover and preserve representative historical landscapes. For example, Charleston County has adopted a preservation ordinance which addresses archaeological resources during design review.[21] A somewhat similar ordinance is under consideration in Berkeley County.[22] Hopefully, these and other South Carolina communities can develop preservation ordinances that channel growth without endangering their archaeological heritage.

As preservationists become more involved with heritage tourism, growth planning, and downtown revitalization, they will be increasingly called upon to devise innovative strategies for public participation. According to preservationist Gregory Paxton, "The key word in shaping a successful future for historic preservation may be partnerships" with tourism bureaus, planners, downtown development commissions, natural conservation groups, and affordable housing advocates.[23] This national partnership trend is encouraging evidence that different economic interests will accept the need to consider the priorities of others.

Historically accurate reconstructions of people, places, and things support heritage tourism and are the lifeblood of cultural exhibits, dioramas, and festival programs that educate the American public about local prehistory and history.[24] Along these lines, archaeologist Loretta Neumann notes that "archaeological programs . . . not only protect the national heritage, but are also labor intensive (and therefore create jobs, jobs, jobs)."[25] Among the recommendations of a recent Society of American Archaeology work group were to a) establish a means for recognizing public education activities as a significant archaeological activity; b) encourage the development of post-secondary curricula, publication outlets, professional development, and career opportunities in public education and outreach; and c) promote archaeology education to Native Americans and others whose past archaeologists study.[26]

As educators and scientists who study historical landscapes, archaeologists can help communities become better acquainted with their heritage resources and better equipped to manage them, from designing educational and recreational programs to developing historical perspectives on local land use and landscape loss,[27] and from guiding site inventory/assessment efforts to assisting in the design of preservation ordinances.

How can South Carolina foster successful partnerships between archaeologists and other groups? One step may be for community planners, as well as state agencies and regional research and development boards, to include archaeologists on their community planning teams and in-house staff training programs. Another option may be to supplement government conservation assistance and information by aggressively publicizing an "answer line" network of professional and avocational archaeologists who volunteer as contacts. Communities requesting specific information or immediate assistance with preservation or

heritage issues and projects could be referred by state and federal agencies and commissions to the archaeology network.[28]

Conservation of historical landscapes stimulates South Carolina's economy by promoting heritage tourism, urban revitalization, and environment-friendly industry. Community themes based on historic contexts offer a useful framework for integrating local historical and archaeological sites into community development plans.

Although landscapes and viewscapes are important cultural, educational, and financial community assets, historic preservation is still an underused (and narrowly focused) option for community development. Whether through intent or ignorance, historical landscapes—especially archaeological sites—are routinely sacrificed to achieve the dubious benefits of economic growth.

This trend can and must be reversed. If prosperity and traditional landscapes are to coexist, community leaders must become better informed about alternatives to the loss of their local heritage. Flexible blends of traditional and newer landscapes requires a conservation perspective compatible with managed land use. Communities that keep failing to protect their historical landscapes do so at the risk of continued decay or unplanned growth.

As specialists in recognizing and evaluating the buried past, archaeologists can help communities achieve a more balanced focus on landscape conservation and heritage tourism. Archaeologists can build positive relationships in their communities, generate local interest in the past, and promote site conservation.[29] In turn, by becoming better informed about their cultural resources, local residents can place themselves in a stronger position to save, shape, and share their heritage.

NOTES

1. Kovacik and Winberry 1989.
2. Knutson 1992.
3. South Carolina Dept. of Parks, Recreation, and Tourism 1990; South Carolina Dept. of Parks, Recreation, and Tourism 1991.
4. Vartorella 1991.
5. South Carolina Sea Grant Consortium 1992:2, 4.
6. Doug DeNatale, personal communication 1991.
7. Smith 1992.
8. Becker 1992.

9. Judge and Smith 1991; Smith and Judge 1992.
10. Jeff Anzevino, quoted in Beaumont 1996.
11. Handy 1992.
12. Handy 1992.
13. Anonymous 1995:56–57. These sentiments are shared by Ken Driggers, personal communication 1991.
14. South Carolina Sea Grant Consortium 1992:5.
15. Ken Driggers, personal communication 1991.
16. Ken Driggers, quoted in Smith 1992.
17. Anonymous 1995:56.
18. Nancy Meriwether, personal communication 1992.
19. U.S. Department of the Interior 1990.
20. Nancy Meriwether, personal communication 1992.
21. Stine 1992a.
22. South Carolina Dept. of Archives and History n.d.
23. Paxton 1992.
24. Chappell 1989.
25. Neumann 1992.
26. Messenger 1994.
27. National Park Service 1990, 1991, 1992.
28. Anzalone 1987.
29. Zimmer, Wilk, and Pyburn 1995.

Works Cited

Anonymous
1995   *Targeting Environmental Priorities in Agriculture: Reforming Program Strategies.* Office of Technological Assessment, Washington, D.C.

Anzalone, Ronald D. (compiler)
1987   Archeology at the Local Level. Ms. on file, Advisory Council on Historic Preservation, Washington, D.C.

Beaumont, Constance
1996   The Statehouse: Developers of Sprawl Slap Opposition with Litigation. *Preservation News* (Jan.–Feb.):31.

Becker, Robert
1992   South Carolina's Rural Life: Can It Be Saved? *Coastal Heritage* 6(6):2.

Chappell, Edward A.
1989   Social Responsibility and the American History Museum. *Winterthur Portfolio* 24(4):247–65.

Handy, Ben
1992   Preservation Reaches Out for Cultural Diversity. *Historic Preservation News* (June). Washington, D.C.

Judge, Christopher, and Steven D. Smith
1991   *Acquiring the Past for the Future: The South Carolina Heritage Trust Status Assessment of Cultural Resource Sites.* Research Manuscript Series 213, South Carolina Institute of Archaeology and Anthropology, Univ. of South Carolina, Columbia.

Knutson, Lawrence L.
1992   Vacation Travel Likely To Be Up. *The State,* May 20. Columbia.

Kovacik, Charles F., and John J. Winberry
1989   *South Carolina: The Making of a Landscape.* Univ. of South Carolina Press, Columbia. Originally published in 1987 as *South Carolina: A Geography.* Westview Press, Boulder and London.

Messenger, Phyllis
1994   The Future of the Past: SAA Maps a Long-Term Strategy. *Archaeology and Public Education Newsletter* 5(2):1, 3, 11. Society for American Archaeology, Public Education Committee, Washington, D.C.

National Park Service
1990   *Federal Archeology Report,* June.
1991   *Federal Archeology Report,* Sept.
1992   *Federal Archeology Report,* Mar.

Neumann, Loretta
1992   Current Archaeological Issues in Congress and the Administration. *Society for American Archaeology Newsletter* 10(2):3.

Paxton, Gregory
1992   Develop Partnerships for Successful Preservation. *Historic Preservation News,* May 1992. Washington, D.C.

Smith, Bruce
1992   Study Finds Good, Bad in Coastal Tourism. *The State,* Apr. 8, 1992. Columbia.

Smith, Steven D., and Christopher Judge
1992   The South Carolina Heritage Trust Ranking System for Archaeological Site Acquisition. *Southeastern Archaeology* 11(2):140–48.

South Carolina Dept. of Archives and History
n.d.   Berkeley County Preservation Ordinance. Ms. on file, Historic Programs Division, Columbia.

South Carolina Dept. of Parks, Recreation, and Tourism
1990 *South Carolina Out-of-State Visitor Survey By Region, 1987–1988.* Report on file, Division of Engineering and Planning Research and Statistics Section, Columbia.
1991 *1991 Year-End Summary: Travel Trends, December–November.* Report on file, Division of Engineering and Planning Research and Statistics Section, Columbia.

South Carolina Sea Grant Consortium
1992 South Carolina's Rural Life: Preserving A Culture. *Coastal Heritage* 6(6).

Stine, Linda France
1992a *Revealing Historic Landscapes in Charleston County: Archaeological Inventory, Contexts, and Management.* Submitted to the Charleston County Planning Dept. South Carolina Institute of Archaeology and Anthropology.

United States Dept. of the Interior
1990 *The Secretary of the Interior's Standards for Rehabilitation [revised].* National Park Service, Washington, D.C.

Vartorella, W. Craig
1991 Profitable Preservation. *Chicora Foundation Research* 5(3). Chicora Foundation, Columbia.

Zimmer, Julie, Richard Wilk, and Anne Pyburn
1995 A Survey of Attitudes and Values in Archaeological Practice. *Society for American Archaeology Newsletter*, Nov.–Dec., p. 10.

18. Integrating a Landscape Perspective with Cultural Resource Management in South Carolina

LINDA F. STINE

As explored in this volume, "Landscape" is interpreted in diverse ways. For Cultural Resource Management (CRM), a landscape is an *entity* that can be identified, nominated to the National Register, preserved, used for public education, and/or serve as a place for recreational activities. An anthropologist views landscape as formed by a series of interactive social and natural processes. These processes can be understood and interpreted to the public, even if much of the physical evidence has been destroyed or adjusted through land use over time. "Landscape" is also an *analytical construct* that can effectively interrelate diverse data sets discovered through archaeological, historical, and geographic research. As such it can aid in construction of research design, interpretation, and evaluation of historical properties.

In this chapter the range of known historical resources in South Carolina is discussed. A sample of historical archaeological sites in the piedmont and lowcountry is selected to illustrate that variation. Using the landscape framework, a strategy for management of these cultural resources is presented.

Historic Site Files: Problems and Potential

The statewide storehouse of archaeological site files is maintained at the South Carolina Institute of Archaeology and Anthropology (SCIAA), University of South Carolina, Columbia. Scholars may gain access to these files after SCIAA approval of a brief research proposal and giving one day's notice. These files contain data about a site's location in time and space. Additional information, such as management recommendations and site evaluation, is included. This data base is a tremendous resource, but uneven in quality. The data has been collected over many years, managed by different agencies, and contributed to by diverse individual researchers. Inclusion of South Carolina Statewide Survey data in the SCIAA files is haphazard. Many standing buildings nominated or placed on the National Register of Historic Places (NRHP) by the Survey Branch at the South Carolina State Historic Preservation Office (SHPO) do not have a corresponding site file number at SCIAA. In the past, standing structures survey and archaeological site survey were planned, undertaken, and reviewed separately. The South

Carolina SHPO is developing methods to better integrate the survey, interpretation, and management of these types of historic properties.[1]

Many of the earliest archaeological site forms are incomplete. As a result, many of these records do not contain pertinent management information nor do they describe attempts to interpret site function. Most of the recent forms have been completed by Cultural Resource Management (CRM) contractors, who must complete site assessments of eligibility to the NRHP. This includes information such as possible site functions. In his study of the 2,622 site files recorded between 1990 and 1992, Keith Derting, information manager at SCIAA, discovered that 3 percent stemmed from academic research, 0.6 percent from amateurs, and 96.4 percent from compliance-related projects. The site files have recently been reviewed for accuracy as part of a collaboration with the South Carolina Department of Natural Resources, Water Resources Division, the SHPO, and SCIAA. As part of the development of a statewide Geographic Information System (GIS), Water Resources is digitizing archaeological site file data to guide state agency management of these resources.[2]

The data base still exists primarily on paper. This makes it difficult to extract the relative range and frequency of historic sites in South Carolina. The use of a standardized form has helped direct data description, but recorders have often opted for generalized categories, as refined analysis usually follows filling out the SCIAA forms. The actual range of site types in the state is probably underrepresented in the site files. Historic sites can have multiple functions, can date to different periods of use, and can be viewed differently by different groups of people. Archaeologists tend to divide sites into the larger domain of "historic scatters." If above- or below-ground features are associated, the archaeologist chooses from a series of nested domains, such as the following: "historic scatter/industrial site/tar kiln"; "historic scatter/plantation/slave quarters/house," etc. This is why most archaeological data bases use the component as the level of analysis, not the site.

Some digital data bases already exist for parts of the state. For example, archaeologists for the Francis Marion National Forest, in conjunction with New South Associates, have developed a digital data base for all sites found on their forest lands.[3] This data base is used in this chapter to help estimate the range and variation in historic sites in the lowcountry. File data concerning historic site components, encoded for the Charleston Planning Office, will be used to contribute data from lands outside the Francis Marion National Forest in Charleston.[4] Although not computerized, the site files for York County will be discussed to represent the piedmont. The discussion of piedmont and lowcountry sites as recorded by September 1992 will serve as indicators of the types and range of variation in South Carolina historical archaeological sites.

Piedmont Example: York County

The paper files for York County serve as a point of comparison to lowcountry data. This piedmont county includes part of the greater Charlotte area and has been investigated by private enthusiasts, university researchers, and CRM contract archaeologists. A series of Duke Power and South Carolina Department of Highways and Public Transportation projects are completed, assuring that a good sample of the county's resources have been recorded. In addition, The Schiele Museum of Natural History has been actively researching sites in the region, as has the Museum of York County. As of September 23, 1992, York contains a total of 278 site forms. Only about 14 percent (n = 39) describe a historic component and/or site.

This part of the upcountry has historical archaeological evidence of settlements dating from the early eighteenth through the mid-twentieth centuries. Myriad site types are described in the files and associated archaeological reports ("grey literature"). Archaeologists have been using similar categories to describe these sites. This is due, in part, to standard categories promulgated for South Carolina archaeological site forms.

It is interesting that not one plantation site has been recorded in this piedmont county, even though we know that plantations existed in the back-country of South Carolina.[5] No slave quarters have been recorded in the York County archaeological site files. Perhaps these sites have not been recognized by field archaeologists as plantation sites. Some of the sites classified as homesites may in fact represent plantations instead of farmsteads and/or urban houses. Fewer large plantations were located in the upcountry of South Carolina, and the data base may reflect that difference. However, it may also represent the simplistic assumptions of some researchers; that the piedmont region was solely settled by farmers, the lowcountry by plantation owners.

Standard site categories include historical scatters, homesites, towns, industrial sites, and "other":

1. *Historical scatters*—generally sites that have not been investigated enough to be clearly interpreted (38YK17, 38YK23, 38YK35, 38YK41, 38YK60, 38YK121, 38YK153, 38YK155, 38YK159, 38YK160, 38YK210, 38YK230, 38YK231, 38YK257, 38YK259).
2. *Homesites*—remains that include remnants of a house, such as a chimney fall (38YK7, 38YK20, 38YK157, 38YK221, 38YK222, 38YK225, 38YK234, 38YK235, 38YK 248) or even standing buildings (38YK21, 38YK38).
3. *Towns*—generally describe middens or scatters found in areas of historically mapped, eighteenth-century Catawba towns (Sucah/Wateree 38YK147, Weyanne/ Kingstown 38YK148, Noostee Town 38YK149, Nasaw/Weyapee 38YK150).
4. *Industrial sites*—incorporates data from a nineteenth-century steatite quarry (38YK53), three eighteenth- to nineteenth-century ironworks (38YK215, 38YK216, 3YK217), and a ca. 1832 grist mill (38YK253).
5. *Other*—includes a possible fort (38YK18) dating from 1760, four cenotaphs on Kings Mountain dating from 1780, a Civil War gun emplacement (38YK239), and a possible eighteenth- to nineteenth-century trading post (38YK252).

One can see from table 18.1 below that only one in ten of the historical components in York have been considered as eligible for nomination to the NRHP. Two of these sites are homesites (one is a standing structure); the other two sites are iron furnaces. This compares to over half (53.8 percent) that are considered potentially eligible and/or in need of additional fieldwork before final evaluation. Table 18.1 also shows the broad spectrum of these potentially eligible sites. About a third of the sites and components have been judged unworthy of nomination to the NRHP. Not unexpectedly, the majority in this category consists of historical scatters, followed by homesites. Only one industrial site (an iron furnace) was not considered eligible.

TABLE 18.1
NUMBER AND PERCENTAGE OF YORK COUNTY EVALUATIONS
OF HISTORICAL ARCHAEOLOGICAL RESOURCES

Site Type	Eligible		Additional Work		Ineligible		Destroyed		Total	
Scatter	0		6	(28.6%)	9	(69.9%)	0		15	(38.5%)
Homesites	2	(50.0%)	5	(23.8%)	3	(25.0%)	1		11	(28.2%)
Towns	0		4	(19.0%)	0		0		4	(10.2%)
Industrial	2	(50.0%)	2	(9.5%)	1	(7.7%)	0		5	(12.8%)
Other	0		4	(19.0%)	0		0		4	(10.2%)
Totals:	4	(10.2%)	21	(53.8%)	13	(33.3%)	1	(2.6%)	39	(99.9%)

Although a single county site has been recorded as destroyed, the actual condition of most of these sites is unknown. Many of the sites considered not eligible in a compliance project have probably been destroyed through subsequent land-altering activities. No further research is required by law at sites that are not considered eligible for listing on the NRHP.

Lowcountry Example: Charleston County

The range and variation of historic site components in the lowcountry is much easier to estimate due to digitization of site file data.[6] The distribution of sites in all non–United States Forest Service lands in Charleston County is first examined, then compared to United States Forest Service (USFS) data from Charleston and Berkeley Counties.

Table 18.2 illustrates the distribution of sites in Charleston and environs as of April 1991, based on SCIAA site file records. One can see that the majority of sites in the region are related to historical occupations, although a comparable number of prehistoric sites have been recorded. It is unfortunate that the chronological placement of close to 20 percent of the sites remains unknown.

How many of these numerous types of components have been considered eligible for nomination to the NRHP? Table 18.3 has been constructed to demonstrate the distribution for all

TABLE 18.2
DISTRIBUTION OF CHARLESTON
COUNTY SITES

Site Type	Number	Percent
Historic	308	35.98
Prehistoric	256	29.90
Multi	126	14.72
Unknown	166	19.40
Totals	856	100.00

NOTE: Excludes USF S data.

TABLE 18.3
NATIONAL REGISTER OF HISTORIC PLACES
STATUS OF CHARLESTON AREA SITES

Evaluation	Number	Percent
On NRHP	65	9.2
Eligible	73	10.3
PE (Work Needed)	301	42.6
Not Eligible	195	27.6
Destroyed	21	3.0
Unknown	52	7.4
Totals	706	100.1

Charleston area sites (exclusive of USFS sites). One can see that almost half of the sites have not been investigated enough to make a determination of NRHP eligibility.[7]

As in the piedmont case, many of the sites determined as not eligible for nomination to the NRHP are probably destroyed; part of a golf course, highway, or housing development. The majority of sites listed on the NRHP are related to standing structures discovered during South Carolina Standing Structures surveys, although some prehistoric sites, such as shell rings and middens, are also listed. Sites such as the early Charles Towne settlement (38CH1) and Willtown Bluff (38CH58/482); forts (e.g., 38CH50), powder magazines (e.g., 38CH69/71), and breastworks (e.g., 38CH190); and a few plantation house ruins (e.g., 38CH127) have been placed on the NRHP.[8] No archaeological industrial sites have been placed on the NRHP except for those related to maritime industries (e.g., 38CH1049). An examination of the range of functional site types in the region shows that the diversity of sites in the region are underrepresented on the NRHP. The distribution of these components by chronological period is shown in table 18.4.

Table 18.4 has been constructed for those historic site components that have an assigned time period. A total of 693 components have about an even distribution between the antebellum and postbellum periods. It is interesting that very few

TABLE 18.4
DISTRIBUTION OF COMPONENTS BY CHRONOLOGICAL PERIOD,
CHARLESTON COUNTY JURISDICTIONAL LANDS

Period	Date Range	Number	Percent
Contact	1526-1700	9	1.3
Colonial	1700-1780	121	17.5
Antebellum	1780-1860	253	36.5
Civil War	1860-1865	34	4.9
Postbellum	1865-1940	276	39.8
Totals		693	100.0

contact and Civil War–period components have been recorded. Component numbers begin to increase for the colonial period, but these sites still fall behind the later periods in representation.

One wonders if the distribution is representational for historic land use and population numbers or indicative of collection biases. For example, contact and early colonial sites tend to have more ephemeral features and smaller assemblages.[9] In addition, a great number of these sites were discovered during CRM surveys and never underwent block excavations. Many early components may also have been lumped with larger collections found on antebellum and postbellum sites, especially if these sites were only investigated at a reconnaissance or assessment survey levels. Materials from these projects are often simply cataloged and counted, without much refined analysis.

To understand the possible variety of components found on lowcountry historical sites table 18.5 has been constructed. This illustrates the range of identified site functions in the lowcountry. These data are exclusive of general middens, shell middens, burials, and modern house components. By far the most numerous components relate to plantations, not unexpected in Charleston and its environs. This category includes all sites that retain the main house structure. Again, most of the plantations recorded as structures have not been assessed in regard to archaeological potential,

although Fick is attempting to address that problem. Her survey of Charleston area buildings, objects, and landscapes will be integrated with an archaeological assessment of the recorded sites in the county.[10]

The number of site files with information on slave quarters is a surprising 7.1 percent, very low

TABLE 18.5
RANGE OF COMPONENTS IN CHARLESTON

Type	Number	Percent
Causeway	2	0.6
Church/Manse	8	2.4
Dump	1	0.3
Encampment	1	0.3
Farmstead	47	13.9
Industrial	39	11.5
Maritime	14	4.1
Military	43	12.7
Plantation	122	36.1
Slave Quarters	24	7.1
Towns	5	1.5
Urban	32	9.5
Totals	338	100.0

NOTE: Excludes USFS sites.

when considered against the recorded 36.1 percent plantations. Again, this could be due to the fact that many sites are recorded at the initial survey level, making it difficult to define slave occupations. In addition, many ephemeral slave sites, especially those on the periphery of the plantations, may have been described as nonsignificant historical scatters or middens during survey. This may also be the explanation for the relatively low number of identified farmstead components (13.9 percent). If no structures were present and little historic research was accomplished before survey, a farmstead often appears in the records as a "nonsignificant historic scatter in a plowed field, with a little whiteware and glass." Researchers have pointed out that many small farm sites are, by their very nature, low in artifact quantity. In addition, plowing should be viewed as a cultural feature, not just a destructive process, when determining integrity.[11] In the earlier years of South Carolina archaeology, few researchers were interested in tenant or small farm owner sites dating from the late nineteenth and early twentieth centuries. Interest in these sites has steadily increased over the years with a concomitant increase in determinations of potential eligibility and eligibility for the NRHP.

Charleston has a wide range of industrial sites (11.5 percent of components). These include kilns for making brick, lime, and tar. Phosphate mining sites have also been located. Charleston includes sites related to damming riverways, windmills, taverns, stores, railroad yards, a gas station, and even an airstrip. It is interesting that Charleston files only include two recorded tar kilns. As one will see below, this is in direct contrast to the number of tar kilns found on USFS lands. This is due to differences in land use and settlement strategies. The lands northwest across the Cooper River from Charleston were generally colonized later than those east of the Ashley River. The western lands were not as productive for rice agriculture, but offered inducements for lime, brick, and tar making with their natural resources.[12] Many of these properties have been incorporated into USFS jurisdictional lands.

It should be mentioned that urban sites are grossly underrepresented in these numbers. First, most urban sites recorded during SHPO-sponsored, standing structure surveys still do not have SCIAA site numbers. Second, in the early years of program development (1970s) at The Charleston Museum, archaeologists maintained their own site numbering and filing system, with no systematic attempt at coordination with the statewide site files. Museum personnel have recently remedied this situation by coordinating their records with the SCIAA site file system.[13]

The diversity of sites found in the immediate Charleston area, and their underrepresentation on the NRHP, is a trend visible in the USFS data for the Francis Marion Forest (on file Francis Marion Forest and SCIAA). The USFS data is not directly comparable. The forest data has been arranged by site number; site function seems to have been assigned on the basis of most prevalent site use. Recall the previous data set was based upon site component distributions, thus these data sets cannot be statistically compared. They can be described and do serve to illustrate trends in lowcountry data.

Table 18.6 depicts the range of variation in Charleston and Berkeley Counties. One can see that this region holds fewer urban sites, towns, and military sites than the preceding Charleston data set. This west Cooper region also contains a somewhat reversed plantation-to-farmstead ratio and many more industrial sites. The highest number of industrial sites are tar kilns (n = 109), compared to the two recorded in Charleston County's jurisdiction. Although tar kilns appear to be a unique resource in one data set, they are very common occurrences in the USFS information. It is important to realize that present-day county lines crosscut environmental zones, drainages, and historic polities—such as illustrated by these data. Managers and other researchers must realize that archaeological data cross-cuts jurisdictional boundaries. When considering settlement patterning, land use changes, and when evaluating significance, archaeologists must look at the regional picture in diverse ways.

TABLE 18.6
HISTORICAL SITE TYPES IN CHARLESTON (CH) AND BERKELEY (BK) COUNTIES,
FRANCIS MARION FOREST

Site Type	No. CH	percent	No. BK	percent
Plantations	34	22.6	28	7.3
Scatter	46	30.6	143	37.2
Homesite	37	24.6	65	16.9
Cemetery	5	3.5	6	1.6
Bridge	7	4.6	21	5.5
Tar Kiln	15	10.0	94	24.5
Isol. Structure	2	1.3	14	3.6
Road	1	0.6	0	0.0
EW/Embank	1	0.6	2	0.5
Fish Weir	0	0.0	1	0.2
Milldam	0	0.0	1	0.2
Town	0	0.0	1	0.2
Church	1	0.6	4	1.0
Isolat. Finds	1	0.6	4	1.0
Totals	150	99.4	384	99.7

NOTE: Reflects data collected up to Sept. 23, 1992.

The range of recorded site types can be examined in light of the National Register of Historic Places (NRHP). Table 18.6 lists the number of sites considered by USFS personnel and contractors as potentially eligible for nomination to the NRHP, as needing additional work before evaluation, and as probably not eligible for nomination. These three categories are those used by the USFS for CRM management purposes.

About half of the *potentially eligible* historic archaeological sites in the Charleston portion of the forest are plantations (47.6 percent). Only about one-fifth of the potentially eligible Berkeley forest sites are plantations (19.5 percent). The variety of sites found in Berkeley and rated as potentially eligible tends to be distributed between historical scatters (32 percent), homesites (19.5 percent), and

tar kilns (11.7 percent). Charleston also has examples of historical scatters (23.8 percent) and homesites (14.3 percent), but much fewer tar kilns (3.2 percent) in this NRHP category. *Additional work* category sites fall mostly into those one would expect: homesites (41.9 percent Charleston County (CH), 26.3 percent Berkeley County (BK)), historical scatters (29 percent CH, 28.9 percent BK), and tar kilns (6.4 percent CH, 26.3 percent BK). Those sites considered *probably not eligible* for nomination to the NRHP are ranked as follows: historical scatters (39.3 percent CH, 41.7 percent BK), tar kilns (19.6 percent CH, 31.6 percent BK), housesites (26.8 percent CH, 13.8 percent BK), cemeteries (7.1 percent CH, 1.8 percent BK), industrial sites (3.6 percent CH, 6.9 percent BK), plantations (1.8 percent CH 0.5 percent BK), and so forth. One expects historical scatters to be highest ranked in this last category due to their generic nature. Tar kilns have been problematical, as are brick and other kiln sites, in terms of the NRHP. Researchers are still trying to decide what kinds of research questions to ask, how to fruitfully, physically study these sites, and how to determine their significance.[14]

Looking at table 18.7 in another light, the relative internal ranking of three of the site types can be seen. This is produced in table 18.8. It appears as if the majority of plantation sites have been considered potentially significant, as opposed to the majority of tar kiln sites. Although this may be

partially due to relative factors of intactness, clarity, and so forth, it is more likely due to whether a particular research domain is currently viewed as important or not.[15]

Comparison of Lowcountry and Piedmont Sites

An examination of the data comparing piedmont and lowcountry sites shows a number of trends. First, there is a great difference in the sheer number of sites and components listed. York County has

TABLE 18.7
FRANCIS MARION NATIONAL FOREST SITE EVALUATIONS BY TYPE

Type	Potentially Eligible		Add. Work		Probably Not Eligible		Total	
	CH	BK	CH	BK	CH	BK	CH	BK
Plant.	30	25	3	2	1	1	34	28
Scatter	15	41	9	11	22	91	46	143
Homesite	9	25	13	10	15	30	37	65
Cemetery	1	2	0	0	4	4	5	6
Bridge	0	0	0	0	1	0	1	0
Indust.	2	4	2	10	11	69	15	94
Isol. Struc.	2	7	0	2	0	5	2	14
Road	1	0	0	0	0	0	1	0
Earthwork	0	2	1	0	0	0	1	2
Fish Weir	0	0	0	0	0	1	0	1
Milldam	0	1	0	0	0	1	0	2
Fort/pall.	0	0	0	1	0	0	0	1
Town	0	0	1	0	0	0	0	0
Church	1	2	0	0	0	0	1	2
Iso.Find	0	0	3	0	0	0	0	1
Totals	63	128	31	38	56	218	150	384
(%)	42.0	33.3	20.6	9.9	37.3	56.8	99.9	100

NOTE: Reflects data collected up to Sept. 23, 1992.

TABLE 18.8
RELATIVE ELIGIBILITY OF FOUR SITE TYPES, CHARLESTON (CH) AND
BERKELEY (BK) COUNTIES, SOUTH CAROLINA

Site Type	Potentially Eligible		Add. Work		Probably Not Eligible		Total	
	%CH	%BK	%CH	%BK	%CH	%BK	%CH	%BK
Plantations	88.2	89.3	8.8	7.1	2.9	3.6	99.9	100.0
Homesites	24.3	38.5	35.1	15.4	40.5	46.2	99.9	100.1
Tar Kilns	13.3	16.0	13.3	10.6	73.3	73.4	99.9	100.0

only a total of 39 recorded historic sites, even though the data base includes a number of CRM and academically inspired surveys. Charleston and Berkeley have a large number of recorded sites in the files. Those lands falling outside the jurisdiction of the National Forest in Charleston have at least 308 historical components; 126 more are listed in SCIAA files as multicomponent (historic/prehistoric). The files at the Francis Marion National Forest list information about 150 historic sites in Charleston County, 384 in Berkeley County. Population densities have varied across the state; regional variation may be influencing actual archaeological site distributions. These data also reflect the higher number of archaeological surveys performed in the lowcountry due to federally mandated programs: USFS, Corps of Engineers, and related South Carolina Coastal Council CRM projects. (As an archaeologist recently stated, it is too bad we do not have a piedmont council overseeing the natural and cultural heritage for that region of the state.)

At SCIAA, after stepping back and looking at the map of the state and then comparing the size of the county file drawers, it is obvious that federally funded or influenced programs (i.e., Section 106, related to the National Historic Preservation Act of 1966, as amended, see Stine and Stine this volume) have produced the overwhelming majority of site forms. On the other hand, noncoastal counties that have seen few Section 106 projects do not have many sites listed. Those noncoastal sites, recorded by amateurs, students, and researchers, tend to be

prehistoric sites. Historic sites are incidentally recorded as part of a multicomponent prehistoric site, or are sites that represent a house or fort site deemed important in the local area.

A comparative look at the types of sites found in the two regions is interesting. One finds that plantation sites make up a large part of those recorded in the lowcountry, with farmsteads/homesites being more common in the upcountry. No plantation sites were recorded in York County archaeological site files. Again, how much this is due to differential settlement pattern and land use and how much due to researchers biases remains to be seen. A much broader variety of site and/or component types has been recorded for the lowcountry than for the piedmont. This may reflect the differences in sheer number of sites recorded or, again, lack of knowledge or the influence of bias in the archaeological community.

For example, archaeological sites representing the important piedmont textile industry have yet to be located or recorded by archaeologists in York County. Tar and charcoal production were common industries in pine-covered portions of the lowcountry. They were also important industries in comparable parts of the piedmont and the midlands, but few have been recorded north of the fall line.[16]

These obvious lacunae in the site file data suggest needed areas of improvement. More sites need to be discovered, all sites need to be assessed for potential National Register of Historic Places eligibility, and more eligible sites need to be actually nominated to the National Register. This is not simply a South Carolina problem; the National Park Service is encouraging archaeologists to work more closely with the various SHPOs to place more archaeological sites on the NRHP. Sprinkle has shown that placing such sites on the NRHP can actually entail less digging, saving time, money, and labor to preserve the resources.[17] To aid these endeavors, three major tasks should be undertaken as follows:

1. Archaeologists and managers should make a concerted effort to locate, survey, evaluate, report, and manage historic sites in South Carolina.
2. A strong effort should also be made to increase communication and joint projects between standing structure preservationists and historical archaeologists.
3. A preservation plan should be developed with help from the archaeological community to isolate those areas of the state that are in most need of systematic survey. This plan should describe the evolving history of land use and social interactions across the state through time and space. Priorities should be set listing areas in most need of archaeological and structural survey, with development of associated historical contexts.

The South Carolina SHPO and South Carolina's Council of Professional Archaeologists are working together to educate the professional community about the needs described above. The SHPO is actively fostering communication within its divisions by hosting a series of retreats and interdepartmental meetings. The SHPO is also encouraging and supporting the funding of federal grant applications to hold symposia, develop bibliographies, and publish abstracts. The SHPO and SCIAA also support the digitization of the archaeological site files and are actively promoting the development of preservation programs in other agencies. Besides federal grant programs, there are a number of federal and state agency partnership programs that provide matching support for survey, excavation, and public interpretation at historic proper-

ties.[18] The landscape approach can be effectively used in developing such preservation plans and educational programs.

Themes to Guide Future Research in South Carolina

Historical archaeologists, historians, and geographers interested in study of South Carolina's landscapes have pointed to some of the power, problems, and potential of a landscape approach in this book. The following themes, to help guide future research, have been drawn from this volume's chapters and earlier discussions. At a symposium cosponsored by the Council of South Carolina Professional Archaeologists, South Carolina SHPO, SCIAA, and the University of South Carolina Department of Anthropology held at the University of South Carolina in September 1991, professionals, students, and interested citizens discussed the landscape concept and cultural resource management needs for South Carolina's historic properties. An additional symposium on the topic was held at the Society for Historical Archaeology meetings in Kingston, Jamaica, in January 1992. Based on transcripts and notes from these symposia, a series of pertinent questions and discussion have been compiled below. Some of the specific questions are directed to CRM personnel, others to preservation planners, and others to the general community.

1. What Constitutes a Historical Archaeological Site in South Carolina?

Discussion: There has been some past debate as to whether specific types of sites and/or sites dating from the twentieth century should be recorded in the site files at SCIAA as historical archaeological sites. Is a liquor still an archaeological site? Is a 1920s gas station and its surroundings an archaeological site? The general consensus is that structures, objects, and sites dating from fifty years ago to the time of first European and Native American contact (ca. 1565) should be considered as historic properties.[19]

If one accepts the broad definition that an archaeological site is a matrix containing evidence of past human activities, then even a few whiteware sherds found in a plowed field should be treated as an archaeological site. In years past these types of finds were often ignored as unimportant evidence of a farmer's lunch. Historical archaeologists have since recognized that such sites may contain important structural and disposal features related to farm occupations.[20]

Landscape features can also be part of an archaeological site. For example, rice berms, oak allees, boat landings, and gardens often contain few if any artifacts. These types of sites, however, are loaded with information about past historic processes and can be considered as features related to a particular archaeological site. Roads, bridges, and cemeteries have been considered archaeological sites. Archaeology has been effectively used to help reconstruct garden areas and walkways, for example, as well as to uncover and date structures.

Standing structures are buildings that are part of an archaeological site. Archaeology can provide information about activities that took place at the site and also can help to date the structure. All too often a building's foundation is renovated without calling in an archaeologist. Once the original builder's trenches are destroyed or kitchen middens bulldozed away, the archaeologist can offer little assistance in answering important questions about site chronology, social processes, etc. Historic property managers using federal assistance, grants, licensing, or funding may also find that their project must meet section 106 of the National Historic Preservation Act (as amended) requirements. If this possibility is not considered well in advance, managers may find themselves scrambling for additional dollars to fund archaeological fieldwork.

The added expense of archaeological investigations at historic properties with standing structures can be mitigated. Preservationists are becoming more creative in finding solutions to funding problems. The key is to locate a strong support base in the local community, including among profes-sional archaeologists. Many archaeologists will gladly serve on local foundation boards or give advice about protection of archaeological resources. Site managers can work with archaeologists with research interests related to a particular historic property to host fieldschools, paid in full or in part, by university funding.

For example, Samford University in Alabama held a fieldschool in 1995 at the state-owned Wheeler Plantation Home Site, near Courtland, Alabama. The Alabama Historical Commission donated site personnel hours, some housing, and some equipment to the fieldschool. Samford University allowed the field director (Linda Stine) to use up to 80 percent of fieldschool tuition fees to fund housing and pay for supplies. The administration recognized the importance of archaeology as a discipline, as a "hands-on" educational tool, and as a source for inexpensive media coverage. Three television segments were broadcast about the fieldwork, and numerous articles appeared in regional newspapers. Students paid for their own field equipment and pooled resources for meals. The site manager arranged for interested local volunteers to participate in the fieldschool. Many of these volunteers also generously provided food and drink to the fieldschool participants. The local support group, the General Joe Wheeler Home Foundation, also provided funds for metal conservation and curation of artifacts.

2. How Can a Landscape Approach Help to Identify the Historic Archaeological Sites Present throughout the State of South Carolina?

Discussion: The use of a landscape approach in development of research designs helps archaeologists to broaden their perspectives. In their discussion of the South Carolina landscape, Kovacik and Winberry offer a diachronic overview of economic and social trends.[21] This kind of study allows an archaeologist to determine what types of sites might be present in the state at any particular period and place. The South Carolina Statewide Survey of Historic Places Manual developed by Archives and

History also serves as a guide.[22] A more complete picture of the range of possible site types is developed before the archaeologist enters the field. A landscape approach is relational, thus researchers ask questions such as:

1. Who lived at the site and when did they live there?
2. Why did they live there?
3. How did they make their living?
4. What transportation networks were necessary?
5. What is the range of site types that should be connected to the particular site studied?
6. What social mechanisms were in place?
7. How does the site compare and relate to others in the region?
8. Which natural and social processes affected site formation?
9. How did these processes affect site formation?
10. What methods would best derive the information needed to answer these types of questions?

This list of possible questions can be adapted to fit the particular research design of individual archaeologists. They can also be broadened to incorporate a regional study, as opposed to study of a particular site. Thus, a landscape perspective leads to asking more questions about the variety of site types and site functions, and therefore to the identification of more historic archaeological sites.

Survey archaeologists often estimate site boundaries by simply drawing a circle around the area containing positive shovel tests. This unsophisticated "method" is of little help in management or interpretation. A landscape approach enables the archaeologist to think about relative and effective scale. Archaeologists are forced to define their criteria for determining positive shovel tests, features, loci, and sites. The researcher's perspective is reoriented to isolating particular loci, then seeing the relationship between those loci, natural resources, and open spaces—loci boundaries do not shift, but site boundaries can shift in tandem with the scale of analysis and related research design.

3. How Can a Landscape Approach Be Used to Evaluate the Significance of Historic Archaeological Sites?

Discussion: As discussed in this volume, a landscape approach can help to evaluate site significance in four major ways as follows:

First, a relational, landscape approach forces managers to examine a site at various scales of significance, fitting NRHP criteria of possible local, state, and national significance. A site such as a Civil War earthwork may not be considered significant if examined solely on the grounds of its particular qualities of integrity, clarity, rarity alone.[23] However, if examined in light of these qualities at a regional level, the earthwork may be seen as vital to understanding the historic landscape—in terms of how it relates to other Civil War sites of the region and/or country. The opposite is also true; for example, a certain site that may seem rare for a particular region, such as a tar kiln in Charleston County's jurisdiction, is seen as common on USFS adjacent lands. As discussed during our symposia, one should not forget that some types of sites remain significant even if a number of them have been recorded in the state. One example used was the Megalithic tombs in Europe. The fact that archaeologists have recorded and investigated a number of these tombs does not mean that a newly discovered tomb cannot offer substantially new information about this category of resources. Many of the cultural resources in South Carolina may fall into this category.

Second, by guiding researchers to take a relational, broader approach, a landscape perspective helps to increase awareness of the possible range of site types in a region. This improves site identification, increasing the data base in the area. This in turn gives CRM researchers more information to help determine site significance.

Third, research design formation is improved with a landscape perspective. As discussed by Butler and Hardesty, significance should be determined by explicitly stating arguments linking a site to specific historical archaeological questions that address substantive issues in the discipline.[24] Landscape processes and formation questions have been and are important, substantive issues in the discipline. Sites that can add explicitly stated, important information toward answering those questions can be justifiably seen as significant sites, worthy of nomination to the NRHP.

Fourth, the NRHP now recognizes rural landscapes as potentially worthy of nomination to the NRHP. A landscape approach helps to identify historic landscapes and provides a framework for evaluation of their significance. South Carolina contains many remnants of its rural past. Some of the state's rural landscapes may prove worthy of nomination to the NRHP.

4. How Can a Landscape Approach Improve Management of Historic Archaeological Sites?

Discussion: Managers will find that this approach helps in three major ways:

First, being relational, a landscape approach can guide managers in planning. It identifies what types of sites might be present and indicates how these site might be interrelated. It also helps managers make decisions about the relative importance of specific site types.

Second, public interpretation and use of historic sites is enhanced by this approach. The general public can readily understand questions about how the natural and cultural processes of the past helped to form the present landscape. Displays can be constructed illustrating how the present lands might have once been used and viewed by historic peoples. Portions of the physical landscape can also be used for recreation. For example, a greenway along a series of Civil War earthworks or forts can serve as a pleasant bike and/or hiking trail (cf. Vicksburg, Mississippi). Visitors can also understand why certain portions of the park, such as actual fortifications, should not be walked upon and or be allowed to erode.

Third, local planners and managers will find that a landscape perspective facilitates discussions about how natural and cultural resources are interrelated. This improves their ability to plan, to interpret, and to preserve historic properties in their region.[25] The educational and economic benefits of this type of planning are clear. Current trends in environmental planning include developing urban wildlife corridors. These are greenways connecting habitats such as marsh and lakes within an urban area. The potential integration of preservation greenways and conservation wildlife corridors is an appealing idea.

5. What Are Some of the Problems of a Landscape Perspective, and How Can We Avoid Them?

Discussion: This is a large topic, of much concern to some of the symposia participants. There are two major issues related to this topic: data base construction and the misuse of the landscape concept.

In order to readily implement a landscape approach the SCIAA site files and the Standing Structure Survey files at Archives and History must be digitized into a useful data base. Such a program has begun and must be maintained. This will give managers and researchers the needed information on the range of site types, their location, and other necessary data for significance evaluations. Without this type of data base, it is very difficult to determine the relative significance of certain types of sites. Construction of digital data bases is time consuming and labor intensive. Standards of data entry are being developed, and guidelines to avoid misuse of information are being formulated. Possible biases in its construction are also be identified. This data base must be updated periodically to remain useful.[26]

With regard to the landscape concept, discussants raised the specter of CRM archaeologists being taken to task for not having written report sections detailing every type of historic landscape in a region or for not identifying such landscapes. Researchers must clearly differentiate between two related concepts. The first is that of a landscape as an entity to observe, record, and evaluate; the second is that of landscape as an analytical tool to help synthesize data about the region under study.

Archaeologists can think of landscape as an

entity in the same light as historical archaeological sites. They already observe land use patterns and should investigate the spatial and temporal relationships between historic sites on a particular project. Archaeologists are already well prepared to identify such landscapes and to justify their significance. Their significance does not, however, lie simply in the fact of their existence. As with any historic property, a historic landscape must be linked to specific arguments demonstrating how these data will add to the theoretical and substantive knowledge of the discipline. Some identified rural landscapes may prove to be unworthy of nomination to the NRHP. Federal guidelines already exist to help researchers identify and evaluate such resources.[27] As an analytical tool, landscape theory should stand in the same light as other important theories in the discipline. It is not a mandated approach; it should serve as an alternative possibility, and/or be used in conjunction with historical archaeology and theory.

6. How Can We Guarantee that "Alternative Voices" Will Be Heard in South Carolina Historical Archaeology?

Discussion: A particular landscape may have been perceived differently by various types of human groups. This is true when studying landscapes through time or even at one particular time period. A landscape approach naturally forces scholars to think about points of view and perspective.

Few historical archaeology papers have been written directly concerning Native American views of the land. We recognize that this book does not cover all of the multitude of possible paper topics generated by the landscape. Landscape studies are in their infancy in this state. The papers in this volume discussing the interrelationship of geography, history, and anthropology underline the effectiveness of a landscape perspective in interdisciplinary research. This promotes a holistic view of South Carolina's past and discussion of diverse perspectives, including Native American views. Discussions also highlight the need for more systematic survey of a greater variety of site types, related to different social groups.

The creation of a preservation plan for historical archaeology in South Carolina, impelled by a landscape approach, will ensure that the state's diverse sites will be systematically researched.

Landscape Perspectives: General Considerations and Conclusions

A landscape approach helps to join different types of sites together, whether studied through time or during one period. For example, it pulls together the vision of the main house, brick kilns, slave villages, rice berms, oak allees, roads, fields, and tar kilns often found across the same plantation lands. It also enhances one's ability to understand the social relations between the plantation inhabitants and the relationship of land use to natural and social forces. Interesting questions can be raised, such as how a slave might have viewed the landscape as opposed to the overseer or owner. One can also wonder how a site such as a brick kiln was differentially viewed by worker and manager.

This approach also ties together two forms of preservation activities that are often kept separated, namely, architectural survey and assessment and archaeological survey and assessment. A structure does not simply become part of an archaeological site once it burns down. Extant buildings and landscape features are parts of archaeological sites. NRHP evaluations of standing portions of sites and of rural landscapes follow the same standard criteria of significance as do archaeological sites (36CFR60). There are very different substantive and theoretical issues involved with these domains that should not be ignored. Nonetheless, the South Carolina SHPO and SCIAA are beginning to formalize the way they trade information about historic properties.

Many state historic preservation offices are structured as separate divisions: there might be architecture, national register, archaeology, and grants sections. Many include environmental review/section 106 as a separate division. Individuals often do not know what specific criteria their fellow workers use for determining significance.

That is why the South Carolina SHPO has instigated an interdisciplinary task force on significance.[28] Each division maintains a separate series of topographic and/or county maps with site location information. Corresponding division data are also maintained in separate file drawers. It would be best if they could computerize their survey and site files and develop a mutual "View Only" system. This would allow fellow researchers to see and use the data without being able to tamper with their respective data bases. It would lead to more efficient use of these data bases. This system would foster communications and improve a state's historic preservation office's ability to evaluate historic properties quickly and cogently—whether these properties are landscapes, sites, buildings, districts, or objects. The SHPO is actively investigating ways to best share its data while protecting its data base.

Preservation Plan for Historical Archaeology

This data base project establishes a clear need for a preservation plan for historical archaeology in South Carolina. Although the SHPO is actively seeking such a plan, no specific strategy for producing a plan has been formulated. To date, this kind of management plan is supported, but state personnel are waiting for nongovernment archaeologists to apply for a Survey and Planning Grant to fund authorship of a preservation plan for South Carolina archaeology.[29] A preservation plan will clarify what historic contexts are needed the most in future synthesis volumes. This volume provides a selection of useful contexts for preservationists and archaeologists, but the topic has proven to be larger than the current state data base readily handles. A preservation plan will focus the research efforts of archaeologists in the state. Such a plan will guide those involved in preservation and compliance level studies of historic landscapes. The archaeological community should be drafted into helping formulate this plan. It could be fostered with Survey and Planning Grants and/or other avenues of funding.

A preservation plan for historical archaeology should incorporate the three basic parts of the federally mandated historic contexts: common cultural themes, defined geographic areas, and defined time periods.[30] Themes can be grounded in local history or be statewide in scope. A good example of such a document is the archaeological plan for Louisiana.[31] This type of plan can be amended easily to include a landscape perspective.

A landscape perspective fits into a preservation plan in the following manner. The preservation plan would divide the state into specific geographic regions with corresponding chronological periods of study. A landscape perspective would be applied to understanding the key patterns of land use, social interaction, economic development, and so forth, for each region for each time period. This analysis would illuminate pertinent themes for each region of study.[32] Organized under each theme, specific site types and components would be discussed. Their frequencies would be compared when SCIAA site files have been computerized. If the survey data is also computerized, standing structure information could be incorporated as well. Relevant issues of social inequality, settlement pattern changes, industrial growth, transportation, etc., would be discussed under pertinent themes. This would provide a guide for future research, point out gaps in the data base, and help in determining NRHP significance. It would also increase awareness of the need to nominate more historic archaeological sites to the NRHP.

The historical archaeological community of South Carolina recognizes the need to synthesize the results of its diverse scholarship. Development of a preservation plan for historical archaeology will guide an ongoing synthesis by providing a well-organized, common framework. Such a guide will be greatly enhanced by incorporating a landscape perspective.

The discussions and data generated by this specific project provide the general archaeological and preservation communities with a greater understanding of the concept of landscape. Researchers and managers from diverse regions can apply a host of new questions and perspectives, fostered by the landscape approach.

NOTES

1. For example, Fick 1992; Stine 1992a. Derting and Leader 1995 outlines SCIAA responsibilities and describe site file access procedures. See Stine and Stine, this volume, note 2 for information on the National Register of Historic Places.
2. Keith Derting, personal communication 1992; see also Derting and Leader 1995; Scurry and Carlson 1995.
3. Robert Morgan and Robert Wise, personal communication 1992.
4. Stine 1992a.
5. Joseph, this volume; Kovacik and Winberry 1989.
6. Stine 1992a, Bob Wise, personal communication 1992.
7. Stine 1992a:28–29.
8. Stine 1992a:Appendix D.
9. Joseph, this volume.
10. Fick 1992; Stine 1992a.
11. Stine 1989a; Joseph, this volume.
12. Stine 1992a, Wayne, this volume.
13. Martha Zierden, curator of historical archaeology at The Charleston Museum, states that all of The Museum's sites now have corresponding SCIAA forms and numbers. This includes urban sites recorded in the 1970s (Martha Zierden, personal communication 1996).
14. Wayne, this volume; Harmon and Snedeker, this volume.
15. Joseph, this volume; Harmon and Snedeker, this volume; Stine and Stine, this volume.
16. Charles Kovacik, personal communication 1991; Harmon and Snedeker this volume.
17. Sprinkle 1995.
18. Contact the SHPO for information on grants and federal partnership programs (e.g., U.S. Forest Service program "Passports in Time"). See also Derting, Pekrul, and Rinehart 1991; Derting and Leader 1995; Scurry and Carlson 1995; Smith and Judge 1992; Tippett and Market 1995.
19. Henry 1995 discusses the importance of twentieth-century sites. See also Hardesty 1995.
20. For example, Brockington et al. 1985.
21. Kovacik and Winberry 1989.
22. South Carolina Department of Archives and History 1990.
23. See Glassow 1977; Hardesty 1995.
24. Butler 1987; Hardesty 1995.
25. Drucker, this volume.
26. Derting and Leader 1995; Scurry and Carlson 1995; Tippett and Market 1995.
27. McClelland et al. 1990.
28. Archives and History personnel in three divisions—NRHP, Statewide Survey, and Environmental Review—began regular meetings as of February 1996 to discuss intradepartmental issues of significance.
29. Lee Tippett, Environmental Review archaeologist, personal communication 1996.
30. See the National Park Service Resources Division's series, Planning Questions, Interpreting the Secretary of the Interior's "Standards for Preservation Planning" No. 1–12.
31. Steven D. Smith, Philip Rivet, Kathleen Byrd, and Nancy Hawkins 1983, *Louisiana's Comprehensive Archaeological Plan.*
32. See, for example, Stine 1992a.

WORKS CITED

Brockington, Paul, Jr., Michael Scardaville, Patrick H. Garrow, David Singer, Linda France, and Cheryl Holt
1985   *Rural Settlement in the Charleston Bay Area: Eighteenth and Nineteenth Century Sites in the Mark Clark Expressway Corridor.* Submitted to the South Carolina Dept. of Highways and Public Transportation. Garrow and Associates, Atlanta.

Derting, Keith, and Jonathan Leader
1995   Information Management Within SCIAA: A South Carolina Perspective. In *Archaeological Site Management: A Southeastern Perspective,* edited by David G. Anderson and Virginia Horak, pp. 72–81. Readings in Archaeological Resource Protection Series No. 3. Interagency Archaeological Services Division, Atlanta, Georgia.

Derting, Keith, Sharon L. Pekrul, and Charles J. Rinehart (compilers)
1991   *A Comprehensive Bibliography of South Carolina Archaeology.* Research Manuscript Series 211.

South Carolina Institute of Archaeology and Anthropology, Univ. of South Carolina, Colombia.

Fick, Sarah
1992   *Architectural and Archaeological Survey of Charleston County.* Submitted to the Charleston County Planning Office by Preservation Consultants, Charleston.

Glassow, Michael.
1977   Issues in Evaluating the Significance of Archaeological Resources. *American Antiquity* 42:413–20.

Hardesty, Donald L.
1995   Research Questions and Information. *CRM* 18(6) Supplement:4–8.

Henry, Susan L.
1995   The National Register and the 20th Century: Is there Room for Archaeology? *CRM* 18(6) Supplement:9–12.

Kovacik, Charles F., and John J. Winberry
1989   *South Carolina: The Making of a Landscape.* Univ. of South Carolina Press, Columbia. Originally published in 1987 as *South Carolina: A Geography.* Westview Press, Boulder and London.

McClelland, Linda F., J. Timothy Keller, Genevieve Keller, and Robert Melnick
1990   *Guidelines for Evaluating and Documenting Rural Historic Landscapes.* National Register Bulletin 30. Washington, D.C.

Scurry, James D., and Ruth E. Carlson
1995   Improving Site Recording Accuracy in a GIS: A South Carolina Example. In *Archaeological Site File Management: A Southeastern Perspective,* edited by David G. Anderson and Virginia Horak, pp. 82–87. Readings in Archaeological Resource

Protection Series No. 3. Interagency Archaeological Services Division.

Smith, Steven D., and Christopher Judge
1992   The South Carolina Heritage Trust Ranking System for Archaeological Site Acquisition. *Southeastern Archaeology* 11(2):140–48.

Smith, Steven D., Philip Rivet, Kathleen Byrd, and Nancy Hawkins
1983   *Louisiana's Comprehensive Archaeological Plan.* State of Louisiana Dept. of Culture, Recreation and Tourism, Office of Cultural Development, Division of Archaeology.

Sprinkle, John H., Jr.
1995   A Site Form for Important Sites—Converting Archaeological Reports into National Register Nominations. *CRM* 18(6) Supplement:13–16.

Stine, Linda France
1989a   *Raised Up in Hard Times: Factors Affecting Material Culture on Upland Piedmont Farmsteads Circa 1900–1940.* Ph.D. diss., Dept. of Anthropology, Univ. of North Carolina, Univ. Microfilms, Ann Arbor.
1992a   *Revealing Historic Landscapes in Charleston County: Archaeological Inventory, Contexts, and Management.* Submitted to the Charleston County Planning Dept. South Carolina Institute of Archaeology and Anthropology.

Tippett, Lee (editor), and Andy Market (compiler)
1995   *Archaeological Abstracts from the Review and Compliance Files of the South Carolina State Preservation Office.* South Carolina State Historic Preservation Office, Columbia.

BIBLIOGRAPHY

Adams, Jane Helen
1987   *The Transformation of Rural Social Life in Union County, Illinois, in the Twentieth Century*. Ph.D. diss., Dept. of History, Univ. of Illinois, Urbana-Champaign.

Adams, Natalie P.
1990   *Early African-American Domestic Architecture from Berkeley County, South Carolina.* Master's thesis, Dept. of Anthropology, Univ. of South Carolina, Columbia.
1992   Elite Ideology and African-American Resistance: Architectural Change at South Carolina Slave Settlements. Paper presented at the Society for Historical Archaeology Meetings, Kingston, Jamaica.

Adams, William H.
1977   *Silcott, Washington: Ethnoarchaeology of a Rural American Community.* Reports of Investigations 54. Laboratory of Anthropology, Washington State Univ., Pullman.

Adams, William H., and Sarah Jane Boling
1989   Status and Ceramics for Planters and Slaves on Three Georgia Coastal Plantations. *Historical Archaeology* 23(1):69–96.

Affleck, Richard M.
1990   *Power and Space: Settlement Pattern Change at Middleburg Plantation, Berkeley County, South Carolina.* Master's thesis, Dept. of Anthropology, Univ. of South Carolina, Columbia.

Affleck, Richard, and Natalie Adams
1991   Plantation Settlement Pattern and Slave Architecture from the South Carolina and Georgia Lowcountry, 1670 to 1865. Paper presented at the symposium entitled Plantation Archeology of the Virginia and Maryland Tidewater Region and the Lowcountry of Georgia and South Carolina: A Synthesis and Comparison. 1991 Annual Meeting of the Society for Historical Archaeology Richmond, Virginia.

Alderson, William T., and Shirley Payne Low
1976   *Interpretation of Historic Sites.* 4th ed., American Association for State and Local History, Nashville.

Allan, Linda K., and Christopher T. Espenshade
1990   *Archeological Resources Survey of Selected Portions of the Wambaw and Witherbee Districts, Francis Marion National Forest, Berkeley County, South Carolina.* Submitted to the United States Forest Service, Francis Marion National Forest, South Carolina. Brockington and Associates, Atlanta.

Allen, Kathleen, Stanton Green, and Ezra Zubrow
1990   *Interpreting Space: GIS and Archaeology.* Taylor and Francis, London and New York.

Amer, Christopher, William Barr, David Beard, Elizabeth Collins, Lynn Harris, William Judd, Carl Naylor, and Mark Newell
1993   *The Malcolm Boat (38CH803): Discovery, Stabilization, Excavation, and Preservation of an Historic Sea Going Small Craft in the Ashley River, Charleston County, South Carolina.* Research Manuscript Series No. 217, South Carolina Institute of Archaeology and Anthropology.

Ames, Kenneth
1986   Meaning in Artifacts: Hall Furnishings in Victorian America. In *Common Places, Readings in American Vernacular Architecture,* edited by Dell Upton and John Michael Vlach, pp. 240–60. Univ. of Georgia Press, Athens.

Anbinder, Tyler
1992   *Nativism and Slavery: The Northern Know Nothings and the Politics of the 1850s.* Oxford Univ. Press, New York.

Ancrum, William
1810   Journal of William Ancrum July 4, 1810–Aug. 5, 1810. Ms. on file, South Caroliniana Library, Univ. of South Carolina, Columbia.

Anderson, David G., and J. W. Joseph
1988   *Prehistory and History Along the Upper Savannah River: Technical Synthesis of Cultural Resource Investigations, Richard B. Russell Multiple Resource Area.* Russell Papers 1988. Interagency Archeological Services, National Park Service, Atlanta.

Anderson, David G., and Jennalee Muse
1982   The Archaeology of Tenancy in the Southeast: A View from the South Carolina Lowcountry. *South Carolina Antiquities* 14:71–82.
1983   The Archaeology of Tenancy (2): A Reply to Trinkley. *Southeastern Archaeology* 2:65–68.

Anderson, David G., and Patricia A. Logan
1981   *Francis Marion National Forest Cultural Resources*

Overview. United States Forest Service, Dept. of Agriculture, Columbia.

Anonymous

1992   Archaeology at Santa Elena. *Federal Archeology Report* 5(1):20.

1995   *Targeting Environmental Priorities in Agriculture: Reforming Program Strategies.* Office of Technological Assessment, Washington, D.C.

Anthony, Carl

1976   The Big House and the Slave Quarters, Part I: Prelude to New World Architecture. *Landscape* 21(1):8–19.

Anthony, Ronald W.

1989   *Cultural Diversity at Mid to Late 18th Century Lowcountry Plantation Slave Settlements.* Master's thesis, Dept. of Anthropology, Univ. of South Carolina, Columbia.

Anthony, Ronald, and Lesley M. Drucker

1984   *Hartwell Destination Park: An Archaeological Study of a Piedmont Locality, Oconoee County, South Carolina.* Resource Studies Series 74. Carolina Archeological Services, Columbia.

Anzalone, Ronald D. (compiler)

1987   Archeology at the Local Level. Ms. on file, Advisory Council on Historic Preservation, Washington, D.C.

Arnold, J. Barto, III

1990   The Survey for the *Zavala,* a Steam Warship of the Republic of Texas. In *Underwater Archaeology Proceedings from the Society for Historical Archaeology Conference,* edited by J. Broadwater, pp. 105–9. Tucson.

Ashe, Thomas

1911   Carolina, or a Description of the Present State of that Country [1682]. In *Narratives of Early Carolina, 1650–1708,* edited by Alexander S. Salley, pp. 135–59. Charles Scribner's Sons, New York.

Atkinson, James R., and Jack D. Elliott Jr.

1978   *Nance's Ferry: A 19th Century Brick and Lime Making Site.* Dept. of Anthropology, Mississippi State Univ., Starkville.

Babson, David W.

1987   Plantation Ideology and the Archaeology of Racism: Evidence from the Tanner Road Site (38BK416), Berkeley County, South Carolina. *South Carolina Antiquities* 19(1, 2):35–47.

1988   *The Tanner Road Settlement: The Archaeology of Racism on Limerick Plantation.* Volumes in

Historical Archaeology, Conference on Historic Sites Archaeology, vol. 4, edited by Stanley South. South Carolina Institute of Archaeology and Anthropology, Columbia. Reprint of 1987 Master's thesis, Dept. of Anthropology, Univ. of South Carolina, Columbia.

Bailey, Louise, and Elizabeth Cooper

1983   *Biographical Directory of the South Carolina House of Representatives, 1775–1790,* 3:339–41. Univ. of South Carolina Press, Columbia.

Baker, C. Michael, and Linda Hall

1985   An Archaeological Evaluation of Three Proposed Alternate Sites for the Gastonia Municipal Airport. Ms. on file, Delta Associates P. E., Richmond, Virginia.

Baker, Donald G.

1983   *Race, Ethnicity and Power.* Routledge and Kegan Paul, London.

Barr, William B.

1995   Childsbury and Ashley Ferry Town: Elements of Control in the Economic Landscape of Colonial South Carolina. In *Underwater Archaeology Proceedings from the Society for Historical Archaeology Conference,* edited by Paul Forsythe Johnston, pp. 88–93. Tucson.

Barrett, John G.

1987   *The Civil War in North Carolina.* Univ. of North Carolina Press, Chapel Hill.

Barrows, Harlan

1923   Geography as Human Ecology. *Annals of the Association of American Geographers* 13:1–14.

Bartlett, Richard A.

1974   *The New Country, a Social History of the American Frontier, 1776–1890.* Oxford Univ. Press, New York.

Bastian, Beverly

1982   *Fort Independence: An Eighteenth Century Homesite and Militia Post in South Carolina,* National Park Service, Atlanta.

1987   Historical and Archaeological Investigations at the United States Post Office/Courthouse Annex, Charleston, South Carolina. Ms. on file, United States Dept. of the Interior, National Park Service, Atlanta.

Beard, David V.

1988   *An Archaeological Survey of Selected Submerged Cultural Resources in Maryland.* Division of Archaeology, Maryland Geological Survey. Submitted to the Maryland Historical Trust, Baltimore.

1989   A Preliminary Reconnaissance of the Paul Pritchard Shipyard Site, Hobcaw Creek, Charleston County, S.C. Ms. on file, South Carolina Institute of Archaeology and Anthropology, Columbia.

1990a   Reconnaissance Survey Report: Underwater Archaeological Investigations of the Lexington Plantation Kiln Site Causeway in Wagner Creek, Charleston County, South Carolina. Ms. on file, South Carolina Coastal Council, Charleston.

1990b   *Underwater Archaeological Investigations of the Cedar Grove Plantation Causeway in the Ashley River, Dorchester County South Carolina.* Submitted to the South Carolina Coastal Council. South Carolina Institute of Archaeology and Anthropology, Columbia.

1990c   *Underwater Archaeological Investigations of the Lexington Kiln Site Causeway in Wagner Creek, Charleston County South Carolina.* Submitted to the South Carolina Coastal Council. South Carolina Institute of Archaeology and Anthropology, Columbia.

1991a   Causeways and Cribbing: Now You *Can* Get There from Here. In *Underwater Archaeology Proceedings from the Society for Historical Archaeology Conference,* edited by John Broadwater, pp. 73–77. Tucson.

1991b   *Preliminary Archaeological Investigations of the Hobcaw Creek Plantation Vessel Located in Hobcaw Creek, Charleston County South Carolina.* Submitted to the South Carolina Coastal Council. South Carolina Institute of Archaeology and Anthropology, Columbia.

Beaumont, Constance
1996   The Statehouse: Developers of Sprawl Slap Opposition with Litigation. *Preservation News* (Jan.–Feb.):31.

Becker, Robert
1992   South Carolina's Rural Life: Can It Be Saved? *Coastal Heritage* 6(6):2.

Bellows, Barbara
1993   *Benevolence among Slaveholders: Assisting the Poor in Charleston, 1670–1860.* Louisiana State Univ. Press, Baton Rouge.

Bender, Barbara
1992   Theorising Landscapes, and the Prehistoric Landscapes of Stonehenge. In *Man* 27:735–55.

1994   *Landscape and Politics.* Blackwell, Oxford.

Bennet, John
1969   *Northern Plainsmen.* Aldine, Chicago.

1976   *The Ecological Transition.* Pergamon Press, London.

Berry, Brian
1964   Approaches to Regional Analysis: A Synthesis. *Annals of the Association of American Geographers* 54:2–11.

Berry, C. B.
1968   Horry County's Oldest Industry. *The Independent Republic Quarterly* 1(5).

Bianchi, Travis L.
1974   *Archaeological Investigations of South Carolina Highway Department's Proposed Connector from Port Royal to Ladies Island.* Research Manuscript Series 59. South Carolina Institute of Archaeology and Anthropology, Univ. of South Carolina, Columbia.

Binning, Cecil
1933   *British Regulation of the Colonial Iron Industry.* Univ. of Pennsylvania Press, Philadelphia.

Birnie, Joseph
1974   *The Earles and the Birnies.* Whittet and Shepperson, Richmond, Virginia.

Black, George R.
1864   "Black Family History, [ca. 1863–1864]." P MSS., Black Collection. South Caroliniana Library, Columbia.

Blackall, Henry
1888   Nails. *American Architect and Building News* 24 (660):71–74.

Blassingame, John
1972   *The Slave Community: Plantation Life in the Antebellum South.* Oxford Univ. Press, New York.

1977   *Slave Testimony.* Louisiana State Univ. Press, Baton Rouge.

Bleser, Carol K.
1981   *The Hammonds of Redcliffe.* Oxford Univ. Press, New York.

Bloch, Marc
1953   *The Historian's Craft.* Vintage Books, Random House, New York.

Blumer, Herbert
1969   *Symbolic Interactionism: Perspective and Method.* Prentice Hall, Englewood Cliffs, New Jersey.

Blumin, Stuart
1989   *The Emergence of the Middle Class: Social Experience in the American City, 1760–1900.* Cambridge Univ. Press, Cambridge, England.

Bond, Stanley C., Jr.
1987 The Development of the Naval Stores Industry in St. Johns County, Florida. *The Florida Anthropologist* 40(3):187–202.

Borchert, James
1980 *Alley Life in Washington: Family, Community, Religion, and Folklife in the City, 1850–1970*. Univ. of Illinois Press, Urbana.

Botkin, Benjamin A. (editor)
1945 *Lay My Burden Down: a Folk History of Slavery*. Univ. of Chicago Press, Chicago.

Breeden, James O. (editor)
1980 *Advice Among Masters: The Ideal in Slave Management in the Old South*. Greenwood Press, Westport.

Brevard Papers
1778 Partnership agreement, Mar. 3, 1778, of Isaac Hayne and William Hill. Brevard Papers, North Carolina State Dept. of Archives and History, Raleigh.
1817 Unsigned note, Dec. 8, 1817. Brevard Papers, North Carolina State Dept. of Archives and History, Raleigh.

Bridgens and Allen Insurance Map
1852 An Original Map of the City of Charleston. Map on file, the South Carolina Historical Society, Charleston.

Brigham, Albert Perry
1915 Problems of Geographic Influence. *Annals of the Association of American Geographers* 5:3–25.

Brockington, Paul E., Jr.
1987 *A Cultural Resource Survey at Snee Farm, 38CH917*. Ms. on file at Brockington and Associates, Atlanta.

Brockington, Paul, Jr., Michael Scardaville, Patrick H. Garrow, David Singer, Linda France, and Cheryl Holt
1985 *Rural Settlement in the Charleston Bay Area: Eighteenth and Nineteenth Century Sites in the Mark Clark Expressway Corridor*. Submitted to the South Carolina Dept. of Highways and Public Transportation. Garrow and Associates, Atlanta.

Brooker, Colin
1990 Tabby Structures on Spring Island. In *The Second Phase of Archaeological Survey on Spring Island, Beaufort County, South Carolina. Investigations on an Isolated Sea Island*, edited by Michael Trinkley, pp. 129–51. Research Series 20, Chicora Foundation, Columbia.

Brookfield, H. C.
1964 Questions on the Human Frontiers of Geography. *Economic Geography* 40:283–303.

Brooks, Mark, Richard D. Brooks, Kenneth Sassaman, George Lewis, and Glen Hanson
1989 *Archaeological Resource Management Plan of the Savannah River Archaeological Research Program*. Savannah River Archaeological Research Program, South Carolina Institute of Archaeology and Anthropology, Columbia.

Brooks, Richard D.
1981 *Initial Historic Overview of the Savannah River Plant, Aiken and Barnwell Counties, South Carolina*. Research Manuscript Series 170, South Carolina Institute of Archaeology and Anthropology, University of South Carolina, Columbia.
1986 The Ashley Plantation (1876–1950): Research Domains and Results. *South Carolina Antiquities* 18 (1, 2):9–14.
1988a *Synthesis of Historical Archaeological Sites on the Savannah River Plant, Aiken and Barnwell Counties, South Carolina*. South Carolina Institute of Archaeology and Anthropology, Columbia.
1988b *250 Years of Historic Occupation on Steel Creek, Savannah River Plant, Barnwell County, South Carolina*. Submitted to the Savannah River Operations Office, U. S. Department of Energy. Savannah River Archaeological Research Program, South Carolina Institute of Archaeology and Anthropology, Columbia.

Brown, Donald E.
1991 *Human Universals*. McGraw-Hill, New York.

Brownell, Blaine, and David Goldfield
1977 *The City in Southern History*. Kennikat Press, Port Washington, New York.

Burl, Aubrey
1979 *Prehistoric Avebury*. Yale Univ. Press, New Haven.

Butler, J. Robert
1966 Geology and Mineral Resources of York County, South Carolina. *South Carolina Division of Geology Bulletin* 33. Columbia.
1981 Geology of the Blacksburg South Quadrangle, South Carolina. In *Geological Investigations of the Kings Mountain Belt and Adjacent Areas in the Carolinas*, edited by J. W. Horton, Jr., J. R. Butler, and David M. Milton, pp. 65–71. Carolina Geological Society Field Trip Guidebook. Columbia.

Butler, William B.
1987   Forum: Significance and Other Frustrations in the
        CRM Process. *American Antiquity* 52(4):820–29.

Butzer, Karl
1982   *Archaeology as Human Ecology: Method and
        Theory for a Contextual Approach.* Cambridge
        Univ. Press, England.

Calhoun, Jeanne, and Martha Zierden
1984   *Charleston's Commercial Landscape, 1803–1860.*
        Archaeological Contributions 7. The Charleston
        Museum, Charleston.

Calhoun, Jeanne, Elizabeth Paysinger, and Martha
        Zierden
1982   *A Survey of Economic Activity in Charleston,
        1732–1770.* Archaeological Contributions 2, The
        Charleston Museum, Charleston.

Calhoun, Jeanne, Elizabeth Reitz, Michael Trinkley, and
        Martha Zierden
1984   *Meat in Due Season: Preliminary Investigations of
        Marketing Practices in Colonial Charleston.*
        Archaeological Contribution 9, The Charleston
        Museum, Charleston.

Calhoun, Jeanne, Martha Zierden, and Lesley Drucker
1987   Home Upriver: Rural Life on Daniels Island,
        Berkeley County, South Carolina. Booklet on file,
        South Carolina Dept. of Highways and Public
        Transportation, Columbia.

Capers and Huger
1849   List of 72 Rice Field Negroes. William Ravenel
        Papers, South Carolina Historical Society,
        Charleston.

Cappon, Lester
1932   Iron Making—a Forgotten Industry of North
        Carolina. *North Carolina Historical Review*
        9:331–48.

Carchedi, Guglielmo
1977   *On the Economic Identification of Social Classes.*
        Routledge and Kegan Paul, London.

Carpenter, James G.
1973   *The Rice Plantation Lands of Georgetown County,
        South Carolina: A Historical Geographic Study.*
        Master's thesis, Dept. of Geography, Univ. of
        South Carolina, Columbia.

Casagrande, Joseph B., Stephen I. Thompson, and Philip
        D. Young
1964   Colonization as a Research Frontier. In *Process
        and Pattern in Culture, Essays in Honor of Julian
        H. Steward,* edited by Robert A. Manners, pp.
        281–315. Aldine, Chicago.

Cassedy, Daniel, Patrick Garrow, Jeffrey Holland, and
        Edward Turber
1992   Additional Archaeological and Architectural
        Investigation for the Grace Memorial Bridge
        Replacement, Charleston, South Carolina. Ms. on
        file, Garrow and Associates, Raleigh, North
        Carolina.

Catesby, Mark
1977   The Natural History of Carolina, Florida, and the
        Bahama Islands; Containing the Figures of Birds,
        Beasts, Fishes, Serpents, Insects, and Plants . . .
        [Originally published 1754]. In *The Colonial
        South Carolina Scene, Contemporary Views, 1697–
        1774,* edited by H. Roy Merrens, pp. 87–109.
        Tricentennial Edition. Univ. of South Carolina
        Press.

Chang, K. C.
1967   *Rethinking Archaeology.* Random House, New
        York.
1972   *Settlement Patterns in Archaeology.* Module in
        Anthropology, Module 24. Addison-Wesley
        Publishing, Reading, Massachusetts.

Chappell, Edward A.
1989   Social Responsibility and the American History
        Museum. *Winterthur Portfolio* 24(4):247–65.

Charleston City Directories
1859   *The Charleston Directory.* Means and Turnbull,
        compilers. Evans and Cogswell, Charleston. On
        file at the South Carolina Historical Society,
        Charleston.
1860   *Directory of the City of Charleston, 1860.* Eugene
        Ferslew, compiler. Evans and Cogswell, Charles-
        ton. Microfilm copy available at the South
        Carolina Historical Society, Charleston.

Charleston City Ward Book
1853   Microfilm copy available from Charleston City
        Archives.

The Charleston Daily Courier
1853   *The Charleston Daily Courier,* Feb. 14, 1853.
1857   Untitled transcript of newspaper article on file at
        Middleton Place Plantation and Gardens,
        Charleston.

Cheeves, Langdon (editor)
1897   *Collections of the South Carolina Historical Society,*
        vol. 5. Jones, Book and Printer, Richmond.

Cherry, John
1987   Power and Space: Archaeological and Geographic
        Studies of the State. In *Landscape and Culture:
        Geographical and Archaeological Perspectives,*

edited by J. M. Wagstaff, pp. 146–72. Basil Blackwell, Oxford.

Chestnutt, David (editor)
1985   *The Papers of Henry Laurens,* vol. 10. Univ. of South Carolina Press, Columbia.

Chisholm, Michael
1970   *Rural Settlement and Land Use.* 2d ed., Univ. Library of Geography. Aldine Publishing, Chicago. Originally published 1962, Hutchinson, London.

City Gazette and Daily Advertiser
1784   *City Gazette and Daily Advertiser,* July 19, 1784. Charleston.
1789   *City Gazette and Daily Advertiser,* Aug. 17, 1789. Charleston.
1795   *City Gazette and Daily Advertiser,* May 12, 1795. Charleston.
1800   *City Gazette and Daily Advertiser,* June 16, 1800. Charleston.

Clarke, David L. (editor)
1977   *Spatial Archaeology.* Academic Press, London.

Clarke, Mary
1968   *Pioneer Iron Works.* Chilton Book, New York.

Clawson, Marion
1970   *Uncle Sam's Acres.* Greenwood Press, Westport. Originally published 1951, Dodd, Mead and Co., New York.

Clowse, Converse D.
1971   *Economic Beginnings in Colonial South Carolina 1670–1730.* Univ. of South Carolina Press, Columbia.

Cobb, Charles, Jeffrey Holland, and Eugene Burr
1990   *Final Report: Phase II Archaeological, Historical, and Architectural Investigations in the Grace and New Market Alignments: Grace Memorial Bridge Replacement, Charleston, South Carolina.* Submitted to the South Carolina Dept. of Highways and Public Transportation by Garrow and Associates, Atlanta.

Coclanis, Peter A.
1985   The Sociology of Architecture in Colonial Charleston: Pattern and Process in an 18th Century Southern City. *Journal of Southern History* 18:607–23.
1989   *The Shadow of a Dream: Economic Life and Death in the South Carolina Lowcountry 1670–1920.* Oxford Univ. Press, New York.

Collard, Elizabeth
1967   *Nineteenth Century Pottery and Porcelain in Canada.* McGill Univ. Press, Montreal.

Combes, John D.
1974   Charcoal Kilns and Cemetery at Parris Mountain State Park. Univ. of South Carolina, S.C. Institute of Archeology and Anthropology. *Notebook* 6(1):3–17.

Commissioners of Fortifications
1755–70 Journal of the Commissioners of Fortifications. Cited in research notes of Harriet Stoney Simons. Ms. on file, South Carolina Historical Society, Charleston.

Conzen, Michael P.
1990   Preface and Introduction. In the *Making of the American Landscape,* edited by Michael Conzen, pp. vii–ix and 1–3. Unwin Hyman, Boston.

Cooper, Thomas
1815   *The Emporium of Arts and Sciences, New Series,* vol. 1. Kimber and Richardson, Philadelphia (June 1813) 1(1):5–444.

Cooper, Thomas, and Lousi McCord
1874   *Statutes at Large of South Carolina.* On file, Univ. of South Carolina, Columbia.

Cosans, Betty, and Susan Henry
1978   *Archaeological Assessment of the Charleston Center Project Area, Charleston, South Carolina.* Ms. on file, Government Offices, City of Charleston.

Cosgrove, Denis E.
1985   *Social Formation and Symbolic Landscape.* Barnes and Noble, Totowa, New Jersey.
1990   "...Then We Take Berlin": Cultural Geography 1989–90. *Progress in Human Geography* 14:560–68.

Cosgrove, Denis E., and Peter Jackson
1987   New Directions in Cultural Geography. *Area* 19:95–101.

Council of Safety
1903   Papers of the Second Council of Safety of the Revolutionary Party in South Carolina, November 1775–March 1776. *South Carolina Historical and Genealogical Magazine* 4(1):13–25.

Council of South Carolina Professional Archaeologists
1992   Membership List. Ms. on file, South Carolina Institute of Archaeology and Anthropology, Columbia.

Courtenay, James
1828   Lexington, the Property of A. S. Willington, Esq. McCrady Plat Map Collection no. 6137. Charleston County Register of Mesne Conveyance, Charleston.

Cowan, Thomas
1987   William Hill and the Aera Ironworks. *The Journal of Early Southern Decorative Art* 13(2):1–31.

Cox, Lee
1985   *Preliminary Survey to Analyze the Potential Presence of Submerged Cultural Resources in the Delaware and Susquehanna Rivers.* Master's thesis, Dept. of History, East Carolina Univ., Greenville, North Carolina.

Coxe, Daniel, Esq.
1976   *A Description of the English Province of Carolina, by the Spainards call'd Florida, and by the French La Louisiane.* Originally published 1772. Reprint, Univ. Presses of Florida, Gainesville.

Coxe, Tench
1814   *A Statement for the Arts and Manufactures of the United States of America for the Year 1810.* A. Corman, Philadelphia.

Crass, David, and Mark Brooks (editors)
1995   *Cotton and Black Draught: Consumer Behavior on a Postbellum Farm.* Savannah River Archaeological Research Papers 5. Occasional Papers of the Savannah River Archaeological Research Program, South Carolina Institute of Archaeology and Anthropology, Univ. of South Carolina, Columbia.

Cremin, Aedeen
1992   Landscape Archaeology as a Central Paradigm in Historical Archaeology. Paper presented at the Society for Historical Archaeology Meetings, Kingston, Jamaica.

Cressey, Pamela, and John F. Stephens
1982   The City Site Approach to Urban Archaeology. In *Archaeology of Urban America,* edited by Roy Dickens, pp. 41–62. Academic Press, New York.

Cressey, Pamela, John F. Stephens, Steven Shephard, and Barbara Magid
1982   The Core-Periphery Relationship and the Archaeological Record in Alexandria, Virginia. In *Archaeology of Urban America,* edited by Roy Dickens, pp. 143–74. Academic Press, New York.

Cronon, William
1983   *Changes in the Land: Indians, Colonists, and the Ecology of New England.* Hill and Wang, New York.

Cross, John K.
1973   Tar Burning, A Forgotten Art? *Forests and People* 23(2):21–23.

Crumley, Carole L.
1979   Three Locational Models: An Epistemological Assessment for Anthropology and Archaeology. In *Advances in Archaeological Method and Theory,* vol. 2, edited by Michael B. Schiffer, pp. 141–73. Academic Press, New York.

1987   A Dialectical Critique of Hierarchy. In *Power Relations and State Formation,* edited by Thomas C. Patterson and Christine Ward Gailey, pp. 155–69. American Anthropological Association, Washington, D.C.

Crumley, Carole L. (editor)
1994   *Historical Ecology: Cultural Knowledge and Changing Landscapes.* School of American Research, Santa Fe.

Crumley, Carole, and William Marquardt
1990   Landscape: A Unifying Concept in Regional Analysis. In *Interpreting Space: GIS and Archaeology,* edited by Kathleen Allen, Stanton Green, and Ezra Zubrow, pp. 73–79. Taylor and Francis, London.

Crumley, Carole, and William Marquardt (editors)
1987   *Regional Dynamics: Burgundian Landscapes in Historical Perspective.* Academic Press, New York and San Diego.

Cutbush, James
1814   *The American Artist's Manual: or, Dictionary of Practical Knowledge in the Application of Philosophy to the Arts and Manufactures.* Johnson and Warner, Philadelphia.

Daniels, Stephen, and Denis Cosgrove
1988   Introduction: Iconography and Landscape. In *The Iconography of Landscape,* edited by Denis Cosgrove and Stephen Daniels, pp. 1–10. Cambridge Univ. Press, New York.

Davis, William Morris
1906   An Inductive Study of the Content of Geography. *Bulletin of the American Geographical Society* 38:67–84.

Deagan, Kathleen
1974   *Sex, Status and Role in the Mestizaje of Spanish Colonial Florida.* Ph.D. diss., Dept. of Anthropology, Univ. of Florida, Gainesville.

1981   Downtown Survey: The Discovery of 16th Century St. Augustine in an Urban Area. *American Antiquity* 46:626–33.

1983   *Spanish St. Augustine: the Archaeology of a Colonial Creole Community.* Academic Press, New York.

Deetz, James
1977   Material Culture and Archaeology—What's the

Difference? In *Historical Archaeology and the Importance of Material Things,* edited by Leland Ferguson. Special Publications Series No. 2, Society for Historical Archaeology, Tucson.

1990   Prologue: Landscapes as Cultural Statements. In *Earth Patterns,* edited by William Kelso and Rachel Most, pp. 1–4. Univ. Press of Virginia, Charlottesville.

Delgado, James P.

1986   Tasting Champagne. In *Archaeology in Solution, Proceedings of the Seventeenth Annual Conference on Underwater Archaeology,* edited by John W. Foster and Sheli O. Smith, pp. 104–7. Tucson.

Denslow, Julie Sloan, and Christine Padoch (editors)

1988   *People of the Tropical Rainforest.* Univ. of California Press, Berkeley.

DePratter, Chester, and William Green

1990   Origins of the Yamasee. Paper presented at the Southeastern Archaeological Conference, Mobile.

Derry, Anne, H. Ward Jandl, Carol D. Shull, and Jan Thorman

1977   Guidelines for Local Surveys: A Basis for Preservation Planning. *National Register Bulletin 24* [revised by Patricia L. Parker 1985]. National Park Service, U.S. Department of the Interior, Washington D.C.

Derting, Keith, and Jonathan Leader

1995   Information Management Within SCIAA: A South Carolina Perspective. In *Archaeological Site Management: A Southeastern Perspective,* edited by David G. Anderson and Virginia Horak, pp. 72–81. Readings in Archaeological Resource Protection Series No. 3. Interagency Archaeological Services Division, Atlanta, Georgia.

Derting, Keith, Sharon L. Pekrul, and Charles J. Rinehart (compilers)

1991   *A Comprehensive Bibliography of South Carolina Archaeology.* Research Manuscript Series 211. South Carolina Institute of Archaeology and Anthropology, Univ. of South Carolina, Columbia.

Dew, Charles

1966   *Iron Maker to the Confederacy: Joseph R. Anderson and the Tredegar Iron Works.* Yale Univ. Press, New Haven, Connecticut.

Diamond, John

1823   The Plat of 500 Acres of High Land in St. Thomas Parish, Formerly Called Addison's Ferry. McCrady Plat Map Collection no. 4353. Charles-

ton County Register of Mesne Conveyance, Charleston, South Carolina.

Dickens, Roy (editor)

1983   *Archaeology of Urban America: The Search for Pattern and Process.* Academic Press, New York.

Dickens, Roy, and William Bowen

1980   Problems and Promises in Urban Historical Archaeology: The MARTA Project. *Historical Archaeology* 14:42–57.

Dickinson, Martin, and Lucy Wayne

1990   *Four Men's Ramble: Archaeology in the Wando Neck, Charleston County, South Carolina.* Submitted to Dunes West Development of Charleston, SouthArc, Gainesville.

Dobson, Edward

1850   A Rudimentary Treatise on the Manufacture of Bricks and Tiles; Containing an Outline of the Principles of Brickmaking, and Detailed Accounts of the Various Processes Employed in the Making of Bricks and Tiles in Different Parts of England. 1971 reprint edited by Francis Celoria. *Journal of Ceramic History* 5.

Douglas, Elisha

1971   *The Coming of Age of American Business: Three Centuries of Enterprise 1600–1700.* Univ. of North Carolina Press, Chapel Hill.

Drago, Edmund

1990   *Initiative, Paternalism, and Race Relations.* Univ. of Georgia Press, Athens.

Drayton, John

1802   *A View of South Carolina, as Respects Her Natural and Physical Concerns.* W. P. Young, Charleston.

Dreppard, Charles

1946   Spikes, Nails, Tacks, Brads, and Pins. *Early American Industries Association Chronicle* 3(8).

Drucker, Lesley M.

1981   Socio-economic Patterning at an Undocumented Late 18th Century Lowcountry Site: Spiers Landing, South Carolina. *Historical Archaeology* 15(2):58–68.

Drucker, Lesley M., and Ronald W. Anthony

1986   On the Trail: An Examination of Socioeconomic Status at Late Historic Piedmont Farmsteads. *South Carolina Antiquities* 18(1, 2):15–24.

Drucker, Lesley M., Ronald W. Anthony, Susan Jackson, S. Krantz, and Carl R. Steen

1984   *An Archaeological Study of the Little River-Buffalo Creek Special Land Disposal Tract, Clarks Hill Lake, McCormick County, South Carolina.*

Submitted to the U.S. Army Corps of Engineers, Savannah District. Resource Studies Series 75. Carolina Archeological Services, Columbia.

Drucker, Lesley M., Woody C. Meizner, and James B. Legg

1982   *The Bannister Allen Plantation (38Ab102) and Thomas B. Clinkscales Farm (38Ab221): Data Recovery in the Richard B. Russell Multiple Resource Area, Abbeville County, South Carolina.* Russell Papers. Submitted to the National Park Service, Carolina Archaeological Services, Columbia.

Dryer, Charles

1920   Genetic Geography. *Annals of the Association of American Geographers* 10:3–16.

Dunbar, Willis F.

1980   *Michigan, a History of the Wolverine State.* Revised edition by George S. May. William B. Eerdmans, Grand Rapids.

Duncan, James S.

1980   The Superorganic in American Cultural Geography. *Annals of the Association of American Geographers* 70:181–98.

Duncan, James, and Nancy Duncan

1988   (Re)Reading the Landscape. *Environment and Planning D: Society and Space 6.* pp. 117–26.

Dunnell, Robert

1987   Geography and Prehistoric Subsistence. In *Landscape and Culture: Geographical and Archaeological Perspectives,* edited by J. M. Wagstaff, pp. 56–76. Basil Blackwell, Oxford.

1992   The Notion Site. In *Space, Time and Archaeological Landscapes,* edited by J. Rossignol and L. Wandsnider pp. 21–42. Plenum Press, New York.

Dunnell, Robert C., and William S. Dancey

1983   The Siteless Survey: A Regional Scale Data Collection Strategy. In *Advances in Archaeological Method and Theory,* vol. 6, edited by Michael Schiffer, pp. 267–87. Academic Press, New York.

Eaton, Clement

1966   *A History of the Old South.* The MacMillan Company, New York.

Ebert, James

1986   *Distributional Archaeology: Non-site Discovery Recording and Analytical Methods.* Ph.D. diss., Dept. of Anthropology, Univ. of New Mexico.

Edgar, Walter

1981   *Sleepy Hollow: The Study of a Rural Community.* Univ. of South Carolina, Columbia.

Edgerton, Robert

1971   *The Individual in Cultural Adaptation.* Univ. of California, Berkeley.

Ehrenreich, Robert M., Carole L. Crumley, and Janet Levy (editors)

1995   *Heterarchy and the Analysis of Complex Societies.* Archaeological Papers of the American Anthropological Association. No. 6. American Anthropological Association, Washington, D.C.

Elliott, Daniel

1990a   Lost City Survey. *LAMAR Briefs* 15, Lamar Institute, Athens.

1990b   *The Lost City Survey: Archaeological Reconnaissance of Nine Eighteenth Century Settlements in Chatham and Effingham Counties.* LAMAR Institute, Athens.

1991   Lost and Found: Eighteenth Century Towns in the Savannah River Region. *Early Georgia* 19(2):61–92.

Elmore Papers

1799–   Elmore Papers. On file, Caroliniana Library,
1850   Univ. of South Carolina, Columbia.

Entrikin, J. Nicholas

1991   *The Betweeness of Place.* Johns Hopkins Univ. Press, Baltimore.

Errante, James R.

1989   The Significance of Waterscapes in the Context of South Carolina's Tidal Rice Growing Plantations. In *Critical Approaches to Archaeology and Anthropology, Annual Papers of the University of South Carolina Anthropology Students Association,* vol. 4, edited by Kathleen Bolen, Kathy Forbes, and Ruth Trocolli, pp. 74–78. Univ. of South Carolina, Columbia.

1991   Underwater Archaeological Sites. In *Acquiring the Past for the Future: The South Carolina Heritage Trust Statewide Assessment of Cultural Sites,* edited and authored by Christopher Judge and Steven Smith, with contributions by James R. Errante, pp. 71–77. South Carolina Institute of Archaeology and Anthropology, Research Manuscript Series 213, Columbia.

1993   *Waterscape Archaeology: A Survey for 18th Century Boat Landings.* Master's thesis, Dept. of Anthropology, Univ. of South Carolina, Columbia.

Eschman, D., and M. Marcus

1972   The Geologic and Topographic Setting of Cities. In *Urbanization and Environment,* edited by

T. Detwyler, and M. Marcus et. al. Duxburg Press, Belmont, California.

Espenshade, Christopher T., and Ramona Grunden
1991   *Archaeological Survey of the Brickyard Plantation Tract, Charleston County, South Carolina.* Brockington and Associates, Inc., Atlanta, Georgia.

Faust, Drew Gilpin
1982   *James Henry Hammond and the Old South: A Design for Mastery.* Louisiana State Univ. Press, Baton Rouge.

Ferguson, Leland G.
1980   Looking for the "Afro" in Colono-Indian Pottery, In *Archaeological Perspectives on Ethnicity in American: Afro-American and Asian-American Culture History,* edited by Robert Schuyler, pp. 14–28. Bayood Monographs in Archaeology no. 1, Baywood Publishing Company, Farmingdale, New York.

1985   Struggling with Pots in Colonial South Carolina. Paper presented at the Eighteenth Annual Meeting of the Society for Historical Archaeology, Boston, Massachusetts.

1986   Slave Settlement and Community Patterns Along the East Branch of the Cooper River: Plans for Research. *South Carolina Antiquities* 18(1, 2):25–32.

1992   *Uncommon Ground: Archaeology and Early African America, 1650–1800.* Smithsonian Institution Press, Washington, D.C.

Ferguson, Leland, and David Babson
1986   *Survey of Plantation Sites along the East Branch of Cooper River: A Model for Predicting Archaeological Site Location.* Ms. on file, Dept. of Anthropology, Univ. of South Carolina, Columbia.

Ferguson, Terry, and Thomas Cowan
1986   *The Early Ironworks of Northwest South Carolina: A Final Report of Investigations Conducted from 1985–1986.* Submitted to the South Carolina Dept. of Archives and History, State Historic Preservation Office, Columbia.

1987   *Investigations into the Ironworks of South-Central North Carolina: A Final Report of Investigations Conducted from 1986–1987.* Submitted to the North Carolina Division of Archives and History, State Historic Preservation Office, Raleigh.

Fick, Sarah
1992   *Architectural and Archaeological Survey of Charleston County.* Submitted to the Charleston County Planning Office by Preservation Consultants, Charleston.

Fields, Barbara
1982   Ideology and Race in American History. In *Region, Race, and Reconstruction,* edited by J. Morgan Kousser and James M. McPherson, pp. 143–77. Oxford Univ. Press, New York.

1990   Slavery, Race and Ideology in the United States of America. *New Left Review* 181:95–118.

Fields, Mamie Garvin, and Karen Fields
1983   *Lemon Swamp and Other Places.* The Free Press, New York.

Fish, Suzanne, Stephen Kowaleski (editors)
1990   *The Archaeology of Regions: A Case Study for Full-Coverage Survey.* Smithsonian Institution Press, Washington, D.C.

Fisher, Charles
1987   The Ceramic Collection from the Continental Army Cantonment at New Windsor, New York. *Historical Archaeology* 21:48–57.

Flannery, Kent V.
1974   Culture History Versus Cultural Process: A Debate in American Archaeology. In *New World Archaeology: Theoretical and Cultural Transformations,* compiled by Ezra B. W. Zubrow, Margaret C. Fritz, and John M. Fritz, pp. 5–8. W. H. Freeman, San Francisco. Originally published in *Scientific American* (Aug. 1967).

Fleetwood, Rusty
1982   *Tidecraft: An Introductory Look at the Boats of the Lower South Carolina, Georgia, and Northeastern Florida: 1650–1950.* Coastal Heritage Society, Savannah.

Fleure, H. J., and H. J. Peake
1927   *Corridors of Time.* Oxford Univ. Press, Oxford.

Force, Peter
1840   *American Archives: Fourth Series* 1–6. M. St. Clair Clarke and Peter Force, Washington.

Ford, Frederick A. (compiler)
1861   *Census of the City of Charleston, South Carolina, for the Year 1861.* Evans and Cogswell, Charleston. On file at the Charleston Library Society, Charleston.

Forney, Sandra J.
1984   Chronological Placement of Materials Associated with the Naval Stores Industry within the National Forests in Florida. Paper presented at the annual meeting of the Society for Historical Archeology, Williamsburg.

Fox-Genovese, Elizabeth
1988   *Within the Plantation Household: Black and White Women of the Old South.* Univ. of North Carolina Press, Chapel Hill.
France, Linda G.
1985   Stratification in South Carolinian Society in 1900. In *Current Research in the Historical Archaeology of the Carolinas,* edited by Jack Wilson Jr., pp. 88–102. Chicora Research Foundation Series 4, Columbia.
Fraser, Walter J., Jr.
1989   *Charleston! Charleston!* Univ. of South Carolina Press, Columbia.
Fuller, George N.
1916   *Economic and Social Beginnings of Michigan, a Study of the Settlement of the Lower Peninsula during the Territorial Period, 1805–1837.* Wynkoop Hallenbeck Crawford Co., Lansing.
Gardner, Robert
1963   *Small Armsmaker.* New York.
Garrow, Patrick H.
1984   The Identification and Use of Context Types in Urban Archaeology. *Southeastern Archaeology* 3(2):91–96.
Gazette of the State of South Carolina
1779   *Gazette of the State of South Carolina,* Nov. 24, 1779. Charleston.
Genovese, Eugene
1974   *Roll, Jordan, Roll.* Pantheon Books, New York.
Giddens, Anthony
1979   *Central Problems in Social Theory.* Univ. of California Press, Berkeley.
Glassie, Henry
1968   *Pattern in the Material Culture of the Eastern United States.* Univ. of Pennsylvania Press, Philadelphia.
1975   *Folk Housing in Middle Virginia: Structural Analysis of Historic Artifacts.* Univ. of Tennessee Press, Knoxville.
Glassow, Michael.
1977   Issues in Evaluating the Significance of Archaeological Resources. *American Antiquity* 42:413–20.
Glen, James
1761   Naval stores. Handout prepared for the Berkeley County Historical Society. Ms. on file, United States Dept. of Agriculture, National Forests in North Carolina, Asheville.
Goodyear, Albert C., L. Mark Raab, and Timothy C. Klinger

1978   Archaeological Research Design. *American Antiquity* 43(2):159–73.
Gould, Richard A.
1983   Looking Below the Surface. In *Shipwreck Anthropology,* edited by Richard Gould, pp. 3–22. Univ. of New Mexico Press, Albuquerque.
Gould, Stephen J.
1981   *The Mismeasure of Man.* W. W. Norton, New York.
Graham, Frank D., and Thomas J. Emery
1945   *Audel's Masons and Builders Guide #1.* Theo. Audel, New York.
Graham Papers
1835   Letter of William Alexander Graham Jr. to William Alexander Graham Sr., Feb. 25, 1835. MS 65–721. Southern Historical Collection, Chapel Hill.
1839   Letter of William Alexander Graham Jr. from Vesuvius Furnace, May 23, 1839. MS 65–721. Southern Historical Collection, Chapel Hill.
Grant, E.
1987   Industry: Landscape and Location. In *Landscape and Culture: Geographical and Archaeological Perspectives,* edited by J. M. Wagstaff, pp. 96–117. Basil Blackwell, Oxford.
Graves, Charles
1854–   Plantation Diary. Planter, Prince William Parish,
55   Granville County, South Carolina. Ms. on file, South Carolina Historical Society, Charleston.
Gray, Marlessa A.
1983   *"The Old Home Place,"* An Archaeological and Historical Investigation of Five Farm Sites Along the Savannah River, Georgia and South Carolina. Russell Papers 1983. Submitted to the Interagency Archeological Services, National Park Service, Atlanta.
Green, Stanton W.
1976   What is a Site? Paper presented at the Archaeological Colloquium Series, South Carolina Institute of Archaeology and Anthropology, Univ. of South Carolina, Columbia.
1992   Review of *The Archaeology of Regions,* edited by Suzanne K. Fish and Stephen A. Kowalewski *Winterthur Portfolio* 26(1):82–85.
Green, Stanton W., and Stephen M. Pearlman (editors)
1980   *The Archaeology of Frontiers and Boundaries.* Academic Press, Orlando.
Green, Stanton, Roy Stine, and Linda Stine
1992   Infinite Landscapes: The Role of View in

Landscape Archaeology. Paper presented at the Anthropology of Human Behavior Through Geographic Information and Analysis: An International Conference, Univ. of California, Santa Barbara.

Green, William
1991   *The Search for Altamaha: The Archaeology and Ethnohistory of an Early 18th Century Yamasee Indian Town.* Master's thesis, Dept. of Anthropology, Univ. of South Carolina, Columbia.

Gregorie, Anne King (editor)
1950   *Records of the Court of Chancery of South Carolina, 1671–1729.* The American Historical Association, Washington, D.C.

Gregory, Derek, and John Urry (editors)
1985   *Social Relations and Spatial Structures.* St. Martin's Press, New York.

Grettler, David J.
1990   *The Landscape of Reform: Society, Environment, and Agricultural Reform in Central Delaware, 1790–1840.* Ph.D. diss., Dept. of History, Univ. of Delaware, Newark.
1991   Farmer Snug and Farmer Slack: The Archaeology of Agricultural Reform in Delaware, 1780–1920. Paper presented at the 1992 Annual Meeting of the Society for Historical Archaeology, Kingston, Jamaica.

Grimes, Kimberly
1985   A Site History of 1927, 1919 Pickens Street. *Notebook,* South Carolina Institute of Archaeology and Anthropology, Columbia.
1989   Investigating Elite Lifeways at the Turn of the Nineteenth Century: A Model from Charleston. Paper presented at the Fifteenth Annual Conference on South Carolina Archaeology, Archeological Society of South Carolina, Columbia.

Grimes, Kimberly, and Martha Zierden
1988   *A Hub of Human Activity: Archaeological Investigations of the Visitor's Reception and Transportation Center.* Archaeological Contributions 19, The Charleston Museum, Charleston.

Grimes, Kimberly, Dale Rosengarten, Martha Zierden, and Elizabeth Alston
1987   *Between the Tracks: The Heritage of Charleston's East Side Community.* Leaflet no. 30, The Charleston Museum, Charleston.

Gunn, Joel, and Carole L. Crumley
1991   Global Energy Balance and Regional Hydrology:

A Burgundian Case Study. *Earth Surface Processes and Landforms* 16(7):579–92.

Gunn, Joel, William J. Folan, and Hubert R. Robichaux
1995   A Landscape Analysis of the Candelaria Watershed in Mexico: Insights into Paleoclimated affecting Upland Horticulture in the Southern Yucatan Peninsula Semi-Karst. *Geoarchaeology* 10:3–42.

Guralnik, David B.
1982   *Webster's New World Dictionary of the American Language.* Warner Books, New York.

Gurcke, Karl
1987   *Bricks and Brickmaking.* Univ. of Idaho Press, Moscow.

Hall, Wesley, and Tucker Littleton
1979   *A Cultural Resource Survey of Selected Portions of the Croatan National Forest, N.C.* Coastal Zone Resources Division of Ocean Data Systems, Wilmington.

Hamer, Friedrich Peter
1982   *Indian Traders, Land and Power—Comparative Study of George Galphin on the Southern Frontier and Three Northern Traders.* Master's thesis, Dept. of History, Univ. of South Carolina, Columbia.

Handy, Ben
1992   Preservation Reaches Out for Cultural Diversity. *Historic Preservation News* (June). Washington, D.C.

Hardesty, Donald L.
1995   Research Questions and Information. *CRM* 18(6) Supplement:4–8.

Hargrove, Thomas H. (editor)
1987   *A Cultural Resource Survey at the U.S. Marine Corps Air Station, Cherry Point, N.C.* Archaeological Research Consultants, Chapel Hill.

Harmon, Michael A., and Rodney J. Snedeker
1988   Tar Kiln Variability and Significance. Paper presented at the Southeastern Archeological Conference, New Orleans.
1989   Croatan National Forest Draft Cultural Resources Overview: Carteret, Craven and Jones Counties, North Carolina. Ms. on file, U.S. Dept. of Agriculture, National Forest Service, Asheville.

Harmon, Michael A., and Rodney J. Snedeker, and A. Scott Ashcraft
1995   *Archaeological Investigation of 31CV160: A Coastal Plain Tar Kiln.* Croatan National Forest, Craven County, North Carolina, USDA National Forests in North Carolina, Asheville.

Harrington, J. C.
1950 Seventeenth Century Brickmaking and Tilemaking at Jamestown, Virginia. *The Virginia Magazine of History and Biography* 58(1):16–39.

Harris, Lynn
1991a South Carolina's Sport Diver Program. Ms. on file, South Carolina Institute of Archaeology and Anthropology, Columbia.
1991b *Laurel Hill Barge Number 2*. Research Manuscript Series 214. South Carolina Institute of Archaeology and Anthropology, Univ. of South Carolina, Columbia.
1992 *The Waccamaw–Richmond Hill Waterfront Project 1991*. South Carolina Institute of Archaeology and Anthropology, Univ. of South Carolina, Columbia.

Hart, James Frazer
1975 *The Look of the Land*. Prentice-Hall, Englewood Cliffs.
1977 Land Rotation in Appalachia. *Geographical Review* 67:148–66.

Hart, Linda F.
1986 Excavations at the Limerick Tar Kiln Site— 38BK472. Ms. on file, U.S. Forest Service, Francis Marion National Forest, McClellanville.

Hartley, Michael O.
1984 *The Ashley River: A Survey of Seventeenth Century Sites*. Research Manuscript Series 192. Institute of Archeology and Anthropology, Univ. of South Carolina, Columbia.

Hartshorne, Richard
1939 *The Nature of Geography*. Association of American Geographers, Lancaster.

Harvey, David
1990 Between Space and Time: Reflections on the Geographical Imagination. In *Annals of the Association of American Geographers* 80:418–34.

Hayden, Dolores
1995 *The Power of Place: Urban Landscapes as Public History*. MIT Press, Cambridge, Massachusetts.

Heintzelman, Andrea J.
1986 Colonial Wharf Construction: Uncovering the Untold Past. *The Log of Mystic Seaport*. Winter issue.

Henry, Susan L.
1995 The National Register and the 20th Century: Is there Room for Archaeology? *CRM* 18(6) Supplement:9–12.

Herbst, Jergen
1961 Social Darwinism and the History of American Geography, *Proceedings of the American Philosophical Society* 105:538–44.

Herman, Bernard L.
1989 Rethinking the Charleston Single House. Paper presented to the Vernacular Architecture Forum, St. Louis, Missouri.

Herold, Elaine
1978 *Preliminary Report on the Research at the Heyward-Washington House*. On file, The Charleston Museum, Charleston.
1980 *Historical and Archeological Survey of Willtown Bluff Plantation, Charleston County, South Carolina*. The Charleston Museum, Charleston.
1981a Historical Archaeological Report on the Meeting Street Office Building Site. Ms. on file, The Charleston Museum, Charleston.
1981b *Archaeological Research at the Exchange Building, Charleston, S.C.: 1979–1980*. Ms. on file, The Charleston Museum, Charleston.
1984 Archaeological and Historical Research at 33 Broad Street, Charleston, S.C. Ms. on file, The Charleston Museum, Charleston.

Herold, Elaine B., and Elizabeth Thomas
1981a History of the Charleston Center Area. Ms. on file, The Charleston Museum, Charleston.
1981b Historical Archaeological Survey of the First Citizens Bank and Trust Project on South Market Street, Charleston, SC. Ms. on file, The Charleston Museum, Charleston.

Herold, Elaine B., and Kay R. Scruggs
1976 *An Archaeological and Historical Survey of the Grove and Flagg Plantations*. The Charleston Museum, Charleston, South Carolina.

Hibbard, Benjamin Horace
1965 *A History of the Public Land Policies*. Univ. of Wisconsin Press, Madison.

Hilligan, Jacob C.
1790 *The Charleston Directory and Revenue System*. T. B. Bowen, Charleston, South Carolina.

Hirsh, Eric, and Michael O'Hanlon (editors)
1995 *The Anthropology of Landscape: Perspectives on Place and Space*. Clarendon Press, Oxford.

Hockensmith, Charles D.
1986 Euro-American Petroglyphs Associated with Pine Tar Kilns and Lye Leaching Devices in Kentucky. *Tennessee Anthropologist* 11(2):100–31.

Hodder, Ian

1986   *Reading the Past: Current Approaches to Interpretation in Archaeology.* Cambridge Univ. Press, Cambridge.

1987   Converging Traditions: The Search for Symbolic Meanings in Archaeology and Geography. *Landscape and Culture: Geographical and Archaeological Perspectives,* edited by J. M. Wagstaff, pp. 134–45. Basil Blackwell, New York.

1990   *The Domestication of Europe.* Blackwell, London.

Hodder, Ian, and Charles Orton

1976   *Spatial Analysis in Archaeology.* Cambridge Univ. Press, Cambridge.

Holcomb, Brian

1978   *Winton (Barnwell) County, South Carolina: Minutes of County Court and Will Book 1, 1785–1791.* Southern Historical Press, Easley, South Carolina.

Hollings, Marie F.

1978   *Brickwork of Charleston to 1780.* Master's thesis, Dept. of History, Univ. of South Carolina, Columbia.

Honerkamp, Nicholas

1987   Household or Neighborhoods: Finding Appropriate Levels of Research in Urban Archaeology. Paper presented at the 1987 Meetings of the Society for Historical Archaeology, Savannah.

Honerkamp, Nicholas, and Charles H. Fairbanks

1984   Definition of Site Formation Processes in Urban Contexts. *American Archaeology* 4(1):60–66.

Honerkamp, Nicholas, and Martha Zierden

1989   *Charleston Place: The Archaeology of Urban Life.* The Charleston Museum Leaflet no. 31, Charleston.

1996   The Evolution of Interpretation at Charleston Place. In *Digging for the Truth: Public Interpretation of Archaeological Sites,* edited by John Jameson, National Park Service [in press].

Honerkamp, Nicholas, and Martha Zierden (editors)

1984   Archaeological Approaches to Urban Society: Charleston, South Carolina. *South Carolina Antiquities,* vol. 16.

Honerkamp, Nicholas, and R. Bruce Council

1984   Individual versus Corporate Adaptation in Urban Contexts. *Tennessee Anthropologist* IX(1):22–31.

Honerkamp, Nicholas, R. Bruce Council, and M. Elizabeth Will

1982   *An Archaeological Investigation of the Charleston Convention Center Site, Charleston, South Carolina.* Ms. on file, U.S. Department of the Interior, National Park Service, Atlanta.

Horlbeck Brothers

1770   Papers. Cited in Research Notes of Harriet Stoney Simons. Collections of the South Carolina Historical Society, Charleston.

1856–75 Day Book. Ms. on file, South Carolina Historical Society, Charleston.

Horne, Robert

1911   A Brief Description of the Province of Carolina, by Robert Horne [1666]. In *Narratives of Early Carolina, 1650–1708,* edited by Alexander S. Salley Jr., pp. 63–74. Charles Scribner's Sons, New York.

Horton, J. Wright, and J. Robert Butler

1981   Geology and Mining History of the Kings Mountain Belt in the Carolinas—A Summary and Status Report. In *Geological Investigations of the Kings Mountain Belt and Adjacent Areas in the Carolinas,* edited by J. W. Horton Jr., J. R. Butler, and David M. Milton, pp. 194–207. A Carolina Geological Society Field Trip Guidebook. South Carolina Geological Survey, Columbia.

Hudgins, Bert

1961   *Michigan, Geographic Backgrounds in the Development of the Commonwealth.* By the author, Detroit.

Hudson, John C.

1969   A Locational Model of Rural Settlement. *Annals of the Association of American Geographers* 59:365–81.

Huger, Sarah E.

1812   Letter to Mrs. Daniel Horry. Pinckney-Lowndes Papers, South Carolina Historical Society, Charleston.

Ingerson, Alice

1994   Tracking and Testing the Nature/Culture Dichotomy in Practice. In *Historical Ecology: Cultural Knowledge and Changing Landscapes,* edited by Carole L. Crumley, pp. 43–66. School of American Research Press, Santa Fe.

Irving, John B., M.D.

1932   *A Day on the Cooper River.* 1969 reprint, R. L. Bryn Co., Columbia, South Carolina.

Jackson, James Brinckerhof

1984   *Discovering the Vernacular Landscape.* Yale Univ. Press, New Haven.

Jackson, Peter H.
1989   *Maps of Meaning.* Unwin Hyman, London.

Jackson, Susan H., and Lesley M. Drucker
1985   *An Archaeological Inventory Survey of Development Parcels in Four State Parks of the Richard B. Russell Multiple Resource Area, Abbeville and Anderson Counties, South Carolina.* Resource Studies Series 79. Carolina Archaeological Services, Columbia.

James, Preston E.
1972   *All Possible Worlds: A History of Geographical Ideas.* Bobbs-Merrill, Indianapolis.

James, Preston, and Geoffrey Martin
1981   *All Possible Worlds: A History of Geographical Ideas.* Second Edition. Wiley and Sons, New York.

Jewitt, Llewellyn
1970   *The Ceramic Art of Great Britain.* Ward Lock Repairs, London.

Jochim, Michael
1983   *Strategies for Survival: Cultural Behavior in Ecological Context.* Academic Press, New York.

Johnson, Michael P., and James L. Roark
1984a   *No Chariot Let Down.* W. W. Norton, New York.
1984b   *Black Masters.* W. W. Norton, New York.

Johnston, R. J.
1991   *Geography and Geographers: Anglo-American Geography Since 1945.* 4th ed., Edward Arnold, London.

Jones, Olive, and Catherine Sullivan
1985   *The Parks Canada Glass Glossary for the Description of Containers, Tablewares, Flat Glass, and Closures.* Parks Canada, Ottawa.

Jones, Thomas
1844   Survey map of Parkers Island. Microfilm on file, South Carolina Department of Archives and History, Columbia.

Joseph, J. W.
1987   Highway 17 Revisited: The Archaeology of Task Labor. *South Carolina Antiquities* 19(1–2):29–34.
1989   Pattern and Process in the Plantation Archaeology of the Lowcountry of Georgia and South Carolina. *Historical Archaeology* 23(1):55–68.
1991   White Columns and Black Hands: Class and Classification in the Plantation Ideology of the Georgia and South Carolina Lowcountry. Paper presented at the symposium entitled Plantation Archeology of the Virginia and Maryland Tidewater Region and the Lowcountry of Georgia and South Carolina: A Synthesis and Comparison. 1991 Annual Meeting of The Society for Historical Archeology, Richmond, Virginia.

Joseph, J. W., and George F. Tyson Jr.
1989   *A Phase I Cultural Resources Survey of the Virgin Islands Port Authority Property, Estate Negro Bay, St. Croix, U.S.V.I.* New South Associates Technical Report 5. Submitted to Bioimpact. New South Associates, Stone Mountain, Georgia.

Joseph, J. W., and Mary Beth Reed
1991   *An Inventory of Archeological Resources and Recommended Preservation and Research Plan, McLeod Plantation, James Island, South Carolina.* New South Associates Technical Report 59. Submitted to Jaeger/Pyburn. New South Associates, Stone Mountain, Georgia.

Joseph, J. W., and Rita Elliott
1995   *Restoration Archaeology at the Charleston County Courthouse site, (38CH1498), Charleston, South Carolina.* MS on file, County of Charleston.

Joseph, J. W., Guy G. Weaver, Patrick H. Garrow, Mary Beth Reed, and Jonathon A. Bloom
1989   *Nineteenth to Twentieth Century Agriculture in Southern Illinois: Pope County Farmstead Thematic Study, Shawnee National Forest,* edited by Charles C. Cobb, Patrick H. Garrow, and Guy G. Weaver. Submitted to the U.S. Forest Service, Shawnee National Forest. Garrow and Associates, Atlanta.

Joseph, J. W., Mary Beth Reed, and Charles E. Cantley
1991   *Agrarian Life, Romantic Death: Archeological and Historical Testing and Data Recovery for the I–85 Northern Alternative, Spartanburg County, South Carolina.* New South Associates Technical Report 39. Submitted to the South Carolina Dept. of Highways and Public Transportation. New South Associates, Stone Mountain, Georgia.

Joseph, Katherine A.
1987   Agricultural Construction on the East Branch of the Cooper River 1770–1825. Paper presented at the 1987 Southeastern Archaeological Conference, Charleston.

Joyce, Jane Sally
1981   *A Settlement Pattern Study of the War Eagle Creek Region, Madison County, Arkansas, During the Pioneer Period.* Master's thesis, Dept. of Anthropology, Univ. of Arkansas, Fayetteville.

Joyner, Charles
1984   *Down by the Riverside.* Univ. of Illinois Press, Chicago.

Judge, Christopher, and Steven D. Smith
1991   *Acquiring the Past for the Future: The South Carolina Heritage Trust Statewide Assessment of Cultural Sites.* Research Manuscript Series 213, South Carolina Institute of Archaeology and Anthropology, Univ. of South Carolina, Columbia.

Jurney, David H., Susan A. Lebo, and Melissa M. Green
1988   *Historic Farming on the Hogwallow Prairies, Ethnoarchaeological Investigations of the Mountain Creek Area, North Central Texas.* Report submitted to the U.S. Army Corps of Engineers, Fort Worth District. Archaeology Research Program, Southern Methodist Univ., Dallas.

Keith, Authur, and D. B. Sterrett
1931   Gaffney–Kings Mountain Folio: U.S. Geological Survey Folio, No. 222, 13 pages.

Kelso, William, and Rachel Most (editors)
1990   *Earth Patterns: Essays in Landscape Archaeology.* Univ. Press of Virginia, Charlottesville.

King, Julia A.
1991   *Recommendations for the Management of Archaeological Resources Historic Snee Farm.* Submitted to Friends of Historic Snee Farm, Charleston, South Carolina.

King's Mountain Iron Company Minute Book
1837–67 Minute Book of the Stock Holders of the King's Mountain Iron Company. South Carolina, Dept. of Archives and History, Columbia.

Kniffen, Fred
1951   Geography and the Past *Journal of Geography* 51:126–29.
1960   To Know The Land and Its People. *Landscape* 9(3):20–23.
1962   Louisiana House Types. In *Readings in Cultural Geography,* edited by Philip Wagner and Marvin Mikesell, pp. 157–69. Univ. of Chicago Press, Chicago. Originally published in 1936 in *Annals of the Association of American Geographers.*
1965   Folk Housing: Key to Diffusion. *Annals of the Association of American Geographers* 55:549–77.
1974   Material Culture in the Geographic Interpretation of Landscape. In *The Human Mirror: Material and Spatial Images of Man,* edited by Miles Richardson, pp. 252–67. Louisiana State Univ. Press, Baton Rouge.

Knutson, Lawrence L.
1992   Vacation Travel Likely To Be Up. *The State,* May 20. Columbia.

Kovacik, Charles F., and John J. Winberry
1989   *South Carolina: The Making of a Landscape.* Univ. of South Carolina Press, Columbia. Originally published in 1987 as *South Carolina: A Geography.* Westview Press, Boulder and London.

Kryder-Reid, Elizabeth
1994   As Is the Gardener, So Is the Garden: The Archaeology of Landscape as Myth. In *Historical Archaeology of the Chesapeake,* edited by Paul Shackel and Barbara Little, pp. 131–48. Smithsonian Institution Press, Washington, D.C.

Lander, Ernest M., Jr.
1953   Thomas Cooper's Views in Retirement. *The South Carolina Historical and Genealogical Magazine* 54(1):173–84.
1954   The Iron Industry in Ante-Bellum South Carolina. *Journal of Southern History* 20(3):337–55.

Landrum, John
1900   *The History of Spartanburg County.* Franklin Printing and Publishing, Atlanta.

Lanter, David
1991   Design of a Lineage-Based Meta-Data Base for GIS. *Cartography and Geographic Information Systems* 18(4):255–61.

Ledbetter, Jerald, Dean Wood, Karen Wood, Robbie Ethridge, and Chad Braley
1987   *Cultural Resources Survey of Allatoona Lake Area 1.* Submitted to the U.S. Army Corps of Engineers, Mobile.

Leech, Richard W., Jr., and Judy L. Wood
1994   Archival Research, Archaeological Survey, and Site Monitoring Backriver Chatham County, Georgia, and Jasper County, South Carolina. U.S. Army Corps of Engineers, Savannah District.

Lees, William B.
1980   *Limerick, Old and in the Way: Archaeological Investigations at the Limerick Plantation, Berkeley County, South Carolina.* Anthropological Studies 5. South Carolina Institute of Archaeology and Anthropology, Columbia.

Lees, William B., and Kathryn M. Kimery-Lees
1979   The Function of Colono-Indian Ceramics: Insights from Limerick Plantation, South Carolina. *Historical Archaeology* 13:1–13.

Lefebvre, Henri
1991   *The Production of Space*, translated by Donald Nicholson–Smith. Basil Blackwell, Cambridge.

Legg, James B., and Steven D. Smith
1989   *"The Best Ever Occupied . . ." Archaeological Investigations of a Civil War Encampment on Folly Island, South Carolina*. Research Manuscript Series 209. South Carolina Institute of Archaeology and Anthropology, Columbia.

Leighly, John
1937   Some Comments on Contemporary Geographic Method. *Annals of the Association of American Geographers* 27:125–41.

Leone, Mark P., and Parker B. Potter Jr.
1992   Legitimation and Classification of Archeological Sites. *American Antiquity* 57(1):137–45.

Lepionka, Larry
1985   Habersham House Excavations: First Phase. Ms. on file, Historic Beaufort Foundation, Beaufort.
1989   Excavations at 926 Bay Street, Beaufort, South Carolina: A Report on Preliminary Investigations. Ms. on file, South Carolina Institute of Archaeology and Anthropology, Columbia.
1990   Excavations at 926 Bay Street: Preliminary Report on Skeletal Remains. Ms. on file, South Carolina Institute of Archaeology and Anthropology, Columbia.

Lesene, Joab
1961   The Nesbitt Manufacturing Company's Debt to the Bank of the State of South Carolina. *The Proceedings of the South Carolina Historical Association*, 15–22. Columbia.
1970   *The Bank of the State of South Carolina: A General and Political History*. Univ. of South Carolina Press, Columbia.

Lesley, John
1859   *Iron Manufacturer's Guide to the Furnaces, Forge's, and Rolling Mills of the United States*. John Wiley, New York.

Lewis, George S.
1992   Volunteer Partnership Works Well. *Federal Archeology Report* 5(1):9–10.

Lewis, Kenneth E.
1976   *Camden: A Frontier Town in 18th Century South Carolina*. Anthropological Studies 2, South Carolina Institute of Archaeology and Anthropology, Columbia.
1979   *Hampton: Initial Archeological Investigations at an Eighteenth Century Rice Plantation in the Santee Delta, South Carolina*. Research Manuscript Series no. 151. South Carolina Institute of Archeology and Anthropology, Columbia.
1982   Settlement and Activity Patterning on Two Rice Plantations in the South Carolina Low Country. *The Conference on Historic Site Archaeology Papers 1979* 14:1–12. South Carolina Institute of Archaeology and Anthropology, Univ. of South Carolina, Columbia.
1983   Archaeological Investigations in the Interior of McCrady's Longroom, 38CH559, Charleston, S.C. *Notebook* 15(3–4), South Carolina Institute of Archaeology and Anthropology, Columbia.
1984   *The American Frontier: An Archaeological Study of Settlement Pattern and Process*. Academic Press, New York.
1985a   Functional Variation Among Settlements on the South Carolina Frontier: An Archaeological Perspective. In *The Archaeology of Frontiers and Boundaries*, edited by Stanton Green and Stephen Perlman, pp. 251–74. Academic Press, Orlando.
1985b   Plantation Layout and Function in the South Carolina Lowcountry. In *The Archaeology of Slavery and Plantation Life*, edited by Theresa A. Singleton, pp. 35–65. Academic Press, Orlando.
1989a   *General Processes and Particular Variables in the Shaping of Frontier Settlement Patterns*. Illinois Cultural Resources Studies.
1989b   Settlement Function and Archaeological Patterning in a Historic Urban Context: the Woodrow Wilson House in Columbia, S.C. In *Studies in South Carolina Archaeology*, edited by Albert Goodyear and Glen Hanson, pp. 225–52. Anthropological Studies 9, South Carolina Institute of Archaeology and Anthropology, Columbia.
1991a   General Processes and Particular Variables in the Shaping of Frontier Settlement Patterns. In *Landscape, Architecture, and Artifacts: Historical Archaeology of Nineteenth Century Illinois*, edited by Erick K. Schroeder, pp. 1–13. Illinois Cultural Resources Study 15, Springfield.
1991b   Motivations for Colonization and their Effect on Settlement Patterning in Nineteenth Century Michigan. Paper presented at the 1991 Illinois Historical Archaeology Conference, Springfield.

Lewis, Kenneth E., and Donald L. Hardesty
1979   *Middleton Place: Initial Archeological Investigations at an Ashley River Rice Plantation*. Research

Manuscript Series 148. South Carolina Institute of Archeology and Anthropology, Columbia.

Lewis, Kenneth E., and Helen W. Haskell
1980   *Hampton II: Further Archeological Investigations at a Santee River Rice Plantation.* Research Manuscript Series 161. South Carolina Institute of Archeology and Anthropology, Columbia.

Lewis, Lynne
1978   *Drayton Hall: Preliminary Archaeological Investigation at a Lowcountry Plantation.* The Univ. Press of Virginia, Charlottesville.

1985   The Planter Class: The Archaeological Record at Drayton Hall. In *The Archaeology of Slavery and Plantation Life,* edited by Theresa A. Singleton, pp. 121–40. Academic Press, Orlando.

Lewis, Peirce F.
1979   Axioms for Reading the Landscape: Some Guides to the American Scene. In *The Interpretation of Ordinary Landscapes,* edited by Donald W. Meinig, pp. 11–32. Oxford Univ. Press, New York.

Ley, David
1985   Cultural/Humanistic Geography. *Progress in Human Geography* 9:415–23.

Leyburn, James G.
1935   *Frontier Folkways.* Yale Univ. Press, New Haven.

Lieber, Oscar
1856   *Report on the Survey of South Carolina: Being the First Annual Report to the General Assembly of South Carolina, Embracing the Progress of the Survey During the Year 1856.* R. W. Gibbes, Columbia.

1858   *Report on the Survey of South Carolina: Being the Second Annual Report to the General Assembly of South Carolina, Embracing the Progress of the Survey During the Year 1858.* R. W. Gibbes, Columbia.

Lightfoot, Kent G., and Antoinette Martinez
1995   Frontiers and Boundaries in Archaeological Perspective. In *Annual Review of Anthropology,* vol. 24, edited by William Durham, E. Valentine Daniel, and Bambi Schieffelin, pp. 471–92. Annual Reviews, Palo Alto, California.

Lincoln County Deeds
1786   Book 17:26, 32. Lincoln County Courthouse, Lincolnton.

1793   Book 19:78. Lincoln County Courthouse, Lincolnton.

Linder, Suzanne L.
1982   *They Came by Train and Chose to Remain: The Importance of Moore County Railroads, 1850–1900.* Richmond Technical College, Hamlet.

Littlefield, Daniel C.
1981   *Rice and Slaves: Ethnicity and the Slave Trade in Colonial South Carolina.* Louisiana State Univ. Press, Baton Rouge.

Lloyd, Nathaniel
1925   *A History of English Brickwork.* H. Greville Montgomery, London, England.

Lofgren, O.
1981   Manniskan i landskapet-landsapet i manniskan. *Tradition och miljo,* edited by L. Honko and O. Lofgren, pp. 235–61. Lund.

Loftfield, Thomas C.
1991   *Archeological/Historical Reconnaissance of Three Soil Compaction Study Plots near Pinecliff in Croatan National Forest, Craven County, North Carolina.* Dept. of Anthropology, Univ. of North Carolina at Wilmington. Submitted to the U.S. Dept. of Agriculture, National Forests in North Carolina, Croatan National Forest, Asheville.

Longwoods International
1991   Executive Summary: South Carolina's Position in the U.S. Touring Vacation Market. Longwoods Travel USA. Submitted to the South Carolina Dept. of Parks, Recreation, and Tourism.

Lossing, Benson
1859   *The Pictoral Field-Book of the Revolution.* Harper Brothers, New York.

Lounsbury, Carl
1994   *An Illustrated Glossary of Early Southern Architecture and Landscape.* Oxford Univ. Press, New York.

Lovingood, Paul E., Jr., and John C. Purvis
n.d.   The Nature of Precipitation: South Carolina, 1941–1970. South Carolina Crop and Livestock Reporting Service, U.S. Dept. of Agriculture. Ms. on file, Dept. of Geography, Univ. of South Carolina, Columbia.

Lowenthal, David
1961   Geography, Experience, and Imagination: Towards A Geographical Epistemology. *Annals of the Association of American Geographers* 51:241–60.

1977   The Bicentennial Landscape: A Mirror Held Up to the Past. *Geographical Review* 67:253–67.

1985   *The Past Is a Foreign Country.* Cambridge Univ. Press, New York.

Marquardt, William H., and Carole L. Crumley
1987   Theoretical Issues in the Analysis of Spatial Patterning. In *Regional Dynamics, Burgundian*

Landscapes in Historical Perspective, edited by
Carole L. Crumley and William H. Marquardt,
pp. 1–18. Academic Press, San Diego.

Mathews, Maurice
1954   A Contemporary View of Carolina in 1680. *South
Carolina Historical Magazine* 55:153–59.

McAlester, Virginia, and Lee McAlester
1984   *A Field Guide to American Houses.* Albert A.
Knopf, New York.

McClelland, Linda F., J. Timothy Keller, Genevieve Keller,
and Robert Melnick
1990   *Guidelines for Evaluating and Documenting Rural
Historic Landscapes.* National Register Bulletin
30. Washington, D.C.

McCurry, Stephanie
1988   *Defense of Their World: Gender, Class, and the
Yeomanry of the South Carolina Low Country,
1860–1980.* Ph.D. diss., Dept. of History, State
University of New York, Binghamton. Univ.
Microfilms, Ann Arbor.

McCuster, John, and Russell Menard
1985   *The Economy of British America, 1607–1789.* Univ.
of North Carolina Press, Chapel Hill.

McElligott, Carroll Ainsworth
1989   *Charleston Residents 1782–1794.* Heritage Books,
Bowie, Maryland.

McGreevy, Patrick
1994   *Imagining Niagara: The Meaning and Making of
Niagara Falls.* Univ. of Massachusetts Press,
Amherst.

McKivergan, David, Jr.
1991   *Migration and Settlement Among the Yamasee of
South Carolina.* Master's thesis, Dept. of Anthropology, Univ. of South Carolina, Columbia.

Mears and Turnbull (compilers)
1859   *The Charleston Directory.* Walker Evans and Co.,
Charleston, South Carolina.

Meinig, Donald W.
1979a The Beholding Eye, Ten Versions of the Same
Scene. In *The Interpretation of Ordinary Land-
scapes,* edited by D. W. Meinig, pp. 33–48. Oxford
Univ. Press, New York.
1979b Reading the Landscape: An Appreciation of W. G.
Hoskins and J. B. Jackson. In *The Interpretation of
Ordinary Landscapes,* edited by D. W. Meinig, pp.
195–244. Oxford Univ. Press, New York.
1990   Foreword. In *The Making of the American
Landscape,* edited by Michael Conzen, pp. xv–xvi.
Unwin Hyman, Boston.

Meriwether, Robert L.
1940   *The Expansion of South Carolina, 1729–1765.*
Southern Publishers, Kingsport, Tennessee.

Merrens, Harry R.
1964   *Colonial North Carolina in the Eighteenth
Century: A Study in Historical Geography.* Univ. of
North Carolina Press, Chapel Hill.

Messenger, Phyllis
1994   The Future of the Past: SAA Maps a Long-Term
Strategy. *Archaeology and Public Education
Newsletter* 5(2):1, 3, 11. Society for American
Archaeology, Public Education Committee,
Washington, D.C.

Michie, James L.
1990   *Richmond Hill Plantation 1810–1868: The
Discovery of Antebellum Life on a Waccamaw Rice
Plantation.* The Reprint Company, South
Carolina.

Mikesell, Marvin W.
1978   Tradition and Innovation in Cultural Geography.
Annals of the Association of American Geographers
68:1–16.
1979b Reading the Landscape: An Appreciation of W. G.
Hoskins and J. B. Jackson. In *The Interpretation of
Ordinary Landscapes,* edited by D. W. Meinig, pp.
195–244. Oxford Univ. Press, New York.

Miller, David Harry, and Jerome O. Steffen
1977   Introduction. In *The Frontier, Comparative
Studies,* edited by David Harry Miller and Jerome
O. Steffen, pp. 3–10. Univ. of Oklahoma Press,
Norman.

Miller, George
1980   Classification and Economic Scaling of 19th
Century Ceramics. *Historical Archaeology* 14:1–40.
1991   A Revised Set of CC Index Values for Classification and Economic Scaling of English Ceramics
from 1787 to 1880. *Historical Archaeology*
25(1):1–25.

Miller, Henry
1983   *A Search for the "Citty of Saint Maries."* St. Mary's
City Archaeological Series 1, St. Mary's City,
Maryland.
1986   *Discovering Maryland's First City: A Summary
Report on the 1981–1984 Archaeological Excavations in St. Mary's City, Maryland.* St. Mary's City
Archaeology Series 2, St. Mary's City, Maryland.
1988   Baroque Cities in the Wilderness: Archaeology
and Urban Development in the Colonial
Chesapeake. *Historical Archaeology* 22(2):57–73.

1994   The Country's House Site: An Archaeological Study of a Seventeenth-Century Domestic Landscape. In *Historical Archaeology of the Chesapeake,* edited by Paul Shackel and Barbara Little, pp. 65–84. Smithsonian Institution Press, Washington, D.C.

Mills, James O.
1988   Investigations at the Slave Settlement, Richmond Hill Plantation, Georgetown County, South Carolina. In *The Search for Architectural Remains at the Planter's House and Slave Settlement, Richmond Hill Plantation, Georgetown County, South Carolina.* Research Manuscript Series 205, Part 2, South Carolina Institute of Archaeology and Anthropology, Univ. of South Carolina, Columbia.

Mills, Robert
1972   *Statistics of South Carolina.* Originally published 1826. Reprint, Hurlbut and Lloyd, Charleston.
1979   Mills' Atlas of South Carolina Originally published 1825. Reprint, A Press, Greenville.

Mohl, Raymond, and Neil Betten
1970   *Urban America in Historical Perspective.* Weybright and Talley, New York.

Moir, Randall W.
1982   Sheet Refuse: An Indicator of Past Lifeways. In *Settlement of the Prairie Margin: Archaeology of the Richland Creek Reservoir, Navarro and Freestone Counties, Texas, 1980–1981: A Research Synopsis,* edited by Mark L. Raab, pp. 139–52. Archaeological Monographs 1. Archaeology Research Laboratory, Southern Methodist Univ., Dallas.

Moran, Emilio
1979   *Human Adaptability.* Duxbury Press, North Scituate.

Morgan, Philip K.
1982   Work and Culture: The Task System and the World of Lowcountry Blacks, 1700 to 1880. *William and Mary Quarterly* 39(4):563–99.

Moss, Bobby
1970   Cooperville: Iron Capital of South Carolina. *South Carolina History Illustrated* 1 (2):32–35, 64–65.
1972   *The Old Iron District: A Study of the Development of Cherokee County—1750–1897.* Jacobs Press, Clinton, South Carolina.
1981   The Old Iron District—a Legacy of Iron Mining and Manufacturing in South Carolina. In:

Geological Investigations of the Kings Mountain Belt and Adjacent Areas in the Carolinas, edited by J. W. Horton Jr., J. R. Butler, and David M. Milton. Carolina Geological Society Field Trip Guidebook. South Carolina Geological Survey, Columbia.

Nash, Gary
1988   *Forging Freedom: The Formation of Philadelphia's Black Community, 1720–1840.* Harvard Univ. Press, Cambridge, Massachusetts.

National Park Service
n.d.   *Planning Questions 1–12, Interpreting the Secretary of the Interior's "Standards for Preservation Planning."* Resources Division, Preservation Planning Interagency, Washington, D.C.
1989   *The Section 110 Guidelines: Annotated Guidelines for Federal Agency Responsibilities under Section 110 of the National Historic Preservation Act. Working with Section 106.* Advisory Council on Historic Preservation, U.S. Dept. of the Interior, Washington.
1990   *Federal Archeology Report,* June.
1991   *Federal Archeology Report,* Sept.
1992   *Federal Archeology Report,* Mar.

Naveh, Zev, and Arthur S. Lieberman
1984   *Landscape Ecology: Theory and Application.* Springer-Verlag, New York.

Nelson, Lee
1968   Nail Chronology as an Aid to Dating Old Buildings. *History News* 23(11):495–6174.

Neumann, Loretta
1992   Current Archaeological Issues in Congress and the Administration. *Society for American Archaeology Newsletter* 10(2):3.

Neve, Richard
1726   *The City and County Purchaser's and Builder's Dictionary: or the Complete Builder's Guide.* 1969 reprint, Augustus M. Kelley, Publishers, New York.

Newton, Milton B., Jr.
1974   Cultural Preadaptation of the Upland South. In *Man and Cultural Heritage,* edited by Bob F. Perkins, pp. 143–54. Papers in honor of Fred B. Kniffen, Geoscience and Man, V. Baton Rouge.

Newton, Milton B., and Linda Pulliam-di Napoli
1977   Log Houses as Public Occasions: A Historical Theory. *Annals of the Association of American Geographers* 67:360–83.

Nietschmann, B.
1973   *Between Land and Water.* New York, Seminar Press.

Noël Hume, Ivor
1963   *Here Lies Virginia.* Alfred A. Knopf, New York.
1975   *Historical Archaeology.* W. W. Norton and Co., New York.
1980   *A Guide to Artifacts of Colonial America.* Alfred A. Knopf, New York.

Nott, Josiah C., and George Gliddon
1854   *Types of Mankind.* Philadelphia.

Oakes, James
1982   *The Ruling Race: A History of American Slaveholders.* Alfred A. Knopf, New York.

Oakes, Laura S.
1987   Epona in the Aeduan Landscape: Transfunctional Deity Under Changing Rule. In *Regional Dynamics, Burgundian Landscapes in Historical Perspective,* edited by Carole Crumley and William Marquardt, pp. 295–333. Academic Press, San Diego.

Oldmixon, John
1969   *The British Empire in America Containing the History of the Discovery, Settlement, Progress and State of the British colonies on the Continent and Islands of America.* Originally published 1741. Reprint, Economic Classics, New York.

Olmsted, Denison
1827   *Papers on Agricultural Subjects and Professor Olmsteads [sic] Report on the Geology of North Carolina Part 2.* J. Galfs and Son, Raleigh.

Orser, Charles E., Jr.
1986   The Archaeological Recognition of the Squad System in Postbellum Cotton Plantations. *Southeastern Archaeology* 5(1):11–20.
1988   *The Material Basis of the Postbellum Tenant Plantation, Historical Archaeology in the South Carolina Piedmont.* Univ. of Georgia Press, Athens.

Orser, Charles E., Jr., and Annette M. Nekola
1985   Plantation Settlement from Slavery to Tenancy: An Example from a Piedmont Plantation in South Carolina. In *The Archaeology of Slavery and Plantation Life,* edited by Theresa A. Singleton, pp. 67–94. Academic Press, Orlando.

Orser, Charles E., Jr., and Claudia C. Holland
1984   Let Us Praise Famous Men, Accurately: Toward a More Complete Understanding of Postbellum Southern Agricultural Practices. *Southeastern Archaeology* 3:111–20.

Orser, Charles E., Jr., Annette M. Nekola, and James L. Roark
1982   *Exploring the Rustic Life: Multidisciplinary Research at Millwood Plantation, a Large Piedmont Plantation in Abbeville County, South Carolina, and Elbert County, Georgia.* Russell Papers. Submitted to the National Park Service. Mid-American Research Center, Loyola Univ. of Chicago.

Orvin, Maxwell Clayton
1961   *In South Carolina Waters 1861–1865.* Charleston.
1973   *Historic Berkeley County, South Carolina, 1671–1900.* Comprint, Charleston.

Ottosen, Ann I., and Timothy B. Riordan
1986   *Report on Investigations Phase I Research and Recovery Program for Historic Resources Cultural Resource Effects Mitigation Plan, Rocky Mountain Pumped Storage, Floyd County, Georgia.* Submitted to the Georgia Power Company, Atlanta.

Otto, John Solomon
1984   *Cannon's Point Plantation, 1794–1860.* Academic Press, New York.

Palmetto Project
1992   South Carolina Sets Sail on a Year of Discovery. *Palmetto Progress,* Mar. 1992. Charleston.

Parkins, Almon Ernest
1918   *The Historical Geography of Detroit.* Michigan Historical Commission, Lansing.

Paskoff, Paul
1980   Labor Productivity and Managerial Efficiency against a Static Technology: The Pennsylvania Iron Industry, 1750–1800. *Journal of Economic History* 15:129–35.
1983   *Industrial Evolution: Organization, Structure, and Growth of the Pennsylvania Iron Industry, 1750–1860.* Johns Hopkins Univ. Press, Baltimore.

Paxton, Gregory
1992   Develop Partnerships for Successful Preservation. *Historic Preservation News,* May 1992. Washington, D.C.

Payne, Robert
1840   Plat of Three Tracts of Land belonging to John and Patrick O'Neill. South Carolina Historical Society, Charleston.
1857   Plan of a Part of Elm Grove Plantation Situate on the South Side of Wando River, Christ Church Parish. Deed Book A, Page 145, Charleston County Records of Mesne Conveyance, Charleston, South Carolina.

Payne, Ted M.
1986   The Early Industrial Period in Laurens, South
        Carolina: An Historical and Archaeological Study
        for the Relocation of Highway US 221. Ms. on
        file, South Carolina Dept. of Highways and Public
        Transportation, Columbia.

Payne, Ted M., and Richard H. Hulan
1986   US 221 Relocation, City of Laurens, Laurens
        County, South Carolina. Ms. on file, South
        Carolina Dept. of Highways and Public Transpor-
        tation, Columbia.

Pease, Jane H., and William H. Pease
1990   *Ladies, Women, and Wenches: Choice and
        Constraint in Antebellum Charleston and Boston.*
        Univ. of North Carolina Press, Chapel Hill.

Perkerson, Medora Field
1952   *White Columns of Georgia.* Rinehart, New York.

Perry, Percival
1947   *The Naval Stores Industry in the Ante-Bellum
        South: 1789–1861.* Ph.D. diss., Dept. of History,
        Duke Univ.

Petit, James Percival (editor)
1967   *South Carolina and the Sea,* vol. 1. Compiled by
        the Historic and Research Committee of the
        Maritime and Ports Activities Committee.
        Walker, Evans and Cogsell, Charleston.

Petition of Mechanics and Workingmen of the City of
        Charleston Praying more effectual Legislation for
        the prevention of slaves hiring out of their own
        time and other purposes.
1858   Slavery Petitions, General Assembly, South
        Carolina Dept. of Archives and History.

Petty, Julian J.
1975   *The Growth and Distribution of Population in
        South Carolina.* Originally published 1943, South
        Carolina State Planning Board, Columbia.
        Reprint, The Reprint Co., Spartanburg, South
        Carolina.

Pielou, Edith
1984   *The Interpretation of Ecological Data: A Primer on
        Classification and Ordination.* Wiley and Sons,
        New York.

Plummer, G. L.
1983   *Georgia Rainfall: Precipitation Patterns at 23
        places 1734–1982.* Georgia Academy of Science,
        Athens.

Polhemus, Richard
n.d.   Gillon Street Delft Site (38Ch70). Ms. on file,
        Information Management Division, South
        Carolina Institute of Archaeology and Anthro-
        pology, Columbia.

Polk, Harding J., II
1984   A Tale of Two Wharves. Ms. on file, Texas A&M
        Univ., College Station.

Poplin, Eric
1989   *True Blue Plantation. Archaeological Data
        Recovery at a Waccamaw Neck Rice Plantation.*
        Submitted to Heritage Plantation by Brockington
        and Associates of Atlanta.
1992   Variations in Structure: A Comparison of
        Absentee and Principal Residence on Rice
        Plantations in the Low Country of South
        Carolina. Paper presented at the Society for
        Historical Archaeology Meetings, Kingston,
        Jamaica.

Poplin, Eric, and David Beard
1991   *Archaeological Survey and Testing in a 23 Acre
        Tract in the Archdale Subdivision, Dorchester
        County, South Carolina.* Report on file,
        Brockington and Associates, Atlanta.

Poplin, Eric, and Michael Scardaville
1991   *Archaeological Data Recovery at Long Point
        Plantation (38CH321) Mark Clark Expressway
        (I-526), Charleston County, South Carolina.*
        Submitted to the South Carolina Dept. of
        Highways and Public Transportation by
        Brockington and Associates of Atlanta.

Porcher, Anne Allston (editor)
1944   Minutes of the Vestry of St. Stephen's Parish,
        South Carolina. *The South Carolina Historical
        and Genealogical Magazine* 45:157–72.

Potter, Parker, Jr.
1991   What is the Use of Plantation Archaeology?
        Historical Archaeology 25(3):94–107.
1992   Critical Archaeology: In the Ground and on the
        Street. *Historical Archaeology* 26(3):117–29.

Powell, John
1887   *Fifth Annual Report of the Bureau of American
        Ethnology for 1883–1884.* United States Govern-
        ment Printing Office, Washington, D.C. Pp. 199–
        201.

Power, Tracy, Jr.
1991   *"An Affair of Outposts, in Which the Subordinate
        Officers and the Troops on the Spot Did the Best
        They Could": The Battle of Secessionville, 16 June
        1862.* Ms. on file, South Carolina State Historic
        Preservation Office, Dept. of Archives and
        History, Columbia.

Powers, Bernard
1994 *Black Charlestonians: A Social History, 1822–1885.* Univ. of Arkansas Press, Fayetteville.

Pred, Allan
1990 *Making Histories and Constructing Human Geographies: The Local Transformation of Practice, Power Relations, and Consciousness.* Westview Press, Boulder.

Price, Cynthia
1979 *19th Century Ceramics in the Eastern Ozark Border Region.* Center for Archaeological Research Monograph Series 1. Southwest Missouri State Univ., Springfield.

Price, Marie, and Martin Lewis
1993 The Reinvention of Cultural Geography. *Annals of the Association of American Geographers* 83:1–17.

Prunty, Merle, Jr.
1955 The Renaissance of the Southern Plantation. *Geographical Review* 45:459–91.

Raab, L. M., and T. C. Klinger
1977 A Critical Appraisal of "Significance" in Contract Archaeology. *American Antiquity* 42:629–34.

Racine, Philip (editor)
1990 *Piedmont Farmer: the Journals of David Golightly Harris, 1855–1870.* Univ. of Tennessee Press, Knoxville.

Radford, John Price
1974 *Culture, Economy and Urban Structure in Charleston, 1860–1880.* Ph.D. diss., Clark University. Univ. Microfilms, Ann Arbor.

Ramsay, David
1858 *Ramsay's History of South Carolina.* Newberry, South Carolina.

Ransom, James
1966 *Vanishing Iron Works of the Rampos: The Story of the Forges, Furnaces, and Mines of the New Jersey–New York Border Area.* Rutgers Univ. Press, New Brunswick.

Rappaport, Roy
1968 *Pigs for the Ancestors.* Yale Univ. Press, New Haven.

Rasmussen, Wayne D.
1975 Introduction, U.S. Land Policies, 1783–1840. In *Agriculture in the United States, a Documentary History,* vol. 1, edited by Wayne D. Rasmussen, pp. 273–80. Random House, New York.

Rauschenberg, Bradford L.
1991 Brick and Tile Manufacturing in the South Carolina Low Country, 1750–1800. *Journal of Southern Decorative Arts* 17(2):103–13.

Ravenel, Edmund
1835 Notes Relating to the Purchase of Grove Plantation in St. Thomas's from Col. John Gordon, Feb. 1835. William Ravenel Papers, South Carolina Historical Society, Charleston.

Receipt Book
1798– Receipt Book, Hill and Hayne Ironworks, 1798–
1803 1803 (part of Sheriff's Receipt Book, 1803–1812, William Edward Hayne), South Carolina Dept. of Archives and History, Columbia.

Records on the British Public Records Office
1752 *Records on the British Public Records Office Relating to South Carolina,* vol. 25, 34–35. South Carolina Archives and History, Columbia.

Reed, Mary Beth, Patrick Garrow, Gordon Watts, and J. W. Joseph
1989 *Final Report: An Architectural, Archaeological, and Historical Survey of Selected Portions of Charleston and Mount Pleasant: Grace Memorial Bridge Replacement, Charleston, South Carolina.* Submitted to Parsons, Brinckerhoff, Quade, and Douglas. Report on file, Garrow and Associates, Atlanta.

Reinhard, Karl
1989 Parasitological and Palynological Study of Soil Samples from the John Rutledge House. In *Investigating Elite Lifeways through Archaeology,* edited by Martha Zierden and Kimberly Grimes, pp. 166–74. Archaeological Contributions 21, The Charleston Museum, Charleston.
1990 Pollen Analysis of the Miles Brewton House, Charleston, South Carolina. Ms. on file, The Charleston Museum, Charleston.

Reitz, Elizabeth
1986a Urban/Rural Contrasts in the Vertebrate Fauna from the Southern Coastal Plain. *Historical Archaeology* 20(2):47–58.
1986b Urban Site Formation Processes and the Faunal Record. Paper presented at the 43d annual Southeastern Archaeological Conference, Nashville.
1987 Vertebrate Fauna and Socioeconomic Status. In *Consumer Choices in Historical Archaeology,* edited by Suzanne Spencer-Wood, pp. 101–19, Plenum Press, New York.

Reitz, Elizabeth, and Martha Zierden
1991 Cattle Bones and Status from Charleston, South

Carolina. In *Perspectives in Zooarchaeology: Essays in Honor of P. W. Parmalee,* edited by Bonnie Styles, James Purdue, and Walter Klippel, pp. 395–408. Illinois State Museum Publications, Springfield.

Relph, Edward
1970   An Inquiry into the Relations between Phenomenology and Geography. *Canadian Geographer* 14:193–201.

Renfrew, Colin, and John F. Cherry (editors)
1986   *Peer Polity Interaction and Sociopolitical Change.* Cambridge Univ. Press, Cambridge.

Resnick, Benjamin
1984   *The Archaeology, Architecture, and History of the Williams Place: A Scotch Irish Farmstead in the South Carolina Piedmont.* Conference on Historic Sites Series, vol. 3, edited by Stanley South. South Carolina Institute of Archaeology and Anthropology, Columbia.

Resnick, Stephen, and Richard Wolff
1981   Classes in Marxian Theory. *Review of Radical Political Economy.* 13:1–18.

Richards, Julian
1990   *The Stonehenge Environs Project.* Historic Buildings and Monuments Commission for England, London.

Richardson, Miles
1974   The Spanish American (Colombian) Settlement Pattern as a Societal Expression and as a Behavioral Cause. In *Man and Cultural Heritage,* edited by H. J. Walker and W. G. Haag, pp. 35–51. Geoscience and Man, vol. 5. School of Geoscience, Baton Rouge.

Roberts, B. K.
1987   Landscape Archaeology. In *Landscape and Culture: Geographical and Archaeological Perspectives,* edited by J. M. Wagstaff, pp. 77–95. Basil Blackwell, New York, and T. J. Press Ltd., Padstow, Cornwall, Great Britain.

Robin, C. C.
1966   *Voyage to Louisiana by C. C. Robin, 1803–1805.* Originally published 1807. Reprint, Pelican Publishing Company, New Orleans.

Robinson, Kenneth N.
1988   Archeology and the North Carolina Naval Stores Industry: A Prospectus. Ms. on file, Office of State Archeology, Raleigh.
1991   Archeological Data Recovery at Weed's Lightwood Plant: An Early Twentieth Century Naval Stores Distillery, Cumberland County, North Carolina. Submitted to the North Carolina Dept. of Transportation, Raleigh.

Rodeffer, Michael J., and Stephanie L. Holschlag
1979   *Greenwood County: An Archaeological Reconnaissance.* Lander College, Greenwood. Report on file, South Carolina Institute of Archaeology and Anthropology, Columbia.

Rogers, George C.
1980   *Charleston in the Age of the Pinckneys.* Univ. of South Carolina Press, Columbia.

Rogers, Virgil
1990   *Soil Survey of Savannah River Plant Area, Parts of Aiken, Barnwell, and Allendale Counties, South Carolina.* U.S. Dept. of Agriculture, Washington, D.C.

Roper, Donna
1979   *Archaeological Survey and Settlement Pattern Models In Central Illinois.* Scientific Paper 14. Illinois State Museum, Springfield.

Rosengarten, Dale, Martha Zierden, Kimberly Grimes, Ziyadah Owusu, Elizabeth Alston, and Will Williams III
1987   *Between the Tracks: Charleston's East Side During the Nineteenth Century.* Archaeological Contributions 17, The Charleston Museum, Charleston.

Rowntree, Lester
1996   The Cultural Landscape Concept in American Geography. In *Concepts in Human Geography,* edited by Carville Earle, Kent Mathewson, and Martin Kenzer. Rowman and Littlefield, Lanham, Maryland.

Rubertone, Patricia, and Joan M. Gallagher
1981   *Archaeological Site Examination: A Case Study in Urban Archaeology.* Atlanta Russell Papers 1988. MS on file, U.S. Dept. of the Interior, National Park Service, Washington.

Salley, A. S., Jr.
1911   Letters of Thomas Newe, 1682. *Narratives of Early Carolina.* C. Scribner's Sons, New York.
1912   *Journal of the Commissioners of the Navy of South Carolina: October 9, 1776–March 1, 1779.* Historical Commission of South Carolina, Columbia.

Samuels, Marwyn S.
1979   The Biography of Landscape: Cause and Culpability. In *The Interpretation of Ordinary Landscapes: Geographical Essays,* edited by D. W. Meinig, pp. 51–88. Oxford Univ. Press, New York.

Sanborn Insurance Company
1888   Sanborn Fire Insurance Company Map of the City of Charleston. On file at the South Carolina Historical Society, Charleston.

Sassaman, Ken, Mark Brooks, Glenn Hanson, and David Anderson
1989   *Technical Synthesis of Prehistoric Archaeological Investigations on the Savannah River Site, Aiken and Barnwell Counties, South Carolina.* Savannah River Archaeological Research Program, Aiken.

Sauer, Carl Ortwin
1927   Recent Developments in Cultural Geography. In *Recent Developments in the Social Sciences,* edited by E. C. Hayes, pp. 186–87. J. P. Lippincott, Philadelphia.
1931   Cultural Geography. *Encyclopedia of the Social Sciences* 6:621–24.
1963a   Foreword to Historical Geography. In *Land and Life: A Selection from the Writings of Carl Ortwin Sauer,* edited by John Leighly, pp. 351–79. Univ. of California Press, Berkeley. Originally published in 1941.
1963b   The Morphology of Landscape. In *Land and Life: A Selection from the Writings of Carl Ortwin Sauer,* edited by John Leighly, pp. 315–50. Univ. of California Press, Berkeley. Originally published in 1925 in Univ. of California Publications in Geography (vol. 2, no. 2):19–53.

Savage, William W., Jr., and Stephen I. Thompson
1979   The Comparative Study of the Frontier: An Introduction. In *The Frontier, Comparative Studies,* vol. 2, edited by W. W. Savage and S. I. Thompson, pp. 3–24. Univ. of Oklahoma Press, Norman.

Scardaville, Michael
1985   Historical Background. In *Rural Settlement in the Charleston Bay Area: Eighteenth and Nineteenth Century Sites in the Mark Clark Expressway Corridor,* Paul Brockington, Michael Scardaville, Patrick H. Garrow, David Singer, Linda France, and Cheryl Holt, pp. 24–78. Submitted to the South Carolina Dept. of Highways and Public Transportation by Garrow and Associates, Atlanta, Georgia.

Schaefer, Fred K.
1953   Exceptionalism in Geography: A Methodological Examination. *Annals of the Association of American Geographers* 43:226–49.

Sharrock, F. W., and D. K. Grayson
1979   "Significance" in Contract Archaeology. *American Antiquity* 44:327–28.

Schiffer, Michael
1976   *Behavioral Archaeology.* Academic Press, New York.

Schoepf, Johann D.
1968   *Travels in the Confederation 1783–1784.* Originally published 1788. Reprint, Burt Franklin Publisher, New York.

Schuyler, Robert (editor)
1982   Urban Archaeology in America. *North American Archaeologist* 3(3).

Scott, E.
1969   *Negro Migration During the War.* Arno Press/The New York Times, New York.

Scurry, James D.
1982   Archeological Investigations at Redcliffe Plantation, Aiken, South Carolina. *Notebook* 14(3–4):1–27.

Scurry, James D., and Ruth E. Carlson
1995   Improving Site Recording Accuracy in a GIS: A South Carolina Example. In *Archaeological Site File Management: A Southeastern Perspective,* edited by David G. Anderson and Virginia Horak, pp. 82–87. Readings in Archaeological Resource Protection Series No. 3. Interagency Archaeological Services Division.

Scurry, James D., J. Walter Joseph, and Fritz Hamer
1980   *Initial Archeological Investigation at Silver Bluff Plantation, Aiken County, South Carolina.* South Carolina Institute of Archeology and Anthropology Research Manuscript Series 168. Columbia.

Sellers, Leila
1970   *Charleston Business on the Eve of the American Revolution.* Arno Press, New York.

Service, Elman R.
1975   *Origins of the State and Civilization: The Process of Cultural Evolution.* W. W. Norton, New York.

Severens, Kenneth
1988   *Charleston: Antebellum Architecture and Civic Destiny.* Univ. of Tennessee Press, Knoxville.

Shackel, Paul, and Barbara Little
1994   Introduction: Plantation and Landscape Studies. In *Historical Archaeology of the Chesapeake,* edited by Paul Shackel and Barbara Little, pp. 97–100. Smithsonian Institution Press, Washington, D.C.

Sharrer, G. Terry
1981   Naval stores, 1781–1881. In *Material Culture of*

the Wooden Age, edited by Brooke Hindle, pp. 241–361. Sleepy Hollow Press, Tarrytown, New York.

Shepard, Charles, and E. F. Jones
1866   *Report Upon The Property of the Magnetic Iron Company of South Carolina, (Formerly the Swedish Iron Manufacturing Company,) situated in the districts of York, Union, and Spartanburg.* Courier Job Press, Charleston.

Shlomowitz, Ralph
1979   The Origins of Southern Sharecropping. *Agricultural History* 53:557–75.
1982   The Squad System on Postbellum Cotton Plantations. In *Toward a New South? Studies in Post–Civil War Southern Communities,* edited by Orville Vernon Burton and Robert C. McMath Jr., pp. 265–80. Greenwood Press, Westport, Connecticut.

Shoemaker, Edward
1990   *Strangers and Citizens: The Irish Immigrant Community of Savannah, 1837–1861.* Ph.D. diss., Dept. of History, Emory Univ., Atlanta.

Silver, Christopher
1979   A New Look at Old South Urbanization: The Irish Worker in Charleston South Carolina, 1840–1860. In *South Atlantic Urban Studies,* vol. 3, edited by Samuel M. Hines and George W. Hopkins, pp. 141–72. Univ. of South Carolina Press, Columbia.

Simons, Harriett Stoney
n.d.   Research notes. Ms. on file, South Carolina Historical Society, Charleston.
1934   Brick in Provincial South Carolina, with Particular Reference to the Period 1740–1750. Ms. on file, South Carolina Historical Society, Charleston.

Singleton, Theresa A.
1984   The Slave Tag: An Artifact of Urban Slavery. *South Carolina Antiquities* 16:41–68.

Sloan, Earle
1908   *Catalogue of the Mineral Localities of South Carolina.* South Carolina Geological Survey, Columbia.

Smith, Bruce
1992   Study Finds Good, Bad in Coastal Tourism. *The State,* Apr. 8, 1992. Columbia.

Smith, Charlotte A.
1989   *Cultural Resources Survey of Fiscal Year 1991 Timber Sales, Francis Marion National Forest.* Report on file, U.S. Forest Service, McClellanville.

Smith, D. E. Huger
1950   *A Charlestonian's Recollections, 1846–1913.* Carolina Art Association, Charleston.

Smith, Henry A. M.
1988   *The Historical Writings of Henry A. M. Smith.* 3 Vols. The Reprint Company, Spartanburg, South Carolina.

Smith, James
1982   *Historical Geography of the Southern Charcoal Iron Industry, 1800–1860.* Ph.D. diss., Dept. of Geography, Univ. of Tennessee, Knoxville.

Smith, Julia Floyd
1985   *Slavery and Rice Culture in Low Country Georgia, 1750–1860.* Univ. of Tennessee Press, Knoxville.

Smith, Marvin T. (compiler)
1986   *Archaeological Testing of Sixteen Sites on the Fort Howard Tract, Effingham County, Georgia.* Garrow and Associates, Atlanta.

Smith, Sheli O.
1986   Excavation of the Ronson Ship. In *Archaeology in Solution, Proceedings of the Seventeenth Annual Conference on Underwater Archaeology,* edited by John W. Foster and Sheli O. Smith, pp. 137–38. Society for Underwater Archaeology, Tucson.

Smith, Steven D., and Christopher Judge
1992   The South Carolina Heritage Trust Ranking System for Archaeological Site Acquisition. *Southeastern Archaeology* 11(2):140–48.

Smith, Steven D., David F. Burton, and Timothy B. Riordan
1982   *Ethnoarchaeology of the Bay Springs Farmsteads: A Study of Rural American Settlement.* Resource Analysts, Bloomington, Indiana.

Smith, Steven D., Philip Rivet, Kathleen Byrd, and Nancy Hawkins
1983   *Louisiana's Comprehensive Archaeological Plan.* State of Louisiana Dept. of Culture, Recreation and Tourism, Office of Cultural Development, Division of Archaeology.

Snow, C. P.
1959   *The Two Cultures and the Scientific Revolution.* Cambridge Univ. Press, New York.

South Carolina Dept. of Archives and History
n.d.   Berkeley County Preservation Ordinance. Ms. on file, Historic Programs Division, Columbia.
1990   *Survey Manual.* South Carolina Statewide Survey of Historic Places, State Historic Preservation Branch, State Historic Preservation Office, Columbia.
1991   *Guidelines and Standards for Archaeological*

Investigations. Review and Compliance Branch, State Historic Preservation Office, Columbia.

South Carolina Dept. of Highways and Public Transportation (SCDHPT)

1978a General Highway Map, Berkeley County, South Carolina. Columbia.

1978b General Highway Map, Charleston County, South Carolina. Columbia.

South Carolina Dept. of Parks, Recreation, and Tourism

1990 *South Carolina Out-of-State Visitor Survey By Region, 1987–1988.* Report on file, Division of Engineering and Planning Research and Statistics Section, Columbia.

1991 *1991 Year-End Summary: Travel Trends, December–November.* Report on file, Division of Engineering and Planning Research and Statistics Section, Columbia.

South Carolina Gazette

1740 Notice. Act of Assembly. On file Charleston County Library, Charleston, South Carolina.

1744 Committee on Rice Trade Decline, Dec. 10, 1744. On file Charleston County Library, Charleston.

1747 Advertisement for Sale of Lands. Property of William Bruce, Mar. 2, 1747. On file Charleston County Library, Charleston.

1748 Property of Deborah Fisher, Nov. 21, 1748. On file Charleston County Library, Charleston.

1770 Advertisement for Overseer. Placed by John Moore, Aug. 14, 1770. On file Charleston County Library, Charleston.

South Carolina Provincial Congress

1775 *Journals of the South Carolina Provincial Congress,* Nov. 28, 1775, Dept. of Archives and History, Columbia.

South Carolina Sea Grant Consortium

1992 South Carolina's Rural Life: Preserving A Culture. *Coastal Heritage* 6(6).

South Carolina State Gazette and Columbian Advertiser

1806 *State Gazette and Columbia Advertiser,* Dec. 20, 1806. Columbia.

South Carolina State Free Negro Capitation Tax Books

1860 Microfilm available from Avery Research Center, Charleston.

South Carolina State Plats

1839 State Plats of South Carolina, Columbia Series, Dept. of Archives and History, Columbia.

South Carolina Treasury Ledger

1778– South Carolina Treasury Ledger, 1778–80:305,
80 320. Dept. of Archives and History, Columbia.

South, Stanley

1963 Exploratory Excavation of a Brick Kiln at Town Creek, Brunswick County, N.C. Ms. on file, North Carolina State Dept. of Archives and History, Raleigh.

1971 *Archeology at the Charles Towne Site (38CH1) on Albemarle Point in South Carolina.* 2 vols. Research Manuscript Series 10. South Carolina Institute of Archeology and Anthropology, Columbia.

1977 *Method and Theory in Historical Archaeology.* Academic Press, New York.

1979 Historic Site Content, Structure, and Function. *American Antiquity* 44(2):213–36.

1989 From Archaeology to Interpretation at Charles Towne. In *Studies in South Carolina Archaeology: Essays in Honor of Robert L. Stephensen,* edited by Albert Goodyear III and Glen T. Hanson, pp. 157–68. Anthropological Studies 9, South Carolina Institute of Archaeology and Anthropology, Univ. of South Carolina, Columbia.

South, Stanley, and Michael Hartley

1980 *Deep Water and High Ground: Seventeenth Century Low Country Settlement.* South Carolina Institute of Archaeology and Anthropology Research Manuscript Series 166, Columbia.

1985 Deep Water and High Ground: Seventeenth-Century Settlement Patterns on the Carolina Coast. In *Structure and Process in Southeastern Archaeology,* edited by Roy S. Dickens and Trawick Ward, pp. 263–86. Univ. of Alabama Press, Tuscaloosa.

SouthArc, Inc.

1995 *Cultural Resource Management Plan, Dunes West Archaeological Sites, Charleston County, S.C.* Submitted to Dunes West, Georgia-Pacific Development Company. On file SouthArc offices, Gainesville.

Southerlin, B. G., Christopher T. Espenshade, and Paul E. Brockington Jr.

1988 *Archaeological Survey of Parker Island, Charleston County, South Carolina.* Report on file, Brockington and Associates, Atlanta.

Spartanburg County Cross Index of Deeds

1795– Lands Granted by the South Carolina
1919 Manufacturing Company. South Carolina Provincial Congress. Spartanburg County Courthouse, Spartanburg.

Spaulding, Albert
1960   The Dimensions of Archaeology. In *Essays on the Science of Culture in Honor of Leslie A. White,* edited by Gertrude Dole and Robert Carneiro, pp. 437–56. Thomas Y. Crowell, New York.

Sprinkle, John H., Jr.
1995   A Site Form for Important Sites—Converting Archaeological Reports into National Register Nominations. *CRM* 18(6) Supplement:13–16.

Staski, Edward
1982   Advances in Urban Archaeology. In *Advances in Archaeological Method and Theory,* vol. 5, edited by Michael Schiffer, pp. 97–150. Academic Press, New York.

Steffen, Jerome O.
1979   Insular Vs. Cosmopolitan Frontiers: A Proposal for Comparative Frontier Studies. In *The American West, New Perspectives, New Dimensions,* edited by Jerome O. Steffen, pp. 94–123. Univ. of Oklahoma Press, Norman.
1980   *Comparative Frontiers: A Proposal for Studying the American West.* Univ. of Oklahoma Press, Norman.

Stephan, Nancy
1982   *The Idea of Race in Science: Great Britain 1800–1960.* MacMillian Press, London.

Stevens, Michael (compiler)
1985   *Journal of the House of Representatives 1791.* Univ. of South Carolina Press, Columbia.

Stilgoe, John R.
1982   *Common Landscape of America, 1580–1845.* Yale Univ. Press, New Haven.

Stine, Linda France
1987   Management Summary: Excavation and Analysis of Areas A and B at Snee Farm, Charleston County, South Carolina. Ms. on file, Brockington and Associates of Atlanta and the South Carolina Institute of Archaeology and Anthropology.
1989a   *Raised Up in Hard Times: Factors Affecting Material Culture on Upland Piedmont Farmsteads Circa 1900–1940.* Ph.D. diss., Dept. of Anthropology, Univ. of North Carolina, Univ. Microfilms, Ann Arbor.
1989b   Twentieth Century Gender Roles: Perceptions from the Farm. Paper presented at the 22nd Annual Chacmool Conference, Calgary, Canada.
1990   Social Inequality and Turn-of-the-Century Farmsteads: Issues of Class, Status, Ethnicity, and Race. In *Historical Archaeology of Plantations and Farms,* edited by Charles E. Orser Jr. *Historical Archaeology* 24(4):37–49.
1992a   *Revealing Historic Landscapes in Charleston County: Archaeological Inventory, Contexts, and Management.* Submitted to the Charleston County Planning Dept. South Carolina Institute of Archaeology and Anthropology.
1992b   *Archaeological Data Recovery Seeking a Slave Settlement, Snee Farm, Charleston County, South Carolina.* Submitted to the National Park Service, Southeastern Division. Draft Ms. on file Brockington and Associates, Atlanta.
1992c   Social Differentiation Down on the Farm. In *Exploring Gender Through Archaeology: Selected Papers from the 1991 Boone Conference,* edited by Cheryl Claassen, pp. 103–9. Monographs in World Archaeology No. 11. Prehistory Press, Madison.
1993   Site Destruction or Park Construction: Charleston County's Civil War Sites. In *Site Destruction in Georgia and the Carolinas,* edited by David G. Anderson and Virginia Horak, pp. 49–58. Interagency Archeological Services Division, National Park Service, Atlanta, Georgia.

Stoney, John
1852   Overseer's Day Book for Medway Plantation, Berkeley County. Stoney Family Papers, South Carolina Historical Society, Charleston.

Stoney, Samuel Gaillard
1938   *Plantations of the Carolina Low Country.* Carolina Art Association, Charleston, South Carolina.

Stoney, Samuel Gaillard, and Henry P. Staats
n.d.   Comments on Old Charleston Brickwork. Ms. Submitted to Historic Charleston Foundation and the Southern Brick and Tile Manufacturers Association. Ms. on file, Historic Charleston Foundation, Charleston, South Carolina.

Swank, James
1891   *History of the Manufacture of Iron in all Ages and Particularly in the United States from Colonial Times to 1891.* The American Iron and Steel Association, Philadelphia, pp. 276–78.

Swedlund, Alan C.
1975   Population Growth and Settlement Pattern in Franklin and Hampshire Counties, Massachusetts, 1650–1850. In *Population Studies in Archaeology and Biological Anthropology: A Symposium,* edited by Alan C. Swedlund, *American Antiquity,* Memoir 30:22–33.

Taylor, Richard, and Michael Smith
1978   *The Report of the Intensive Survey of the Richard B. Russell Dam and Lake, Savannah River, Georgia and South Carolina.* Research Manuscript Series 142. South Carolina Institute of Archaeology and Anthropology, Univ. of South Carolina, Columbia.

Terry, George D.
1981   *"Champaign Country": A Social History of an Eighteenth Century Lowcountry Parish in South Carolina, St. Johns Berkeley County.* Ph.D. diss., Dept. of History, Univ. of South Carolina.

Thomas, David H.
1976   Nonsite Sampling in Archaeology: Up the Creek without a Site? In *Sampling in Archaeology,* edited by James Mueller, pp. 61–81. Univ. of Arizona Press, Tucson.

Thompson, Stephen I.
1973   *Pioneer Colonization: A Cross-Cultural View.* Addison-Wesley Modules in Anthropology 33.

Tippett, Lee (editor), and Andy Market (compiler)
1995   *Archaeological Abstracts from the Review and Compliance Files of the South Carolina State Preservation Office.* South Carolina State Historic Preservation Office, Columbia.

Toomer, Anthony
1783–   Plantation Accounts of Anthony Toomer, Esq.
85   Vanderhorst Collections, South Carolina Historical Society, Charleston.

Travis, L.
1974   *Archaeological Investigation of South Carolina Highway Department's Proposed Connector from Port Royal to Ladies Island.* Research Manuscript Series 59. South Carolina Institute of Archaeology and Anthropology, Univ. of South Carolina, Columbia.

Trewartha, Glenn
1948   Some Regional Characteristics of American Farmsteads. *Annals of the Association of American Geographers* 38:169–225.

Trimble, Stanley W.
1974   *Man-Induced Soil Erosion of the Southern Piedmont, 1700–1970.* Soil Conservation Society of America, Ankeny, Iowa.

Trindell, Roger T.
1968   Building in Brick in Early America. *The Geographical Review* 58(3):484–87.
1969   Franz Boas and American Geography. *Professional Geographer* 21:328–32.

Trinkley, Michael
1983a   Analysis of Ethnobotanical Remains. In *An Archaeological Study of the First Trident Site,* edited by Martha Zierden, Jeanne Calhoun, and Elizabeth Pinckney, pp. 88–96. Archaeological Contributions 6, The Charleston Museum, Charleston.
1983b   "Let Us Now Praise Famous Men"—If Only We Can Find Them. *Southeastern Archaeology* 2:30–36.
1986   Ethnobotanical Analysis of Samples from the Aiken-Rhett House, City of Charleston, South Carolina. Ms. on file, Chicora Foundation, Columbia, South Carolina.
1987a   Ethnobotanical Analysis of Samples from the Charleston Center Site, City of Charleston, South Carolina. Chicora Foundation, Columbia, South Carolina.
1987b   *An Archaeological Survey of Longpoint Development: Charleston County, South Carolina: Palmetto Grove Plantation.* Chicora Foundation Research Series 8. Chicora Foundation, Columbia, South Carolina.

Trinkley, Michael (editor)
1989   *Archaeological Investigations at Haig Point, Webb, and Oak Ridge, Dafuskie Island, Beaufort County, South Carolina.* Chicora Foundation Research Series 15. Chicora Foundation, Columbia.
1990a   *The Second Phase of Archaeological Survey on Spring Island, Beaufort County, South Carolina: Investigations of Prehistoric and Historic Settlement Patterns on an Isolated Sea Island.* Chicora Foundation, Columbia.
1990b   *Archaeological Excavations at 38BU96, A Portion of Cotton Hope Plantation, Hilton Head Island, Beaufort County, South Carolina.* Chicora Foundation Research Series 21. Chicora Foundation, Columbia.

Trinkley, Michael, and Olga M. Caballero
1983a   *Additional Archaeological, Historical, and Architectural Historical Evaluation of 38Hr127 and 38Hr131, Horry County, South Carolina.* South Carolina Dept. of Highways and Public Transportation, Columbia.
1983b   *An Archaeological and Historical Evaluation of the I-85 Northern Alternative, Spartanburg County, South Carolina.* South Carolina Dept. of Highways and Public Transportation, Columbia.

Trinkley, Michael, Elizabeth F. Mallin, and Newell O. Wright
1979   *Archaeological Investigations of Brickyard Landing, Colleton County, S.C.* South Carolina Dept. of Highways and Public Transportation, Columbia.

Trinkley, Michael, Natalie Adams, and Debi Hacker
1992   *Plantation Life in the Piedmont: A Preliminary Examination of Rosemont Plantation, Laurens County, South Carolina.* Chicora Foundation Research Series 29. Chicora Foundation, Columbia.

Tuan, Yi-Fu
1974   *Topophilia.* Prentice-Hall, Englewood Cliffs.
1979   Thought and Landscape: The Eye and the Mind's Eye. In *The Interpretation of Ordinary Landscapes,* edited by D. W. Menig, pp. 89–102. Oxford Univ. Press, Oxford.

Tuomey, Michael
1848   *Report of the Geology of South Carolina.* A. H. Johnson, Columbia.

Ullman, E.
1954   Geography as Spatial Interaction. In *Proceedings of the Western Committee on Regional Economic Analysis,* edited by D. Revzan and E. Englebert. Univ. of California Press, Berkeley.

Union County Census
1850   Union District Census. Dept. of Archives and History, Columbia.

United States Census
1850   Products of Industry in the County of Charleston. Census of Manufactures Schedule 5. Microfilm on file, South Carolina Archives, Columbia.

United States Dept. of Agriculture
1941   Climate of South Carolina. *Yearbook of Agriculture 1941: Climate and Man.* Government Printing Office, Washington, D. C.

United States Dept. of the Interior
1990   *The Secretary of the Interior's Standards for Rehabilitation [revised].* National Park Service, Washington, D.C.

Upton, Dell
1990   Imagining the Early Virginia Landscape. In *Earth Patterns,* edited by William Kelso and Rachel Most, pp. 71–88. Univ. Press of Virginia, Charlottesville.

Urlsperger, Samuel (editor)
1972– *Detailed Reports on the Salzburger Emigrants Who*
81   *Settled in America.* 8 vols. Univ. of Georgia Press, Athens.

Vanderhorst, Arnoldus
1780   Losses of Arnoldus Vanderhorst by the British. Vanderhorst Collections, South Carolina Historical Society, Charleston.

Vartorella, W. Craig
1991   Profitable Preservation. *Chicora Foundation Research* 5(3). Chicora Foundation, Columbia.

Vlach, John M.
1975   Sources of the Shotgun House: African and Caribbean Antecedents to Afro-American Architecture. Ph.D. diss., Dept. of Folklore, Indiana Univ., Bloomington.
1978   *The Afro-American Tradition in the Decorative Arts.* Cleveland Art Museum, Cleveland, Ohio.

Wade, Richard C.
1964   *Slavery in the Cities.* Oxford Univ. Press, London.

Wagner, Philip L.
1962   Themes of Cultural Geography. In *Readings in Cultural Geography,* edited by Marvin Mikesell, pp. 1–24. Univ. of Chicago Press, Chicago.
1974   Cultural Landscapes and Regions: Aspects of Communication. In *Man and Cultural Heritage: Geoscience and Man,* vol. 5, edited by Bob F. Perkins, pp. 133–42. Louisiana State Univ., Baton Rouge.
1975   The Themes of Cultural Geography Rethought. *Yearbook of Pacific Coast Geographers* 37:7–14.

Wagner, Philip, and Marvin Mikesell (editors)
1961   *Readings in Cultural Geography.* Univ. of Chicago Press, Chicago.

Wagstaff, J. M.
1987   *Landscape and Culture: Geographical and Archeaological Perspectives.* Basil Blackwell, Oxford.

Walker, Joseph
1966   *Hopewell Village: A Social and Economic History of an Iron Making Community.* Univ. of Pennsylvania Press, Philadelphia.

Wallace, David D.
1951   *South Carolina—A Short History 1520–1948.* Univ. of North Carolina Press, Chapel Hill.

Wallerstein, Immanuel
1980   *The Modern World System II: Mercantilism and the Consolidation of the European World Economy, 1600–1750.* Academic Press, New York.

Waterhouse, Richard
1973   *South Carolina's Elite: A Study of the Social Structure and Political Culture of a Southern Colony 1670–1760.* Univ. Microfilms, Ann Arbor.

Watts, Gordon P., Jr.

1992   *Remote Sensing and Low Water Survey: Back River and New Cut, Chatham County, Georgia, and Jasper Co., South Carolina.* Draft report submitted to the U.S. Army Corps of Engineers, Savannah District by Tidewater Atlantic Research, Little Washington, North Carolina.

Watts, Gordon P., Jr., and Wesley K. Hall

1989   *An Investigation of Blossums Ferry on the Northeast Cape Fear River.* Research Reports 1. East Carolina Univ., Greenville.

Watts, J.

1979   Site survey records, Francis Marion National Forest. Forms on file, U.S. Dept. of Agriculture, Forest Service, McClellanville, South Carolina.

Wayne, Lucy B.

1989   Field notes, archaeological survey, Dunes West, Charleston County, South Carolina. Ms. on file, SouthArc, Gainesville, Florida.

1992   *Burning Brick: A Study of a Lowcountry Industry.* Ph.D. diss., College of Architecture, Univ. of Florida, Gainesville.

Wayne, Lucy B., and Martin F. Dickinson

1989   *Archaeological Survey, Dunes West Development, Charleston County South Carolina.* Submitted to Dunes West Development, Mount Pleasant, South Carolina by Environmental Services and Permitting, Jacksonville.

1990   *Four Men's Ramble: Archaeology in the Wando Neck, Charleston County, South Carolina.* Submitted to Dunes West Development Corporation by SouthArc, Gainesville, Florida.

Weaver, David

1972   *The Transport Expansion Sequence in Georgia and the Carolinas, 1670–1900: A Search for Spatial Regularities.* Ph.D. diss., Univ. of Florida, Gainesville.

Weaver, David C., and James F. Doster

1982   *Historical Geography of the Upper Tombigbee Valley.* Center for the Study of Southern History and Culture, Univ. of Alabama, Tuscaloosa.

Weir, Robert M.

1983   *Colonial South Carolina: A History.* KTO Press, Millwood, New York.

Weldon, Bill

1990a   The Brickmaker's Year. *The Colonial Williamsburg Historic Trades Annual* 2:1–40.

1990b   The Arts and Mysteries of the Colonial Brickmaker. *Colonial Williamsburg, The Journal of the Colonial Williamsburg Foundation* 12(4):7–15.

Westerdahl, C.

1978   *Marinarkeologisk inventering med utanqspunkt fran ettanorrlandskt exempel. C-uppstats arkeologi.* Graduation thesis, Univ. of Stockholm.

1980a   On Oral Tradition and Place Names. *The International Journal of Nautical Archaeology* 9:311–29.

1980b   Nagot om aldre maritim kultur. In *Meddelande XLI–XLII 1978–80. V sterbottens norra fornminnesforensing,* Skelleftea Museum, Skelleftea, pp. 7–12.

1991   Norrlandsleden: The Maritime Cultural Landscape of the Norrland Sailing Route. In *Aspects of Maritime Scandinavia a.d. 200–1200,* Proceedings for the Nordic Seminar on Maritime Aspects of Archaeology, Mar. 13–15, 1989. Edited by O. Crumlin Pederson, Roskilde.

1992   The Maritime Cultural Landscape. *The International Journal of Nautical Archaeology* 21(1):5–14. Published for the Nautical Archaeology Society by Academic Press, Boston.

Wheaton, Thomas R., Jr.

1987   *Archaeological and Historical Investigations of the Barrow Farmstead, Fayette County, North Carolina.* Report submitted to Waste Management by Garrow and Associates, Atlanta.

1989   *Drayton Hall: Archeological Testing of the Orangerie.* Report submitted to the National Trust for Historic Preservation. New South Associates Technical Report 11. Stone Mountain, Georgia.

1992   *An Archaeological Survey of 2,012 Acres in the Wambaw District, Francis Marion National Forest.* Submitted to the U.S. Forest Service, New South, Stone Mountain, Georgia.

Wheaton, Thomas, R., Jr., Amy Friedlander, and Patrick H. Garrow

1983   *Yaughan and Curriboo Plantations: Studies in Afro-American Archaeology.* Soil Systems, Marietta, Georgia.

Wheaton, Thomas R., Jr., and Patrick H. Garrow

1985   Acculturation and the Archaeological Record in the Carolina Lowcountry. In *The Archaeology of Slavery and Plantation Life,* edited by Theresa A. Singleton, pp. 239–59. Academic Press, Orlando.

Wheaton, Thomas R., Jr., Mary Beth Reed, and Mary Elizabeth Gantt

1987   *The Jimmie Green Lime Kiln Site, Berkeley County,*

South Carolina. Submitted to the South Carolina Dept. of Highways and Public Transportation, Columbia. Garrow and Associates, Atlanta.

Wigginton, Eliot
1979   *Foxfire 4.* Anchor Press, Garden City.

Will and Estate Papers of William Hill
1817   Will and Estate Papers of William Hill. On file Dept. of Archives and History, Columbia.

Willey, Gordon
1953   *Prehistoric Settlement Patterns in the Viru Valley, Peru.* Bureau of American Ethnology Bulletin 155. Smithsonian Institution, Washington, D.C.

Willey, Gordon R., and Philip Phillips
1958   *Method and Theory in American Archaeology.* Univ. of Chicago Press, Chicago.

Williams, G. Ishmael, John S. Cable, and Mary Beth Reed.
1992   *An Archeological Survey of 2,195 Acres in the Cainhoy Area, Wambaw and Witherbee Districts, Francis Marion National Forest. Francis Marion National Forest Indefinite Services Survey Report 1.* New South Associates Technical Report 66. Submitted to the U.S. Dept. of Agriculture, Forest Service. New South Associates, Stone Mountain, Georgia.

Williams, Petra
1978   *Staffordshire Romantic Transfer Patterns.* Fountain House East, Jeffersontown, Kentucky.

Williams, Petra, and Marguerite Weber
1986   *Staffordshire II Romantic Transfer Patterns.* Fountain House East, Jeffersontown, Kentucky.

Wilson, David
1988   *Prehispanic Settlement Patterns in the Lower Santa Valley, Peru.* Smithsonian Institution Press, Washington, D.C.

Wilson, Samuel
1911   An Account of the Province of Carolina [1682]. In *Narratives of Early Carolina, 1650–1708,* edited by Alexander S. Salley, Jr., pp. 161–75. Charles Scribner's Sons, New York.

Winberry, John J.
1983   "Lest We Forget": The Confederate Monument and the Southern Townscape. *Southeastern Geographer* 23:107–21.

Winterhalder, Bruce P.
1994   Concepts in Historical Ecology: The View from Evolutionary Theory. In *Historical Ecology: Cultural Knowledge and Changing Landscapes,* edited by Carole L. Crumley, pp. 17–42. School of American Research Press, Santa Fe.

Wobst, Martin
1974   Boundary Conditions for Paleolithic Social Systems: A Simulation Approach. *American Antiquity* 39:147–78.

Wood, Peter H.
1974   *Black Majority: Negroes in Colonial South Carolina from 1670 through the Stono Rebellion.* W. W. Norton and Company, New York.

Worthy, Linda (editor)
1983   *"All That Remains": Traditional Architecture and Historic Engineering Structures of the Richard B. Russell Multiple Resource Area, Georgia and South Carolina.* Russell Papers. Interagency Archeological Services Division, National Park Service, Atlanta.

WPA Folklore Writers Project
1937   Ex-slaves Account Dec. 23, 1937 (Project 1885—Folklore), Elmer Turnage editor. Spartanburg District 4, Work Project Administration Writers Program, United States Archives, Washington.

York County Census
1790   York District, First Federal Census. Dept. of Archives and History, Columbia.
1850   York District Census, Dept. of Archives and History, Columbia.

York County Deeds
1786   Book B:52–193; 152–155, 167–171, 177–193. Dept. of Archives and History, Columbia.
1798   Book E:32–151. Dept. of Archives and History, Columbia.
1815   Book H:3–14, 39–41. Dept. of Archives and History, Columbia.
1825   Book K:50–356. Dept. of Archives and History, Columbia.
1830   Book L:45–352. Dept. of Archives and History, Columbia.

York County Plats
1798   Book 1:449–53. Dept. of Archives and History, Columbia.

Yorkville Enquirer
1859   *Yorkville Enquirer,* Feb. 24, 1859. Yorkville.

Zierden, Martha
n.d.   Archaeological Excavations at the Miles Brewton house. Ms. in preparation, The Charleston Museum.
1981   Preliminary Management Report: Archaeological Survey of Compartment 117, Francis Marion National Forest. Ms. on file, U.S. Dept. of

Agriculture, Forest Service, Columbia, South Carolina.

1984   The Urban Environment: 18th Century Charleston. Paper presented at the 17th annual meeting of the Society for Historical Archaeology, Williamsburg.

1986   The Rural-Urban Connection in the Lowcountry. *South Carolina Antiquities* 18(1–2):33–40.

1990a   The Past and the Present: Urban Archaeology in Charleston, South Carolina. In *Cultural Heritage Conservation in the American South,* edited by Benita J. Howell. Southern Anthropological Society Proceedings 23, Univ. of Georgia Press, Athens.

1990b   Archaeological Excavations at 70 Nassau Street. Notes on file, The Charleston Museum, Charleston.

1990c   Management Summary: Test Excavations at 40 Society Street, The Charleston Museum, Charleston.

1993   *Archaeological Testing at the Stable Building of the Heyward–Washington House.* Archaeological Contributions 23, The Charleston Museum, Charleston.

1996   The Urban Landscape, the Work Yard, and Archaeological Site Formation Processes in Charleston, South Carolina. In *Historical Archaeology and the Study of American Culture,* edited by Bernard Herman and Lu Ann De Cunzo, Winterthur Museum Publications.

Zierden, Martha, and Bernard L. Herman

1996   Charleston Townhouses: Archaeology, Architecture, and the Urban Landscape, 1750–1850. In *Landscape Archaeology: Reading and Interpreting the American Historical Landscape,* edited by Rebecca Yamin and Karen Bescherer Metheny. Univ. of Tennessee Press, Knoxville.

Zierden, Martha A., and Dale Rosengarten

1987   The Archaeological Potential of Charleston's Black Population. Paper presented at the Joint Meeting of the 44th Southeastern Archaeological Conference and 1987 Eastern States Archeological Federation, Charleston, South Carolina.

Zierden, Martha, and Debi Hacker

1986a   *Exploration of the North Entrance of the Joseph Manigault House.* Archaeological Contributions 15, The Charleston Museum, Charleston.

1986b   *Examination of Construction Sequence at the Exchange Building.* Archaeological Contributions 14, The Charleston Museum, Charleston.

1987   *Charleston Place: Archaeological Investigations of the Commercial Landscape.* Archaeological Contributions 16, The Charleston Museum, Charleston.

Zierden, Martha A., and Jeanne A. Calhoun

1982   *Preliminary Report: An Archaeological Preservation Plan for Charleston, South Carolina.* Archaeological Contributions 1, The Charleston Museum, Charleston

1983   *An Archaeological Assessment of the Greenfield Borrow Pit, Georgetown County, South Carolina.* Archaeological Contributions 4, The Charleston Museum, Charleston.

1984   *An Archaeological Preservation Plan for Charleston, South Carolina.* Archaeological Contributions 8, The Charleston Museum, Charleston.

1986   Urban Adaptation in Charleston, South Carolina, 1730–1820. *Historical Archaeology* 20(1):29–43.

1987   Household or Neighborhoods: Finding Appropriate Levels of Research in Urban Archaeology. Paper presented at the 1987 meetings of the Society for Historical Archaeology, Savannah.

1990   An Archaeological Interpretation of Elite Townhouse Sites in Charleston, South Carolina, 1770–1850. *Southeastern Archaeology* 9(2):79–92.

Zierden, Martha, and Kimberly Grimes

1989   *Investigating Elite Lifeways through Archaeology: The John Rutledge House.* Archaeological Contributions 21, The Charleston Museum, Charleston.

Zierden, Martha, and Robert Raynor

1988   *The President Street Site: An Experiment in Public Archaeology.* Archaeological Contributions 18, The Charleston Museum, Charleston.

Zierden, Martha, Elizabeth Reitz, Michael Trinkley, and Elizabeth Paysinger

1982   *Archaeological Excavations at McCrady's Longroom.* Archaeological Contributions 3, The Charleston Museum, Charleston.

Zierden, Martha, Jeanne Calhoun, and Debi Hacker

1986   *Outside of Town: Preliminary Investigation of the Aiken-Rhett House.* Archaeological Contributions 11, The Charleston Museum, Charleston.

Zierden, Martha, Jeanne Calhoun, and Debi Hacker Norton

1985   *Archdale Hall: Investigations of a Lowcountry Plantation.* Archaeological Contributions 10. The Charleston Museum, Charleston.

Zierden, Martha, Jeanne Calhoun, and Elizabeth Paysinger
1983   *Archaeological Investigations at Lodge Alley.* Archaeological Contributions 5, The Charleston Museum, Charleston.

Zierden, Martha, Jeanne Calhoun, and Elizabeth Pinckney
1983   *An Archaeological Study of the First Trident Site.* Archaeological Contributions 6, The Charleston Museum, Charleston.

Zierden, Martha, Jeanne Calhoun, and Elizabeth Reitz
n.d.   Archaeological Investigations of the Charleston Waterfront. Notes on file, The Charleston Museum, Charleston.

Zierden, Martha, Jeanne Calhoun, Suzanne Buckley, and Debi Hacker
1987   *Georgian Opulence: Archaeological Investigation of the Gibbes House.* Archaeological Contributions 12, The Charleston Museum, Charleston.

Zierden, Martha, Kimberly Grimes, David Hudgens, and Cherie Black
1988   *Charleston's First Suburb: Excavations at 66 Society Street.* Archaeological Contributions 20, The Charleston Museum, Charleston.

Zierden, Martha A., Lesley M. Drucker, and Jeanne Calhoun
1986   *Home Upriver: Rural Life on Daniel's Island, Berkeley County, South Carolina.* Submitted to the South Carolina Dept. of Highways and Public Transportation. A Joint Venture of Carolina Archaeological Services/The Charleston Museum, Columbia and Charleston.

Zimmer, Julie, Richard Wilk, and Anne Pyburn
1995   A Survey of Attitudes and Values in Archaeological Practice. *Society for American Archaeology Newsletter,* Nov.–Dec., p. 10.

CONTRIBUTORS

DAVID BEARD has his M.A. degree in Maritime History from East Carolina University. He developed a data base for known and potential underwater and landing archaeology sites while at the South Carolina Institute of Archaeology and Anthropology in Columbia. He continues his research on the various types of plantation landing sites in the lowcountry.

RICHARD D. BROOKS is a historian at the Savannah River Archaeological Research Program. His B.A. is from Kentucky Wesleyan College, and he is a M.A. candidate at the University of South Carolina. He has conducted historical research in the southeastern United States for two decades and is currently researching the development of the British colonial military frontier through a study of Fort Moore and Savanno Town.

THOMAS A. COWAN was the assistant South Carolina folk art coordinator while a graduate student in the applied history program at the University of South Carolina. He has yet to complete his studies, but has his B.A. in History from Wofford College. He was the coordinator of historic trades at Old Salem, Inc., in North Carolina. He continues his research on the industrial archaeology of South and North Carolina.

DAVID COLIN CRASS is a historical archaeologist at the Savannah River Archaeological Research Program. He has his M.A. in Anthropology from the College of William and Mary and a Ph.D. from Southern Methodist University. He has conducted research in the American Southwest and is currently excavating colonial sites in the South Carolina frontier settlement of New Windsor.

CAROLE L. CRUMLEY is a professor of Anthropology at the University of North Carolina at Chapel Hill. Some of her current research interests include the ecological and cultural historical analysis of regions, global-scale historical ecology, epistemology of complex systems, pattern recognition studies, and applications of GIS and remote sensed data in anthropology.

LESLEY M. DRUCKER is the president of AF Consultants, a cultural resource management firm in Columbia. She holds a Ph.D. in Anthropology and has been the president of the Council of South Carolina Professional Archaeologists. She continues to undertake grants, contracts, and other research and education projects in the Carolinas.

JIM ERRANTE has his M.A. from the Anthropology Department, University of South Carolina at Columbia. He has directed both underwater and terrestrial archaeological projects in the Carolinas. Currently Jim is an archaeologist in South Carolina, at the USDA, Department of Natural Resources.

TERRY A. FERGUSON is a professor at Wofford College, South Carolina, where he has received numerous computer laboratory improvement grants. His research interests include the application of geographic techniques in archaeology and investigation of early industrial sites in the Carolinas.

STANTON W. GREEN is the dean of Arts and Sciences, Clarion University. While a professor and chairperson of the Department of Anthropology, University of South Carolina, he continued his research interests in archaeological method and theory, especially pertaining to landscape studies in the Southeast and in Ireland, and in regional and nonsite archaeological techniques. He has co-edited books on geographic techniques in archaeology and on boundaries and frontiers in archaeological research.

MICHAEL A. HARMON is a forest archaeologist at Uwharrie and Croatan National Forests. He has his M.A. in Anthropology from the University of South Carolina, Columbia, and furthered his research interests in Carolina archaeology at the

South Carolina Institute of Archaeology and Anthropology.

J. W. JOSEPH is a native South Carolinian, and received his B.A. in Anthropology from the University of South Carolina and his M.A. in American Civilization and Ph.D. in Historical Archaeology from the University of Pennsylvania. He has been active in the archaeology of southern agrarian sites during the past several years including work on the Walthour Plantation in Georgia, McLeod Plantation and the Finch Farm in South Carolina, and he has served as the historical archaeologist for the technical synthesis of archeological and historical studies carried out for the Richard B. Russell reservoir. He is currently the president and principal archaeologist for New South Associates, a private archaeological and historical consulting firm.

DEE DEE JOYCE is a professor in the Department of Anthropology, College of Charleston. She is a doctoral candidate at SUNY Binghamton, specializing in nineteenth-century southern studies. She focuses on issues of social inequality and landscape studies in urban areas in South Carolina, with an emphasis on the Irish presence in the nineteenth century.

CHRISTOPHER JUDGE has his M.A. in Anthropology from the University of South Carolina at Columbia. He is currently the archaeologist for the Heritage Trust Program, South Carolina Department of Natural Resources. His research interests include the preservation of archaeological sites in South Carolina, and he is active in public education for archaeology.

KENNETH E. LEWIS is a professor in the Department of Anthropology, Michigan State University. He has long-term research interests in South Carolina archaeology, especially the development of early historical settlements, the maintenance of frontiers and boundaries, and landscape studies. He has been associated with the South Carolina Institute of Archaeology and Anthropology and the South

Carolina Department of Archives and History as an archaeologist.

MARY BETH REED received her B.A. in Anthropology from the University of Arizona and her M.A. in American Civilization from the University of Pennsylvania, where she is currently a doctoral candidate. Ms. Reed has been very active in the fields of historical research, architectural history, and land use history and has provided land use studies and analyses of changes in the historic landscape of both urban and rural contexts. Ms. Reed currently is employed by New South Associates as a historian.

RODNEY J. SNEDEKER is a forest archaeologist for the National Forests of North Carolina. He has a long-term interest in promoting the study and preservation of industrial sites in the Carolinas. His experience with the Forest Service continues to foster his interest in historical archaeology and documentary research.

LINDA F. STINE has her M.A. in Anthropology, with a specialization in Historical Archaeology, from the College of William and Mary and her Ph.D. in Anthropology from the University of North Carolina at Chapel Hill. Her research interests include landscape studies and the historical archaeology of the South, especially with regard to African American culture. She has been the environmental review archaeologist for the South Carolina Department of Archives and History, a grants archaeologist at the South Carolina Institute of Archaeology and Anthropology, and a professor of anthropology at several southeastern universities.

ROY S. STINE is a professor in the Department of Geography, University of North Carolina at Greensboro. His has an M.A. in History, from Montana State University; he has a Ph.D. from the Department of Geography, University of South Carolina at Columbia. His research interests include the application of Remote Sensing, Global Positioning Satellites, and Geographic Information Systems, and the relationship of geology and Predynastic settlement at Hierakonpolis, Egypt.

LUCY B. Wayne specialized in Historic Preservation at the College of Architecture at the University of Florida at Gainesville. Dr. Wayne's research interests include the history and distribution of brick making on plantation sites in the lowcountry of South Carolina and the historical archaeology of plantation sites.

JOHN J. WINBERRY is a professor of Geography at the University of South Carolina. He co-authored a seminal work on the development of South Carolina's landscape with Charles Kovacik. His interests include the relationship between geogra-phy and anthropology and the history of geographic thought.

PETER H. WOOD is a professor of History at Duke University. He is known for a ground-breaking work on South Carolina's African American colonial history, as well as numerous other books and articles. He has participated in interdisciplinary projects in the Mid-Atlantic and Southeast.

MARTHA ZIERDEN is the curator of Historical Archaeology at The Charleston Museum. Her M.A. is in Anthropology from Florida State University, Tallahassee. Her research interests include urban archaeology, landscape studies, and museum interpretation.

Index